AF577146

An Introduction to European Porcelain

To Desmond Elliott

An Introduction to EUROPEAN PORCELAIN

Harriet Wynter

Thomas Y. Crowell Company
New York · Established 1834

First published in the United States of America in 1972

Printed in Great Britain

L.C. Card 72-167763

ISBN 0-690-44851-1

Contents

Preface

To-day things are happening so fast in the field of ceramic research, that a book on porcelain may well become slightly out-dated even between the time of the author delivering the manuscript, and the publication of the finished volume. Thus, to justify more books on the subject of antique pottery and porcelain, it is essential for the authors to have carried out their research from the writings and findings of the many specialists who devote their love and attention to the productions of one particular period, factory or area. To-day such research is proving very rewarding and we are all very indebted to such people as the members of the *English Ceramic Circle*, who by their diligent labours are making our tasks easier with new knowledge concerning not only the obscure and little known factories, but also such long established factories as that of Worcester.

Mrs. Wynter has spent long hours in endeavouring to keep up with 'whats new?' in the world of decorative porcelain and in this volume presents an up-to-date review, which should not only prove of immense benefit to both old, and new, collectors, but also give a great deal of pleasure to those who do not necessarily collect, but derive much satisfaction from seeing beautiful pieces of craftsmanship, and learning more of the social background in which such fragile creations were used and enjoyed. Harriet Wynter certainly helps one to cover this approach particularly well.

Many of the pieces of porcelain Harriet Wynter has chosen as illustrations for this new volume are to-day far beyond the purse strings of the average collector, but knowledge acquired in the study and appreciation of such examples can help considerably in the selection of more easily obtainable wares.

JOHN P. CUSHION
Victoria & Albert Museum

Foreword

Lovers and collectors of porcelain, of whatever kind, pass through several stages in their understanding and appreciation of a ware that even to the ignorant can never lack beauty. It is something which has grace, daintiness and endless variety of colour, and it is impossible to look upon it without an interest which in turn demands deeper, instructed knowledge. Superficial beauty apart, there must be an ever-increasing desire to understand something of its story, of its manufacture, and of the sources of its decoration.

It is natural that collectors in our own country, initially at any rate, will be most interested in the English and Welsh porcelains, and here indeed is a lifetime's study in itself. Nevertheless, there will be those who will wish to know more about Continental wares, if only because so many of our own eighteenth century styles of decoration came to us from Holland, France or Germany.

All these facets of porcelain collecting can of course be best studied by handling actual specimens or at least by looking at them in the cabinets of museums and private collectors. At the same time, however, much may be learnt from books of the right kind. Indeed, some careful study of their pages is essential to a proper understanding of the wares that are handled or seen. It is invaluable to know what to lock for and how to recognise it.

Of recent years many new discoveries have resulted from the finding of early documents or references, and from informed, expert excavation of factory sites. Many established theories have been disproved and a great deal of porcelain re-attributed.

If only for these reasons the publication of an up-to-date book on European porcelain is to be welcomed.

Mrs. Harriet Wynter has, I believe, succeeded well in covering a wide subject admirably and at the same time in bringing the information she gives completely up to date. She has not, I think, perpetuated any fallacies. Naturally enough, the expert may well know much that she has to say, though even he will welcome the concise way in which she has presented it. The beginner cannot fail to be greatly helped by a most important feature of the book—the "Characteristics" section at the end of each chapter, which tells him what he most needs to know in the early, and indeed in the later, stages of his pursuit. I am confident that every lover of European porcelain will find much of value and interest in the following pages.

Stanley W. Fisher

Bewdley
Worcestershire

Author's Note

This book is not intended for either the experienced collector or the scholar. It is an introduction and guide for the average person who would like to know about porcelain.

Many books on porcelain have been written. The subject is vast. Books tend to specialise and become technical, and without some prior knowledge the average reader is lost in a maze of terms and apparent contradictions. This book is intended as a link, so that advanced works by specialists may be more readily understood. Voltaire wrote:

> "*L'histoire de la céramique, c'est l'histoire de l'humanité toute entière.*" (The history of ceramics is the history of all humanity.)

In order to assimilate the enormous amount of information it is necessary for a collector to be familiar not only with the backs ground of the factories but also with the cultural background of Europe. Many readers have forgotten their history and I have included such facts which, even appearing irrelevant to the subject, could still refresh the reader's memory, and set his interest in the history of porcelain. I asked the curator of a German museum if he knew anything of the private lives of early porcelain manufacturers. His reply was that they were far too busy trying to make porcelain to have a private life!

I have given more space to the history of the factories and not so much to their products, for in a book of this nature, it is impossible to include everything. In order to maintain the interest for the beginners, I have purposely left out much which I have considered would be of no interest to them. The bibliography provides a selection of books containing more information.

I lay no claim to original material nor to new discoveries, but I offer a digest of currently available information, which is constantly changing according to new publications. I have appended a list giving the characteristics of the products of each factory mentioned in my book which should be accepted as a "rule of thumb" for quick reference. It was only in the nineteenth century that books appeared on the history of porcelain and many romantic stories, now discounted, were born. I have included some of them and I hope that they could be of interest to the reader.

HARRIET WYNTER

Acknowledgements

I am deeply grateful to my friends; collectors, dealers and curators, who have given their valuable time to encourage and instruct me, and especially

Mr. J. P. Cushion, Victoria and Albert Museum; Herr Doktor Ruckert and Herr Doktor Hojer, Bayerisches National Museum, Munich; Mme. M. H. Sauget, Bibliothèque Nationale, Paris; The Bäuml Family at the Staatliche Porzellan-Manufaktur, Nymphenburg; Mr. F. Bramfitt and Mr. J. G. Cliff, The Royal Crown Derby Porcelain Co. Ltd.; Mme. Monique Ricour, Musée des Arts Décoratifs, Paris; Sr. Raffaello Causa, Naples Museum; Mr. L. G. Lovell, Rotheram Museum; Mr. A. Pobedinskaya, Hermitage Museum, Leningrad; Mlle. Brunet, Manufacture Nationale de Sèvres; Mr. T. Robert Copeland and Mr. H. Holdway and Mr. L. R. Whiter, W. T. Copeland & Sons Ltd.; Mr. F. G. Taylor and Mr. J. E. Hartill, Minton Ltd.; Dott. Silvana Pettenati, Museo Civico, Turin; Dr. Wolfgang Scheffler, Staatliche Museum, Berlin; Mr. W. A. Billington, Josiah Wedgwood & Sons Ltd.; Mr. H. V. Percival, Wellington Museum; Mr. C. Shingler and Mr. Henry Sandon, Dyson Perrins Museum, Royal Worcester Porcelain Co. Ltd.; Mr. A. L. Thorpe, Derby Municipal Museum; Mr. Derek Hutchings; Mr. Peter Philp; Messrs. Sotheby & Co; Messrs. Christie, Manson & Woods.

Mr. Bernard Denvir who gave me the benefit of his experience when he edited the book, and Mr. Stanley Fisher, F.R.S.A., who was kind enough to write the foreword. Miss Pat Burrows, who drew the marks, and Mrs. Elsa Ayres who drew the illustrations. Eileen Astley-Hall without whose enthusiasm in the early stages this book might never have been completed.

Factory Marks

Colour Plates

Illustrations

Chapter One

How It Began

[1] THE ORIGINS OF PORCELAIN

"The important ends of man's life include the creation and enjoyment of beauty, both natural and man-made."

SIR JULIAN HUXLEY

PORCELAIN Today is manufactured commercially, under modern factory conditions, with the latest technical equipment; it is freely available and relatively inexpensive. When it was first introduced into Europe it was a rare and costly novelty, owned only by kings and princes, who valued it as highly as precious metals and stones, and who exchanged pieces as diplomatic gifts.

The word "porcelain" is derived from *porcellana*, which in several languages stands for mother-of-pearl. The name "porcelain" or its modifications, was first applied in Europe to any substance that was fragile and opalescent, like mother-of-pearl or fine earthenware, so some of the early references could be misleading.

In 1586, an inventory of minor valuables belonging to Mary Queen of Scots enumerated "*Deux cuillières de porcelaines, garnyes, l'une d'or, et l'autre d'argent.*" (Two porcelain spoons, decorated, one in gold, the other in silver.) Amongst the New Year gifts to Queen Elizabeth 1587–1588, Burghley offered one "porrynger" of white "porslyn" garnished with gold, and Mr. Robert Cecil "a cup of grene pursselyne".

Porcelain was invented in China during the Sung Dynasty

(A.D. 960–1279), although some believe it was in use even before that time. A mysterious and remote area to Europeans, China developed its own art and culture independently, and was a source of wonder and speculation to the limited number of travellers who were allowed within its borders. Marco Polo, one of the first of these, reported the manufacture of porcelain upon his return to Venice in 1295. He described the dull red glow in the sky from the numerous kilns, and how everyone—men, women and children—were employed in some way in its manufacture. Porcelain was abundant and cheap in China and was exported to the Levant overland on the backs of camels and donkeys, and then shipped to Europe. Istanbul (Constantinople) was an active trans-shipment area, hence the magnificent collections owned by the ruling classes and the present-day assemblage, still not completely catalogued, at the Topkapi Museum there.

Interest in Chinese porcelain grew wider when the route round the Cape was taken by Vasco da Gama on his voyage to India in 1498. The sea route to the East was established, and by 1518 the Portuguese were trading direct with China. In 1557 they were presented with the sovereign rights of Macao in gratitude for the dispersal of some troublesome pirates off the Ladrones Islands, and were soon shipping magnificent porcelain, which they sold to the rest of Europe at a handsome profit.

When Philip II of Spain conquered Portugal in 1580, he forbade the export of Oriental goods to the enemies, whose reaction was the formation of their own trading companies. By 1604 the Dutch East India Company had 150 merchant ships, 40 warships and an army of 10,000 men, with which they seized two Portuguese ships, the "San Jago" and the "Caterina", both full of porcelain, which was taken to Amsterdam for auction. After their victory at Malacca in 1615 the Dutch founded their East Indian Colony and excluded the Portuguese from the Oriental trade. Having supplanted the Portuguese, the Dutch vigorously protected their monopoly, and warned the already suspicious Chinese against any other "foreign devils".

The British East India Company, founded 1600, prevented from trading with China direct, established a depot at the Port of Gombron in the Persian Gulf, and made this a great trading centre where the products of India and China were exchanged for those of Europe. From this place Chinese porcelain was first introduced directly into England. Horace Walpole refers to "Gombroon Ware" [*sic*] and it was generally known by this name before it was called "china".

A British man-o'-war which penetrated the Yangtze River endeavoured to establish friendly relations, and according to naval custom fired a broadside in salute. This was misinterpreted by the Chinese, who returned fire for fire, and the visitor beat a hasty retreat. Some years later another British warship repeated the gesture and the ship was boarded. The captain was taken before the Manchu Emperor K'ang Hsi who fortunately was co-operative and granted the British the right to trade in China. By 1753 there were fifty-two London merchants dealing in Oriental goods.

The French Compagnie des Indes Orientales was founded by Colbert in the reign of Louis XIV and had some share in the highly competitive trade. When John Law's Compagnie d'Occident was liquidated, the ensuing scandal caused the government to merge the two companies in 1719 to become the Compagnie Française des Indes.

A late arrival in the field was the infant American Republic which later in the century resolutely set about establishing direct world trade, a freedom they had never previously enjoyed without crippling tariffs. With all their hopes and prayers they provisioned the *Empress of China*, 360 tons, which set sail from New York in February 1785. The voyage was successfully accomplished. The Chinese received them sympathetically, naming them the "Flowery Flag Devils", and considerable trade followed.

K'ang Hsi (1662–1723) had been the first Chinese ruler to encourage trade with the West. The royal pottery at Ching-tê-Chên, where the choicest porcelain was commissioned for the royal use, also supplied merchants with enormous quantities which were decorated by Cantonese artists for foreign commissions. The prosperity of the Canton merchants was advantageous to the Imperial Court, so in 1720 K'ang Hsi permitted the foreigners to reside outside the walls of Canton, and made the Chinese merchants responsible for their good behaviour. Thirteen buildings were constructed by the merchants and leased to foreign interests. Each one was solidly built along a uniform frontage facing south, 300 feet from the river. They were referred to as the *hongs*, meaning places of business, and their builders were known as the *hong* merchants. Great ceremony was attached to the daily raising and lowering of national flags at the waterfront, where sampans and junks unshipped merchandise for the vessels moored ten miles away at the Whampoa anchorage. In 1790 a traveller reported that in the Canton Roads there were forty-six English, three Dutch, two French and six American ships.

The first porcelain the European traders bought in China were examples of pure Chinese art, but later on they ordered special decoration for the European market. They specified heraldic coats of arms which the Chinese interpreted often with unusual spelling, together with their own Taoist or Buddhist symbols and emblems. The Dutch ordered sets of five vases with domed covers, painted in blue, to suit their customers; the Americans ordered portraits of Benjamin Franklin and George Washington and pictures of their ships. The Jesuits, who were still converting the Japanese, ordered pictures of the Crucifixion and other religious studies. The Chinese must have had a curious impression of the Western world.

These examples are known as "Export Porcelain", being quite apart from the natural development of Chinese art styles, although the current Chinese border patterns and designs were usually incorporated.

This "Export Porcelain" is often misleadingly called "Lowestoft" and is confused with the products of the porcelain factory of the same name.

[2] POTTERY

Until porcelain became generally available in Europe, the ceramics produced had reached a very high level of decoration and design, but were thick and opaque and did not have the delicacy demanded by the drinkers of subtle China tea.

Pottery is one of the oldest applied arts. Examples have been found on every archaeological excavation from every known civilisation back to prehistoric man. Pottery is made of clay, formed, then hardened by the heat of the sun or in a kiln. Until the invention of the potter's wheel in ancient Egypt, the shaping was accomplished by one of three methods, by hand, by the ring, or by the coil. Plates, pitchers and bottles were made in these ways and are still being made today in primitive societies. It is interesting that hand work was always performed by women and the wheel used only by men.

When the Romans, who had established great pottery-producing factories all over their Empire, left Northern Europe, local needs were met by itinerant potters who produced comparatively crude examples of their wares. They covered their pots in a brown, yellow or green glaze, and scratched a decoration with whatever was available—a twig, a shell, a piece of iron (*s'graffito*).

By the seventeenth century techniques had so improved that fine slip-wares, highly prized today, were being produced in European potteries. The red clay body was decorated in "slip", a mixture of white clay and water, with wavy and dotted lines and crudely drawn leaves, birds and human figures. Some bore the name of the potter or the name of the customer. English slip-ware was made by among others, a Staffordshire family named Toft.

A mighty industry originating in Germany was the manufacture of stoneware—a coarse form of pottery which is perpetuated today in the decorative beer *steins* mainly made for the tourist trade.

A great influence on English pottery was exerted by two silversmith brothers from Holland, John and David Elers (*c.* 1670–1700), who settled in Bradwell Wood, near Newcastle-under-Lyme, Staffordshire. They guarded their secrets with such senacity that they were said to employ only half-wits so that tpies from other factories could infiltrate only by posing as idiots. The Elers were responsible for establishing a standard of finely-finished lathe-turned red stoneware decorated with geometric patterns or applied sprigs stamped out with metal dies, which set a precedent for the rest of Staffordshire.

Two outstanding English potters in the stone-ware tradition were John Astbury (1686–1743) who worked in the Elers style and John Dwight (*c.* 1637–1743) of Fulham who perfected a beautiful white stoneware. Dwight also believed he had found the secret of porcelain manufacture and applied for a patent to Charles II, but unfortunately never produced any.

Although stoneware required no glaze, an English seventeenth-century invention was a characteristic pitted orange-skin finish called salt-glaze. Simeon Shaw (*History of the Staffordshire Potteries*) describes how the potbank kiln in Staffordshire was constructed to take a week's output, for only one firing was performed each week, usually on Thursday and the pieces were removed on Saturday. A scaffold was constructed alongside the chimney which the firemen ascended, and at the appropriate time flung the salt down the chimney.

The most illustrious of the pottery group is *maiolica*, which is soft, opaque, non-vitrified, earthy fracture, covered with a lead glaze containing tin oxide. Of Oriental origin, it was made by the Moors in Spain, particularly in Valencia, from where it was exported "to all Christendom". Large quantities of this Hispano-Mauresque ware were sent to Italy, where it was believed that it had come from the island of Maiorca, so it acquired the name *maiolica*—not to be confused with majolica which was a nineteenth-century Staffordshire invention for the English lead-glazed wares made. The Italian potters of Orvieto and Faenza eagerly copied and adapted the imported wares and developed a magnificent industry. The town of Faenza gives its name to *faïence*, and *fayence*, the terms subsequently used in France and Germany in the seventeenth century for their types of *maiolica*.

In Holland *maiolica* took the name of Delft, and in England it was made under the name of delft-ware at the main factories at Lambeth, Bristol and Liverpool. The character of these wares was of Chinese-Dutch origin, necessarily crudely decorated, usually in blues in the "delft painter's touch".

All this pottery was notable, not only for its colours and

decoration, but also for its distinctive glaze. This was made of the usual lead base but contained tin oxide. A present-day application is on the household cast-iron bath-tub. The glaze supplied a milky transparent coat to protect the decoration and seal the porous body of the paste. Similar ceramics were being made at the same time all over Europe, but these were too numerous to mention here.

[3] HOW PORCELAIN IS MADE

Chinese porcelain was true porcelain or hardpaste. It was hard, white, translucent and resonant. The Chinese themselves attached no importance to the translucence, but judged the quality of a piece by its resonance. Not so in Europe, where the public were used to earthenware which was thick and opaque, and regarded the translucence of porcelain as its most desirable feature.

Porcelain is the highest expression of the potter's art. The manufacture of porcelain is really the reconstruction by man of a natural phenomenon. It is not pottery, although the tools—the wheel, the dolly—are the same. The basic materials used are different.

HARD PASTE OR TRUE PORCELAIN

Kaolin (china clay) derived from the Chinese *kao-ling*, meaning high ridge, probably from where it originally came, is the fine white powder from which porcelain is made. Kaolin is a product of the decomposition of the mineral feldspar. Feldspar (sometimes called by its French name *petuntse*) is an abundant mineral found in crystalline rocks formed in volcanic heat and pressure. When by subsequent erosion the feldspar is exposed to the influence of air and water and chemical decay, it breaks down and becomes kaolin. The size of the particles is reduced to a minimum by the action of water, probably in a river bed, determining the fine white quality desired.

Man discovered that when feldspar ground to a powder was added to the kaolin, it acted as a flux, the malleability of the kaolin was not impaired, so a shape could be formed and, as in nature, it could be vitrified by being subjected to intense heat. The product of the phenomenon was pure white, translucent, light reflecting, resonant and rock hard.

This then was True Porcelain.

SOFT PASTE OR ARTIFICIAL PORCELAIN

In the search for the formula for true porcelain, the European factories experimented with all kinds of materials, even using ground glass in order to give their products the rock hard finish. They succeeded in producing some lovely wares, which were not porcelain at all, but only resembled it. These were the soft-paste (*pâte tendre*), so called because the body is softer and more porous than that of the hard-paste (*pâte dure*), and they were fired at a comparatively low temperature.

The manufacture of soft-paste was slow and laborious. Chemical analysis was of a very simple kind, so that the impurities which differed in each batch of raw materials could not be detected nor removed. Nor could the temperature of the kilns be accurately controlled, so there was a good deal of waste. The formula was roughly this: flowers of sulphur were added to saltpetre and heated in an oven. When the mixture cooled it was crushed and added to sand, sea salt, gypsum and alum, mixed well, laid over sand and fired for about two days and nights. This was the first firing and produced the "frit"—soft-paste porcelain is sometimes referred to as "frit porcelain". The frit was then mixed with water, chalk and limestone and the result was ready for modelling. This process took about five weeks. The frit composition was not plastic like the malleable kaolin and the modelling was accomplished only by the addition of soap. This highly unstable paste was consigned to the kiln, where the slightest inaccuracy—in temperature or the length of time involved—caused the shape to deform or collapse. These failures were termed "wasters".

BONE CHINA

English bone porcelain is half-way between hard- and soft-paste. Made with the constituents of hard-paste plus bone ash, it is more resistant to acids than the soft-paste. Similar in fracture to the hard-paste, it is not so white. It is fired at 1,250°C in its biscuit state, followed by a cooler "glost" (glaze) firing.

The general use of bone ash reduced manufacturing costs and opened up the possibility of porcelain for all.

THROWING AND TURNING

When the clay was ready for forming it was passed to the potter, who threw a lump on to his wheel, and with a dexterity that only those who have tried to do it themselves will appreciate, gripped the paste with his fingers and thumbs and drew it into shape. He then cut the finished object off the wheel with a piece of wire, and it was set aside to dry "leather hard". The pieces were then finished on the lathe. This process was used for useful wares; cups, saucers, plates, bowls, vases, etc. More complicated shapes were realised in the same manner as figures, which were either hand-pressed or slip-cast.

When the modeller had completed his master's model in modelling clay or wax, it was cut into sections, the number depending on complications involved with undercuts and projections, and plaster-of-Paris moulds were made of them. A completed model cast from the moulds in wax (or lead for Chelsea toys) was retained as a master for the benefit of production continuity—new moulds, etc.

HAND PRESSING

In the English factories of Bow, Worcester, Plymouth and Bristol, and in most of the continental factories, the damp clay was pressed into the moulds with the fingers, then the various moulds making up the section would be keyed together until the plaster-of-Paris mould had absorbed all the water from the clay. The moulds could then be easily lifted off the shrunken clay which would then be in a "leather hard" condition.

SLIP CASTING

Modern factories who still make figures pour slip—that is plastic clay mixed with water and a small quantity of sodium carbonate—into a hole at the base of the model whose various moulds are fitted together for the operation. As soon as the outline of the moulds is filled and dried in contact with the plaster-of-Paris the rest of the slip is poured out, leaving a remarkably even, thin-walled casting, without any finger or tool marks.

Slip casting was used by Staffordshire potters in the manufacture of salt-glazed stoneware from 1740 and used at the old porcelain factories at Chelsea, Girl-in-the-Swing, Longton Hall, Derby and Worcester. Crisp, finely finished detail was possible with this method, but the moulds wore out quicker than the pressing type.

When the leather-hard parts were removed from their moulds they were passed to the "Repairer" who not only cleaned the joins and remodelled any damage but stuck the pieces together with slip, and pressed out any extra pieces with brass dies that were needed to complete the figure.

The flowers and leaves which covered the bases and supporting tree-trunks are all the fantasy of the "Repairers" who, although not recognised as designers, sometimes tried their hand at making original models. The "Repairer" was actually entrusted with making the same models in different sizes as at Derby, or any necessary revisions to the model.

DECORATION

The decoration of a service begins with a 10 inch dinner plate, from which the other pieces are adapted. Decoration can be accomplished in either of the following manners, or in a combination of them:

(*a*) The decoration may be in the white, that is applied reliefs, engravings, embossing, perforations or fret-work—all before glazing. It should be mentioned that high relief mouldings were modelled separately and joined to the main work with liquid slip before firing.
(*b*) The decoration may be executed in colours or gilding, or both.

The coloured decoration could be applied in three ways:

1. Underglaze colours—the most important was blue which came in many shades. It was derived from cobalt (or smalt) and was by far the most popular and successful colour. Powder blue does not imply the shade of blue as is commonly termed these days, but the method whereby the old porcelain makers blew the powdered dry cobalt on to the article to give a mottled blue effect.

2. Enamel colours and gold were applied after glazing, and another cool firing in a "muffle kiln" was carried out to fix the colours permanently. As the glaze on hard-paste is rock hard, the enamel colours applied afterwards stand out from the work and can easily be detected by touch. However, in the case of the soft-paste wares, the porosity of the body allowed not only the glaze, but the colours also to sink in and fuse as one, and in most cases it is impossible to feel anything above the soft glossy coat of the glaze. The colours are thus enriched and protected.

3. Colour glazes. These were used principally by the Chinese, like the celadon green which was intended to imitate jade and which was said to have magical properties which would cause the colour to change should the vessel contain poison. Sometimes coloured glazes were afterwards painted in enamel colours. Ernest Rosenthal (*Pottery and Ceramics*) gives this list of the more common oxides and the colours they produce:

Ferric Oxide	yellow, red, brown, black
Cobalt Oxide	shades of blue, depending on concentration, bluish green when chrome oxide is present
Copper Oxide	green, blue-green, shades of green and red
Manganese Oxide	violet, cream, brown, black
Chrome Oxide	green, pink, red, brown
Nickel Oxide	brown, violet
Uranium Oxide	yellow
Gold (Colloidal)	red, purple
Tin Oxide (in colloidal suspension)	white

THE GLAZE

The Chinese named the glaze the "skin", the kaolin the "bones" and the feldspar the "flesh" of porcelain. The glaze, another name for glass, is a transparent coat, sometimes tinged with colour, which covers the porcelain and gives it the high glassy sheen. The Chinese air-dried their products, then glazed them before the single firing, fusing the glaze with the porcelain. In Europe, the hard-paste was first fired at 600°–900°C, then coated with glaze. The second firing was at the full temperature of 1,350°–1,500°C, causing the simultaneous 'porcelainisation' of the material and the fusion of the glaze, which then became indistinguishable from the body. The feldspathic composition of hard-paste was non-porous and rock hard and required no sealing, so the glaze was purely decorative.

Soft-paste glazes were of a different nature and always remained distinct from the body. The frit compositions were soft and porous and the glazes were necessary to seal the material and to protect it from staining. The unglazed articles were first fired at 1,100°–1,150°C, then a thin glassy, transparent glaze, rich in lead or borax, was applied and the articles re-fired at 1,000°C to melt and fuse the glaze. The excessive fluid nature of the soft-paste glazes caused pools to form in crevices in figures and particularly on the foot rings of saucers—always something to look for when examining soft-paste manufactures.

METHODS OF IDENTIFICATION

Manufacture marks can be classified into five categories:

1. Incised marks, made with a tool, indicating either manufacturer, workman, or recipient.
2. Impressed marks, transfer printed or painted, used by factories for advertisement and protection.
3. Workmen's marks, to aid in settling wages and inspection of faulty work. They could derive from the potter, the repairer or the decorator.
4. Marks to indicate year of manufacture.
5. Mould or pattern numbers, for factory records.

6. Strokes incised with a cutting wheel across the manufacturer's mark to indicate degree of defectiveness (particularly at Meissen).

SUBJECTS

The most exquisite creation of the Oriental potter was the white porcelain of Tê-hua in the Province of Fukien, which we refer to as *blanc-de-chine*. This porcelain was always white and, used for religious ritual vessels, it had to be flawless. It was made into vases, birds, animals, and the God of Contentment—a cheerful, smiling fat gentleman called Pu Tai—and a Madonna figure or Goddess of Mercy, Kuan Yin. The Fukien style was widely imitated at Meissen, Saint-Cloud, Bow and Chelsea.

European potters also followed designs, forms and decorations used by the goldsmiths and silversmiths. Large quantities of useful wares were made, tea bowls and saucers, cups for coffee and chocolate, plates and dishes, teapots, jugs and coffee and chocolate pots.

Sculptors were introduced into the porcelain factory, and they modelled delightful figures after subjects from contemporary life. The figures were originally intended as decorations on the dinner table to replace the sugar models made by the pastry cooks for the elaborate banquets given by the nobility. Ultimately these figures and groups of figures were made to rest on the chimney-piece so they were modelled from the front rather than all round. The subjects of these figures were ladies in panniered dresses, gentlemen in their be-ribboned satin coats, Shepherds and Shepherdesses, workers and peasant folk, allegorical figures representing the five Senses, Muses, and groups representing incidents in classical mythology.

The theatre made an important contribution. Rocks and bushes used on stage inspired the bocage of flowering hawthorn which became the charming background decoration of chimney-piece figures. The great theatrical tradition of the Italian Comedy —*Commedia del l'Arte*—was the inspiration of some of porcelain's most outstanding models. The *Commedia dell'Arte* was composed of traditional stock characters who extemporised in outrageous situation comedy. We are fortunate that some of the plays were recorded by Goldoni.

Arlecchino was the oldest personage in the Italian Comedy. It is believed that his original was the young satyr, a clown in the Greek Old Comedy; an entertainment based on phallic ritual and the ceremonies of Dyonysos known to have taken place from about 500 B.C. Greek art was universally adopted by Imperial Rome and Greek theatrical characters were absorbed and adapted.

The young satyr was a favourite performer at the Games, where he did acrobatics, leaped and danced and amused the audience with his clowning. He wore a repulsive black leather mask with pin-holes for his eyes. The mask was furrowed, covered with warts and bore an ugly animal-like expression. He covered himself with skins, wore the white hat of the peasant and carried a small baton. Some believed he was the protégé of Mercury, whose caduceus the baton resembled. The Greek clown was always a slave. The Renaissance *Arlecchino* was always a servant who constantly cheated his master and practised every vice of man. He seduced, he lied, he stole, he was lewd and obscene, but all was forgiven by the audience for he was always endearingly in trouble.

The first illustration available of *Arlecchino* is of the sixteenth century in which he wears an untidy suit covered in patches, which was the origin of the motley costume familiar on eighteenth-century porcelain models. When the Italian Comedy went to France his name became *Arlequin* and he was sophisticated, witty and elegant, for the public disliked the old vulgarity. The artists who portrayed him were cultured, educated men, who used their intellect to give the character meaning and personality. They made him a clown in the Chaplinesque manner and played upon the emotions of the audience. In England he became Harlequin, who with his fellow players founded the great pantomime tradition.

His master was *Pantalone*, the elderly middle-class Venetian merchant who was always modelled in porcelain leaning forward with his hands under his black coat. He wore a brown mask with a long nose and pointed beard, and his regional accent and mannerisms were exaggerated. Always avaricious and amorous, he was cheated and cuckolded, and his senile antics made him the subject of ridicule. He was the villain of the piece.

Il Dottore was another elderly type. Originally a Doctor of Law and later a Doctor of Medicine, he came from Bologna and in exaggerated Bolognese accents bored the company with lengthy quasi-intellectual dissertations. He was useless as a lawyer and lost whatever cases he undertook, sometimes landing his clients in prison, and as a doctor he was dangerous to his patients. He too was both amorous and avaricious. He wore the long black gown of the university don and a black mask, with a large black nose and the bulging purple cheeks of the dipsomaniac.

Il Capitano was the soldier—a braggart and a coward. A Neopolitan, he caricatured the proud and overbearing Spaniards who were then in occupation. He appeared in military clothing and his flesh-coloured mask had a large nose and magnificent black moustaches.

Scaramuccia, another Neapolitan, was also a caricature of a Spanish type. He was the civilian, cowardly and quarrelsome, and boasted of his most unlikely noble birth. Dressed in black in the Spanish style, his mask gave him enormous moustaches and a monumental nose and a mouth that stretched from ear to ear.

The ladies of the company were always played by women—an attraction at a time when female rôles were usually played by young men. They were unmasked and played attractive straight roles. *Isabella* was the female lead, the daughter of the house, the virtuous wife or sometimes the beautiful courtesan. She was usually talented and musical.

Colombina was the maid, the perky buxom country girl, who was no better than she should be. Flirting vivaciously with all and sundry, her true match was *Arlecchino*.

Other characters developed from the originals as succeeding artists gave their individual interpretations, many of which were reproduced in porcelain.

[4] ARTISTIC STYLES

The first European porcelain products were copies of Chinese imports, partly with the intent to deceive the public as to their origin, and partly because there was no tradition on which to fall back. The designs of goldsmiths and silversmiths were also copied and later the factories developed styles of their own, and specialised in their various fields along the lines of the current art styles.

The artistic styles which influenced porcelain were the baroque, the rococo, the neo-classical and the Empire or neo-Greek.

BAROQUE

This style was introduced in Italy in the seventeenth century and adopted by the Catholic Church as part of the Counter-Reformation. A new spirit was rising, inspiring the artists to express themselves with newly-found technical virtuosity. The style they developed became more "effect" than "form" and every art and artifice were exploited to achieve sensational and rhetorical results. With extraordinary skill, stone was chiselled into delicate flying draperies and audacious techniques in composition expressed the new freedom of design. The greatest exponent of this style was Lorenzo Bernini, whose sculpture in Rome has added much to the lustre of the Eternal City.

The baroque style had little influence in England. The Reformation had been firmly established and the new Jesuit Catholic Revical was not accepted, so few baroque churches were built. Appreciation of Dutch architecture because of William of Orange, watered down the Italian tendency and under the masterful leadership of Inigo Jones and Sir Christopher Wren the English Renaissance style continued. Some architects (including Wren) played with baroque, and altar-pieces, fonts and sepulchral monuments ensued, often melded with rococo.

In France, baroque was adopted for the same reasons as in Italy but without Italian excesses. One of the most brilliant of baroque sculptors in France was Guillaume Coustou (1677–

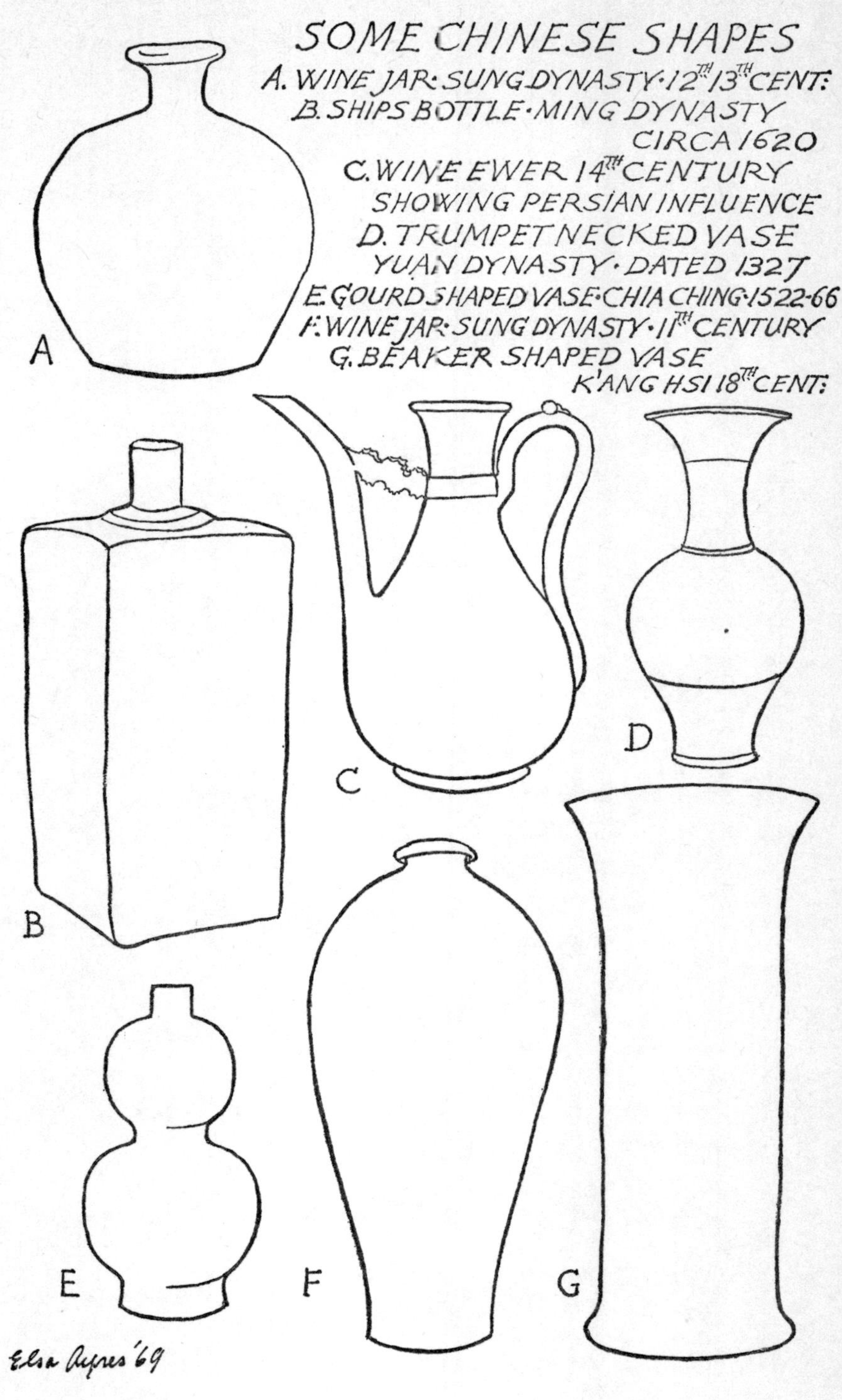
SOME CHINESE SHAPES
A. WINE JAR · SUNG DYNASTY · 12TH 13TH CENT:
B. SHIPS BOTTLE · MING DYNASTY
CIRCA 1620
C. WINE EWER 14TH CENTURY
SHOWING PERSIAN INFLUENCE
D. TRUMPET NECKED VASE
YUAN DYNASTY · DATED 1327
E. GOURD SHAPED VASE · CHIA CHING · 1522-66
F. WINE JAR · SUNG DYNASTY · 11TH CENTURY
G. BEAKER SHAPED VASE
K'ANG HSI 18TH CENT:
A
B
C
D
E
F
G
Elsa Ayres '69

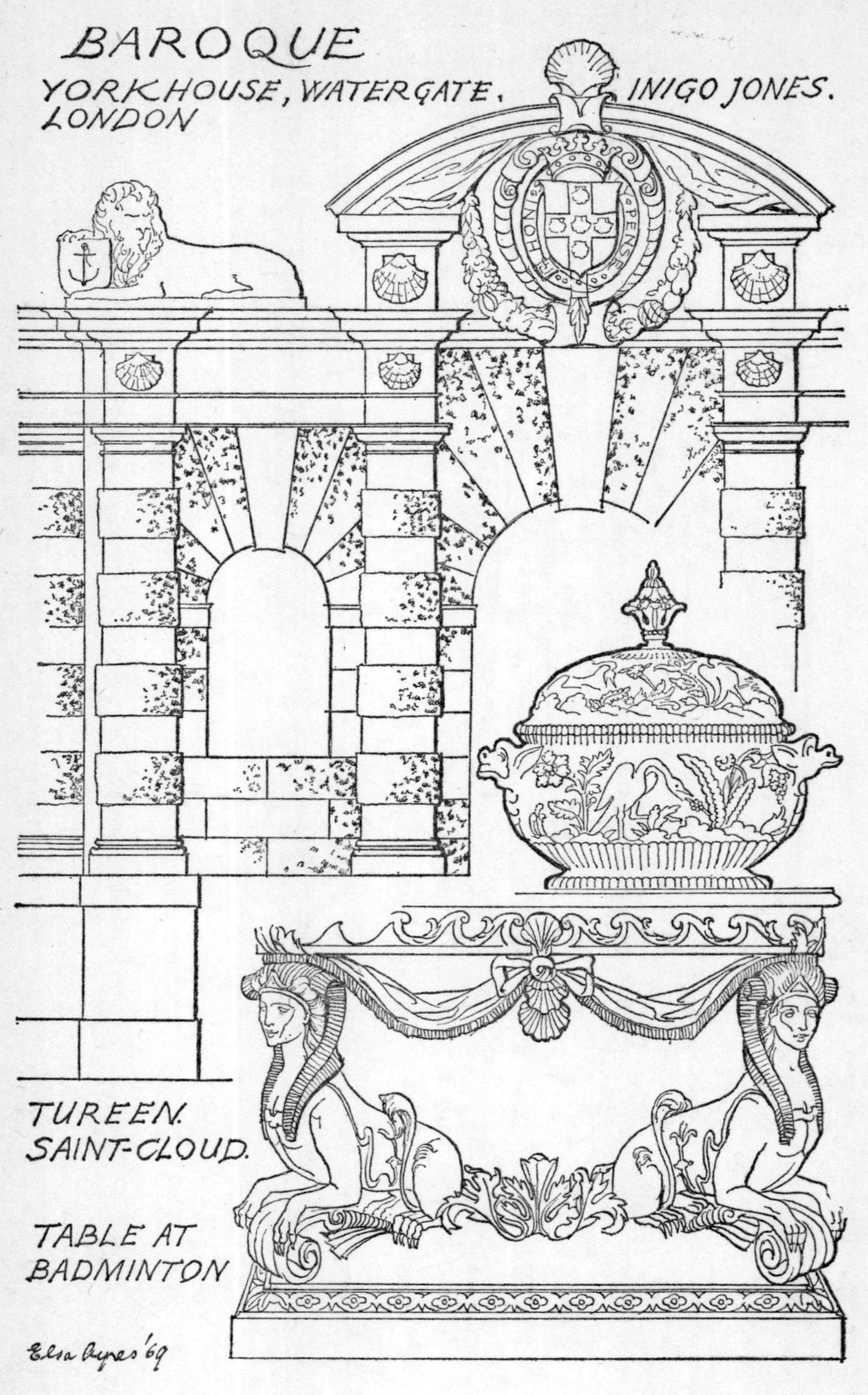
BAROQUE
YORKHOUSE, WATERGATE, LONDON
INIGO JONES.
HONI
PENSE
TUREEN. SAINT-CLOUD.
TABLE AT BADMINTON
Elsa Byres '69

1746), who is known particularly for his "Marly horses", the stone prancing horses with a restraining groom, made originally for the Château de Marly outside Paris, and which now stand on either side of the Champs-Elysées at the Plaçe de la Concorde.

Although the baroque style was eagerly patronised by the Church, joyful in the triumph of the Counter-Reformation, it was lacking in spirituality and was seldom free from sensuality. The fusion of spiritual and temporal things, which seventeenth-century artists used merely for decorative effect, owed nothing to mediaeval simplicity and faith. J. A. Symonds in *The Catholic Reaction* records that on the sculptored monument to Pope Paul III there is a nude figure representing Truth which was a portrait of the Pope's sister, Giulia Bella, who was mistress of Pope Alexander VI (Borgia). Sir Banister Fletcher wrote, "At its best baroque was an assertion of freedom, at its worst a lapse into licence".

The baroque style in porcelain was adopted at Meissen especially by *Modellmeister* Kändler whose exuberant modelling, alarming projections and startling postures, demonstrate the secular development of this art style.

A new style appeared in porcelain soon after 1730. It was a development of the baroque, but more delicate and graceful. It was light, with frivolous overtones, veering to fantasy. Rococo, from the French *rocaille* meaning rock-work, employed the medium of elegant scrolls and free-flowing asymmetrical forms. It was born in France. Sophisticated and elegant, it was synonymous with Louis XV and his Court, and was a decorative art form for the privileged few. The artists Watteau, Fragonard, Boucher and Pillement painted extravaganzas of theatrical unreality suitable for the salon. Their subjects were a mirror of Court life, which was conducted by protocol and orders of precedence and lived in Olympian splendour, removed from the realities of life in the heavily taxed middle and lower classes. Rococo art was an escapist paradox in the "Age of Reason". With so much patronage, cabinet-makers became master craftsmen, and the finest furniture the world has ever seen was

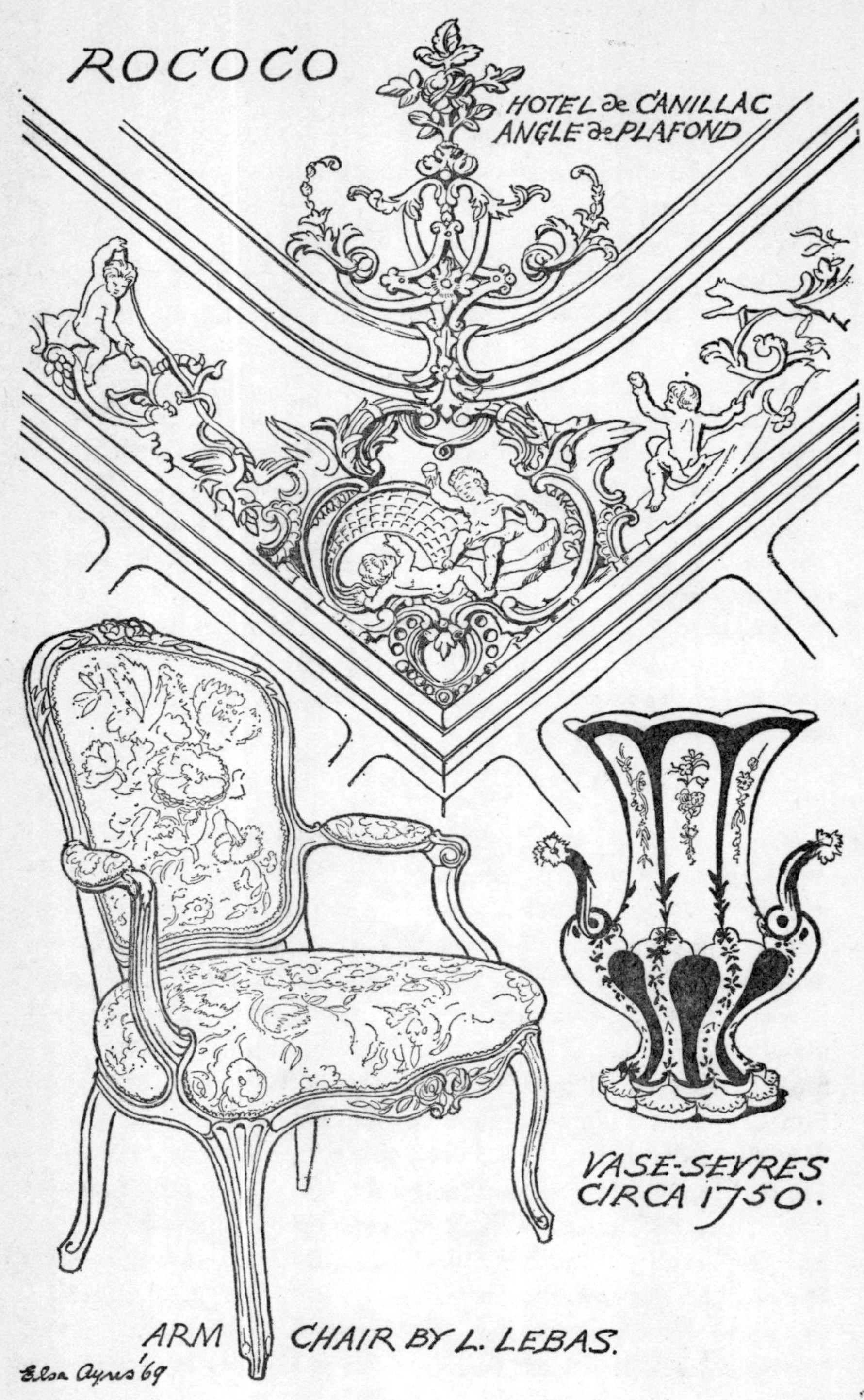
ROCOCO
HOTEL de CANILLAC
ANGLE de PLAFOND
VASE-SEVRES
CIRCA 1750.
ARM CHAIR BY L. LEBAS.
Elsa Ayres '69

eagerly collected. Rococo was like some French wine, it did not travel too well. Its ebullience was watered down in the temperate English climate, and did not reach perfection until furniture in the "French taste" was designed by Chippendale, Adam and Hepplewhite.

However, the lyrical, amusing character of the rococo style suited the tense, fragile porcelain medium and coincided with the finest period for European porcelain. The most outstanding exponent of rococo art in porcelain was Franz Anton Bustelli at Nymphenburg, who was closely followed by the artists at Sèvres.

NEO-CLASSICAL

Towards 1770, the fashion altered and a complete change was enthusiastically received. Simplicity became the keyword, and the fantastic extravagancies of the baroque and rococo were abandoned for the vertical and horizontal lines of the neo-classical style. The adoption of classical forms was inspired by the recent publication of books with illustrations on discoveries at Pompeii and Herculaneum by J. J. Winckelmann, Sir William Hamilton and others.

One of the finest English artists of the period was John Flaxman who became the first professor of sculpture at the Royal Academy. His drawings showed a true understanding of classical form, and whilst not the greatest of sculptors, his art was in contrast to that of the Italian, Canova and the Dane, Thorwaldson, who "fined down" what they saw in nature to appear (as they thought) as if "the spirit alone had wrought it." The results were shallow and meaningless by comparison and whilst generally accepted in their time as typical of the tradition of classical times, this was proved to be wrong when the Elgin Marbles were brought to England and studied at first hand.

The leading English architects of the style were the brothers Robert and James Adam, who, returning to England after a sojourn in Rome, became the toast of the country-house building aristocracy. They discarded the solidity of the Palladian classicism, which was a Renaissance version of the antique, for their own version. Husks and swags and graceful classical

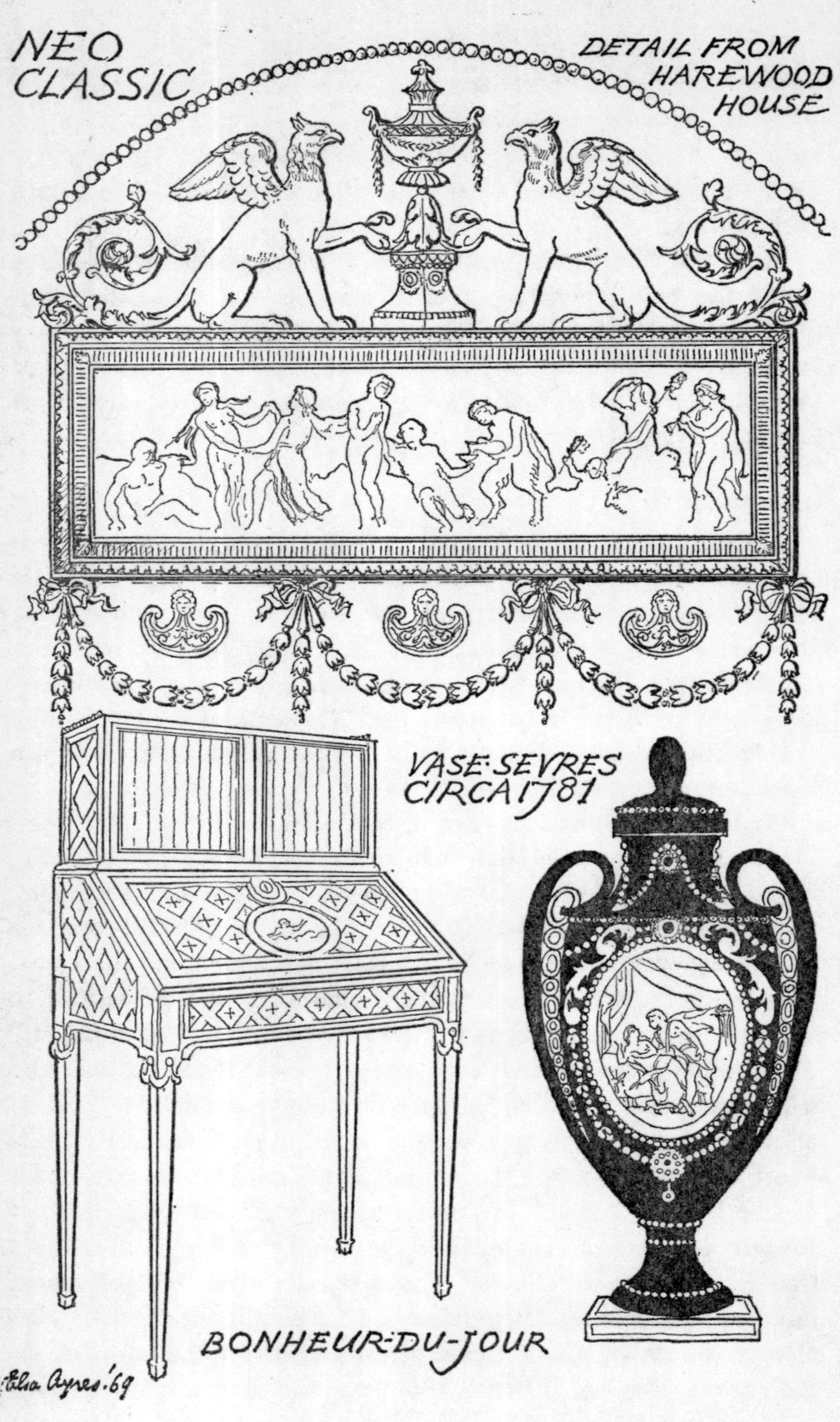
NEO CLASSIC
DETAIL FROM HAREWOOD HOUSE
VASE·SEVRES CIRCA 1781
BONHEUR-DU-JOUR

figures were used tastefully in plaster reliefs or paintings to decorate the interiors of great houses which were given elegant porticos and columns.

English furniture was graceful and light. Square bracket feet became splayed into an elegant shaped apron front. Satinwood was introduced from the West and East Indies, and inlays of variegated woods were used with restraint and taste. Ever conservative, the British finally adapted the best features of the French cabinet-makers' art and created an English style which was superb. The designs of Adam, Hepplewhite and Sheraton need no further explanation.

The Louis Seize style, introduced in France about 1760 (although anticipating the King's reign), was a sentimental, elegant version of the neo-classical, without its severity and with the delicacy of the preceding rococo style. The furniture continued to be magnificent, although the cabriole legs were now straight and fluted and the *bombé* and serpentine *commodes* had developed into simple, rectangular shapes. In the "transition" period details of both were incorporated in the same piece. Leading cabinet-makers included Jean Riesener (1734–1806) and Georges Jacob (1739–1814), who made many pieces for the royal use.

In porcelain, the finest work was made at Sèvres, whose lead was followed by her contemporaries. But the cool breeze of competition was blowing across the Channel. Wedgwood with his business acumen and sense of timing, was mass-producing his Jasper-ware and Queen's-ware in the true neo-classical style. His coloured basalt vases, with white low relief classical friezes, captured the popular imagination, and shipments were being sent all over Europe. It was the beginning of the end for porcelain.

EMPIRE OR NEO-GREEK

This period in art fashion coincided with the French First Empire and Napoleon Bonaparte. It was a development of the earlier neo-classical style, but was pompous and aggressive by comparison. Studied copies of Egyptian motifs were employed and the Napoleonic eagle became a favourite emblem.

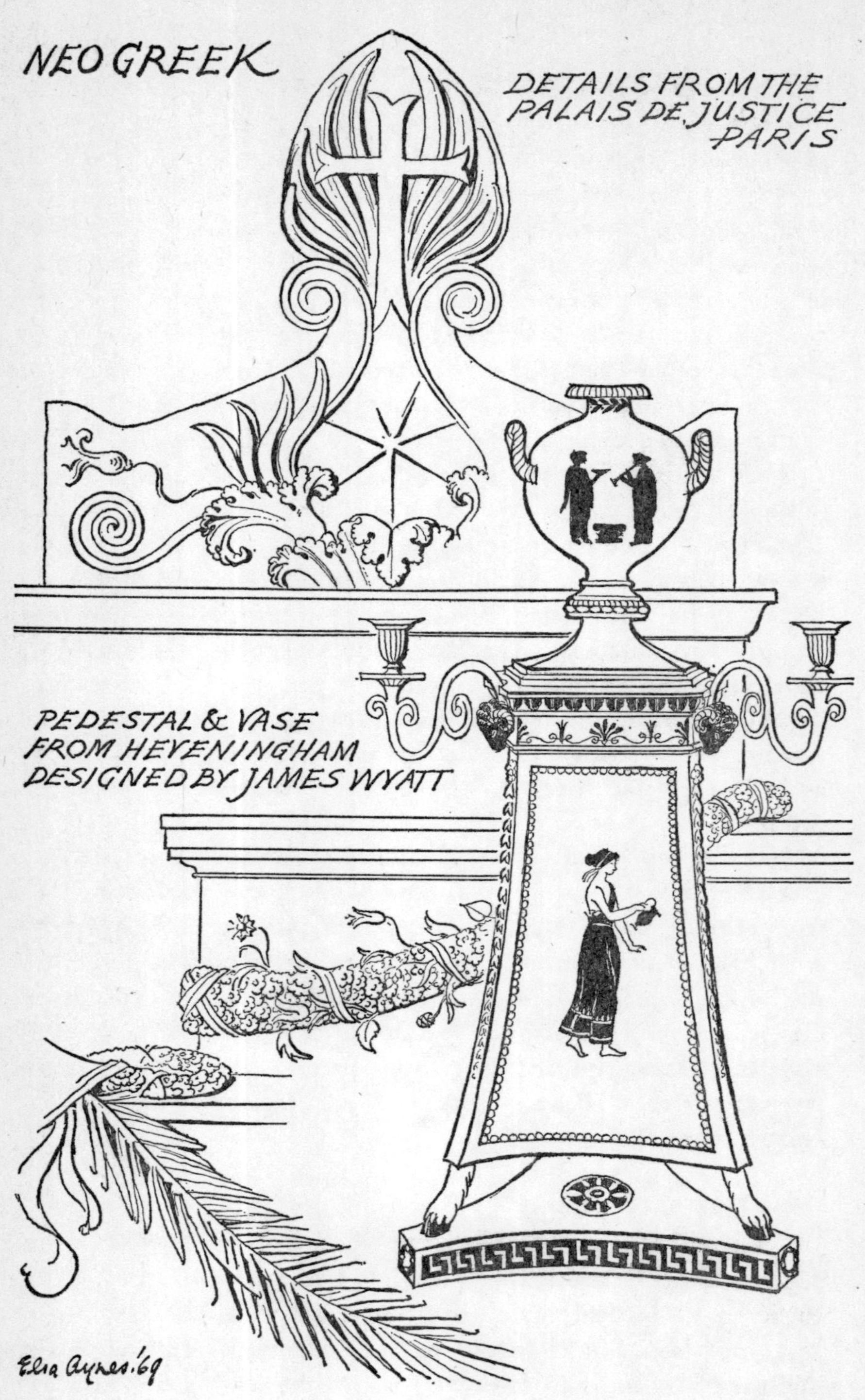
NEO GREEK
DETAILS FROM THE
PALAIS DE JUSTICE
PARIS
PEDESTAL & VASE
FROM HEVENINGHAM
DESIGNED BY JAMES WYATT
Elsa Aynes '69

The English architect, Henry Holland, supplanted Robert Adam in popularity. By this time, the Adam style had become too elaborate and feminine. Horace Walpole, after seeing Holland's work for the Prince of Wales (later Regent) at Carlton House in 1785, wrote, "How sick one shall be after this chaste place, of Mr. Adam's gingerbread and sippets of embroidery"!

Henry Holland introduced the Regency style, ante-dating the actual Regency which was 1811–1820 by about twenty years. He eagerly adopted the French designs and taste which were popular with the Prince and his côterie, and developed a version of the French Directoire style. He never copied the French originals exactly, but modified them into an exciting English fashion. After his death in 1806, the forms degenerated into heavy copies after the antique. "Strong and massy furniture is everywhere vulgar and unpleasing", wrote Archibald Alison.

It was during this period that the feeling for porcelain began to wane. The beautiful white surface of the paste was covered with enamels, and used like a canvas for pictures copied from museums, or painted to represent marble or precious metals. Smothering of porcelain with decoration defeats the purpose of the medium and marks a decline in what was once a superb art form.

In the first quarter of the nineteenth century, a standard bone china paste was generally adopted, and porcelain can now only be judged on the merit of the decoration, and not, as with earlier works, on the product as a whole.

There was, however, one notable exception and that was the superb soft-paste made at Nant Garw and Swansea by Billingsley, the last of the great arcanists.

[5] PORCELAIN IN EUROPE

By the beginning of the eighteenth century, the mania for porcelain had grown to extraordinary proportions. Pewter and silver had been satisfactory for ale and wine, but now that the fashionable demanded tea, coffee and chocolate, they wanted the dainty vessels used by the Chinese. These had to be obtained regardless of cost. On 10th April, 1689, Lord Bristol wrote: "For a white teapot and basin for the wife £4 16s. 9d." Evelyn, about 1685, recorded that "porcelain" saucers, etc., were very popular with fashionable ladies.

The demand was so great that European potters endeavoured to make it themselves. Travellers to China tried to discover the porcelain formula, but the Chinese were wary and parried the question.

It was not until a French Jesuit missionary, Père d'Entrecolles, sent home descriptions of Chinese porcelain manufacture in 1712 and 1722, together with specimens of kaolin and petuntse in the latter year, that research came to be undertaken seriously. The letters were published in 1717 and 1724 under the title of *Lettres édifiantes et curieuses*.

The first porcelain to be produced outside the Orient was at Florence, nursery of Renaissance art and culture. In 1575–1587 a curious greyish-white soft-paste porcelain was made "with the help of a Levantine", probably a Persian. In France at Rouen Louis Poterat is believed to have made some soft-paste porcelain in 1672. Letters patent were granted to Saint-Cloud in 1702, for a process improvement porcelain they had been making since 1693 "as perfect as the Chinese". None of these was true porcelain.

True porcelain was invented by Böttger at Meissen, in 1709 when he discovered the secret of the kaolin-feldspar combination and made true hard-paste porcelain similar to the Chinese for the first time in Europe. The other factories in Germany made hard-paste, for they were started by breakaway workmen from Meissen. The porcelain factories in France which were considered inferior to those of Germany, made only soft-paste until 1769.

The Capodimonte factory was begun in 1743 in Naples by Charles III King of the two Sicilies and his Queen who, in spite of the fact that she was the daughter of Augustus III of Saxony, had no access to the hard-paste formula—and the Capodimonte factory made only soft-paste. The first English factories also made soft-paste. Saint-Cloud inspired the arcanists at Chelsea, and at Bow it was discovered that the addition of calcined animal bones to the paste made it more stable. Other factories in the London area opened and closed and apart from Limehouse, records have been lost and they are now unknown, except where in the excavation for new buildings the remains of a kiln and broken china denote their existence. Until quite recently, early London-made soft-paste was attributed to either Chelsea or Bow, but with the new discoveries many collections will have to be reassessed.

The invention of hard-paste porcelain in England occurred after Cookworthy's discovery of kaolin in Cornwall, and this gave rise to the factories at Plymouth, Bristol, and New Hall, and so to the Staffordshire china industry.

Another English formula was conceived by Benjamin Lund originally at Limehouse and then at Lowdins Glass Works at Bristol, which led to the steatitic paste developed at Worcester, Liverpool and Caughley.

Porcelain was bought by the wealthy for show as well as for daily use. It was fashionable to make a collection. After the social changes following the French Revolution, the demand for luxurious porcelain declined all over Europe and apart from the few which were financially sound, the factories closed. The nineteenth century saw the beginning of a new mass-production porcelain industry which supplied the demands of a wide public. This book is only concerned with the European factories that were founded before 1830.

The early European makers of porcelain were known in their most illustrious state as "arcanists" (from the Latin *arcanum* meaning "mystery"), and it was they who, despite disappointments and financial losses, endeavoured to make porcelain in Europe to supplant the imported Chinese ware. Their costs were high, due to the large proportion of firing breakages, termed, "wasters", and unless they had unlimited financial backing they frequently became bankrupt and their factories were sold. The manufacture marks were altered accordingly, and it is through these changes of marks that pieces of early porcelain can be identified, but, I hasten to add, not entirely. An identifiable mark does not preclude the possibility of forgery. In fact, the last item to be examined is the mark, which should only corroborate the other evidence.

In the beginning the European factories copied the Chinese and then each other, sometimes copying the marks also, but these do not rate as forgeries in the true sense today, for the early copies were sometimes better than the originals, with the added *panàche* of their own. Decoration alone is insufficient evidence except possibly for the identity of the artist. Independent decorators bought porcelain in the white from several factories simultaneously, and there was also a drift of painters from factory to factory. The most important clue for the identification of porcelain is the appearance and qualities of the paste or body. Scientific knowledge was limited and chemical analysis primitive. The potters employed local or other materials (as the history of the factory tells us) from which only large ferrous impurities could be magnetically removed, and depending on the formula, the resulting paste assumed a special identity which through experience the collector is able to recognise.

The style of the example should also be considered, for each factory had its own specialities and according to the date at which the piece was presumed to be manufactured, so it must conform to the art form which was in fashion at the time.

Different colours were invented at recorded dates and can be confirmed. There is a variation in colouring from factory to factory which only experience can make apparent.

From these remarks the reader will appreciate that identification of early porcelain is not a simple matter to be learned from a book. Even the experts have been known to differ on what is after all a matter of opinion based on years of experience. The story of porcelain, however, is so fascinating that a passing curiosity in the subject could be converted into a passionate interest.

Chapter Two

Germany and Austria

BY THE BEGINNING of the eighteenth century the power of the Holy Roman Empire had declined and had lost its original significance. Voltaire wrote that it was neither holy, Roman nor an Empire. It now consisted of Austria, Bohemia and Hungary and an association of individual German Principalities from which the traditional Electors were drawn. The title Holy Roman Emperor was now embarrassingly reduced to Emperor of the Romans.

The Austrian Empire under the Hapsburgs struggled to maintain its hereditary dignities, but the rest of the German Principalities rebelliously sought their own independence.

They were all suspicious of each other and of their neighbours. They admired and envied the French Court of Louis XIV at Versailles, and sought to emulate its elegance, after the barbaric conditions prevalent in their own lands following the Thirty Years War.

The disastrous Thirty Years War had only ceased in 1648, when half the population of the German States had been annihilated and the country completely exhausted by waves of pillaging soldiery. Wolves were said to roam in Saxony and conditions were pitiful.

The Princes of Germany sought the re-establishment of order. Frederick I invited the French Huguenots persecuted by Louis XIV to immigrate to Prussia to swell the decimated population, and 300,000 foreigners were absorbed. In 1700, one-third of the population of Berlin was French.

Prussia, a separate Kingdom under the redoubtable Hohenzollerns, emerged as a highly disciplined and militaristic machine, and soon gained ascendancy over the other German States, rivalling the Empire, whose lands included large areas which were necessary to Prussia's expansionist programme.

When the young Maria Theresa succeeded to the Imperial throne on the death of the Emperor in 1740, Frederick the Great invaded Silesia, and the rest of Europe joined in what was intended to be the dismemberment of the Austrian Empire. Maria Theresa fled to Hungary and appealed for help in an impassioned speech from the Palace balcony. The sight of the young defenceless woman with her child in her arms, roused the chivalry of the Hungarians, who enthusiastically went to her aid, and Austria was saved. However, Prussia retained Silesia.

The German Princes built their palaces in the style of Versailles, and modelled their Courts in its image. The arts were cultivated, music, poetry and painting were encouraged and appreciated. Handel, Haydn, Mozart and Beethoven could not have been born in a more receptive era. Private orchestras and ballet companies were formed, and theatricals were performed by visiting *Commedia dell 'Arte* companies and by the members of the Court themselves.

A mania for porcelain soon swept through Germany. Oriental examples were eagerly collected and special porcelain rooms were constructed in order to display them to advantage. The pieces were arranged on gilded consoles in a large mass in the baroque style to give a striking effect. It was the age of absolutism, and a fine collection of porcelain was an impressive method of proclaiming the owner's superiority.

The German Princes were envious of the successful Meissen factory and resented the high prices they were called upon to pay. They tried unsuccessfully for years to start their own individual factories, believing that they would be able to compete with Meissen, but when they ultimately did start to manufacture, with the help of Meissen defaulters, they discovered that porcelain was expensive to produce and the projects were generally abandoned.

The defaulting Meissen arcanists who were responsible for the formation of these factories in fact performed a great service to the world at large, for they broke the Meissen monopoly and enabled so much more exquisite porcelain to be made. They included Christoph Konrad Hunger (*c.* 1700–1760), Josef Jacob Ringler (1730–1804), Samuel Stöltzel (*d.* 1737), Johann Benckgraff (1708–1753), Nikolaus Paul (*c.* 1770) and Christian Daniel Busch (*d.* 1790).

Christoph Konrad Hunger, a gilder and enameller at Meissen with Johann Friederich Böttger (1682–1719) escaped to Vienna in 1717. He persuaded Du Paquier (*d.* 1751) to entice Stöltzel, the kiln master at Meissen, and the two men established the formula for Vienna porcelain which was first made in 1719. Hunger left in 1719 and went to Venice where he helped the Vezzi brothers to establish their factory. He returned to Meissen in 1727, and from there he appeared in Sweden at Rorstrand and in 1737 at Copenhagen. From 1744 to 1748 he was at St. Petersburg, after which there is no further record. He called himself an arcanist, but he had little personal success in that profession. He was a fine enameller and gilder, and there are several signed pieces of his work.

Josef Jakob Ringler began at Vienna as a painter in about 1744, and through his friendship with Du Paquier's daughter learned the secrets of the arcanum. Ringler was the most influential porcelain maker of his time. Honey in *European Ceramic Art* lists his wanderings: Künersberg (1747–1748), Höchst (1750–1751), Strasbourg (1751–?), Neudeck-Nymphenburg (1753-1757), Schrezheim (1757), Ellwangen (1758–1759), Ludwigsburg (1759–1802).

Johann Benckgraff, a potter, learned the secrets of kiln construction from Ringler, and helped in the formation of Wegley's Berlin factory in 1752, and then Fürstenberg in 1753. An opportunist, he was involved in the theft of clay and a kiln model which he disposed of to rival concerns.

Nikolaus Paul was concerned with Weesp, Fulda, Kloster-Veilsdorf and others. His associate, Christian Daniel Busch, worked at Kelsterbach, Frankenthal and Strasbourg.

From these beginnings, Europe's finest porcelain was created. It sometimes seems a curious paradox to non-Germans that art forms such as music, poetry and porcelain should be so perfectly developed by what we have come to accept as a militaristic nation. However, during the eighteenth century the German states were not a nation and were not aggressive until Frederick the Great of Prussia led the way to Bismarck, Kaiser Wilhelm and Hitler. The ideology of the *Nibelungen* where men are heroes who fight to conquer and then idealise their experiences in poetry and music was adopted in the nineteenth century and to German thought explains the inconsistency. Tennessee Williams in *The Night of the Iguana* called it "the logic of contradictions".

[1] MEISSEN, Saxony 1710—Present Day

Meissen or Dresden? There is some confusion in the public mind about these two descriptions. There was, and is, only one porcelain factory in Saxony, and this is at Meissen. No porcelain was ever made in Dresden, the capital of Saxony. Decorating establishments were founded in or around Dresden, and enjoying the privilege of the porcelain reputation of their city, bought large quantities in the white from the Meissen factory, fourteen miles away, and finished and marked it for sale as "Dresden China". "Dresden Shepherdess" has, however, become part of the language, and Honey (*Dresden China*) suggests that it would be pedantic to insist on the correct term of Meissen. Although this is a strong argument, it adds to the confusion. It would perhaps be simpler to continue the custom in the antique trade of describing porcelain made in the eighteenth century by the name of Meissen, and all the later works, whether completely or partly finished at Meissen, by the name of Dresden.

Augustus II, Elector of Saxony, King of Poland, surnamed "the Strong" from his great bodily strength, possessed a taste for intellectual pursuits and was a great patron of the arts. Finding the Meissen residence of his ancestors too restricted for his magnificent plans, he removed his Court to Dresden, where he built superb palaces and public buildings—this at a time when most of Northern Europe was in a state of semi-barbarism.

An apothecary from Berlin, Johann Friedrich Böttger arrived in Saxony from Prussia where he had been persecuted by

Frederick the Great because it was believed that he was a successful alchemist. He was taken before Augustus but his fate was no better and he was virtually imprisoned and put to work.

After years of unsuccessful experiments, Augustus became impatient, but was persuaded to transfer Böttger to the laboratory of E. W. von Tschirnhaus, who was then seeking the formula for true porcelain. Böttger ironically placed this sign over his door, "*Es macht der Gott der grosse Schöpfer aus einem Goldmacher einem Töpfer*" (It pleased the Lord to change a Goldmaker into a Potter).

In 1708 Böttger produced a hard red stoneware which he called *Jaspis-Porzellan* in imitation of the Chinese seventeenth century Yi-hsing wares. Augustus the Strong immediately perceived the importance of this discovery, and removed Böttger to the fortress of Albrechtsburg at Meissen, where although provided with every comfort and luxury he was closely guarded so that he might not escape with his valuable secret. Augustus then established the Saxon Porcelain factory there in 1710, with Böttger as Director.

Red stoneware was produced successfully. It had the opacity, grain and toughness of pottery and was polished and gilded and mounted in silver. Glittering colour glazes were also used, which gave the ware the appearance of Chinese lacquered work. It was first placed on the market at the Easter Fair at Leipzig in 1713.

Böttger finally succeeded in producing true porcelain in 1709. His was the honour of the second invention after the Chinese. He had had no help from Père d'Entrecolles, whose letters had arrived later, but brilliantly he had solved the problem of the kaolin-flux combination. Curiously enough, he never used feldspar as it was not located at Siebenlehner in Saxony until 1722, when it was introduced into the formula by Höroldt. Böttger used alabaster or marble instead.

Kaolin was discovered in Saxony by accident. A rich Iron Master of the Erzebirge, Johann Schnorr, while riding near Aue noticed that his horse's hooves continually stuck into the soft white earth. The general use of hair powder at that time prompted Schnorr to take a sample of the earth, and subsequently he had hair powder made from it, which was widely sold. Böttger discovered to his great joy that it was the kaolin for which he had been searching.

Great secrecy was observed, and kaolin continued to be known in commerce as *Schnorrische weisse Erde* (Schnorr's white earth). Exportation was forbidden under severe penalties, and it was transported to the factory in sealed barrels. The workmen were sworn to secrecy, and the motto *Geheim bis ins Grab* (secret unto death), was printed in large letters all over the factory. Nevertheless, men did escape from the factory, and with them the secret spread and rival establishments were formed. The most serious defection was in 1719 when Samuel Stöltzel, who had been in charge of the paste and kilns, left to join one of the Meissen gilders, Christoph Konrad Hunger, in Vienna.

The designs were copies of Chinese and Japanese models, but the potting was thick and heavy. The quality was considerably improved later, and some very fine work was achieved by Böttger under the most primitive and inadequate conditions. There were considerable difficulties in painting the earliest white porcelain. The ideal was a range of colours equal to the Chinese, and above all an underglaze blue and a pale yellow—a colour reserved in China for the Emperor alone, but it was some time before satisfactory results could be obtained.

Augustus the Strong founded his "Japanese Palace" in Dresden in 1717, to house his great collection of Oriental porcelain (to which were later added examples of the products of the Meissen factory). He coveted forty-eight Oriental vases which were in the possession of Frederick of Prussia in his Charlottenburg Palace near Berlin. It is said that there was nothing to distinguish them but their enormous size, and ultimately Augustus exchanged them for twelve "big men" from his personal guard of Dragoons. The vases became known as the *Dragonervasen*.

Augustus gave little financial support to the factory and Honey suggests that this was because of Böttger's failure to produce great vases in blue and white like the Chinese. Böttger was essentially a chemist, with little artistic or executive ability. He was a poor manager and could not control the workmen, who through lack of sufficient funds were not paid regularly. Financial difficulties prevented the building of a large kiln, and quantities of unfired porcelain were allowed to accumulate. Although Böttger had been formally granted his freedom in 1715, the years of virtual imprisonment had undermined his health. He had become a heavy drinker, his troubles at the factory aggravated the situation, and he died at the age of thirty-seven on 13th March, 1719.

After Böttger's death, Augustus the Strong appointed a Commission to set the factory in order, with powers to hire and fire workmen or officials where necessary. He provided capital and the staff were properly paid, and almost immediately the reforms brought good results and the business prospered. A happy event was the return of Stöltzel from Vienna, begging for reinstatement. He brought a young enameller who had worked with him for some time, and this young man, whose name was Johann Gregor Höroldt (1691–1775), was to become the greatest influence on Meissen porcelain during his life time. An artist of ability, he had an instinct for porcelain and designed and selected what was suitable for it. He was just the man the factory needed. His talents were soon recognised, and under his management standards were generally improved and the factory grew in strength until it had no rival outside China.

Höroldt's first task was to satisfy the King's demand for underglaze blue, and with the help of the arcanist David Köhler a beautiful blue from cobalt was produced. Large vases were made for the decoration of the King's palace and these were boldly painted from freely adapted Chinese designs. On his deathbed in 1725, Köhler is said to have passed on the formula for the underglaze blue, but the true recipe was lost and Köhler's clear blue was never reproduced until modern times.

By 1731, Höroldt had perfected a large range of enamel colours which included yellows, greens, greys, lilac, crimson and purple, which he recorded. In 1731 he was appointed *Hof Kommisar* with a salary of 1,000 thalers, and in the same year the sculptor Johann Joachim Kändler (1706–1775), whose plastic work was to play so important a part in the story of Meissen, was engaged as a modeller. But the full flowering of the superb artistic and technical quality of Meissen was due to the inspired direction of one man—Höroldt. Being a painter, Höroldt saw to it that the shapes of the wares were simple and uncluttered so that they would form a suitable medium for exquisite miniature painting. It was under his direction that the delicate paintings of harbour scenes were created, some by his own hand. The figures in the foreground were quite tiny, with an important background of masts and buildings.

Chinoiseries were popular. These were fanciful Chinese scenes taken from travel books. Deliciously quaint, they bore no resemblance to the paintings on the original Chinese porcelain. The greatest exponent of this medium was the artist Adam Friedrich von Löwenfinck (1714–1754), who was apprenticed at Meissen in 1726. He was a painter of great originality; his *chinoiseries* in particular show great dash and innovation and his silhouetted figures are exceptional. With his handling of the excellent colours (including a remarkable black) and using delicate brush strokes, he created compositions notable for their strong clean line. He also painted flowers and the best produced at Meissen between 1726 and 1737 have been attributed to him.

Other artists produced exquisite copies in miniature of old Flemish paintings and two magnificent styles of the naturalistic type of flower painting known as *Deutsche Blumen*, and the stylised Oriental flowers which were known as *Indianische Blumen*. Table-ware with borders in low relief, in the style of silver made their appearance. These border patterns, which resemble basketwork and were called *ozier*, have been extensively copied, but on their first appearance in 1732 they were greeted with great excitement.

Among the objects produced at Meissen were the much admired porcelain boxes which were used for snuff. These were exquisitely executed and only the finest artists were allowed to work on them. The decoration was frequently a miniature portrait and these boxes, termed *galanteries*, frequently had a hidden compartment in which there was another painting of an erotic or pornographic nature, known as a *scène galante*. Frequently mounted in gold or silver these Meissen boxes were never marked, and the copyists at Höchst, Fürstenberg, Nymphenburg, etc., obligingly did not mark theirs either, hoping that their work would be mistaken for Meissen.

Kändler the sculptor resented Höroldt's superior position. He lost no opportunity to cause friction, and derided the constantly repeated painted wares produced so successfully. The Commission were conscious of the value of both men, and sought to keep the peace.

Augustus the Strong died in 1733 and was succeeded by his son, Augustus III, who inherited his love of beauty and extravagance without his talent. He really preferred paintings to porcelain, and amassed a large collection, but his ambitious Minister, Count Heinrich von Brühl (1700–1763) took over the direction of the factory and under his protection it enjoyed its greatest period until the beginning of the Seven Years War in 1756.

Brühl's commissions to the factory for services and decorative pieces for his personal use were a constant stimulus for new ideas and designs. Brühl recognised Kändler's genius and encouraged him to develop the Meissen style which led the rest of Europe.

Kändler, an artist of the German baroque, was the first to realise the special qualities of porcelain for modelling purposes, as well as the potentialities of its shiny glaze and palette of colours. He modelled his figures boldly and dramatically with deep hollows and exaggerated projections, and used the play of light and shadow to great effect. Kändler's subjects are never pretty-pretty. Virile, almost brutal, they are exquisitely and satirically executed. To observe the leer on the face of his laughing Buddha can be an uncomfortable experience. He introduced allegorical subjects, the Five Senses, the Continents, the Seasons, the Elements, the Arts, the Months, subjects from the theatre, figures from contemporary life, animals and birds. His inventions were endless, each more ingenious and original than the last. An important work was the Swan Service for Count Brühl. This consisted of a great number of table-wares heavily ornamented with swans, nymphs and dolphins modelled in high relief. The famous Band of Monkeys, each holding musical instruments, was produced and was said to have been a parody of the Court Orchestra. These were copied by many factories

The Meissen Commission became alarmed when they discovered that independent decorators were selling rejected Meissen wares as the finished products of the factory. Until that time, only pieces intended for the Royal use were marked (with the letters AR for Augustus Rex), so in self-protection they caused the mark KPM for *Königliche Porzellan Manufaktur* to be painted in underglaze blue on every completed piece. This was found to take too long, so in 1724 the electoral swords, the insignia of Saxony, became the factory emblem.

An important customer for vast quantities of coffee cups and saucers for Turkey was Manassus Athanas. He was concerned that the Meissen mark might be considered a Christian symbol in an Islamic country, so the Commission allowed his orders to be completed with a caduceus (the staff carried by Mercury). In 1732 he ordered no fewer than 2,000 dozen coffee cups.

The *hausmaler*, as the independent decorators were called, because they worked at home, produced original decorative work, which today is as highly prized as that from the Royal factory. Their specialities were *chinoiseries* in gold, *schwarzlot*—monochrome paintings in black, and special subjects obviously to order.

The main centres of the *hausmaler* were the cities of Breslau, Vienna, Augsburg, Bayreuth and Pressnitz. Considerable doubt still exists about the origin of some of this work. Only perfect pieces were decorated at Meissen and all imperfect pieces were supposed to have been destroyed. These, however, had a happy knack of reaching the *hausmaler* who decorated them. Usually a *hausmaler* piece can be recognised because the paste is either discoloured, the glaze spotted or cracked, or the shape spoiled in the firings.

Another source of porcelain for the *hausmalers* was second-rate Chinese hard-paste imported in the white. To add to the difficulties, Chinese decorators in China copied *hausmaler* decorations, and to attribute a piece correctly requires considerable knowledge and skill.

In 1738, on Kändler's instigation, new French designs after Watteau were adopted, and the tiny figures in the harbour scenes were superseded by large figures without detailed backgrounds. *Putti*, Lovers and Shepherds were exquisitely executed, usually in monochrome. A large service (actually consisting of seventeen services!) was made in this manner in a beautiful leaf green, as a wedding present for the King's daughter, Maria Amalia Christina, when she married Charles IV King of Naples, founder of the Capodimonte porcelain factory.

Jonas Hanway, a merchant of great individuality (he introduced the use of the umbrella into England), passing through Dresden in 1750, wrote:

"There are about 700 men employed at Meissen in the manufactory, most of whom have not more than ten German crowns a month, and the highest wages are forty, so that the annual expense is not estimated above 80,000 crowns. This manufactory being entirely for the King's account, he sells yearly to the value of 150,000 crowns, and sometimes 200,000 crowns (£35,000) besides the magnificent presents he occasionally makes, and the great quantity he preserves for his own use. They pretend they cannot execute fast enough the commission which they receive from Asia, as well as from all parts of Europe, and are consequently under no necessity of lowering the enormous prices. However, this must be the consequence ere long, if the English and the French continue to make such great improvement in this art. It is with great satisfaction that I observe the manufacture of Bow, Chelsea and Stepney so improved."

The finest work at Meissen was achieved before the Seven Years War (1756–1763). Brühl's inept politics had caused the displeasure of Frederick the Great of Prussia, and totally unprepared, Saxony was soon overrun.

Frederick had long wanted a porcelain factory of his own, and had gazed enviously at Meissen. Once before, in 1745 during the Silesian war, he had occupied Meissen, but had done no damage except to ship large quantities of finished china back to Berlin and raid the petty cash. On that occasion Augustus III the "Porcelain King", had fled with his paintings and large porcelain vases to the fortress of Königsheim, leaving the archives and his Queen to the mercy of the conqueror.

The Seven Years War was a different matter. Augustus III fled to Warsaw and the faithful workmen destroyed kilns and equipment. Höroldt and his arcanists fled to Frankfurt. Frederick had planned to dismantle the factory and transport it to Berlin, but Wegely, the Director of the Berlin factory viewed the wreckage and voted it impracticable.

In order to re-start the factory, an astute Meissen arcanist, Georg Michael Helbig (1715–1775), dealt with Frederick (for which he was later condemned as a traitor, but was reprieved). Frederick ordered several large services and frequently prepared the designs himself. The results of his *eigene invention* were sometimes very feeble, for his taste ran to a mixture of baroque, rococo and classical styles. Kändler remained at Meissen throughout the war and executed much work for Frederick. He had become obsessed with the idea of making a life-sized equestrian figure of Augustus but the Factory Commission wisely showed no interest in this over ambitious project. However, Kändler worked on his giant model at home, and ruined himself in the process. It was believed that he remained behind so that he could continue his statue, which incidentally was never completed. The head alone was preserved.

After the peace in 1763, the establishment was restored to some degree of eminence under Christian Wilhelm Ernst Dietrich (1712–1774), a Dresden professor of painting, and the sculptor Michel-Victor Açier (1736–1795) from Paris, who in 1765 introduced the neo-classical style.

Both Augustus III and Brühl died in 1763, and a new Commission was formed. Höroldt returned, but was too old to adapt himself to the changes and was pensioned off in 1765 after forty-five years' service. Kändler continued for another ten years, until he died in 1775.

The period 1763–1774 is known as the "Academic" period, and the mark in use was a dot between the hilts of the swords.

1774–1813 was the Marcolini period, when a star was added in the same manner. Count Camillo Marcolini (1739–1814) was appointed Director by the new Elector, Friedrich Augustus III, and under his guidance some order was maintained.

The monopoly the factory had enjoyed was over, and competition was rife throughout Germany, France and England; it was unable to pay its own expenses and became a drain on the Sovereign's privy purse. When Josiah Wedgwood went there in about 1790, so convinced was he of its capabilities under good management that he offered £3,000 a year to be allowed to assume control. His offer was proudly refused.

To add to the difficulties, the beds of fine clay at Aue were almost exhausted, and an inferior material brought from Zittan had to be substituted.

The lead had now been taken by Sèvres, and although fine artists were employed, no new styles were created. The general policy was mass production to meet the demands of a competitive market, and the wares were carelessly finished. A meretricious process was invented towards the end of the eighteenth century, when real lace was dipped in slip and when the piece was fired, the lace burned away leaving its pattern in the fired clay.

The troubles at the factory increased with the advent of the nineteenth century. Markets were lost in Russia and Turkey and in 1813 during the Napoleonic wars, Meissen was once more laid waste by foreign troops. The factory was at its lowest ebb, Marcolini resigned on the verge of collapse and died soon after in Prague.

In the Cartwright Collection at Aynhoe there is an historical service found by General William Cartwright on the field of Waterloo. Complete with red leather travelling case, this beautiful Meissen service was believed to have belonged to Napoleon and abandoned in the retreat.

The factory limped through the Biedermeyer period, about 1820–1845, which was the German *bourgeois* version of the Empire style, when quality of workmanship declined. From about 1860, well into the twentieth century, eighteenth-century moulds and models were revived which caused consternation amongst collectors as they could be mistaken for the originals.

Decorating establishments sprang up all round and in the city of Dresden, and considerable quantities of white porcelain bought from the Meissen factory were decorated and sold as Dresden china. These are not to be confused with the earlier *hausmaler*. The most successful of these was a Madame Wolfsohn and her successors, who added the Augustus Rex mark AR and probably persuaded the unwary public that the porcelain was genuine early Meissen. After twenty-five years the Meissen factory at last took action against her. She was restrained from using the AR mark, and switched to the word "Dresden", sometimes surmounted by a crown. From her workshop came pairs of vases with quatrefoil decoration in yellows, blues and greens, services for tea and dessert and miniature tea and dinner services.

Other imitators were Meyer and Sohn, who used the letter M between the swords; A. Hamaan, who used a crowned D or a fish, and Carl Thieme, who used the letter T above crossed sticks.

The factory moved from Albrechtsburg in 1860–1864 to new premises built by the Saxon Government at Triebischtal, where it flourished after initial difficulties.

The factory re-opened after the Second World War and started reproducing the most popular models of the eighteenth century.

MEISSEN CHARACTERISTICS

1. Always hard-paste.
2. Böttger paste slightly grey or yellowish. 1720–1750 greenish with moons. After 1750 paste clear, hard white, translucent and quite perfect.
3. Original glaze comparatively thick, later glaze clear and brilliant.
4. Strong colours in large areas.
5. Decoration—flawlessly executed in brilliant enamel colours. Magnifying glass examination should reveal finest detailed miniature painting.
6. Crossed swords mark applied underneath unglazed base about 1724. Because of obliteration in firing, small mark was placed on the rear of the base from about 1745.
7. Before 1800, one stroke across mark implied the piece was

sold undecorated. After 1800 the number of strokes defined degrees of defectiveness; two strokes meant minor defects, three strokes more serious defects, and four strokes indicated that it was not sold to the public direct, but cheaply to the workmen.

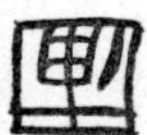

1720–1725, in underglaze blue. So-called Chinese mark on blue and white.

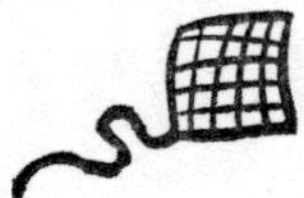

1720–1725, in underglaze blue. So-called "Kite" mark on blue and white.

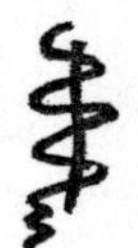

1723, in underglaze blue. So-called "caduceus" mark used for Turkish market.

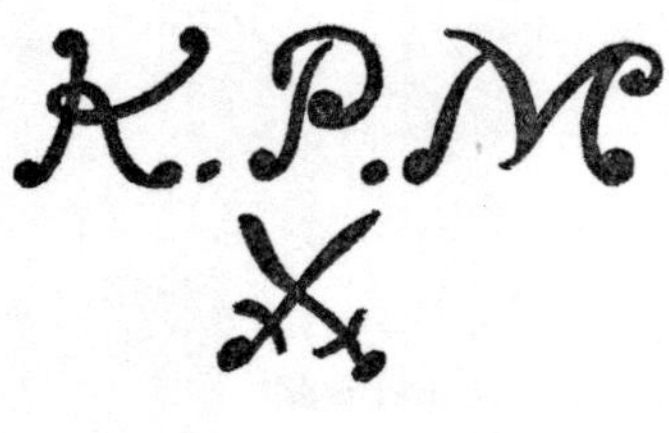

1723–1724, in underglaze blue. "Königliche Porzellan Manufaktur".

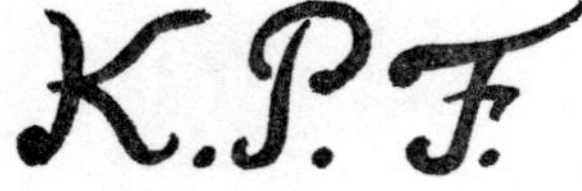

1723–1724, in underglaze blue. "Königliche Porzellan Fabrik".

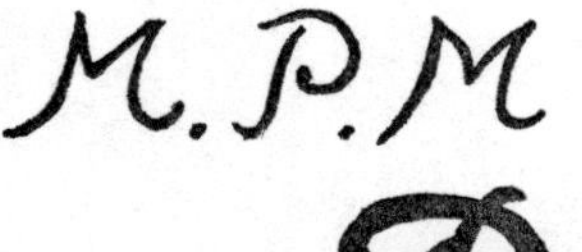

1723–1724, in underglaze blue. "Meissner Porzellan Manufaktur".

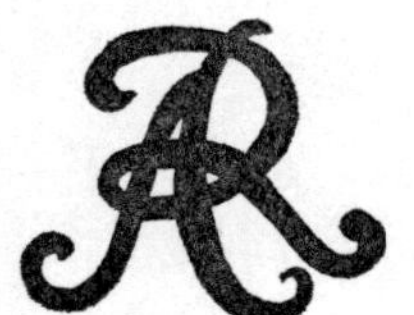

Cypher for "Augustus Rex" *1725–1730*, in underglaze blue.

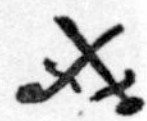

Adopted *1724*, usually blue or black enamel. Carefully drawn.

Variations of the crossed swords mark

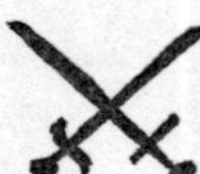

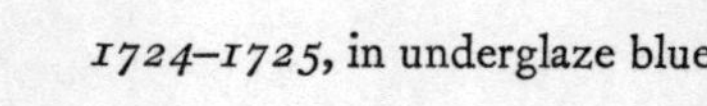

1724–1725, in underglaze blue.

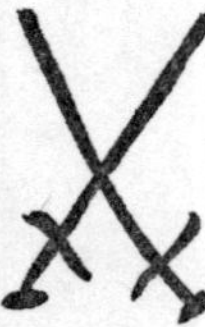

1724–1725, in underglaze blue.

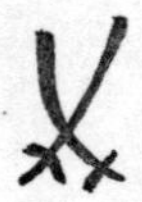

1725–1763, in underglaze blue.

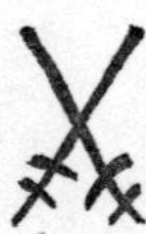

1725–1763, in underglaze blue.

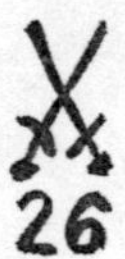

1725–1763, in underglaze blue and gold.

1725–1763, in underglaze blue.

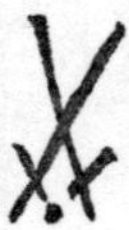

1725–1763, in underglaze blue.

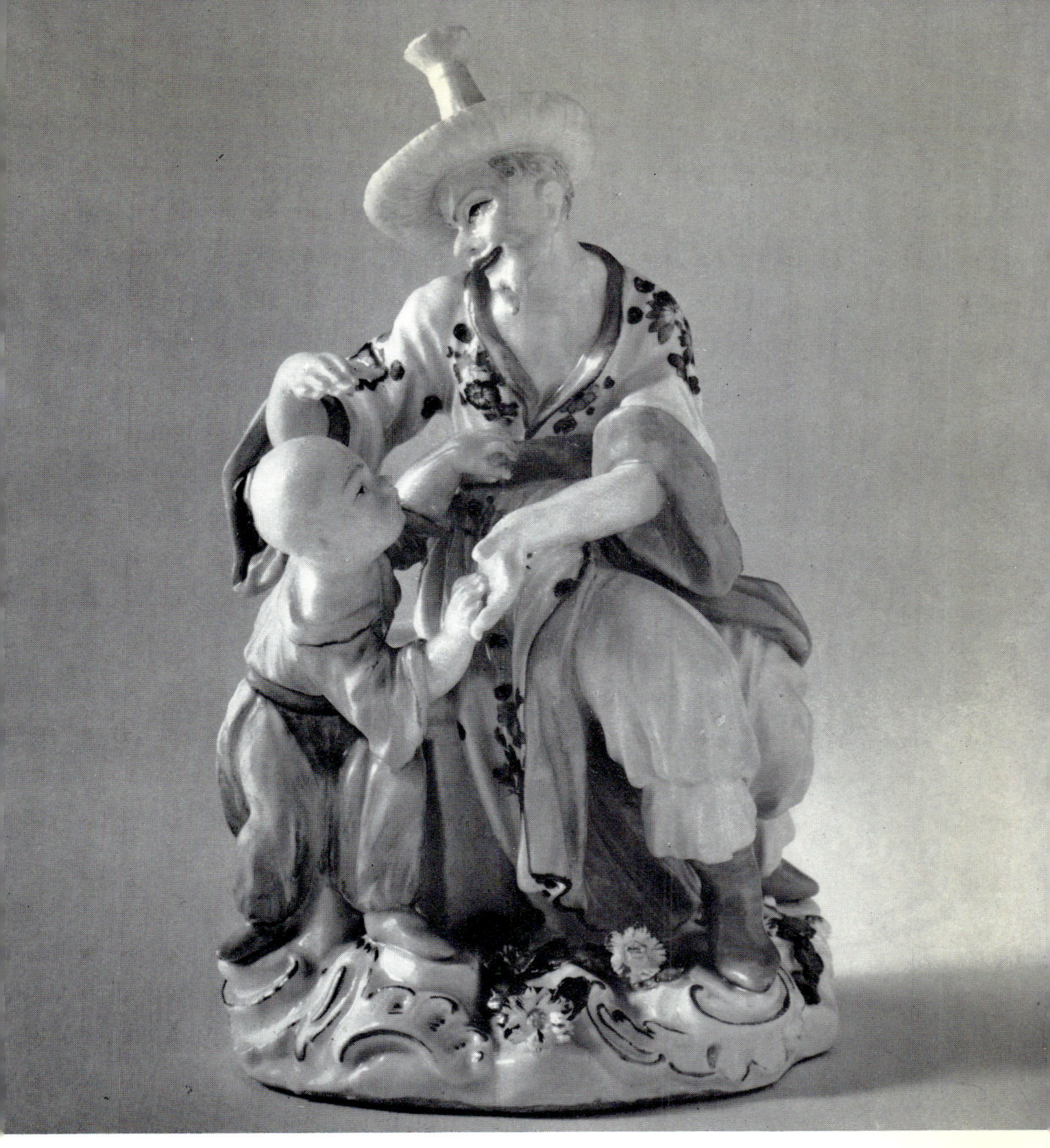

MEISSEN

Chinoiserie Group by Kändler, Meyer and Reinicke, *c.* 1760

Formerly in the collection of the late Hon. Mrs. Nellie Ionides

By courtesy of John Barry

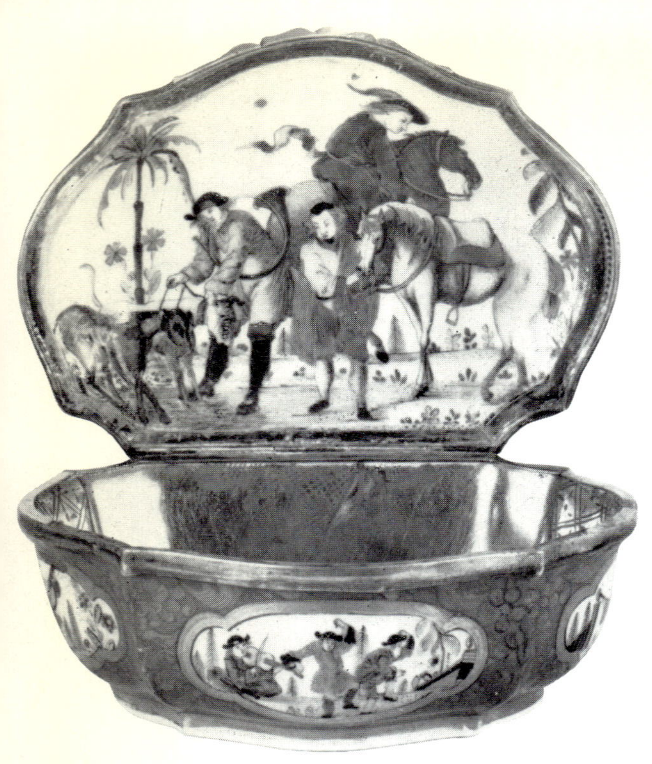

An extremely rare Meissen silver-mounted, red-ground Box of bombé form, decorated in so-called *Löwenfinck* style with pseudo-chinoiserie figures at varying pursuits. Size 3½ ins., *c.* 1730. Once in the author's collection

Sotheby & Co.

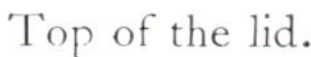

Top of the lid.

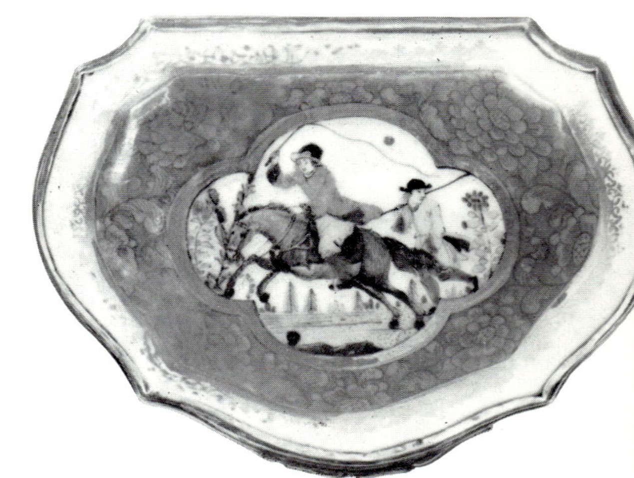

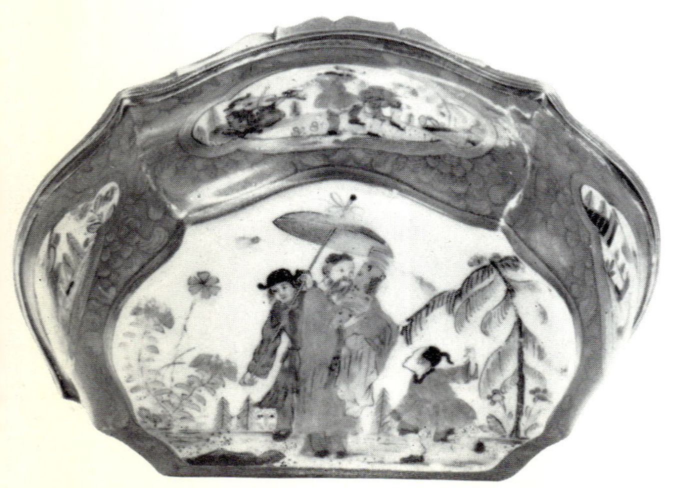

Base of the box.

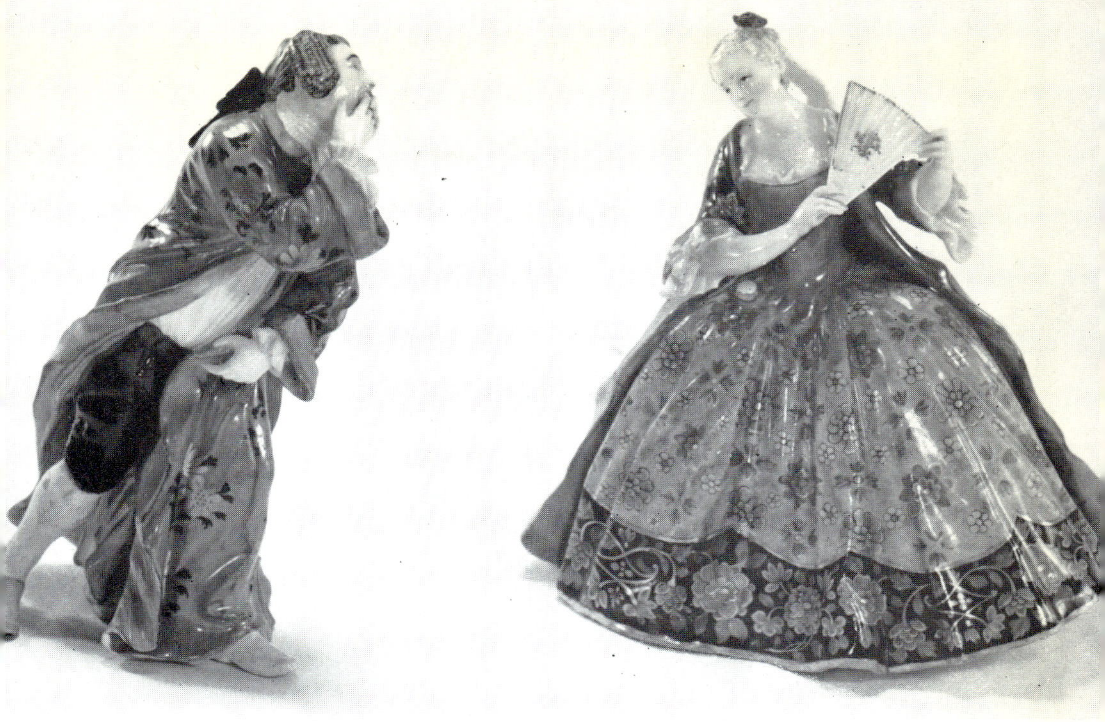

MEISSEN. Porcelain Group by Kändler, 1737

Both from Kunstgewerbe Museum Berlin

VIENNA. Tureen with cover and stand, *c.* 1725 Du Paquier Period

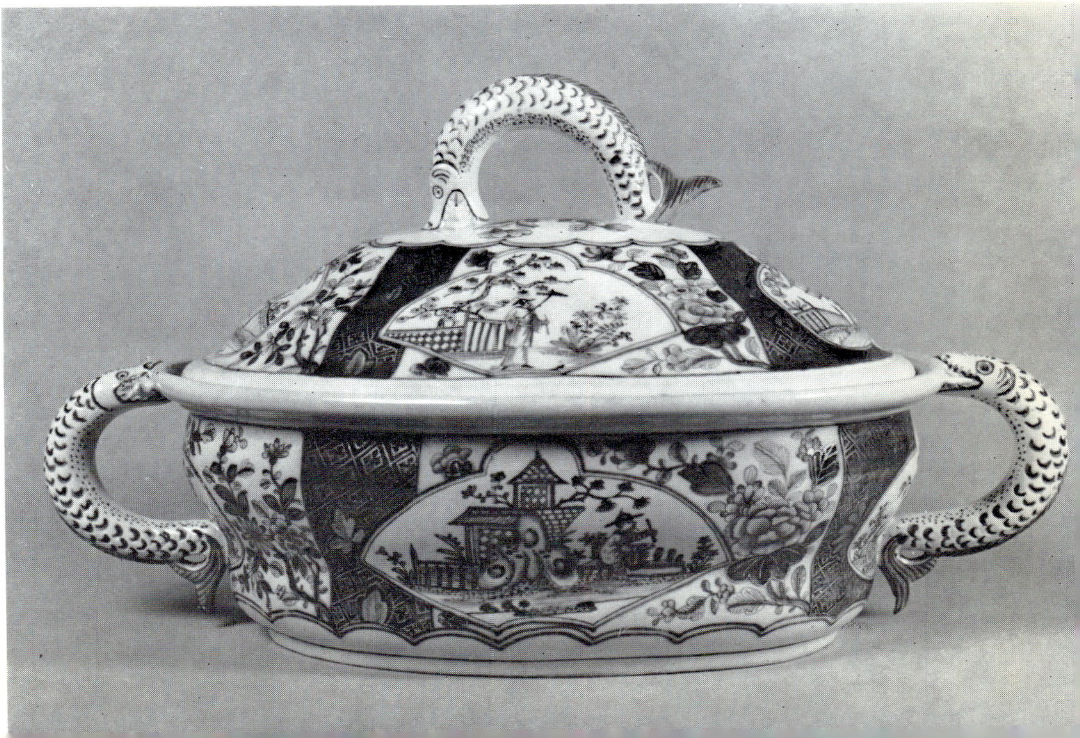

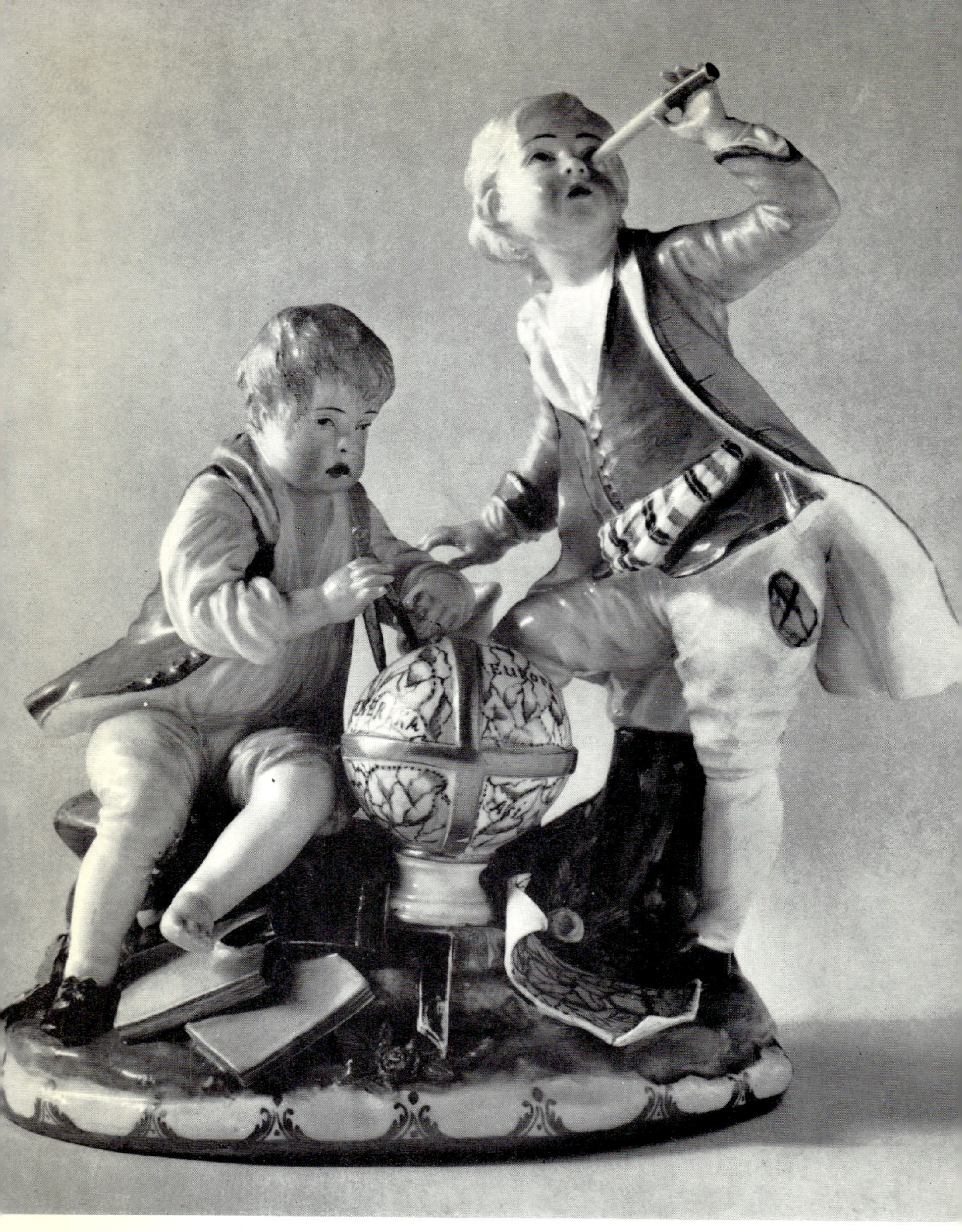

VIENNA. Group of two children representing Navigation, *c.* 1770

By courtesy of John Barry

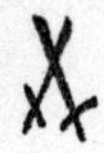

1725–1763, in underglaze blue.

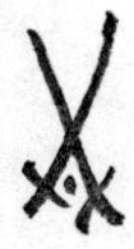

1763–1774, in underglaze blue. Mark of the "dot" period.

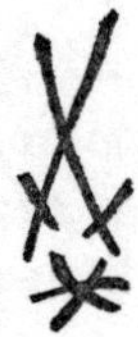

1774–1814, in underglaze blue. Mark of the "Marcolini" period.

1774–1814, incised (on biscuit). Mark of the "Marcolini" period.

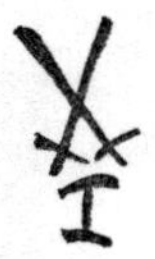

1814–1818, in underglaze blue.

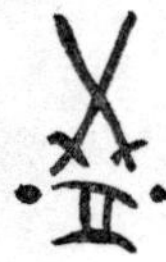

About *1818*, in underglaze blue.

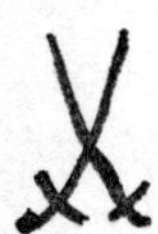

1818–1924, in underglaze blue.

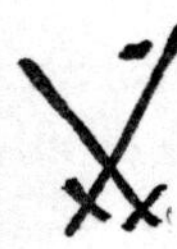

Since *1924*, in underglaze blue.

[2] VIENNA 1718–1864

A Dutchman, Claudius Innocentius Du Paquier, began experimenting with porcelain in Vienna as early as 1716, but it was not until 1718 that he was granted the monopoly of the manufacture and sale of porcelain for a term of twenty-five years, throughout the territory of the Holy Roman Emperor Charles IV.

In 1717, the enameller-gilder Christoph Konrad Hunger, who claimed to have access to the arcanum, but who knew nothing about porcelain production and caused a great deal of trouble thereby, left Meissen to join Du Paquier. Achieving little success, Hunger probably suggested to Du Paquier that Samuel Stöltzel would be a convenient addition to the works. Du Paquier is reported to have disguised himself and met Stöltzel secretly in a coffee house and to have offered him a thousand thalers to work in Vienna. Stöltzel defected in 1719, and capable kiln-master that he was, the Vienna factory began to make good porcelain soon after his arrival.

The porcelain made during this period was of fine quality, but the paste was of a greying hue, and very little is available for the modest collector.

Du Paquier was a poor business man, and the affairs of the factory deteriorated. Unable to pay his workmen, his difficulties increased, and Stöltzel, who had been lured by high wages, now found that the promises were not fulfilled. He therefore applied to his former employers at Meissen for reinstatement, where he was welcomed with open arms, together with the young enameller Höroldt, with whom he had worked at Vienna.

The factory was continued on a reduced scale, but even so, by 1727 Du Paquier was bankrupt. Supported by State loans until 1744 when his patent expired, he was then forced to sell to the State but continued in a managerial capacity until his death in 1751.

The porcelain made by Du Paquier is very beautiful and highly regarded by the connoisseur. The forms are those of silverware in the baroque style, and do not really follow those of Meissen as much as one would expect from the fact that Meissen workmen were employed. Chinese subjects were very popular and were painted in *schwarzlot*. This was a style of decoration invented by the glass decorators of the seventeenth century in which the design was painted with a fine brush in delicate black enamel, sometimes with touches of red or gold, and details scratched in with a needle and highlights wiped off, in the manner of an etching. Many decorators were also *hausmalers* and vice versa, and individualistic and unusual designs were made. Figures were few and mainly used as plastic decorations on vases. Applied masks were a frequent motif, as were spouts in the form of animal heads.

The factory came under the influence of the Empress Maria Theresa and a new Director was found in Mattheus Mayerhofer (1744–1764).

STATE PERIOD FROM 1744–1864

For the first ten years the surplus porcelain produced by Du Paquier was either decorated, often in a style at variance with the shape, or disposed of by lottery. The mark adopted was the shield, representing the arms of Austria, either impressed or incised. After 1749, when a new white clay from Hungary was introduced, the shield was painted in underglaze blue and thereafter became the regular trade mark. Unoriginal designs were competently executed after Sèvres and Meissen, and copies made of patterns produced at Nymphenburg and Frankenthal.

The original plastic work of this period was excellent. The *Modellmeister* from 1747 until his death in 1784, was Johann Josef Niedermeyer who was responsible for most of the figures made at the time. His subjects are charming doll-like figures in the rococo style on scrolled bases. Honey describes them (*Dictionary of European Ceramic Art*): "They are marked by certain common features in posture and expression, in particular the feet placed close together and the small heads, with smiling faces, held back in a peculiarly vivacious manner." Anton Grassi (1755–1807), engaged in 1778, was responsible for some attractive groups, but his later neo-classical work became dry and academic.

During the Seven Years War the factory profited at the expense of Meissen and was considerably enlarged. However this was followed by financial crises due to immoderate expenditure on experimental work, and the factory was offered for sale in 1784. No buyer could be found, so the State appointed Konrad von Sorgenthal, a wool manufacturer, as the new Director, and under his dynamic leadership it began to enjoy some financial stability.

Georg Perl (*d.* 1807), a chemist, invented the method of gilding in relief, and some attractive wares were decorated with classical designs in this manner. An excellent dark blue, a deep violet and a pale lilac lustre were introduced by arcanist and painter Joseph Leithner. The entire surface of the porcelain was covered with ground colour, leaving spaces for paintings after Rubens and Angelica Kauffman, or small sprigs of flowers. The perfection of the colours and the competence of the execution combined to achieve the elegance and refinement found in Sorgenthal Vienna.

After 1810, the work became pretentious and overloaded with ornament.

Later in the nineteenth century Sorgenthal designs were revived, but without the original craftsmanship.

The factory closed in 1864.

VIENNA CHARACTERISTICS

DU PAQUIER 1719–1744

1. Hard-paste, creamy in tone, inclined to be greenish.
2. Silver forms, and baroque shapes, applied masks and acanthus leaves, etc.
3. Decoration, *chinoiseries* and baroque scrollwork *Laub-und-bandelwerk* (leaf and strap-work).
4. Colours, typical Vienna brick red, *schwarzlot*, gold, pink.
5. Figures rare.
6. No factory mark.

STATE PERIOD 1744–1784

1. Paste whiter than Du Paquier, but uneven in quality.
2. Factory mark adopted, incised, impressed or painted *Bindenschild*—shield of arms of Austria.
3. Figures made of singular quality in the rococo style with scrolled bases, animal groups.
4. Useful wares in rococo style with excellent decorations. Subjects after Teniers, cupids after Boucher, battle scenes after Rugendas, figures after Watteau.

SORGENTHAL AND AFTER 1784–1864

1. Factory mark. After 1783, in addition to the shield, the last two numerals of the date were impressed, and after 1800, the last three, of which the 8 was shown larger. Not to be confused with workmen's marks.
2. Neo-classical styles. Excellent quality of painting and productions deteriorating after 1810 into usual over-decorated variety.
3. Forms and decoration after the antique.
4. Colours: brick red, dark blue, dark violet, light lustre mauves, bluish-green and flat pink.
5. Figures made in creamy biscuit, also busts of the Emperor and the composer Haydn, as well as those after the antique.
6. Old Vienna porcelain frequently over-decorated in late nineteenth century with intent to deceive.

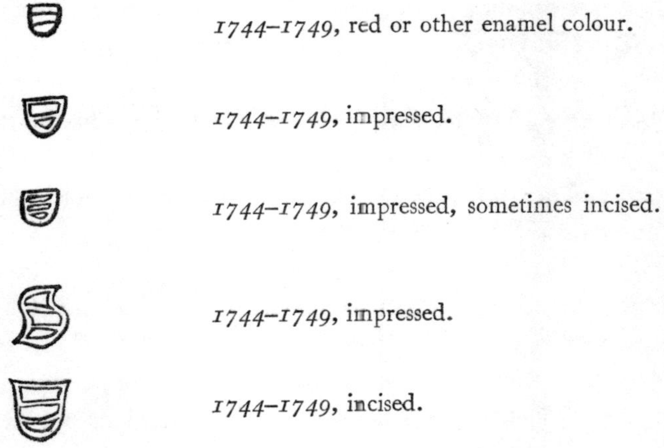

1744–1749, red or other enamel colour.

1744–1749, impressed.

1744–1749, impressed, sometimes incised.

1744–1749, impressed.

1744–1749, incised.

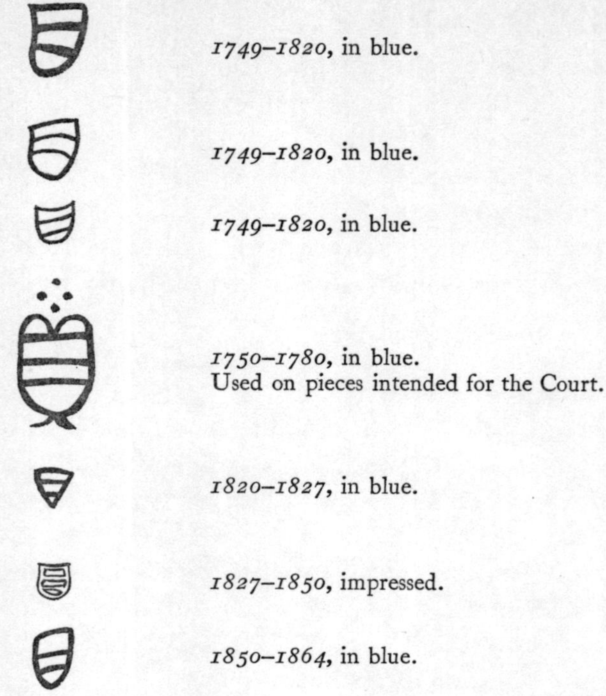

1749–1820, in blue.

1749–1820, in blue.

1749–1820, in blue.

1750–1780, in blue.
Used on pieces intended for the Court.

1820–1827, in blue.

1827–1850, impressed.

1850–1864, in blue.

[3] HÖCHST, NEAR MAINZ 1750–1796

An accomplished painter from Meissen, Adam Friedrich von Löwenfinck (1714–1754), together with two business men from Frankfurt on Main, Johann Christoph Göltz (1660–1757) and Johann Felician Clarus (*c.* 1750), started a factory here in 1746 to make porcelain, for which they were granted the sole privilege for fifty years from the Elector Friedrich Karl of Mainz.

Beautiful *faïence fine* decorated by Löwenfinck was made for the first few years. There is no record that Löwenfinck knew the secrets of the arcanum, but perhaps he gave his partners to understand that he did. He quarrelled with Göltz in 1749 and left for Strasbourg.

Göltz became the sole owner. In 1750 he engaged Johann Benckgraff of Vienna, who represented himself as an arcanist, but still no porcelain was produced until J. J. Ringler, arrived in the same year. During his stay at Höchst, a group of his colleagues, led by Benckgraff, made him drunk, and when he was quite inebriated stole his papers containing the formulae and processes which he always carried on his person. Ringler's secrets of the arcanum were sold to the rest of Europe and new porcelain factories mushroomed everywhere, particularly in Germany. Ringler left Höchst in disgust, and Benckgraff, now an arcanist, followed in 1753. Göltz died in 1757, and the manufacture of *faïence* was discontinued.

The factory was administered by a local official, and it was not until 1765, when the Elector Emmerich Joseph became chief stockholder, that the affairs of the factory were put in order.

The succeeding Elector, Friedrich Karl Joseph, having tried unsuccessfully to sell out, continued his support. The factory was declining. Financial difficulties followed by political crises, culminating in the French invasion of 1796, caused it finally to close down. The moulds and fittings were sold in 1798. These were ultimately bought by Damm in about 1830, who reproduced the old Höchst models in earthenware. In 1904 the moulds were used for forgeries in porcelain.

The Höchst paste was gradually developed into a beautiful creamy-white consistency of excellent quality with a brilliantly clear glaze. The modeller Johann Simon Feilner (*d.* 1798) was employed at Höchst between 1749 and 1753 and is credited with some square-based allegorical groups. Johann Friedrich Lück (*d.* 1797), a repairer, left Meissen in 1757 and is believed to have worked at Höchst for a few months. Many figures in the rococo style have been attributed to him, although some doubt exists as to whether he could have made so many in such a short time. Lorenz Russinger (*c.* 1740–1810) was chief modeller from 1758 to 1767 and introduced the neo-classical style.

The artist who established Höchst as one of the best in Germany was the talented sculptor Johann Peter Melchior (1742–1825), who was *Modellmeister* from 1767 to 1779. George Ware, in *German and Austrian Porcelain*, quotes G. B. McClellan, an outstanding American collector of German porcelain, who wrote, "Melchior was the third in ability and chronologically the last of the famous trinity of porcelain modelers which includes, besides himself, Kändler and Bustelli. . . . While lacking the charm of Bustelli and the marvellous variety of Kändler, his work has an individuality quite its own and is forceful, graceful and distinguished. Without him Höchst would have been little more than a follower of Meissen. Thanks to his achievements it stands out as one of the great factories."

Melchior continued Russinger's development of the neo-classical style under the inspiration of French artists. His Teutonic versions of subjects by Boucher and Falconet are pleasing and individual and in the true tradition of German modelling. The flesh tones were painted a delicate pink and the bases were typical moss-covered mounds. The later models, probably finished after his departure, were over-decorated and the flesh tones painted a crude pink.

Melchior was influenced by his friend Goethe and by the current strain of sentimentality in German thought. His subjects of children, well observed and beautifully executed, show his warm approach and his excellent artistry. His spirited rendering of religious, pastoral and mythological groups ensure his position in porcelain history. Melchior in his later years also modelled some fine figures in the beautiful creamy toned Höchst biscuit, as well as reliefs of Goethe and the Elector Emmerich Joseph. He left Höchst for Frankenthal in 1779. His successor Josef Reiss (*c.* 1750–*c.* 1820) was responsible for some figures with over-large heads which were not popular, and figure work was abandoned.

Functional productions made at Höchst followed the fashions of the period. The first range made between 1750 to about 1765 were rococo in style and unoriginal in conception. Copies of the designs of other factories, including Meissen and Frankenthal, consisted of the popular *chinoiseries* and rococo scroll work and *Deutsche Blumen*. From about 1765 to 1780 landscapes after Teniers and scenes from popular plays were painted, encircled by bluish garlands or ribbons of blue or green. This framing was also used for popular cameo heads and classical subjects. During the final period up to 1796 a blue border with excessive gilding was frequently produced.

Rococo scrolled handles and helmet jugs were popular and the later classical style introduced severer forms with applied masks and flat bottomed saucers. Honey describes the prominent colours, "yolk-of-egg yellow, a bright blue and a clean red", in his *Dictionary of European Ceramic Art.*

The mark adopted for Höchst was a five or six-spoke wheel painted in red or blue or gold. After 1762 it was applied in underglaze blue. The Electoral Crown was added from about 1765 to 1774 and is generally believed to have been included when the pieces were intended for Royal use.

Höchst has been copied and forged incessantly. To add to the difficulties of attribution, the Höchst artists painted on Chinese and Nymphenburg porcelain, adding the wheel mark. Later copies were extremely glossy and the decoration inferior.

HÖCHST CHARACTERISTICS

1. Hard-paste, fine creamy-white.
2. Glaze milky but brilliant.
3. Colours: clean red, bright blue, yolk-of-egg yellow, purplish-red monochrome.
4. Domestic ware, fanciful scrolled handles and shapes in early period, developing into severer yet sympathetic classical styles.
5. Figures, sentimental children and Teutonic versions of French Louis Seize models.
6. Factory mark, five, or six-spoke wheel in red, blue or gold. After 1762 in underglaze blue. 1765–1774 surmounted by crown.

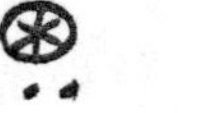

1750–1765, in red enamel.

1750–1765, in red enamel.

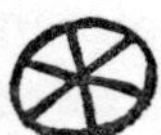

1762–1796, in underglaze blue.

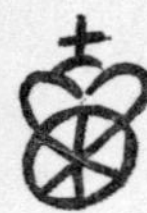

1765–1774, in underglaze blue. (Electoral hat or crown).

[4] NYMPHENBURG 1747—PRESENT DAY

When the Elector Max III Joseph, nicknamed "*der gute Vielgeliebte*" (jolly good fellow) ascended the throne of Bavaria in 1745 at the age of eighteen, his kingdom was in debt to the tune of 35 million florins following defeat in the war of the Austrian Succession and the Spanish war.

Taking as his example the efforts of Louis XIV of France and Colbert who had been faced with a similar national calamity, he threw all his energies into the development of Bavaria's natural resources. He encouraged the mining industry and afforestation schemes and generally induced a feeling of optimism in an otherwise depressed and insignificant State.

In 1747, he married Maria Anna Sophia, a daughter of Augustus III Elector of Saxony, where the porcelain factory of Meissen was the envy of all Europe. "*Guter Max*" as Max III Joseph was known affectionately, decided to have a porcelain factory of his own, and encouraged by his Electress gave his patronage to a *faïence* potter named Franz Ignaz Niedermayer who claimed that he had found the porcelain formula.

Niedermayer was established at the Renaissance Palace of Neudeck where he carried out extensive experiments without success. Alterations were made to the building and two kilns were constructed and after considerable expenditure without producing any porcelain Max III Joseph withdrew his support. The factory had attracted the attention of Graf Sigismund von Haimhausen (1708–1793), an energetic and capable nobleman who had studied mineralogy, and had travelled all over Europe. His great gift was his ability to handle people, and choose the right man for the job. He poured his own money into the porcelain factory without success until the arrival in Munich in 1753 of Joseph Jacob Ringler, whom he invited to join the undertaking. Ringler solved the technical difficulties and very soon a beautiful hard-paste was produced using kaolin from Passau.

1754 was indeed a significant year for Nymphenburg, for it was then that the sculptor Franz Anton Bustelli (1723–1763) was engaged, whose work was to establish the fame of Nymphenburg for all time. Practically nothing is known of the private life of Bustelli. No records were known until the early part of this century when a Director of the Bavarian National Museum, Dr. Hofmann, discovered his seal with his signature. Until then, his name had only been vaguely known, sometimes spelt Bastelli or Pustelli, and his work had been attributed to his successor Auliczek.

Bustelli was born in the Swiss Canton of Tessin at Locarno in 1723. From the beginning his work showed a mature understanding of his material and suggested a slight Italian influence which has led some scholars to believe that he may have worked previously at the Italian factories of Capodimonte or Doccia. He was admitted to the arcanum by Rupert Härtl (1715–1792), who had surreptitiously learned the secret processes from Ringler, whom he succeeded as Manager from 1754 to 1761.

Härtl was an excellent Manager, and under his care the factory grew in strength until 300 workmen were employed. While the range of delicate colours has been attributed to Bustelli, Honey asserts that Härtl the chemist was probably the inventor (*Dictionary of European Ceramic Art*).

Graf von Haimhausen successfully persuaded the Elector to re-interest himself in the factory, and it became known as the *Kurfürstliche Porzellanfabrik*. In 1761, it was removed to more convenient premises in three pavilions in one of the two wings of the grace and favour houses which joined the summer palace of Nymphenburg. Härtl was replaced by Joseph von Linprun (*d.* 1787) in 1763–1773, who steered the factory through the prosperous period from 1763 to 1767 and through the great decline, when after financial crises the staff was reduced to eighty persons. Bustelli spent only two years at the new premises, for he died at the early age of forty-one in 1763.

During his eight and a half years with the porcelain factory he was responsible for the production of over 150 models, including six large groups. His palette of colours was exquisitely and delicately used, down to the smallest detail of expression and costume. His talent lay in his treatment of the porcelain medium itself. Judiciously he allowed part of his model to remain uncoloured, so that the brilliance of the white porcelain was clearly remarked. The figures were so skilfully modelled, the fluid lines incorporating slight exaggerations of feature and dress, that the high-lights and shadows make enamel colours superfluous. The rococo scrolled bases he modelled were not a decorative afterthought, but a subtle yet important part of the composition. It was this extraordinary understanding of his material that has placed Bustelli's work far above that of any other eighteenth-century artist.

Other factories endeavoured to tempt him away, notably Ludwigsburg, but without success. A mature and genial craftsman, he was a brilliant exponent of the fragile, brittle and superficial rococo style, which seemed to suit the nervous quality of the porcelain medium so admirably. He was a man of his time. Porcelain was the new vibrant material which appealed to young artists. The rococo style which suited him to perfection was going out of favour in the 1760's and one wonders had he lived a normal lifespan, whether he would have been able to adapt himself to the neo-classical style and improve upon his early spectacular achievements. As it was, his career was like a comet, bursting in a brilliant flame, to burn itself out in its own intensity of spirit.

Although he designed the plastic work for services and other useful wares, Bustelli was in his element in the miniature world of the figurine. His subjects were taken from the social life of the period. There were Artisans, Chinamen, Children, busts of Children, Ladies and Gentlemen of the Court (including a magnificient one of the Graf von Haimhausen), groups and animals, and especially figures from the *Maschera*—the members of the Italian Comedy.

His treatment has an unexpected French elegance, and although obviously influenced by the Bavarian wood carver, Franz Ignaz Gunther, it betrays none of the usual Teutonic characteristics. This may seem surprising for an artist tucked away in a small porcelain factory in the heart of Bavaria. However, Haimhausen saw to it that he had access to his own fine collection of original works in addition to the engravings by Callot and Watteau.

Bustelli's Italian Comedy figures bear no relationship to the engravings from Augsburg which were found in his effects. He modelled his subjects from the ladies and gentlemen of the Bavarian Court, who, dressed in the most exquisite and costly costumes, played the *Commedia dell 'Arte* for their own amusement. His Columbines, Isabellas and Lucindas wear their costumes as naturally as peacocks and birds of paradise wear their plumage. His Capitani, Pantalones, Scaramouches and Harlequins strike their traditional poses, but with an extraordinary vitality which recalls the breathless excitement of a first night, in the true spirit of the theatre. The curtain fell on the gay rococo style when Bustelli died.

His successor, a competent Bohemian sculptor Dominikus Auliczek (1734–1804) introduced the neo-classical style. Influenced by his friend, the artist Wincklemann, he produced large unpainted figures of the immortals, and followed the tendency of the period to simulate in porcelain the style of sculptured marble statuary. His most interesting work was his range of birds and animals.

Upon the death of Max III Joseph in 1777, the Palatinate became absorbed into Greater Bavaria under the Elector Karl Theodor, who was more interested in his own porcelain factory at Frankenthal until it was closed for political and economic reasons in 1799, and the moulds and materials were transferred to Nymphenburg, together with many of the artisans and artists. Among these was the sculptor Peter Melchior, who succeeded Auliczek as *Modellmeister* from 1799 until 1822 when some of the earlier magnificence of the Nymphenburg factory was revived.

Melchior's work at Nymphenburg was in the neo-classical form and always modelled in biscuit, and bore no resemblance to his familiar earlier styles at Höchst and Frankenthal. Busts, reliefs, portraits of contemporaries and groups of figures reflected the calm and benevolent serenity of his later years.

The great porcelain era at Nymphenburg was now past and despite the interest shown by King Ludwig I, the factory declined. His architect Friedrich Gärtner was appointed manager, and was followed in 1848 until 1856 by a painter Eugen Napoleon Neureuther.

In 1856 the establishment ceased to be a Royal Factory, and was leased to a private company headed by Albert Bäuml, whose heirs are in possession today.

Under the Bäuml family, the factory regained some of its former eminence, reproducing the successful earlier models as well as a range of new ones. With great diligence and application they unlearned the nineteenth-century techniques which had crept into the works, and relearned the eighteenth-century methods. Apart from the paste which for economic reasons can no longer be reproduced (although the kaolin still comes from the Passau seam which now extends into Czechoslovakia), the painting and modelling are still performed in the same premises in the same workrooms and in the same methods as those used by Bustelli.

Central heating has replaced the quaint tiled stoves in the long, low sunlit studios. The kilns are thermostatically controlled and fired by electricity instead of timber from the Bavarian forests. The quiet atmosphere of creative artists at work and the mass of orders from all parts of the globe augur well for those who dare to place craftsmanship and quality first, in the true tradition of their illustrious past.

NYMPHENBURG CHARACTERISTICS

1. Hard-paste, pure white, close grained, without imperfections. After 1767 greyish with flaws.
2. Glaze clear, sometimes green in hollows.
3. Delicate pink and blue borders reminiscent of lace.
4. Meissen style decorative subjects. Flowers, fruit, birds, landscapes, *ozier* borders.
5. Original forms of *rechaud*, a food warmer, two elegant

receptacles surmounting each other, the lower containing the pastille burner.

6. Mark, the *Rautenschild*, shield mark of the arms of Bavaria. After 1773, defective pieces sold uncoloured bear one or two wheel cuts to show "seconds" and "thirds" in the manner adopted at Meissen to cope with competition from *hausmaler*.

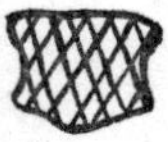

1754–1765, impressed (Bustelli period).

1765–1780, impressed (Auliezek period).

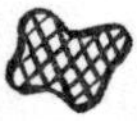

1780–1790, impressed.

1780–1790, impressed.

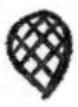

About *1800*, impressed. Lozenges change form from this time.

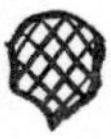

1810–1850, impressed.

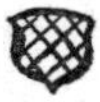

Middle of nineteenth century—impressed.

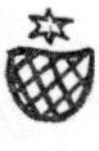

1850–1862, impressed.

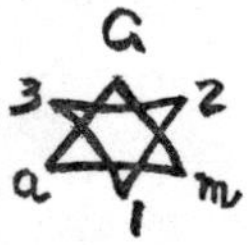

1763–1767, in blue (a Hexagram mark).

[5] FÜRSTENBERG
1747–1859 Royal—State
1859–Present Day Private

A porcelain factory was founded in the castle of Fürstenberg in 1747 by Karl I Duke of Brunswick, in order to compete with his royal contemporaries. No materials, workers or trained arcanists were available, and nothing was produced until 1753 when some artists were acquired from Höchst. These were Johann Benckgraff, arcanist, Johann Simon Feilner, *Modellmeister* and chemist, and Johann Zeschinger (1723–*c.* 1770), decorator. Benckgraff died soon after his arrival, and the many financial and production difficulties that followed had to be settled before the factory could operate successfully.

At first the raw materials arriving from distant Passau were full of impurities, and the paste and glaze were grey and imperfect with nasty black spots. Many pieces had to be overpainted to hide these defects. It was not until 1770 that a white body with brilliantly clear glaze after the manner of Meissen was achieved.

Because of difficulties with the paste only a limited number of figures were produced by *Modellmeister* Feilner. These included Greek Gods, Italian Comedy and Miners, all before 1768 when he was discharged from the factory for laziness and insubordination. W. B. Honey states, "the special excellence of Feilner's art lies in the vigorous characterisation of his figures shown especially in the heads". (*Dictionary of European Ceramic Art*). These figures were on simple mound bases with applied flowers in the manner of Meissen.

The best period of the factory followed from about 1768 onwards when figure work was neglected and many fine decorators painted and signed important picture plaques.

The painting establishment was moved in 1774 to the Duke's palace at Brunswick where an academy for porcelain and *faïence* painters had been established since 1756.

From about 1770 onwards figures of no great artistic merit were again produced.

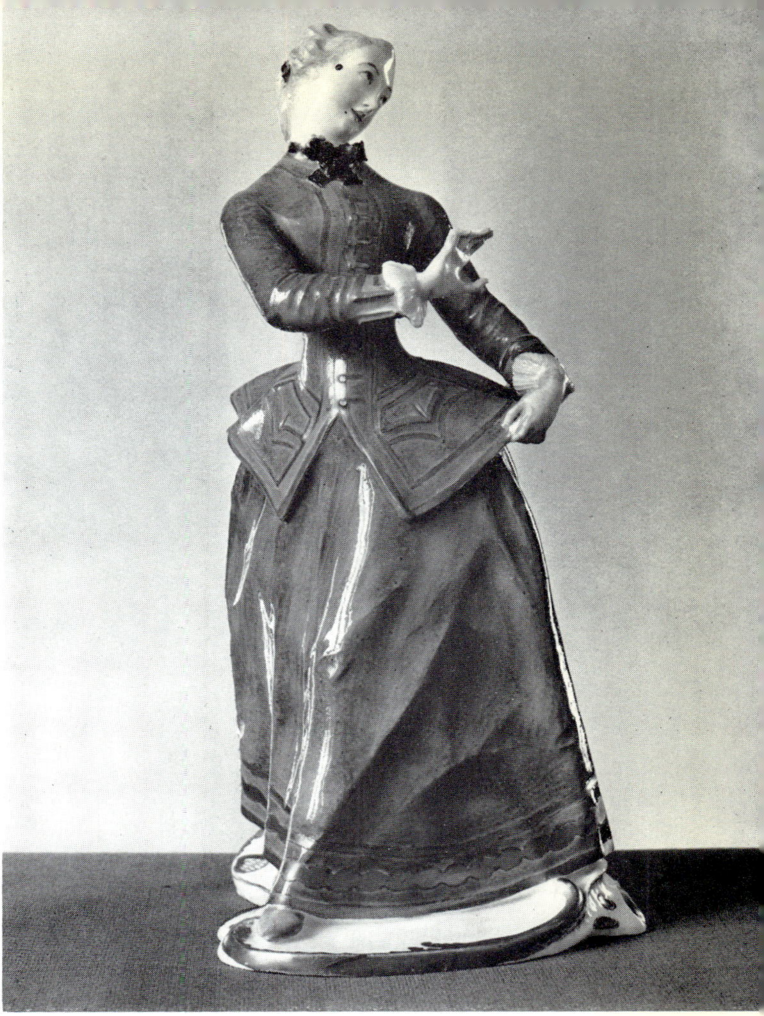

NYMPHENBURG. "Julia", from the Italian Comedy, by F. A. Bustelli, *c.* 1756

Bayerische Museum, Munich

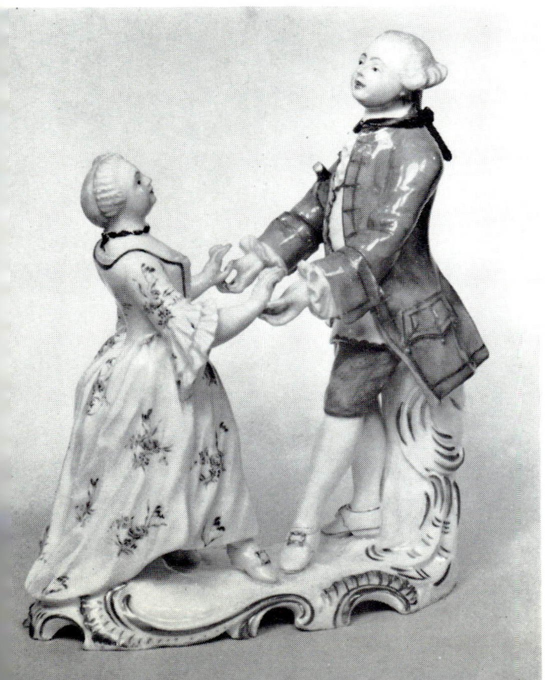

HÖCHST. A Group of "The Dancing Lesson", $6\frac{3}{4}$ ins. high. Red wheel mark

Christie's

NYMPHENBURG.
"Scaramouche", from the Italian Comedy, by F. A. Bustelli, *c.* 1756

Bayerische Museum, Munich

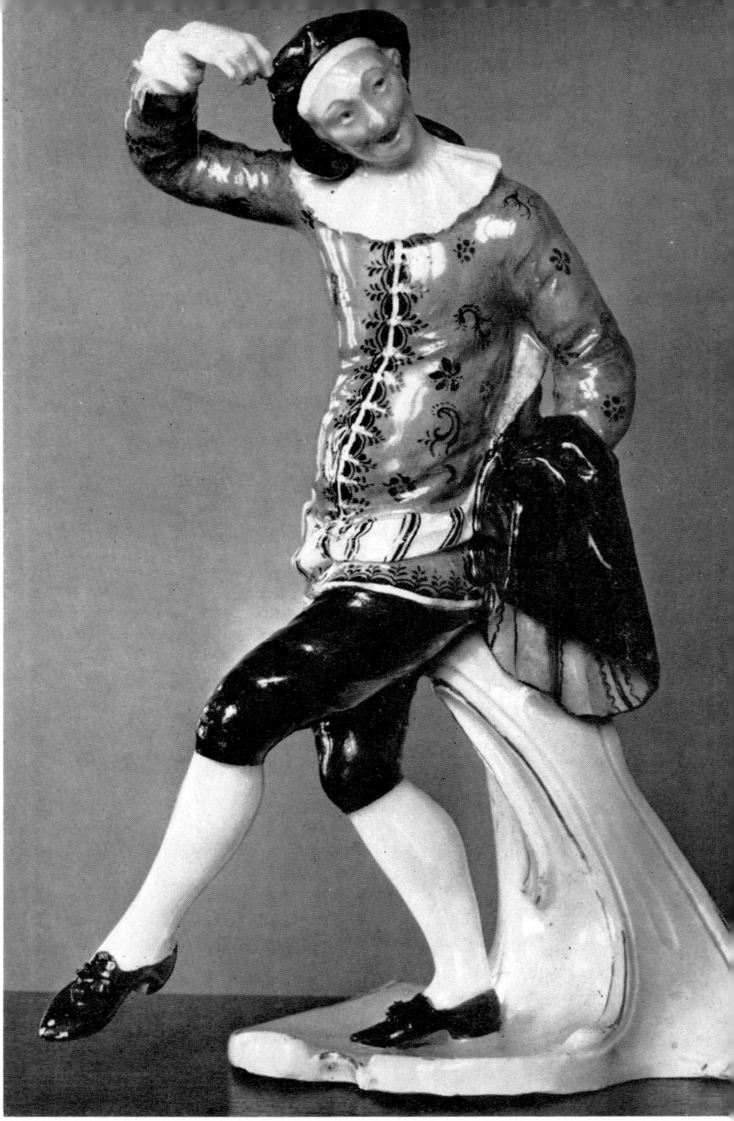

Two FURSTENBERG figures by Feilner. "The Dowser", 8 ins. high, unmarked, and "The Borer", $7\frac{3}{4}$ ins. high

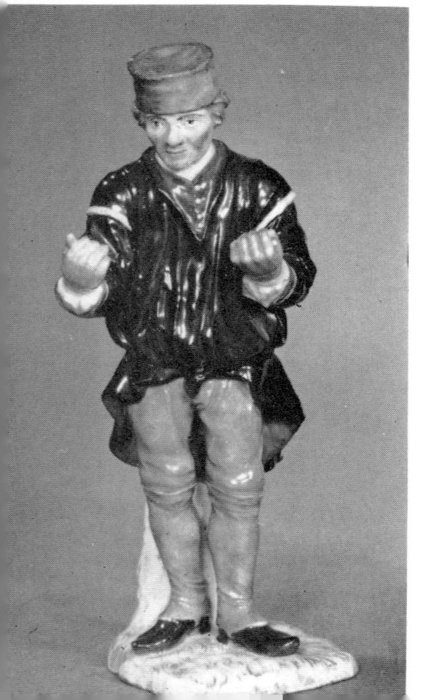

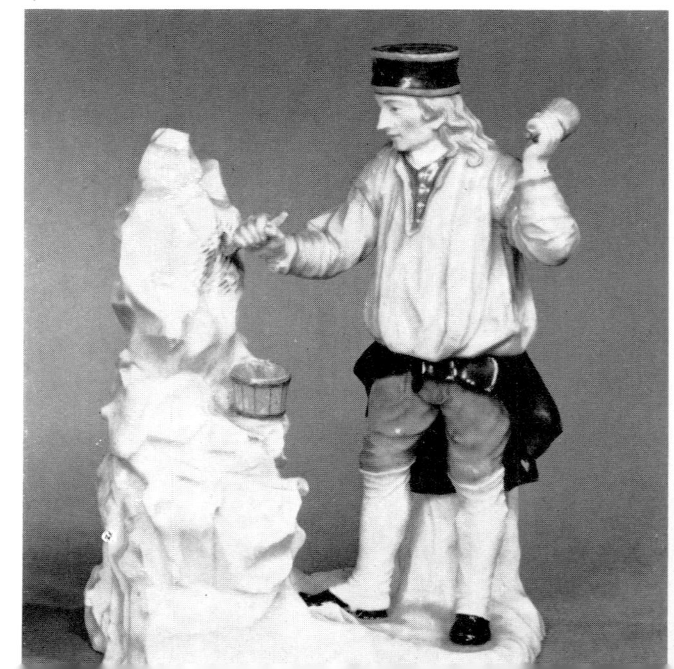

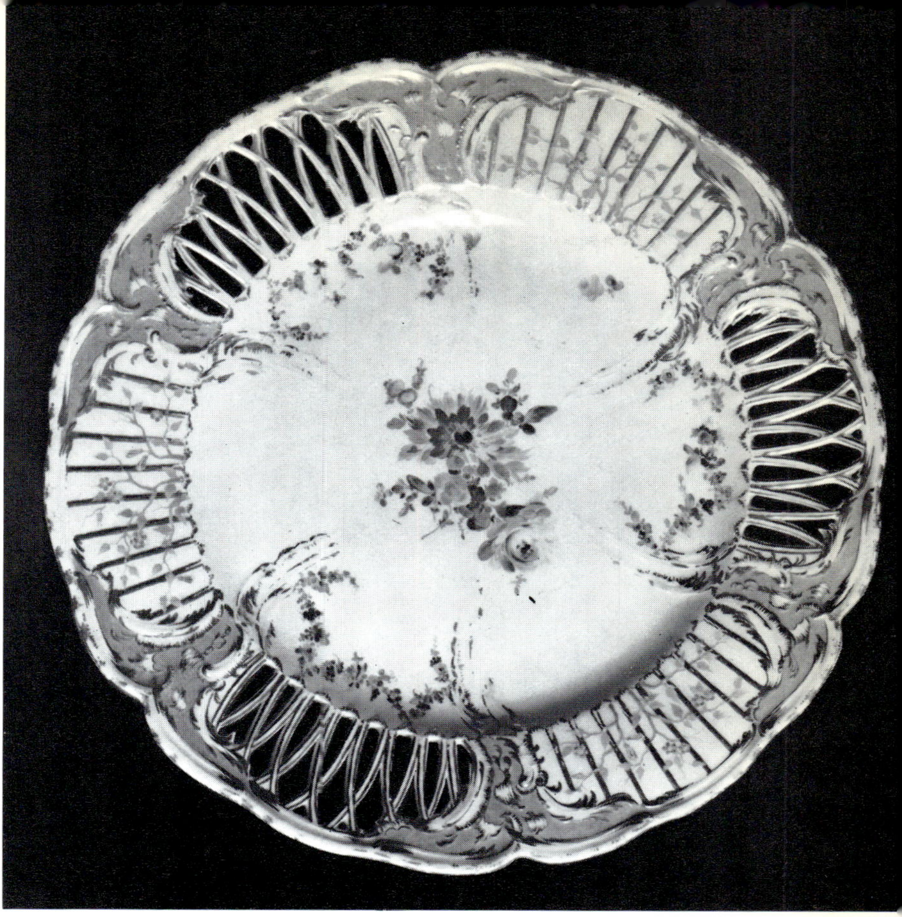

BERLIN. A plate from the Ansbacher Service, (*Reliefzierat mit Spalier*), 1766

Kunstgewerbe Museum, Berlin

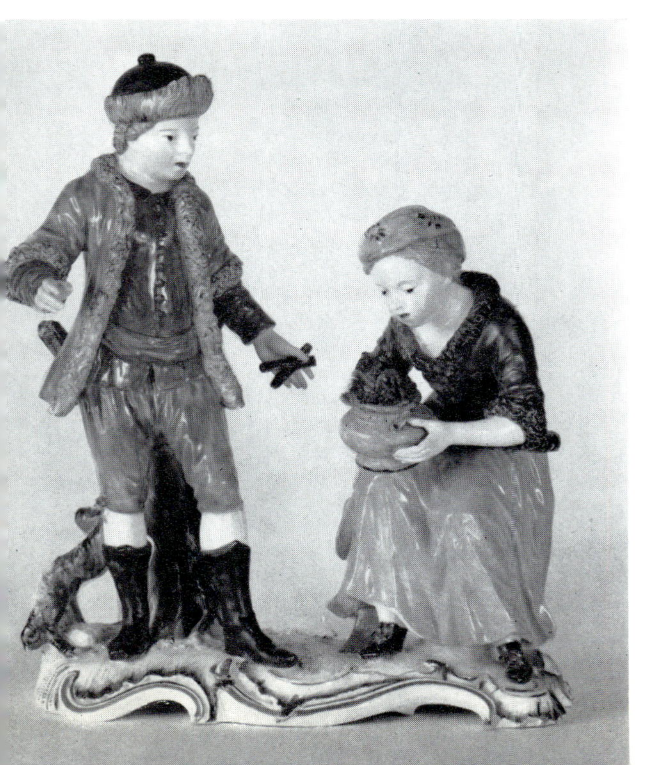

FRANKENTHAL. A Group depicting "Winter," *c.* 1755–59, by Johann Wilhelm Lanz

Kunstgewerbe Museum, Berlin

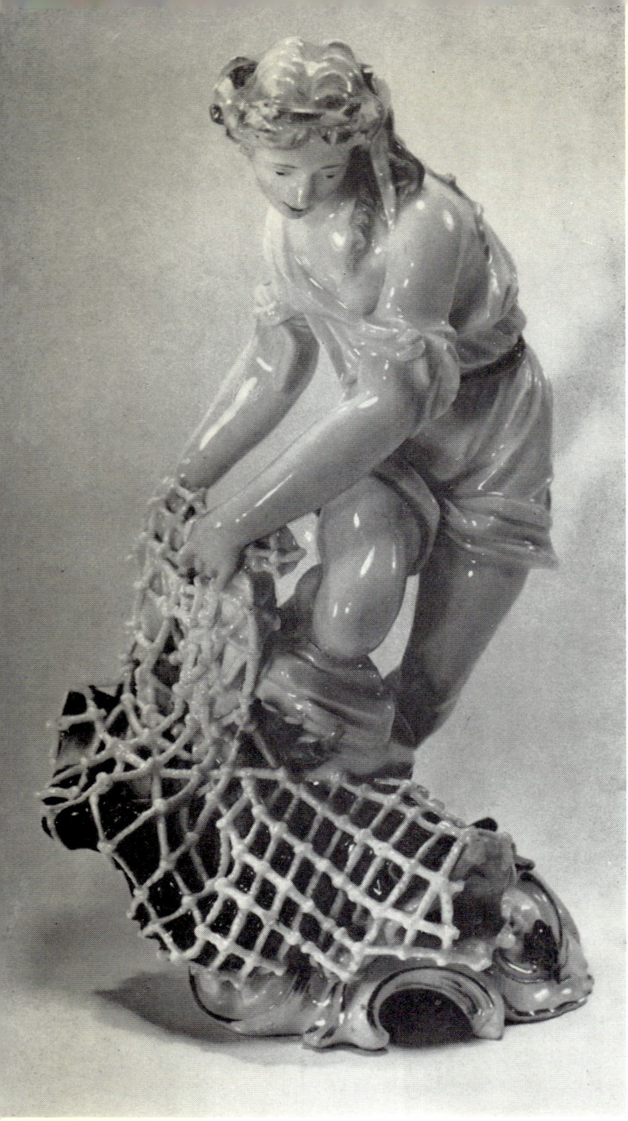

LUDWIGSBURG
"Fischerin" by Johann Christian Wilhelm Beyer, *c.* 1764

Kunstgewerbe Museum, Berlin

LUDWIGSBURG
"Bacchantengruppe"

Kunstgewerbe Museum, Berlin

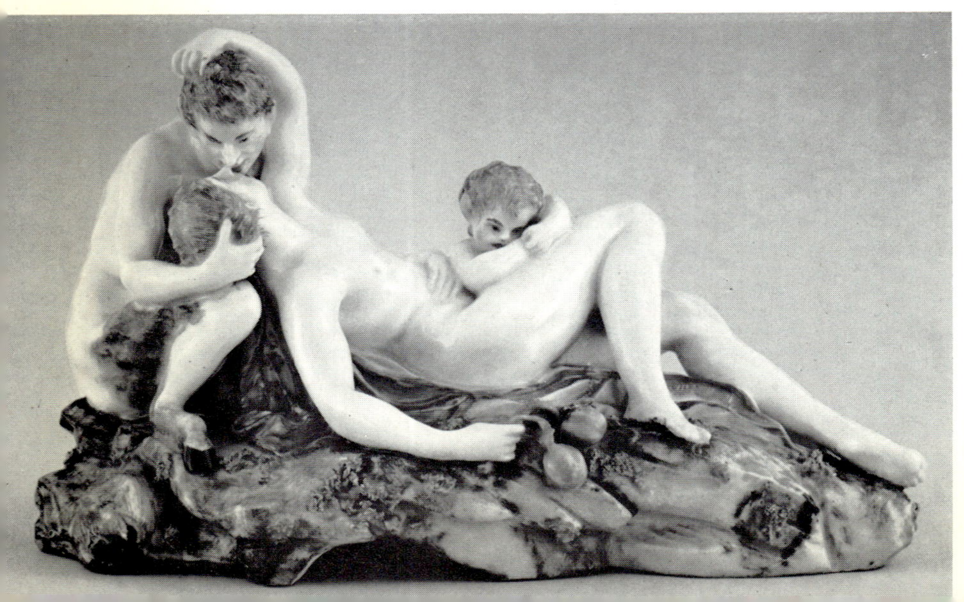

In about 1775 Feilner's miners and comedy figures were reproduced in a smaller size than the originals and with scrolled rococo bases.

The best modeller at Fürstenberg after Feilner was Johann Christoph Rombrich (1758–1794), who created some charming miniature figures and copies of Meissen originals, including the Monkey Band, and many copies of bronze originals in the Duke's collection. He was also responsible for biscuit medallions and busts of his famous contemporaries. Another modeller was Anton Karl Luplau (1765–1795), who designed the famous "Woman Looking for a Flea".

It was the sets of vases, usually in multiples of five, made after 1760, together with the services of table-wares, which make this factory rank with its great eighteenth-century contemporaries.

Many designs were freely adapted from the products of Meissen, Berlin and Sèvres, but curiously enough Fürstenberg was one of the few Continental factories that adopted the English styles of Wedgwood, Chelsea and Bow.

The high relief modelling on the borders and handles of the useful wares and vases is of the most individual character; the fine quality elaborate and exaggerated rococo scrollwork is typical.

In 1795 the Frenchman Louis-Victor Gerverot (1747–1829) from Sèvres was appointed Manager, and he influenced the development of the neo-classical style. He introduced basalt, and busts were made in the manner of Wedgwood. He obtained the patronage of Jérôme Bonaparte from 1807–1813 when the Dukedom of Brunswick became part of Westphalia in Napoleon's re-arrangement of Europe. When the Dukedom was restored in 1814, Gerverot was dismissed.

The Empire style followed in the nineteenth century when the porcelain was heavily gilded and completely covered with painting in the style much favoured by Sèvres and Vienna.

The factory mark, a letter F in script in underglaze blue was used on most items. An impressed mark of the running horse of Brunswick was used on biscuit pieces.

The factory passed to a private firm in 1876, and is still in existence making good quality useful wares and copies of the early models.

FÜRSTENBERG CHARACTERISTICS

1ST PERIOD 1753–1768

1. Hard-paste, greyish with black spots and bubbles.
2. Raised borders, applied and painted decoration used to conceal the defects.
3. Colours, washed out purple and runny underglaze blue, pale green, brownish-crimson.
4. Fantastic rococo forms for table-ware and fanciful scrollwork.
5. Splendidly vigorous figure modelling on simple mound bases with applied flowers.

1768–1795 (BEST PERIOD)

1. Hard-paste, white and clear.
2. Palette extended to dark green, purple, soft brown and clear yellow.
3. Excellent painting on commemorative plaques, sometimes copied from engravings.
4. Figures undistinguished, except smaller copies of earlier models of Comedy and Miners by Feilner on scrolled bases.
5. Factory marks. F in script in underglaze blue. Running horse of Brunswick impressed on biscuit. Gold F on plaques.

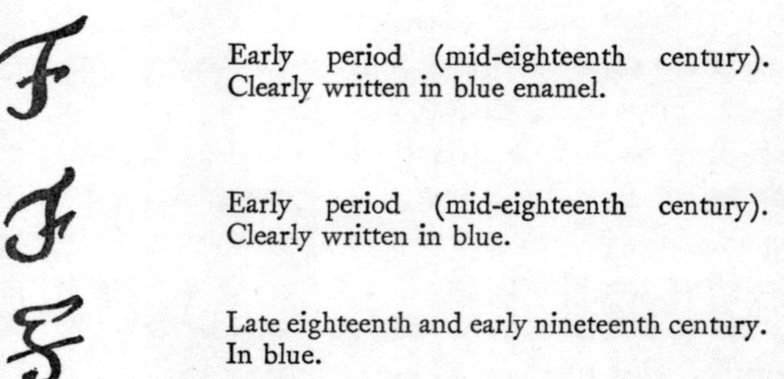

Early period (mid-eighteenth century). Clearly written in blue enamel.

Early period (mid-eighteenth century). Clearly written in blue.

Late eighteenth and early nineteenth century. In blue.

Late eighteenth and early nineteenth century.
In blue.

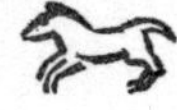

After *1770*, impressed (on biscuit).

Modern, in blue.

[6] BERLIN

1751–1757 Wegely
1763–Present Day Gotzkowsky, Royal and State

Frederick the Great (*d.* 1786) had long been interested in the manufacture of porcelain. Several abortive attempts had already been made in Berlin so when in 1751 a cloth merchant, Wilhelm Kaspar Wegely (*c.* 1770), offered to start a factory, he was given premises, finance and encouragement.

With the assistance of Johann Benckgraff, the arcanist from Höchst and Fürstenberg, production was started late in 1752, but the results were disappointing. Whilst the paste made from the Meissen kaolin from Aue was good and the modelling strong and vigorous, the enamel colours were a failure, for they tended to flake off.

Wegely probably hoped that when Saxony was invaded by Frederick during the Seven Years War (1756–1763), he would be given facilities at the Meissen factory, but Frederick had other ideas. He owed considerable sums to his army contractor, Carl Heinrich Schimmelmann (*c.* 1770), and offered him the Meissen Works, hoping he would ultimately start a factory in Berlin. Schimmelmann owned the factory during the war but did not continue.

Johann Ernst Gotzkowsky (*b.* 1710), a banker, started another Berlin factory in 1761 with the help of Ernst Reichard (*d.* 1764), Wegely's *Modellmeister*. Frederick was enthusiastic. He appropriated materials and equipment from Meissen and forcibly removed many workers to Berlin.

Wraxall wrote in his *Memoirs of the Court of Berlin* in 1777, "There are acts imputable to Frederick over which no casuistry can throw a gloss. Neither the laws of nations nor those of modern war, allow of transporting the male and female manufacturers of a conquered state into the dominions of the invader. This infraction of justice was nevertheless committed at Meissen, in Saxony, famous for the manufacture of porcelain, so generally admired under the name of Dresden china. All the best artists were forcibly sent to Berlin, and there compelled to continue their labours for the benefit of a sovereign the inveterate enemy of their country. They and their descendants, or their scholars, who are still here, have become the involuntary denizens of another soil, the subjects of Frederick II."

Among the artists to move to Berlin were Friedrich Elias Meyer (1723–1785), who became *Modellmeister*, the landscape and figure painters Carl Wilhelm Böhme (1720–1789) and Johann Balthasar Borrmann (1725–1784), and the musician and painter Karl Jacob Christian Klipfel (1726–1786), the King's favourite, to whom are attributed the new wave of mosaic border patterns which heralded the great period of the Berlin factory.

By 1763 Gotzkowsky became financially embarrassed and sold the undertaking with a large stock of unfinished porcelain to the King for 225,000 thalers.

The King now directed his Royal factory and sought to emulate and surpass the rival Meissen Works. He used whatever means in his power to further his aims. Berlin lotteries were instructed to offer porcelain as prizes and Jews were forced to buy a quantity of porcelain before they were permitted to marry. This edict was still law, although not strictly enforced, until the time of Hitler who reversed it and would not allow Jews to buy any porcelain at all. By this time many Jews had become some of the world's greatest experts on porcelain.

The productions during the Wegely period are now rare. They were frequently unpainted because of the enamel firing problems, but when decorations were applied these consisted of *Deutsche Blumen*, landscapes and Watteau scenes.

The nature of the paste, which was extremely hard and lacking in flux content, enabled large pieces to be fired successfully.

Large vases with flowers, stems and leaves modelled in relief in the rococo style were made, as well as figures imitating models made at Meissen and Sèvres. The mark was a W in underglaze blue.

Under Gotzkowsky the mark used was the letter G, usually in underglaze blue but occasionally painted in black, brown or gold over the glaze. So much glazed porcelain was sold to the King in an unfinished state that, as Honey asserts (*German Porcelain*), it is impossible to distinguish the Gotzkowsky wares with any certainty.

The first change under the King's direction was the character of the paste. Frederick's chauvinism compelled him to seek supplies of kaolin within Prussian borders. Deposits were located in Silesia (newly acquired from Austria), but even when blended with the Aue clay the results were creamy-white, then considered to be a fault. In 1771 deposits in Prussia itself were located at Sennewitz and Marl, from which supplies are still drawn. This kaolin produced a cold blue-white porcelain which was technically perfect.

The finest products of the factory were the magnificent services in creamy paste which were ordered by the King and his friends. New designs were produced employing a mosaic border, said to have been invented by Klipfel. The artists from Meissen seemed to thrive in their new surroundings, and each new design raised the standard of Berlin wares far above those of Meissen, which never recovered its porcelain lead after the ravages of the Seven Years War.

When the cold white paste was introduced in 1771, it coincided with the neo-classical fashion. Severer forms found favour and pierced and beaded borders were invented. Wedgwood's classical motifs were the inspiration of many new *englisch* style borders and shapes.

These new designs were not admired by Frederick. He is said to have ordered a service in the old rococo style in 1784, two years before his death.

During the reign of his successor, Frederick Wilhelm II, the neo-classical style was developed and the porcelain medium as a true art form declined. Parallel with her contemporaries,

Berlin suffered her porcelain to be disguised as marble and mosaics or hidden under heavy gilding.

Among the figure-modellers were the brothers Meyer, Friedrich Elias (1723–1785) who was *modellmeister* from 1761 until 1785, and Wilhelm Christian (1726–1786) who worked from 1766 to 1772. Friedrich Elias continued the rococo style he had learned at Meissen and made many charming figures and groups notable for their small heads. Wilhelm, although his brother's pupil, inclined more to the neo-classical style and was influenced by the French sculptors who worked with him. The two brothers were responsible for many large groups, including the marriage of Louis XVI and Marie Antoinette in 1770, and an enormous group representing Catherine the Great under a canopy surrounded by innumerable groups of classical figures and Russian Peasants, presumed to have been designed by Frederick himself—as a shrewd diplomatic present to his German-born ally.

A later modeller, Johann Gottfried Schadow (1764–1850), made a large table centre group of allegorical figures in honour of the Duke of Wellington after Waterloo, which was ordered by Frederick Wilhelm III at a cost of 28,542 thalers and presented in 1819. It can now be seen at Apsley House.

The mark used from 1763 was a sceptre in many variations in underglaze blue, and KPM for *Königliche Porzellan Manufaktur* was added after 1837. The sceptre, printed in violet-toned blue, was used again from 1870.

The factory continues to the present day and is State owned. Severely damaged during World War II, it has been transferred to Selb in Bavaria.

BERLIN CHARACTERISTICS

WEGELY 1751–1757

1. Hard-paste, white, fine quality.
2. Glaze thin and opaque.
3. Colours flaky. Lacquer colours sometimes used.

4. Figure subjects after Meissen and Vincennes, rather ungainly proportions. Sometimes on high pedestal bases.
5. Useful wares with rococo scrolls in relief enclosing reserves of flowers or marine subjects.
6. Factory mark W in underglaze blue.

GOTZKOWSKY AND ROYAL PERIOD 1761

1. Hard-paste, slightly creamy at first, after 1771 cold white and technically perfect.
2. Dates of notable designs of services:

   1763 *Neuzierat* simple scroll borders with shell handles.

   1764 *Reliefzierat mit Stäben* raised scrolling on irregular border enclosing reeding.

   1765 *Reliefzierat mit Spalier* trellis work of radiating ribs. Six panels of which three are in flame red and gold *mosaïk* and three in flowers, central motif of flowers.

   1767 Potsdam service, same as above but in green and gold.

   1768 *Antikzierat* blue service. Reduced scrollwork, increased reeding and fluting. First of the neo-classical styles.

3. Factory marks. Gotzkowsky G sometimes underglaze blue and sometimes in enamel. 1763—Sceptre in underglaze blue. 1837 onwards—KPM and sceptre in underglaze blue.

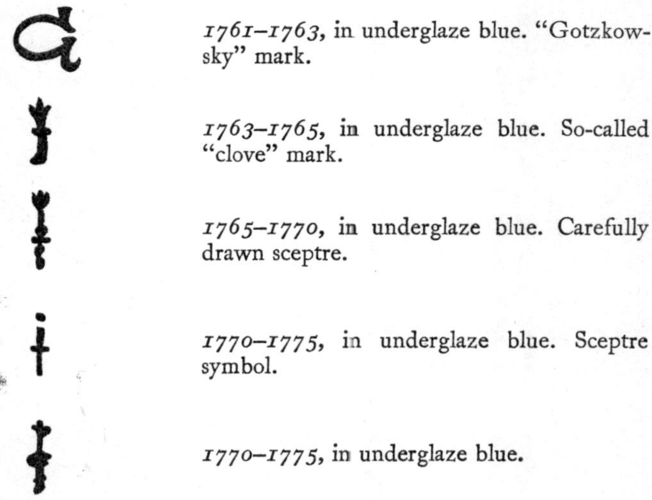

1761–1763, in underglaze blue. "Gotzkowsky" mark.

1763–1765, in underglaze blue. So-called "clove" mark.

1765–1770, in underglaze blue. Carefully drawn sceptre.

1770–1775, in underglaze blue. Sceptre symbol.

1770–1775, in underglaze blue.

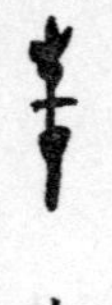

1775–1800, in underglaze blue. In variations, usually thinner.

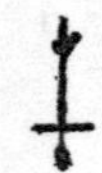

1770–1800, in underglaze blue. Nineteenth century version violet toned.

1832 onwards, printed in red or blue. The "Orb" added at time of decoration.

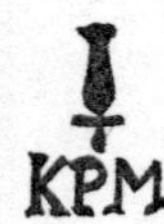

1837–1844, printed (sometimes impressed). On plaques and lithophanes.

1823–1832. Printed in red or brown, "decoration" mark.
1844–1847. In blue, plus band inscribed "Königliche Porzellan-Manufaktur"
1849–1870. The same with or without sceptre,

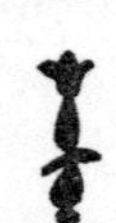

1870 onwards, printed.

[7] FRANKENTHAL, NEAR MANNHEIM 1755–1799

In order to escape the restrictions imposed by royal edict on the manufacture of porcelain in France, other than at the Vincennes factory, Paul Antoine Hannong (1700–1760) left his successful Strasbourg factory to open a new factory in the Palatinate on the other side of the Rhine. With the blessing of the Elector Palatine, he founded the Frankenthal factory and appointed his son, Charles-François-Paul (1732–1757), as Director, while he returned to his Strasbourg factory in order to continue the profitable manufacture of *faïence*.

Charles-François-Paul died in 1757, and his brother, Joseph-Adam (1734–1810), was appointed in his place. He bought his father out in 1759, but the factory was not profitable and he gratefully sold the concern to the main creditor, the Elector Karl

Theodor, in 1762. Adam Bergdoll (*d.* 1797) became Manager, but he had many disputes with his staff and was replaced by Johann Simon Feilner of Fürstenberg, who remained with the concern until 1797.

The Palatinate was the centre of much political strife during that period, and during the wars of 1794–1795 the Elector's factory was confiscated by the French and leased to Peter van Recum. In 1797 the Elector got his factory back, but it was again confiscated in 1797 and leased to Johann Nepomuk van Recum. The factory closed finally in 1799 and the moulds were distributed amongst other factories, including Nymphenburg. Some of the models were reproduced in the nineteenth century in both porcelain and earthenware.

The earliest years at Frankenthal, from 1755–1775, was its finest period. A large number and variety of items were produced, first of all in continuation of the style of Strasbourg (pieces were in fact brought from Strasbourg for finishing). Clay from Passau was employed, and produced a hard creamy-white paste of fine quality, with a thin absorbent glaze which did not mask modelling details, yet caused the colours to "sink in" as in soft-paste. With the use of cheaper kaolin from Alzeyer in 1774, the quality of the paste declined considerably.

A modeller of great distinction was Johann Wilhelm Lanz (*c.* 1720–*c.* 1780) who was with Frankenthal from the very beginning, having come from Strasbourg with the Hannongs. He was responsible for the rococo style, elaborately scroll-based figures. His output was prolific and included Seasons, Continents, *chinoiseries*, Musicians, Italian Comedy and *putti*. His style was somewhat stiff and his figures appear to be posed in an artificial and strained manner, as if waiting for the click of the shutter of an old plate camera. Some of his figures have mound bases, which Honey attributes to his earlier period at Strasbourg. The elaborate scrolls on the later models are outlined in a carmine pink and a favourite colour was a soft apple green. His models have the great charm of artless simplicity. They are well finished and beautifully painted. His other models included equestrian figures, and groups of peasants engaged in simple pleasures, all executed in a naïve and unsophisticated manner.

Lanz was succeeded in 1761 by Johann Friedrich Lück, "repairer" from Meissen. He is credited with figures similar to those produced by Lanz, but with characteristic full-cheeked faces. He also produced some charming slimmer-than-usual *putti* on scrolled bases. These were beautifully modelled; the base itself followed the line of the figure and was an essential part of the whole work. The faces of his many subjects tended to be expressionless, although the modelling was clean and sharp. The cheeks were highly coloured and the hair sketchily painted either all grey or light beige, resembling a wig more than natural growth.

When Karl Theodor purchased the factory in 1762, he appointed the Court sculptor Konrad Linck (1732–1793) as *Modellmeister*, and he remained until 1766; going to Mannheim, he continued to send the factory models and designs for at least another ten years. He introduced the neo-classical style, and his models included many nude figures, mythological subjects including Meleaga and Atalanta, and Apollo and Daphne, after Bernini. He produced portrait busts of Karl Theodor and his wife, Elizabeth August, *putti* and symbolic subjects such as the Twelve Months, the Four Seasons, and the Muses which portrayed beautiful women in delicate pale flesh tones on square plinths, scrolled and gilded and painted with flowers. A famous service produced in 1768 was the *Speiseservice*, which is today reproduced at modern Nymphenburg. It had an *ozier* and ribbed border, decorated with Greek Key patterns, with naturalistic sprays of flowers in purple monochrome.

After Linck's departure, Karl Gottlieb Lück (*d.* 1775) (cousin to Johann Friedrich Lück), who had worked at the Frankenthal factory since 1756, was promoted to *Modellmeister* from 1766 to 1775. Many pretty, humorous, small figures are attributed to him. Table-wares were made in great quantity, elaborately painted, sometimes with battle or hunting scenes. Mythological characters and birds and flowers were also used. The style of Sèvres was closely copied, but its excellence was never achieved.

Lück was succeeded by Adam Bauer (1743–1794) in 1775–1779, who was responsible for groups of figures in the neo-classical taste. Highly coloured cheeks, knees and elbows are typical of his work. He contributed nothing of particular merit.

Johann Peter Melchior of Höchst was appointed in 1779. He repeated his style from Höchst and produced some attractive groups of children. Portrait medallions of the Elector and Goethe were part of his accomplishments. He also produced figures after Watteau, the faces of which have distinct Germanic features. He painted exquisite *Deutsche Blumen*, as well as stylised fruits and flowers but he did not improve on his earlier inspiration at Höchst. Melchior left Frankenthal in 1793.

One of the smaller of the seven great German factories of the eighteenth century, Frankenthal is remarkable in its short history of only forty years for the wide variety and enormous quantity of excellent works which were produced. It came into existence at the best period of the rococo style and was later influenced by the more severe neo-classical style, but closed before the Empire period. A fine collection of Frankenthal work can be seen at the Residenz Museum in Munich.

FRANKENTHAL CHARACTERISTICS

1ST (BEST) PERIOD 1755–1775

1. Hard-paste, creamy white, fine.
2. Glaze exceptionally absorbent and thin.
3. Colours "sunk in" as in soft-paste.
4. Factory marks. Impressed PH for Paul Hannong or a blue lion or shield in underglaze blue. 1762 CT for Charles (Karl) Theodor in underglaze blue. PR and VR in underglaze blue for the van Recums.

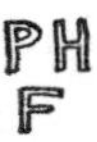

1755–1756, impressed, for "Paul Hannong"

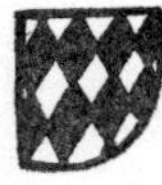

1755–1756–1759, impressed. For "Paul Hannong Frankenthal".

About *1756*, in blue. From arms of Elector Paletine.

1758–1762, impressed. Initials of Joseph Hannong.

iH

1758–1762, impressed.

1762–1793 and *1796*, in blue. "Carl Theodor" period.

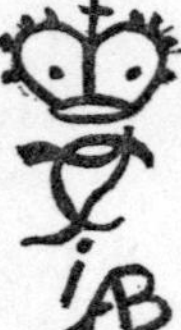

1762–1770, in blue. "Carl Theodor" period with initials of Adam Bergdoll.

1780–1793, in blue. Late "Carl Theodor" period. Sometimes with two or three dots.

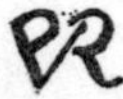

1795, in blue. Mark of Peter van Recum.

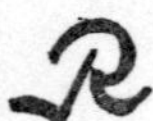

1797–1798, in blue. Mark of Johann Nepomuk van Recum.

[8] LUDWIGSBURG, Württemberg 1756–1824

A porcelain factory was founded in Ludwigsburg, a small town near Stuttgart, by the engineer/architect Bonifacius Christoph Hackher, but production was only started in 1758 when the factory was taken over by Karl Eugen, the Duke of Württemberg (1737–1793). The wandering arcanist from Vienna and Nymphenburg, Josef Jakob Ringler, joined the undertaking in 1759 and remained as Director until 1804. This was his last appointment in a porcelain factory before his death in 1806.

Karl Eugen, a pleasure-loving, ostentatious man, patronised

the factory only to add lustre to his luxurious Court, to which he had already added an excellent ballet company, one of the finest in Europe.

The paste was evolved from the kaolin of Passau, and although rarely white it was particularly suitable for plastic and figure modelling. The earliest designs were copies of Meissen, but the Ludwigsburg artists soon developed a style of their own. The early models were in the rococo style which was then prevalent, and from 1759–1779 the leading designer was Gottlieb Friedrich Riedel (1724–1785), who had previously worked at Meissen, Höchst and Frankenthal. He created classical and mythological subjects and table-ware often decorated with birds. His classical figures included Neptune, Leda, the Continents, Venus and Bacchus, the Seasons and some *putti*. His models frequently included a trellis background in the style of Frankenthal, and his influence was felt in many other contemporary factories. A fine engraver, he left many sketches and engravings which were used long after he had left the factory. In 1779 he went to Augsburg and devoted his time to engraving.

Other artists of this period were Johann Göz (1734–1762), who worked with Riedel from 1759–1762 as "Chief Repairer", and the Court Sculptors Domenico Ferretti (1702–1774) and Pierre-François Le Jeune (1721–1790) who modelled for the factory at various times between 1762 and 1767.

From 1762–1772, the artist Jean-Jacob Louis (1703–1772) of Namur, whose work has been identified by means of an incised L, was, according to Honey, responsible for "finely modelled large figures of birds, particularly some parrots on rococo bases, some groups of animals, a Turk leading a Horse, groups of Lovers, Gardeners and Hunters, and a Lady at a Spinet with an attendant Cavalier (often erroneously called Franziska von Hohenheim and Voltaire)".

From 1764–1767, the Court Sculptor Johann Christian Wilhelm Beyer (1725–1806) became the chief of the modelling department, and his style influenced many figures although they were not actually by his hand. Beyer's work has been identified by a series of engravings which he had published in Vienna, and these included reproductions of seven of his porcelain figures as well as sculpture. During this period, the bases which had previously been rococo scrolled, picked out in brownish crimson or gold, gave way in about 1765 to a rectangular base, usually marbled, in the neo-classical style. The figures modelled during the time of Beyer are considered to be the finest work of the Ludwigsburg factory, and rank amongst the finest of the eighteenth century. Honey says, "the beautiful flowing lines and the monumental forms, no less than the subtle indication of temperament and the playful *negligé* of the costumes, entitle these to rank among the best of all porcelain figures" (*Dictionary of European Ceramic Art*).

In 1767 Beyer left Ludwigsburg to go to Vienna. Beyer's models were a subtle transition from the rococo to the neo-classical style. These included Fishermen, Musicians, Wine Drinkers, Singers, all in vital twisted postures which evoke some of the "strength at play" of the earlier baroque period.

After 1770, the work of the factory declined. It had never been profitable, and when the Duke Karl Eugen, who had declared the factory to be "necessary to the splendour and dignity" of his Court, died in 1793, it deteriorated rapidly. It struggled for another thirty years, until it closed in 1824.

According to Ware (*German and Austrian Porcelain*), the moulds were reported to have been transferred to Regensburg in 1825, and later, in about 1850, to an Amburg pottery, where poor copies were made. Old Ludwigsburg models are still being reproduced in Germany by the Württembergische Porzellan Manufaktur at Schorndorf and marked with the old Ludwigsburg factory marks, usually with WPM beneath.

LUDWIGSBURG CHARACTERISTICS

1. Hard-paste, smoky muddy tone with thin irregular glaze.
2. Figures in rococo style, similar to Frankenthal. Individual development of dancing figures derived from Württemberg ballet.
3. Unoriginal models and painting styles on useful wares, evocative of contemporary eighteenth-century factories.

4. Factory mark, 1759–1793, consisted of two C's back to back sometimes surmounted by a crown in underglaze blue. Later pieces were sometimes marked with a capital L in script sometimes with a crown; three antlers, with or without a crown; the letters FR also with or without a crown and the letters WR usually in gold under the crown.

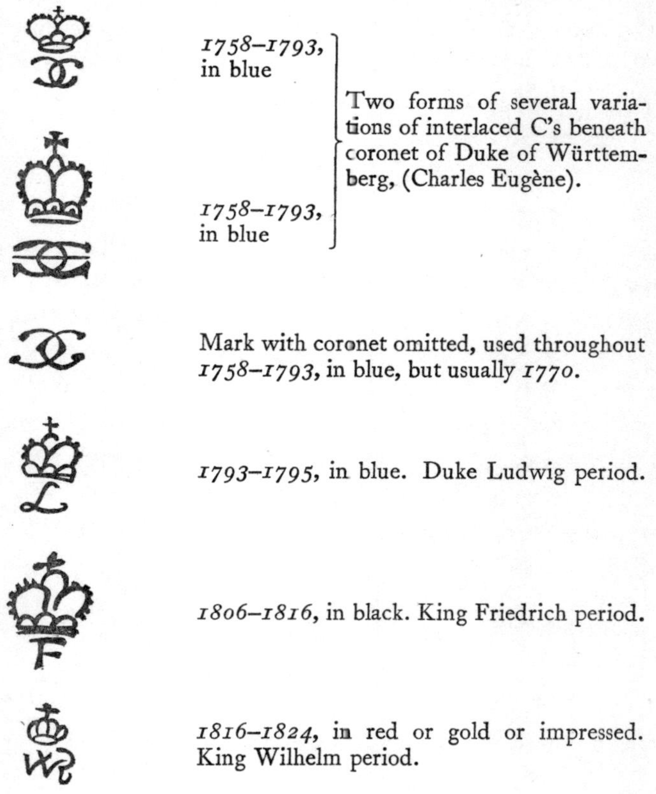

1758–1793, in blue
1758–1793, in blue
Two forms of several variations of interlaced C's beneath coronet of Duke of Württemberg, (Charles Eugène).

Mark with coronet omitted, used throughout *1758–1793,* in blue, but usually *1770.*

1793–1795, in blue. Duke Ludwig period.

1806–1816, in black. King Friedrich period.

1816–1824, in red or gold or impressed. King Wilhelm period.

[9] OTHER FACTORIES IN GERMANY—
Ansbach, Fulda, Kloster-Veilsdorf

There were numerous small factories in Germany in the eighteenth century whose work was interesting but mainly derivative. The following were the most outstanding.

ANSBACH 1758–1860

The arcanist Johann Friedrich Kändler, cousin to the great Meissen Kändler, together with some ex-Meissen workers, began production of a pure white porcelain with an incomparable glaze in a *faïence* factory at Ansbach in 1758.

Their patron, the Höhenzollern Margrave Alexander of Brandenberg, moved them to his hunting castle at Brückberg in 1762, and the next years until 1775 witnessed the production of their finest work in the rococo style, which compares favourably with the best in German porcelain.

The Margrave abdicated in 1791 in favour of his cousin, and the factory declined. It was sold to a private firm in 1807, and so it continued until it closed in 1860.

White and painted figures were made in considerable quantities of unusual quality. Decorative and useful wares were made: plates, monogrammed cups and saucers, coffee pots with spouts made in the form of a female face, and paintings of flowers and landscapes after the style of Meissen. The output was prodigous and examples are much sought after.

The mark used at Ansbach from about 1760–1785 was an A in underglaze blue. This does not represent Ansbach as is commonly thought, but is the initial of Alexander, the Margrave.

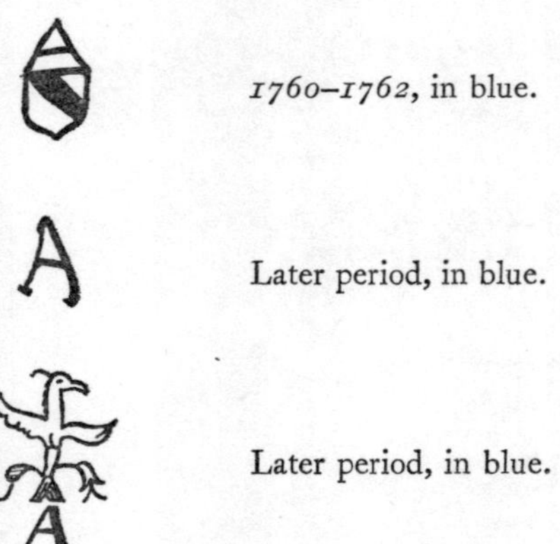

1760–1762, in blue.

Later period, in blue.

Later period, in blue.

FULDA 1765–1790

Under the patronage of Prince Heinrich von Bibra, Bishop of Fulda, the arcanist from Wegely's Berlin, the protegé of

Ringler, Nikolaus Paul, began porcelain production in 1765.

Very fine white porcelain with a sparkling glaze was produced. Many models were copied from Höchst and Frankenthal, and the charming figures are both attractive and distinctive.

The mark was usually a double F with or without a crown in underglaze blue. Sometimes a simple cross was employed.

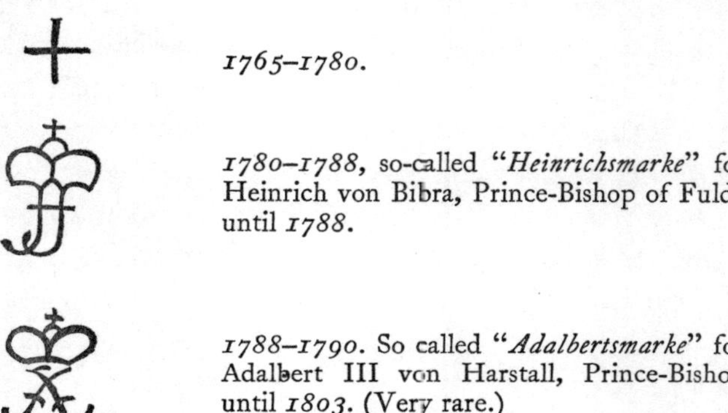

1765–1780.

1780–1788, so-called "*Heinrichsmarke*" for Heinrich von Bibra, Prince-Bishop of Fulda until *1788.*

1788–1790. So called "*Adalbertsmarke*" for Adalbert III von Harstall, Prince-Bishop until *1803.* (Very rare.)

KLOSTER-VEILSDORF 1760–

The most important of the Thuringian porcelain factories, it was founded in 1760 by Prince Friedrich Wilhelm Eugen von Hildburghausen. It was sold by his heirs to the Greiner family of Limbach, and remained in their possession until 1822. The factory is still operating.

The arcanist Nikolaus Paul was employed from 1766 to 1768, and developed a fine milk-white paste. The best period was before 1780 and the models were in the rococo taste. Enamel colours were used with great success and paintings of Birds, Cupids, Festoons, Landscapes and subjects after Watteau, Boucher and Teniers.

The most successful colours were bright clear yellow, a pale yellow-green, a bright blue-green, purple, brown and a magenta used on the edges.

The names of the artists and modellers are unknown, but the work reached an excellent standard. The most outstanding modelled work consisted of Italian Comedy figures after the style of Simon Feilner at Fürstenberg, with which they are frequently confused, and some classical figures, draped or nude, on square, polygonal plain, or marbled bases. There were many other models in the eighteenth-century idiom of Shepherds and Shepherdesses, Ladies and Gentlemen and Children on simply modelled rococo scrolled bases.

Numerous pottery and porcelain factories were started in the Thuringian forest, where fuel and clay were freely available, and which in time became the equivalent of modern Staffordshire, and the area is still producing porcelain and pottery. Other small factories were started in the eighteenth century at Limbach, Gotha, Volkstedt-Rudolstadt, Wallendorf, Ilmenau, Gera, Grossbreitenbach and Rauenstein, which supplied peasant porcelain to a wide middle-class market. The greyish hard-paste was not unattractively decorated in a naïve style in imitation of Meissen with imitated marks.

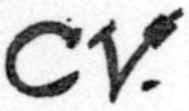

CV *1760–1797.*

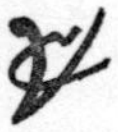

1760–1797.

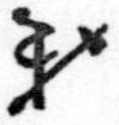

Intended to imitate MEISSEN crossed swords.

Chapter Three

France

> "*La porcelaine et la frêle beauté*
> *De cet émail a la Chine empruntée,*
> *Par mille mains fût pour vous préparée,*
> *Cuite, recuite, et peinte et diaprée.*"
>
> VOLTAIRE; *Oeuvres*, t/10, p. 91

LOUIS XIV (1643–1715) inherited a bankrupt feudal state and bequeathed a bankrupt, war-weary nation. Much has been written about his long despotic reign, his progressive and retrogressive policies—his politics and his mistresses. We are concerned with his patronage of the arts, for all eyes turned in envy to Versailles and the splendour of the Court of the *Roi Soleil.*

He built the palace of Versailles around a charming house constructed for his father who had found the location ideal for an overnight stay when it was too late to return to Paris after a day's hunting. The land was low-lying swamp and the building was fraught with difficulties. Construction could only be achieved by *travail forcé* and many unfortunates died of marsh diseases. The gardens were landscaped by Le Nôtre and the town of Versailles was planned around the palace with wide tree-lined avenues. No expense was spared in the luxurious royal apartments—paintings, sculpture, tapestries, furniture and silver were commissioned and legions of craftsmen were employed to supply carved and gilded wood panelling, parquet flooring and marble staircases. Versailles became the showplace of Europe. Visiting princes patronised the craftsmen, so it was felt that the expense had been justified and business had been brought to France.

Recalling the troubles with the nobles in his father's reign, Louis XIV shrewdly invited them to attend him at Court, now removed from Paris to Versailles, where he could keep them under observation. Those who preferred Paris or their estates were snubbed and could not hope for honours or appointments. Life at the Court of Versailles became a brilliant extravaganza of luxury—entertainments, masques and balls—so resplendent and costly, that it has never been surpassed.

Louis XIV led Europe in style and grandeur, and collected magnificent works of art. Porcelain was being imported from the Orient, and he became the first great European collector. He built the first Trianon, a pavillion in the grounds of Versailles, as a tea house for Madame de Montespan. It was decorated throughout in blue, violet and white to simulate ceramics. Unfortunately these decorations no longer exist.

His chief Minister Colbert, who had been instrumental in reviving the French economy, died in 1683, and the last obstacle to the King's extravagancies was removed. He appointed his favourites, often regardless of talent, to governmental positions and in the hands of these incompetents earlier iniquitous practices reasserted themselves. Continual wars and maladministration brought France to the verge of bankruptcy.

Following the disasters which befell France after the Battle of Blenheim in 1704, Le Duc de Saint-Simon (the contemporary gossip writer) recounted that the Duchesse de Gramont conceived the idea of offering her plate to the King to replenish his impoverished exchequer. She was followed reluctantly by the other members of the Court, who dared not refuse to do so. The courtiers replaced their gold and silver table appointments with *faïence*, and then eagerly turned to porcelain.

French porcelain production had made a hesitant start at Rouen in 1673 and Letters Patent were granted to the Chicaneau family at Saint-Cloud in 1702. No other French factory began until after the publication of the letters received between 1712 and 1722 from Père d'Entrecolles the Jesuit Missionary in China. The first porcelain made in France was not real porcelain at all, but is known as *pâte tendre* (soft-paste) or artificial porcelain. It was not until 1769 that hard-paste or true porcelain, was finally made in France, although it had been invented at Meissen in 1709. Porcelain production in France was originally considered to be an extension of the silversmiths' art, as the basic materials used were regarded as precious metals. Silversmiths and goldsmiths were employed as designers and decorators, and their stamp appears on early productions. Later the porcelain medium became a subject of its own and artists and technicians grew from it.

By the time Louis XV reached his majority at the age of thirteen in 1723, following the *Régence* of Philippe, Duc d'Orleans, the manufacture of soft-paste porcelain was established. An interval of peace, manoeuvred by Cardinal Fleury and Robert Walpole after the Peace of Utrecht, permitted France to reorganise her government and industry. A factory was started at Menneçy in 1734 and at Chantilly in 1735. The King became personally involved in porcelain manufacture at Vincennes in 1745, and from 1753 owned a quarter share in the establishment of the new factory at Sèvres.

Royal edicts were issued in 1745, 1747, 1752, 1753, 1759–1760 and 1766, protecting the monopoly rights of Sèvres against competition.

The foundation of the great Sèvres factory owed much to the patronage of the celebrated Madame de Pompadour, mistress of Louis XV, and her taste and culture were evident in the styles and designs produced. She was the indirect cause of the introduction of the Louis Seize neo-classical style to France. She sent her talented brother Abel Poisson to Italy in 1749 in order to study art and architecture, which led him to the adoption of the classical idiom when he later became Marquis de Marigny and Intendant Général des Bâtiments du Roi (the equivalent of our Minister of Works).

Voltaire wrote, "Barely sixty years ago, Europe imitated Chinese porcelain: we now surpass it because of our great efforts, but these efforts have made it very expensive, and therefore not available to everyone. The great secret of art is that all classes of society may enjoy it without difficulty."

Porcelain was an expensive luxury for the privileged, but with the discovery of kaolin at St. Yrieix in 1765, new factories were opened, at Lunéville, Niderviller, Strasbourg and Paris making the cheaper hard-paste. Their competition increased the mounting difficulties at Sèvres, where the workmen were frequently unpaid and many of them deserted.

Louis XVI continued the Royal patronage, but porcelain was the least of his worries. The legacy of financial chaos of the preceding reigns and the disastrous Seven Years War were causing alarming unrest amongst the population. The American Declaration of Independence in 1776 encouraged the revolutionaries in France to rise, and in 1789 the Bastille was stormed and taken. Austria, whose daughter Marie Antoinette was in mortal danger, was too busy to intervene in the domestic problems of France as she was nervously watching her partners Russia and Prussia in the share out in the last two divisions of Poland.

After the Terror, the country settled down to some sort of order and the new bourgeois society restored the elegant way of life to Paris.

Most of the French porcelain factories had not survived, but the new hierarchy demanded the equipment of gracious living which the remainder hastened to supply. Napoleon assumed the patronage of Sèvres and appointed Brongniart as Director, who reorganised the factory and placed it on a sound financial footing.

As the nineteenth century progressed, social values changed, and the market for porcelain altered accordingly. Porcelain reached the less exacting middle classes, and parallel with the rest of Europe, standards of merit fell.

The value of the livre, which is frequently quoted in the following chapters, is difficult to assess by present-day values. W. H. Lewis (*Memoirs of the Duc de Saint-Simon*) suggests the following rough guide:

1 livre, silver = 1 franc, 17th century = 1 franc, 1914 = 10d
6 livres, silver = 1 Crown, 17th century = 6 francs, 1914 = 5s
4 crowns, silver = 1 gold louis, 17th century = 24 francs, 1914 = 20s

In 1745 (the time of the Dauphin's marriage to the Infanta Marie-Thérèse-Raphaele and the Ball of the Clipped Yew Trees) the Duc de Luynes wrote, "they give in London a guinea for a louis and in Lille a louis for a guinea".

[1] ROUEN, Seine-Inférieure 1673–1696

The first Patent for the manufacture of porcelain in France was issued in 1673 to Louis Poterat (1612–1687), the son of the Rouen *faïence* manufacturer, Edmé Poterat.

Rouen *faïence* was typical of the Louis XIV style, attributed to Jean Bérain (1637–1711) decorated in underglaze blue, with closely packed scrolls, arabesques and a lacy design in inverted scallops known as lambrequins.

Very little Rouen porcelain was made, and about half a dozen attributed pieces are scattered throughout the museums of France and England. The style closely followed that of the *faïence*.

Louis Poterat died in 1696, "crippled in his limbs by the ingredients used in his porcelain". As only he had been involved in the secret manufacture of the porcelain, so the Rouen porcelain died with him.

ROUEN CHARACTERISTICS

1. Soft-paste.
2. Similar in appearance to Rouen *faïence*.
3. Baroque styling.
4. Underglaze blue, lambrequins and arabesques, etc.
5. No factory mark attributable.

[2] SAINT-CLOUD, Seine-et-Oise about 1678–1766

The first real production of porcelain in France took place at the Saint-Cloud factory near Paris. Pierre Chicaneau invented a formula, but although his family claimed that he had made quantities of porcelain before his death in 1678, it cannot be proved.

In 1679, Chicaneau's widow, Berthe Coudray, married Henri-Charles Trou, whose master the Duc d'Orléans, brother of Louis XIV, advanced large sums of money for the factory, which was in the vicinity of his château.

In his *Memoires*, the Duc de Luynes wrote, "It took the fancy of Madame de Parabère (mistress of le Duc d'Orléans) to have some porcelain in her apartment. M. le Duc d'Orléans had some brought from all around at whatever price was asked. This taste for porcelain lasted a long time. They say that M. le Duc d'Orléans gave 1,000,000 livres for it."

Martin Lister, an English professor of medicine and a mineralogist, who travelled in France and visited the factory at Saint-Cloud in 1698, wrote, "I have seen the pottery at Saint-Cloud, and I was delighted with it, for, I swear, I could find no difference between the articles made in this establishment and the most beautiful porcelain of China that I have seen. The glaze of this pottery is in no way inferior to that of the Chinese porcelain, in whiteness, in regularity of surface, and without any faults. The body which constitutes this pottery appeared to me to be completely identical, hard and firm like marble, of the same grain and the same vitrified appearance. They sell this pottery at Saint-Cloud at a high price; they ask several écus for a single chocolate cup. They sell tea services at four hundred écus the service."

In 1700, this anecdote was reported in the *Mercure de France*: "The 3rd September Madame la Duchesse de Bourgogne (mother of Louis XV) having passed by Saint-Cloud and proceeded along the river bank to visit Madame la Duchesse de Guiche, halted her carriage at the door of the house where Messieurs Chicaneaux have established for several years a factory for fine porcelain, which without contradiction has no equal in the whole of Europe. This Princess took pleasure in seeing several beautiful pieces being made. The Princess did not leave until she had expressed her satisfaction by the gratuities she distributed to the workmen."

In 1702 the Chicaneau family were granted Letters Patent, but poor Trou was not mentioned, although he was part owner. It has been suggested that he had died by this time. We read in the Letters Patent, dated 16th May, 1702, that Berthe Coudray and her children, in their application for the privilege of making porcelain, stated that the late Pierre Chicaneau had made extensive experiments and produced porcelain as fine as that of China, and also that he had taught his children the trade and they too were familar with the secret processes. The King gave permission in these documents "to make in the town of Saint-Cloud one or more establishments for the manufacture of all colours, styles and sizes".

The old lady died in 1722, and the factory continued under her son Pierre. When he died in 1741, the arcanum was passed to his sons and daughters and their marriage partners.

In the meantime, a widowed daughter-in-law, Marie Moreau Chicaneau, with her cousin by marriage, Louis-Dominic-François Chicaneau, started an independent factory of the firm's Paris branch at the rue de la Ville-l'Evêque, Faubourg St. Honoré, in the Parish of the Madeleine. The Saint-Cloud Works were nearly burned down in 1737, and again some five years later, in 1742–1743. Marie Moreau died in 1743 and Henri (II) Trou took over both factories. In 1746 Henri (II) died, leaving the factories to his son Henri-François Trou, who in 1764 took Edmé Choudard des Forges into partnership. The concern went into liquidation in 1766, and many of the employees went to Vincennes.

The soft-paste of the porcelain made at Saint-Cloud is its most attractive feature. Usually creamy or ivory tinted, it lends warmth to the subject. The modelling was strong, original and vigorous, and the designs of tureens, toilet pots, dishes, etc., although massive and austere, were never clumsy. Bold gadrooning and reeding were used in the style of silver ware. The productions of the Saint-Cloud factory were frequently mounted in silver, as there was probably an arrangement with the Paris silversmiths. A frequent decoration was the applied Chinese prunus blossom, usually all white and resembling the Chinese *blanc-de-chine* from Fukien. Saucers were of the *trembleuse* pattern, and had high foot rings. Subjects of Chinese *famille verte* inspiration and the Japanese *Imari* and *Arita* were popular.

The factory varied it shapes, but rarely its decoration. The designs in blue, in the style of Bérain, the lambrequins, the arabesques, the geometrical lines and the white reliefs dominated, prolonging during the *Régence* and the reign of Louis XV the baroque style of the preceding reign. Figures played a sufficiently important part, but they were rarely decorated, the modelling was primitive, and they frequently deformed in the firing; the beautiful creamy glaze was unsuitably thick and masked the details.

The factory at Saint-Cloud employed a process for the application of gold leaf to porcelain by engraving. It consisted of a sort of glue made from quince pips, on which they applied the gold leaf by means of the kind of engraving tool used in bookbinding, after which it was re-fired.

Whichever styles were adopted, the Saint-Cloud factory gave then a special identity, a restrained and elegant French taste dominating them all.

SAINT-CLOUD CHARACTERISTICS

1. Always soft-paste.
2. Paste, apart from the early period when it was a cold white, became creamy or ivory tinted. Pieces from the last period became greyish.
3. Modelling strong and form massive.
4. Knobs on lids in the shape of pine cones a peculiarity.
5. Foot rings in saucers very high, leaving a deep hollow in the base.
6. Fine pitting in glaze makes surface look like satin.

7. Plates extremely rare. Due to technical difficulties large flat areas usually became wasters.

8. Factory marks. To about 1722, the sun in blue. 1722–1766, St.C. / T in blue or incised.

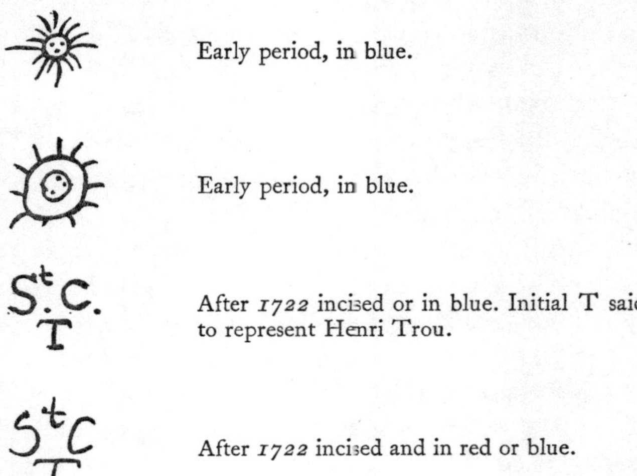

Early period, in blue.

Early period, in blue.

After *1722* incised or in blue. Initial T said to represent Henri Trou.

After *1722* incised and in red or blue.

[3] CHANTILLY, Dept. Oise 1725–1800

The leading spirit behind the Chantilly factory was Louis-Henri de Bourbon, Prince de Condé, who lived in the spectacular white palace at Chantilly. He decided that porcelain should be produced in France, and for this purpose assembled a fine collection of Oriental pieces, particularly the Japanese *Arita* ware, to be used as models for form and decoration. He was very determined about porcelain production, and in 1725 found a capable manager in Ciquaire Cirou (1698–1751). The Prince died in 1740 while his heir was still a minor, so it was the Comte de Charolais, his uncle and guardian, who decided that development of the Park and Château was more important than porcelain production, and neglected the factory. It was during this period that many workers left Chantilly, among them the brothers Dubois, to offer their services to M. Orry de Fulvy, founder of the porcelain factory at Vincennes.

After Cirou's death in 1751 the production passed to Buquet de Montvallier (1709–1760) and de Roussière, and from 1754 to 1760 to Montvallier alone. From 1760 to 1776 Pierre Peyrard, the principal *concierge* of the Château and Treasurer to His Royal Highness, became the *concessionaire*. In 1776 Louis-François Gravant acquired the concession from Peyrard, together with the formulae, kilns, stocks of kaolin, sand, moulds and other utensils, for the sum of 150,000 livres. Madame Gravant was aware that her husband was managing his affairs badly so when she reached her majority on 12th August, 1778 she demanded a legal separation which was accorded to her on 7th September, 1779. She then seized all the furniture, effects and merchandise belonging to her husband, and finally became proprietress of everything that the Gravants had bought from Peyrard.

La Dame Gravant now found herself in a position to expand the business, but as the buildings, the land, the mill and the stream belonged to the Prince de Condé, she demanded from him an indefinite concession, which was granted to her on 14th March, 1781 and for which she paid 150 livres a year in rent. As soon as she had all the rights afforded her, she immediately sold her concession, together with the equipment and stock, to Antheaume de Surval and his wife.

Antheaume de Surval was a lawyer in the *Parlement* and a Tax Collector at Chantilly. He managed the factory for eleven years. In 1792 he sold his concession to Christopher Potter, citizen of London, who gave his address as 3 Prince's Place, Westminster. Potter had already owned a hard-paste factory at Rue de Courcelles Paris, and he set about the expansion of the Chantilly factory. He began to make *faïence* and enjoyed such prosperity that he increased the number of workers to 200. He undertook large productions, and at one time made 9,000 dozen plates each month. He also founded the factories of Montereau and Forges. In 1789 he applied for a monopoly in France for transfer printing, which was refused. His large speculations ran counter to the political atmosphere of the time and he was forced to close down in 1800.

L'Abbé Fauquemprez, in his *Histoire de la manufacture de Chantilly* (p. 97) wrote, "The establishment founded by the Prince de Condé, after having lasted for three quarters of a century and having produced pieces which remain as some of the most remarkable types of our soft-paste porcelain, finally ended in bankruptcy at the hands of an Englishman".

Under Cirou the soft-paste porcelain with the milky tin glaze previously only used on *faïence* was produced in quantity. The use of tin glaze on porcelain is unknown at any other factory, except briefly at Lund's Bristol, and gives the Chantilly ware its individual distinction. The decoration was "Korean", sparse, free-flowing, asymmetrical designs, derived from the 17th century Japanese artist Kakiemon and executed in the French rococo taste. The forms became progressively more European but retained the quaint Oriental flavour.

The second period of Chantilly began in about 1750 when the tin glaze was rejected in favour of the more usual type of lead glaze, which gave the wares a yellowish, creamy tone. The porcelain was still of fine quality. The influence of *faïence* and silver forms is clearly noticeable in Chantilly porcelain. The designs in the second period cover a wider field. Copies of Meissen, *Deutsche Blumen* and the applied Vincennes flowers were freely adopted, but in a different fashion, and the body and glaze gave the Chantilly colours a soft matt finish. During the Sèvres prohibition, which precluded other factories from using polychrome, delightful monochrome decorations after Boucher in dull-bluish crimson were produced.

After 1780 hardly any soft-paste was made in the now accepted Chantilly tradition.

The mark adopted by this factory was a hunting horn in either blue or red. This token of the factory was presumably taken from the great interest in hunting which prevailed in the Chantilly woods.

CHANTILLY CHARACTERISTICS

1. Always soft-paste until the last twenty years. Beware of fraudulent hard-paste copies.
2. Smooth opaque pure white tin glaze. Later works lead glazed and inclined to be yellowish.
3. French silver and *faïence* shapes, followed by Japanese octagonal, melon, pomegranate and peach shapes.
4. Typical clear bright orange Japanese style decoration.
5. Quaint mixture of two asymmetrical styles, French rococo and Japanese.
6. Factory mark, a hunting horn in blue or red.

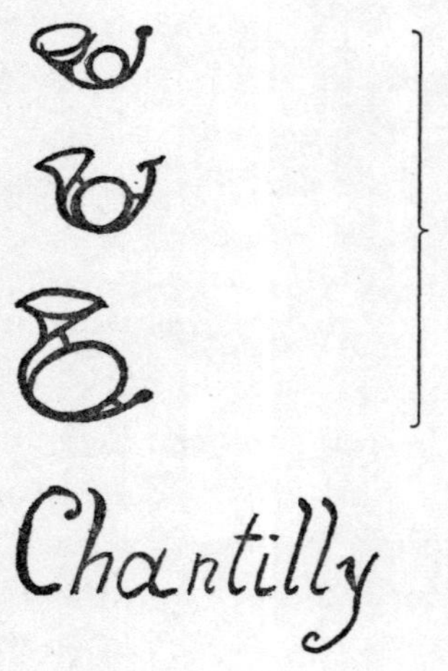

The hunting horn in variations—in red, blue or other colours.

Rare mark usually found with Chantilly sprig decoration.

[4] VINCENNES 1738–1756 SEVRES 1756–PRESENT DAY

The invention of a soft-paste (*pâte tendre*) first produced at Saint-Cloud then at Chantilly was the basis of Vincennes porcelain. The manufacture of porcelain was considered essential not only to replace the Chinese but because of the unprecedented success of Meissen. The Chantilly secrets were sold in 1738 to M. Jean-Louis-

Henri Orry de Fulvy (1703--1751) brother of the *Comptrôlleur-Général*, by two discharged workmen—Robert (*b.* 1709) and Gilles Dubois (*b.* 1713). Premises in a disused riding school attached to the Château de Vincennes and financial assistance were made available to the brothers who continued with their experiments. Some porcelain was made but most of it was spoilt in the firing. The situation became intolerable, for the Dubois could not produce satisfactory results (it has been said that they were often too drunk to work) so they were dismissed in 1741. François Gravant (*d.* 1765) was appointed manager in their place and proved to be competent and reliable. Engaged in 1740 he had learned all the brothers had to impart, and continued his own experiments. He produced workable pastes and glazes, procured new workmen from Chantilly and got production going.

A group of financiers formed a company in 1745 in the name of the sculptor, Charles Adam, with a starting capital of 90,000 livres, and secured the first of its many privileges, the exclusive right for twenty years to produce "porcelain in the style of the Saxon, that is to say painted and gilded with human figures". A process for gilding was bought from Frère Hippolyte, a Benedictine monk; the painter Jean-Adam Mathieu (*c.* 1750– and the sculptor and goldsmith Claude-Thomas Duplessis (*d.* 1774) were engaged and by 1750 the factory was well established, employing about a hundred workmen.

The success of the Vincennes-Sèvres factory owed much to Mme. La Marquise de Pompadour, mistress of Louis XV. Born Jeanne-Antoinette Poisson in 1721, she was carefully reared by her mother, after her father had disappeared to avoid the consequences of a fraudulent deal involving government money. A pretty woman, the mother became a close friend of M. de Tournehem, who protected her and supervised the child's upbringing. Jeanne-Antoinette's education, according to eighteenth-century standards for women, was very enlightened. Quick and clever, witty and talented, she married an official at the Royal Mint (Le Normant d'Etoilles) and led a gay social life. She had many admirers and is reported to have refused them on the grounds that she would be unfaithful with no one but the king. This happy event took place in 1740 and five years later she was installed in Versailles. She became the leader of fashion and in her salon entertained the intellectual élite of the day. Voltaire, Greuze, and Boucher were among her friends whilst her refined taste, quick intelligence and wide interests kept the king enthralled long after their physical attachment had waned. As patroness of the arts she became more and more interested in porcelain and is said to have remarked "not to buy this china as long as one has money is to prove oneself a bad citizen".

In order to interest the King in her beloved porcelain, she invited him to her Château where she had a magnificent greenhouse built, in which an indoor garden was arranged. Imagine the King's surprise when he bent to smell his favourite flower only to find that it was made of porcelain suitably scented. It was an expensive ruse, but it established the fortunes of the factory. The King placed an order for Vincennes flowers for 800,000 livres and his Court were not slow to follow suit. A magnificent bouquet of nearly 500 separate blossoms mounted in ormulu sprays of leaves was sent by the Dauphine Marie-Josèphe to her father the Elector of Saxony in about 1750. The bouquet was in a white vase between two groups of figures, all of Vincennes porcelain. Mme. de Pompadour persuaded the King to transfer the porcelain factory from Vincennes to a new, large building to be specially constructed at Sèvres which could be more conveniently approached from her Château at Bellevue.

The Marquis d'Argenson wrote on 15th January, 1753, "They are taking everything from Vincennes. The porcelain factory is going to be moved to Sèvres, near to the Glassworks. Our King buys, supplying the funds for everything, as if His Majesty had a great deal of money in his coffers. The twelve financiers who have been made Directors are principally friends of the Marquise and the Keeper of the Seals. These persons make out that they are advancing the capital, but they are not. They are buying the processes for porcelain from the old company, it will be a new ruination for the King. They will dissipate it; they will make some curious bagatelles and attract His Majesty to the bait of profit for the State which does not exist; they say that this will save us two millions annually that now go abroad and two more millions of foreign exchange which this will bring us. I do not believe it."

In January 1755, he wrote, "In passing Sèvres I saw the magnificent folly of the new factory for French porcelain in the style of Meissen. It is an immense building, nearly as large as the Invalides; it is built only of bricks. Madame de Pompadour is very interested in it, and she has even interested the King. However, they are selling the pieces at an exorbitant price and the Meissen porcelain is better and cheaper, that of China and Japan is even better".

In 1753 Louis XV became owner of a quarter share in the factory, and it then became known as the "*Manufacture Royale de Porcelaine de France*", and the royal cypher of crossed LL's became the official factory mark, although it had already been in use for some time. It was in the same year that the date letter system was adopted, in which the date letter was put in the space remaining in the centre of the monogram. "A" signified 1753, "B" 1754, and so forth until "Z" which was 1777. Although the French generally only use the letter "K" in foreign words it was included, but "W" which also only appears in foreign words, was left out. Letters were doubled in 1778, beginning with "AA", but the system was discontinued on 17th July, 1793 when it had reached "PP". From this date insignias which applied to the Republic were employed. As a direct result of the King's involvement, further restrictions were placed on porcelain made elsewhere in France, with severe penalties for infringement.

The Duc de Luynes wrote, "Thursday, 9th June, 1757—A few days ago the Dauphin went to the Sèvres porcelain factory. He gave the workmen gratuities and made several purchases for Madame la Dauphine and for those who had the honour to be in his suite. The ladies were there also. The King had been there about a fortnight previously for the second time. This factory, first established at Vincennes, was moved to Sèvres last August. I must have spoken of the enormous building which was built near the old glassworks, which had been moved to the other side of Sèvres, just below Bellevue.

Some time ago, I went to see this Sèvres factory. The builders have prepared an apartment for the King, composed of a large ante-room which will serve as a guardroom; to the left is a large Chapel of which the altar may be seen from all the rooms in the apartment. At the end of the Chapel is a large room and a very large office. Under the building are large cellars, well vaulted and lit, and on the first floor a corridor of such a prodigious length which leads to different rooms, more or less large, depending upon the type or number of workmen. In the painting room, there are 60 who work each in a different medium according to their different talents. They are paid at different rates, and also proportionately. There are some who earn up to a louis per day, and the leading painter who is in charge of the workmen earns 2 louis. The painting appears to have already reached a high standard; the white is extremely beautiful but the difficulty at present is its high price. The painting in blue has increased the price considerably, but it is this type of porcelain which sells best. Vases for flowers sell at 25 louis, soup tureens 50; coffee cups and saucers, 2 louis. The King's apartment was not yet finished when I was there about six weeks ago. They were also working on a shop where they could place the merchandise for sale, and the public were not yet allowed to go in. It was necessary to have a ticket from the Controller-General. At present there are about 500 workmen who have to be housed in the building when it is complete. It is also quite different from the Meissen factory, where there were, before the invasion (Seven Years War) about 1,400 workmen. The King has a part share in the factory; I believe it is a fifth."

Only soft-paste porcelain was made at Sèvres until 1769. The inherent elegance of French taste guided its artists to produce models which, although influenced by Oriental and Meissen originals, were yet unmistakably French. The enamels sank gently and subtly into the porous *pâte-tendre* which, although white, had a creamy texture which was not even impaired by the thick glaze which had to be applied not only to protect the colours but to seal the porous body. It is for soft-paste production that Sèvres is famous. Hults, in a letter of 21st September, 1751 wrote, "Porcelain . . . should be like the inspiration of a pretty woman, that is to say smiling and agreeable".

The light Vincennes style was continued at Sèvres, where dainty enamelled sprigs and sprays of flowers were painted on to plain white porcelain. Porcelain-de-luxe made for presentation purposes was later developed in which strong ground colours were used leaving reserves of white porcelain visible in a sort of cartouche in which flowers or scenes after Boucher and Watteau were painted. The edges of the reserves were outlined with gilding. The first ground colour used was *gros bleu*, invented in 1749 and was a deep underglaze cobalt blue. *Bleu du roi* was a bright blue enamel invented before 1760; *bleu turquin*, a brilliant turquoise enamel which has never been surpassed in modern times, perfected in 1756 by Jean Hellot; *jaune jonquille* dates from 1753, pea green from 1756 and *rose Pompadour*, sometimes called *rose du Barry*, was invented by the chemist Xhrouet in 1757.

Jewelled porcelain perfected in about 1780 by Cotteau, consisted of blobs of enamel to simulate precious stones. Chrome green enamel which was yellow toned and without the slight irridescence which is often seen in copper greens, made its first appearance in 1804.

Porcelain figures made at Vincennes and later at Sèvres were enamelled and glazed in the manner of Meissen. Manufacturing difficulties had been largely overcome and the porcelain was exquisitely finished. Jean-Jacques Bachelier (1724–1805), appointed Director in 1751, decided to sell the figures unpainted and in an unglazed state called biscuit in the following year. The subjects so produced were charming yet sophisticated, and included children, mythological and allegorical subjects, scenes from popular plays. The painter François Boucher was the constant inspiration of both these figures and the designs on table-ware and vases. Madame de Pompadour is reported to have ordered eight models of *enfants d'après Boucher* (children after a Boucher design) in biscuit in 1752, although she already had the same figures in the painted, glazed versions.

The sculptor Etienne-Maurice Falconet (1716–1791) was employed to supervise the modelling department from 1757 to

1766 when he went to Russia. He produced several models, including the famous *Baigneuse* and *La Source*, which have been constantly reproduced. Other sculptors were employed, but with the use of hard-paste and the new neo-classical style the true feeling for porcelain declined.

The *pâte tendre* production of the Sèvres factory was of superb quality, but the French chemists felt that they had not equalled the porcelain which was being imported from Saxony and the Orient. In 1761, Pierre-Antoine Hannong sold the secret formula to the Sèvres factory for a pension of 3,000 livres, which much to their discredit the French Government never paid. They made the excuse that the ingredients, kaolin and feldspar, were unobtainable in France, so although they had a formula, it was unworkable.

A nationwide search was instigated, and a chemist employed by Louis, Duc d'Orléans, found some inferior kaolin near Alençon, from which a grey porcelain was made.

In 1765, the source of the real kaolin in France was discovered. The wife of a poor surgeon, Madame Darnet, remarking on a ravine of white unctuous earth near her home at St. Yrieix near Limoges, thought that it could be used as a substitute for soap. She took a sample to her husband, who being aware of the national search for kaolin, showed it to a pharmacist at Bordeaux, who sent it to the chemist Macquer who immediately recognised it as kaolin. The fortunate find also included quantities of feldspar, and after a series of experiments, *pâte dure* was first produced at Sèvres in 1769, although *pâte tendre* continued to be made simultaneously until 1804.

The discovery did not help the wretched Madame Darnet who in 1825 had to apply to Brongniart, who was then the Director, for some assistance to return to her home at St. Yrieix. Louis XVIII, upon hearing of her plight, granted her a pension from the civil list.

When Louis XVI and Marie Antoinette succeeded to the throne in 1774, they enthusiastically continued the Royal patronage of Sèvres. Hettlinger wrote, "I have already said that an exhibition of porcelains takes place at the end of every year and continues until Epiphany. It is held at the Royal Palace, but the public are allowed to go and examine and buy the pieces. The King occupies in Versailles, besides the State rooms, the 'Petits Appartements', where he passes his private life. Three of these rooms are cleared of their furniture, and the porcelain pieces are exhibited on tables. This year he did not wait until the arrival of the work people but must himself be unpacking the pieces, breaking not a few, and mixing everything up so that it took us hours to put it straight. The King delights in his manufactory at Sèvres, and he said to one of his confidants, 'Our brave Sèvres men will soon be here. I must make haste to shoot some game'."

There was a reduced demand for porcelain due to the political situation which did not favour the purchase of the magnificent show pieces, for which Sèvres had become famous. A contemporary source says, "Every New Year's Day they bring into the galleries at Versailles the newest and choicest pieces of Sèvres porcelain, which the King himself distributes among his great lords for their money; he fixes the prices himself and they are not cheap. We presume that the price must be pretty high on account of the financial situation, but we shall speak about that later on. It is certain that some of the noble lords are not ashamed of taking a cup, or some little ornament, when they think they are not observed. Seeing a count take a cup in this way, Louis XVI sent to him next morning the cashier from Sèvres with the saucer that he had been unable to take and a bill for the pieces. One day the King saw that an Abbé refused to purchase a piece on account of its price but in order to persuade him the King immediately promised him a benefice."

The financial situation deteriorated; the workmen had not been paid for some time, so a group of financiers offered to buy the factory from the King. Louis XVI clung proudly to the Royal factory. "*Je garde la Manufacture de Sèvres à mes frais*"—("I will maintain the factory at my own expense")—he is reported to have said. Not for long, however, for at his death on the guillotine in 1792 it ceased to be a Royal factory and became the property of the Republic. Difficulties increased, for the Republic busily decapitated the customers as well as Regnier the Manager, denounced by a colleague who coveted his job.

The factory remained open somehow, although the work people were frequently unpaid and were once provided with putrid flour in lieu of wages. Napoleon became interested in the factory in 1806 and he appointed Alexandre Brongniart (1770–1847) as Director, who saved the factory from extinction.

Brongniart, a geologist, son of the architect who built the Paris Bourse, was a very able scientist and a competent manager. His most important decision was to cease the manufacture of soft-paste completely. This had been made concurrently with hard-paste since 1769, but was now rejected purely on economic grounds, since the hard-paste porcelain was so much cheaper to produce. At the same time, Brongniart cleared the factory of all the undecorated soft-paste and put it up for auction. There was a scramble to buy it by both Paris and London dealers, who hastened to have it decorated in the most expensive, luxurious Sèvres manner, and so brought about the existence of those semi-frauds which are so hard to recognise. They provided the cypher and date marks and subsequently sold it as genuine eighteenth century soft-paste Sèvres, and many fine collections included a few of these "cuckoos in the nest". "Seconds" and rejects were amongst the porcelain sold under the hammer, pieces which to the discerning eye would now be most suspect. Black specks and discolouration due to inexperienced firing would immediately bring the item under suspicion, and the date marking system was incorrectly used, as it was not fully understood at the time. Finally, the quality of the brushwork would be the deciding factor.

The Sèvres factory continued production into the nineteenth century and moved to new premises at Saint-Cloud in 1876. It is still in existence and making excellent porcelain; the fine museum is worth visiting.

SEVRES

Soft-paste until 1804. Hard-paste 1769 onwards.

CHARACTERISTICS OF SOFT-PASTE

1. Colour floated on in the style of water colours and sunk into the paste in firing, not stippled as in the manner of miniaturists which is a hard-paste characteristic.
2. The gilding stands up thickly as pure leaf gold was used ground up in honey.
3. Glaze creamy and heavy which fills cavities in small pools, sometimes crazed.
4. The biscuit is creamy white, slightly rough to the touch, and does not reflect much light. It shines slightly from within, rather than from the surface. The crossed LLs rarely used, usually only an impressed mark of the repairer.
5. A nail file used on the base should betray a brownish porous paste, not white rock hard porcelain.
6. Painting of the highest merit.
7. Factory mark, crossed LLs with date letter and mark of painter. A—1753, B—1754, and so on, excluding W, until Z—1777. AA—1778. PP—17th July, 1793, after this date mark R.F. for *Republique Française*.

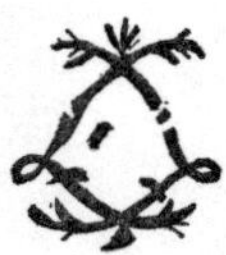

Before *1753*. In blue enamel.

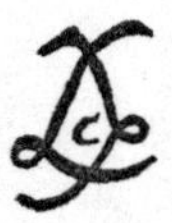

Mark with date letter for *1755*—in blue enamel.

Mark with date letters for *1778*.
Mark used *1769–1793*, in blue and occasionally red.
Mostly on hard-paste. Un-crowned mark with date letters enclosed more usual for soft-paste.

R.F
Sevres

First Republic (*1793–1804*). In blue.

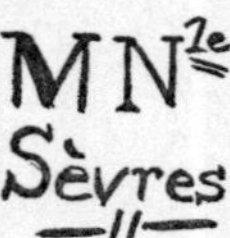

1803–1805, printed in red.

T9 indicates	IX (*1801*)		
X ”	X (*1802*)		
II ”	XI (*1803*)		
÷ ”	XII (*1804*)		
-//- ”	XIII (*1805*)		
ψ ”	XIV (*1806*)		
7 ”	*1807*	From *1801* the indications of date were used once more.	
8 ”	*1808*		
9 ”	*1809*		
10 ”	*1810*		
oz ”	*1811*		
dz ”	*1812*		
tz ”	*1813*		
qz ”	*1814*		
qn ”	*1815*		
sz ”	*1816*		

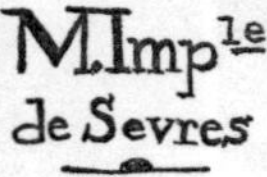

First Empire (*1804–1814*) *1804–1809*, stencilled in red.

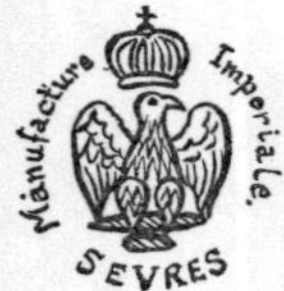

1810–1814, printed in red.

Reign of Louis XVIII (*1814–1824*). Date mark for *1821*. Printed in blue. Showing use of last two numerals to indicate date.

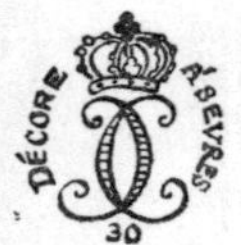

Reign of Charles X (*1824–1830*). In blue.

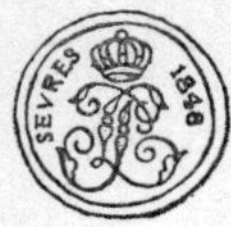

Reign of Louis-Philippe (*1830–1848*). In blue or gold.

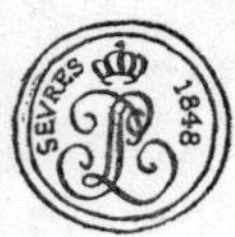

Reign of Louis-Philippe (*1830–1848*). In blue or gold.

Second Republic (*1848–1852*). In red.

Second Empire (*1852–1870*). In red.

1852–1870, in red.

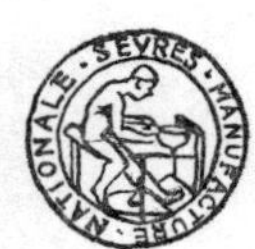

Third Republic (*1871–1940*). In relief or printed underglaze in brown.

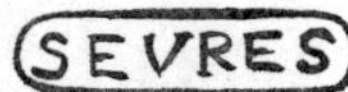

1860–1899, impressed on biscuit.

[5] MENNEÇY, Ile-de-France 1734–1773
SCEAUX—*Faïence* 1748–1794
Porcelain 1763–1772
BOURG-LA-REINE 1773–1806

A pottery was founded by François de Neufville, Duc de Villeroy in Paris in the rue de Charonne in 1734, but due to pressure from the Vincennes monopoly, the factory removed to Menneçy in 1748.

The factory was managed by a *faïencier*, François Barbin (*d.* 1765), and although both *faïence* and porcelain were made, very little *faïence* has survived. Barbin was joined by his son in 1751, and they continued until 1765 when they died within months of each other.

The factory was bought the following year by Joseph Jullien (*d.* 1774) and Symphorien Jacques (*d.* 1798), who had already been leaseholders of the Sceaux pottery for the preceding three years. They ran the two factories concurrently, but disposed of Sceaux in 1772 and Menneçy in 1773, and established a new factory at Bourg-la-Reine.

The sons of the partners joined the firm, Joseph-Léon Jullien in 1774 when his father died, and Charles-Symphorien Jacques in about 1790. The factory continued to operate until 1806, but for about the last twenty years only made *faïence* and semi-porcelain.

The first products of the de Villeroy factory in the rue de Charonne and at Menneçy were yellowish in tone, but soon developed into a milky white tone with a superbly brilliant glaze which Honey so aptly states appears "wet". The porcelain took on a remarkable personality of its own, whilst obviously imitating Saint-Cloud, Chantilly and Vincennes.

There is an appealing femininity about Menneçy, a frailty and a tenderness which are endearing.

The powerful patronage of the duc de Villeroy enabled the Menneçy factory to continue, although even he could not disobey the Vincennes prohibition on gilding. The edges of Menneçy porcelain were therefore painted blue or bluish-pink and never gilded. Typical colours used were a greeny-yellow and a soft brown. The *ozier* pattern was frequently employed and scattered flowers after Meissen and Vincennes were enchantingly interpreted. Figures were made in great numbers, both enamelled and unpainted—Chinamen, Italian Comedy, Children, groups, fruits, birds and animals. The dogs and sheep regard one with a winsome "Buy me" expression. *Galanteries* and "toys" were made in great numbers, but as Honey states in *French Porcelain of the 18th Century*, most of them were unmarked so many may well have been made by a modeller from Menneçy who had set up business on his own at Crépy-en-Valois. Among these are boxes in the shape of a human leg, a bunch of asparagus, animal heads and so on. The inventions were legion and each with a delicate feminine charm.

The first mark used was DV for the Duc de Villeroy, and later Jacques and Jullien registered BR for Bourg-la-Reine.

The porcelain manufactured at Sceaux during the ownership of Jacques and Jullien was very similar to that of Menneçy, but was coarser and more like *faïence* in character. It is interesting that the *faïence* of Sceaux was one of the finest in France, and the thinness and opacity was developed to such a degree of perfection that it rivalled porcelain itself.

MENNEÇY CHARACTERISTICS

1. Paste, yellowish at first, then milky white.
2. Glaze, brilliant and "wet". Surface wavy.
3. Edges painted pink or blue, never gilded.
4. Very feminine shapes; forms simple and graceful.
5. Figures beautifully observed. Children particularly sympathetic with childish expressions.
6. Factory mark, DV until 1773. BR, 1773–1806.

D.V. — From *1735*, in blue.

2 DV — Middle and late period. Incised.

D,V. — Middle and late period. Incised.

SCEAUX

S.X — Mark on porcelain. Incised.

S.X. — Mark on porcelain. Incised.

BOURG-LA-REINE

B.R. Incised.

BR N Incised.

CREPY-EN-VALOIS

C.P. Mark found on white figures.

[6] NIDERVILLER, Lorraine 1754—Present Day

A small *faïence* factory was established at Niderviller in 1754 by the Baron de Beyerlé (Councillor and Treasurer to the King and Director of the Strasbourg Mint), with the help of François-Antoine Anstett (1732–1783) and other Strasbourg potters.

In 1765 a small quantity of hard-paste porcelain was made, from the kaolin deposits at St. Yrieix, and was continued in production alongside the *faïence*. The same models were frequently made in porcelain as well as *faïence*, sometimes indistinguishable from Strasbourg. Tureens with modelled vegetables were made in graceful rococo asymmetry. The plates and dishes were in pierced basket work or with flowing scrolled borders edged with characteristic crimson. The paintings of flowers and figures were capably executed, and supervised by Anstett and his brother François-Michel, and, it is said, often by Madame Beyerlé herself.

An important artist from Lunéville, Charles-Gabriel Sauvage (called Lemire) (1741–1827), was persuaded to join Niderviller as early as 1759. He worked in porcelain as well as *terre-de-Lorraine*, and much of the fame and excellence of this little factory were based on his work. He remained at Niderviller until 1806.

In 1770–1771 the factory became the property of Général-Comte de Custine, and the works were improved and enlarged. Paul-Louis Cyfflé (1724–1806) sold him all his moulds from the Lunéville factory when it closed in 1780. The Comte de

Custine was executed in 1793 during the Revolution, and his estates forfeited.

Niderviller was closed until 1802, when Claude-François Lanfrey (1734–1827), previously Custine's manager, bought it and re-started production. He was the sole owner until the factory closed at his death in 1827. It was later bought by L. W. Dryander, and his successors are still in production producing amongst other items copies of the old models from the original moulds which are still in existence.

The first productions of the Niderviller factory were indistinguishable from the contemporary wares made at Strasbourg, although they are finer in execution and in paler, daintier colours. They were in the rococo style, which by then was going out of fashion. Later, useful wares were made in imitation of the Paris factories, with Bourbon sprigs and naturalistic flowers, and are hardly distinguishable from them.

An original decoration at Niderviller, copied by her contemporaries, was the *décor bois*, a *trompe l'oeil* painting to simulate wood graining. This was usually accompanied by a reserve containing a crimson landscape.

The most prominent works of the factory were the figures by Lemire and Cyfflé. Cyfflé's work differed from that of Lemire in that his models were unpretentious, sentimental subjects. Lemire's first models were reminiscent of Cyfflé's technique, but he developed a superb style of his own and was at his best in the classical idiom. His splendid nude figures were moulded in pure white biscuit, which had a sugar-like transparency with a slight gloss. He is famous for his classical groups and allegorical subjects particularly the one made in 1770 in honour of Marie-Antoinette who stayed at the castle of Strasbourg on her way to Paris for her marriage to the Dauphin, afterwards Louis XVI.

NIDERVILLER CHARACTERISTICS

1. Hard-paste, similar to Paris.
2. Characteristic biscuit, pure white with sugar-like transparency and slight gloss.

3. Shapes and decoration of useful wares similar to rococo Strasbourg and later neo-classical Paris.
4. Factory marks. Beyerlé 1765–1770, BV. Custine 1770–1793, two C's back to back, sometimes surmounted by crown in enamel. Similar mark used at Ludwigsburg in underglaze blue.

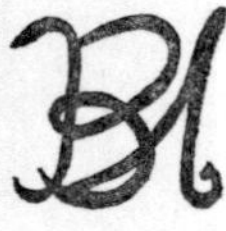

Beyerlé mark. *1754–1770*, in manganese brown.

1770–1793, in blue or brown.

Mark of C. F. Lanfrey. *1793–1827*, usually stencilled in blue.

LE MIRE PERE Signature of Lemire, incised.

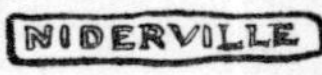

1780–1800, impressed in relief on an applied label.

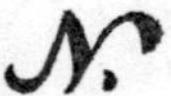

1780–1800, in black. Possibly earlier also.

[7] STRASBOURG (HAGUENAU), Alsace
Faïence 1709–1781
Porcelain 1753–1755, 1762–1781

Charles-François Hannong, probably of Spanish origin, born at Maastricht in Holland in 1669, established a factory at Strasbourg in 1709. His speciality was pipes. With the collaboration of a painter from the factory at Ansbach, Jean-Henri Wachenfeld, he introduced the manufacture of *faïence*. Wachenfeld left in 1722, and under Hannong's direction the business flourished.

Another factory was established in 1724, at Haguenau where the source of their clay lay. The first products were fired in the pipe furnace in primitive conditions, but this *faïence* developed into one of the most beautiful ever made. The two thriving factories were left to his son, Paul-Antoine, in 1737.

The international success of the factory owed everything to the energy and foresight of Paul-Antoine. He introduced the method of decoration and styling to *faïence*, which until then had only been used for porcelain, and produced a variety which was elegant and fine, and was eagerly bought for use in the great châteaux and castles.

Not content with his *faïence* production, he turned to the manufacture of porcelain, with the help of J. J. Ringler in about 1753. The Strasbourg factory is particularly interesting to the collector as it made the first hard-paste porcelain in France and originated a style of flower painting which was copied throughout France and Germany.

Haguenau was placed under the direction of Adam von Löwenfinck, the superb Meissen painter, from 1750 until his death in 1754, when he was succeeded by his wife Maria Seraphia. Von Löwenfinck's influence on the Haguenau production was considerable. His talent and taste were everywhere apparent. His previous experience at Ansbach, Fulda and Höchst dictated the freely adapted forms and shapes and imaginative rococo styling as well as an excellent colour sense.

The Royal Edicts which gave a monopoly to the newly-founded factory at Vincennes prevented the Hannongs from making any more porcelain in France, so in 1755 they crossed into the Palatinate, now Bavaria, and founded a porcelain factory at Frankenthal.

When Paul-Antoine died in 1760, his son, Pierre-Antoine inherited Strasbourg and Haguenau and his other son, Joseph-Adam was left the Frankenthal porcelain factory. Pierre-Antoine was incompetent, so he sold out to his brother Joseph-Adam in 1762, who now became the sole owner of Strasbourg and Haguenau, having recently disposed of the Frankenthal factory to the Elector Palatine. Pierre-Antoine offered the secrets of the manufacture of hard-paste porcelain to the Directors of the Sèvres factory, by whom he was miserably treated, and never paid.

In the Sèvres prohibition Alsace had been treated as part of France, but this was amended and Alsace was now declared to be foreign, so Joseph-Adam recommenced the manufacture of porcelain at Strasbourg. He was chiefly concerned with services for every day use and his decorations were Chinese designs and flowers. Gilding was very rare.

Joseph-Adam had many financial difficulties, particularly with the French tax collectors, who increased the tax on porcelain "entering France" from Alsace by ten times. His patron, the Cardinal de Rohan, died in 1779 and his heirs demanded repayment of loans. The factories were closed in 1781 and in order to escape imprisonment Joseph-Adam fled to Germany. He applied to Louis XVI in 1782, and to the National Assembly in 1791, for compensation, which was refused, and he is said to have died miserably in Munich in the early nineteenth century.

STRASBOURG PORCELAIN CHARACTERISTICS

1. Hard-paste, faulty, imperfect.
2. Thickly potted, clumsy.
3. Similar to Frankenthal in inspiration, but coarser.
4. Defects in glaze concealed by haphazard decoration.
5. Designs similar to *faïence*.
6. Factory marks LM and HL.

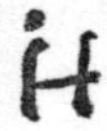

For porcelain marks see FRANKENTHAL.
1721–1740, in blue.

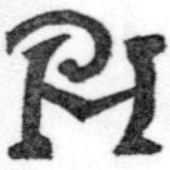

1740–1760, in blue underglaze.

[8] ARRAS, Pas de Calais, 1770–1790
AND
ST. AMAND-LES-EAUX, Nord

ARRAS

A factory was founded in 1770 by Joseph-François Boussemaert (*d.* 1773) to make soft-paste porcelain.

The factory was taken over by four ladies, the Demoiselles

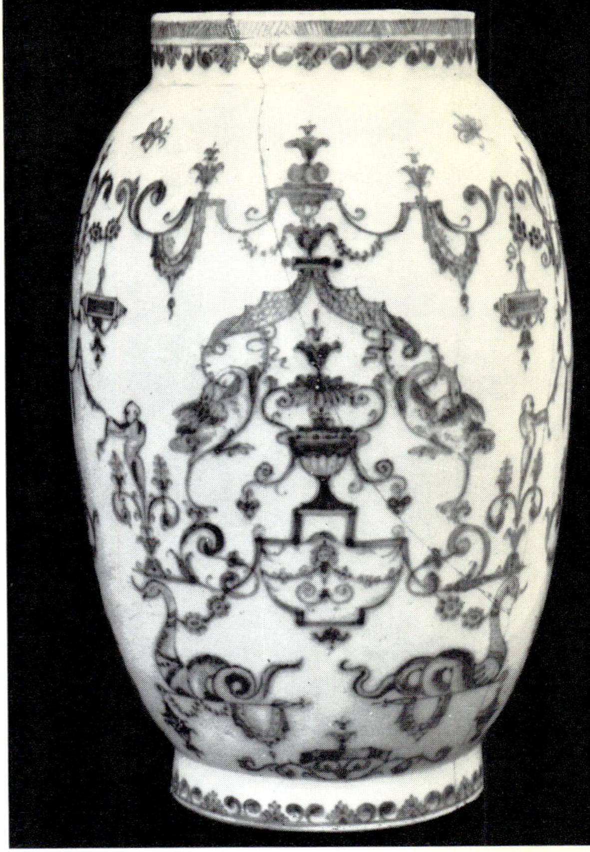

St. CLOUD, but could be ROUEN. Vase *décor Bérain* (blue and white), late seventeenth century. Height 8 ins.

Musée des Arts Décoratifs, Paris

St. CLOUD

Cream-jug, height $5\frac{1}{2}$ ins., and scent bottle. Soft-paste porcelain, eighteenth century

Musée des Arts Décoratifs, Paris

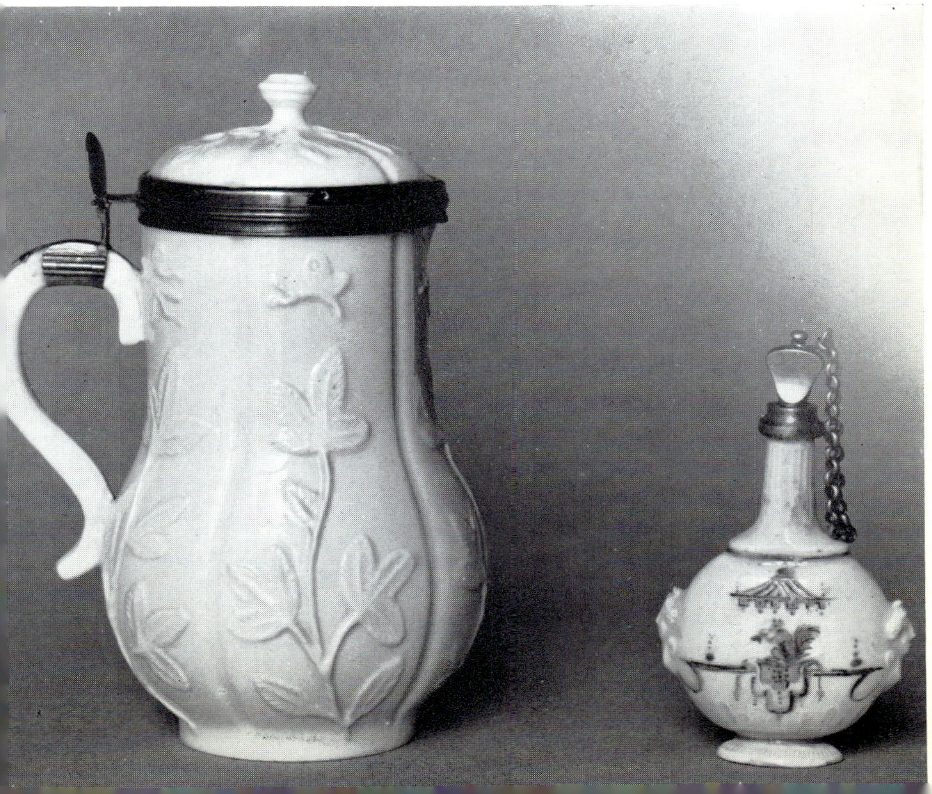

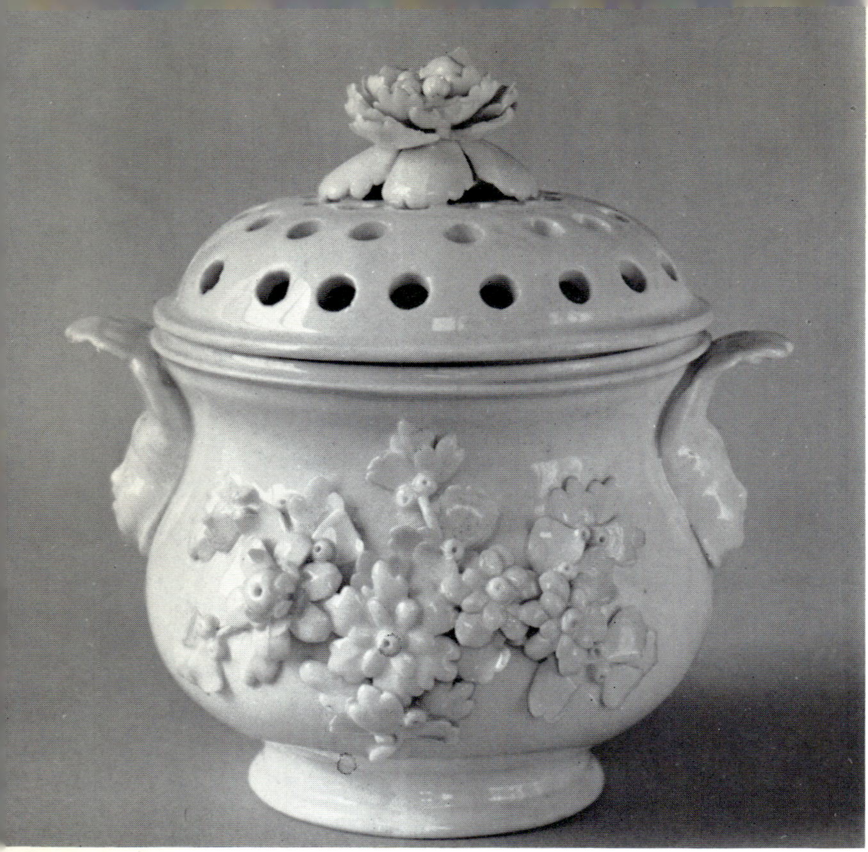

St. CLOUD. *Pot-pourri* vase glazed in white in imitation of *blanc-de-Chine*, eighteenth century. Height $6\frac{1}{2}$ ins.

CHANTILLY. Cup, $2\frac{1}{2}$ ins. high, and saucer 5 ins. diameter, decoration *chauve souris* (green and blue), eighteenth century

Musée des Arts Décoratifs, Paris

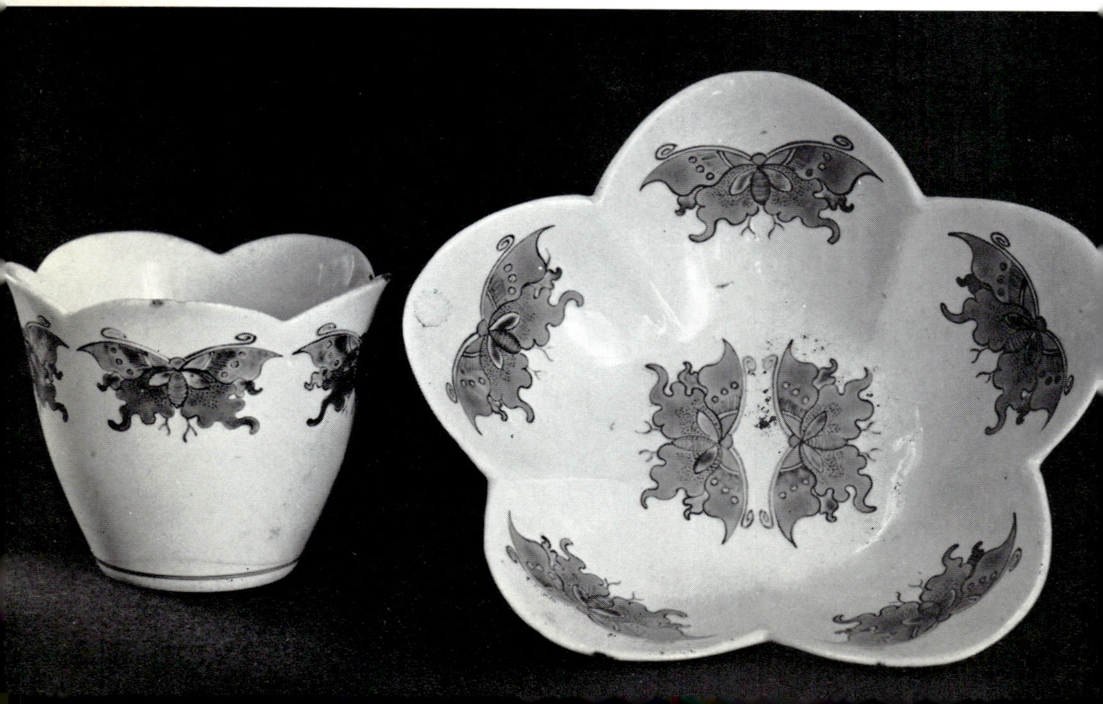

CHANTILLY
Toilet pot, *c.* 1744–50. Height 5 ins.

Musée des Arts Décoratifs, Paris

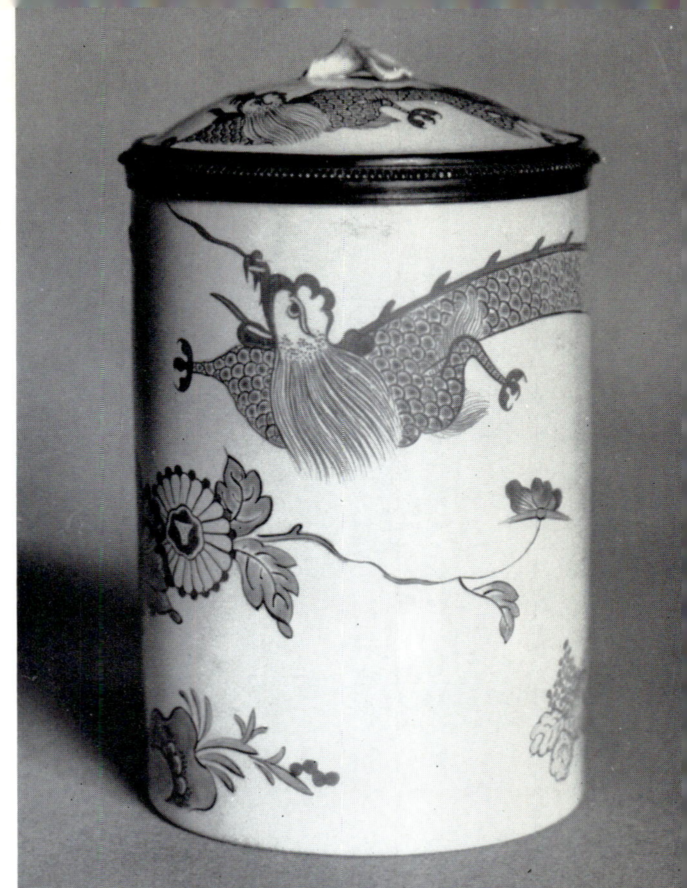

VINCENNES (SEVRES)
"The Flute Lesson", in biscuit. Model after Boucher, 1752. Height $9\frac{1}{4}$ ins. Length $9\frac{1}{4}$ ins.

Musée des Arts Décoratifs

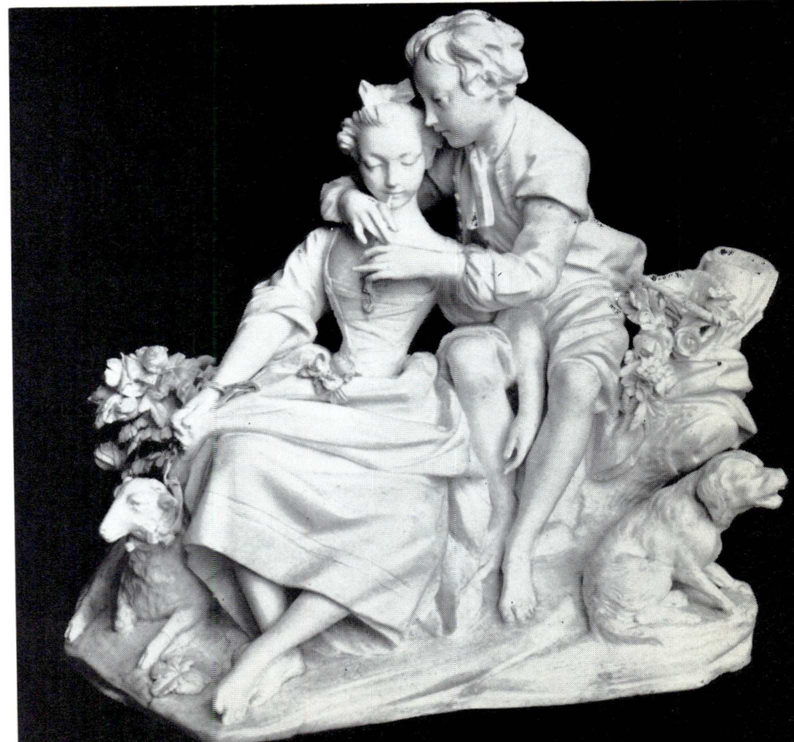

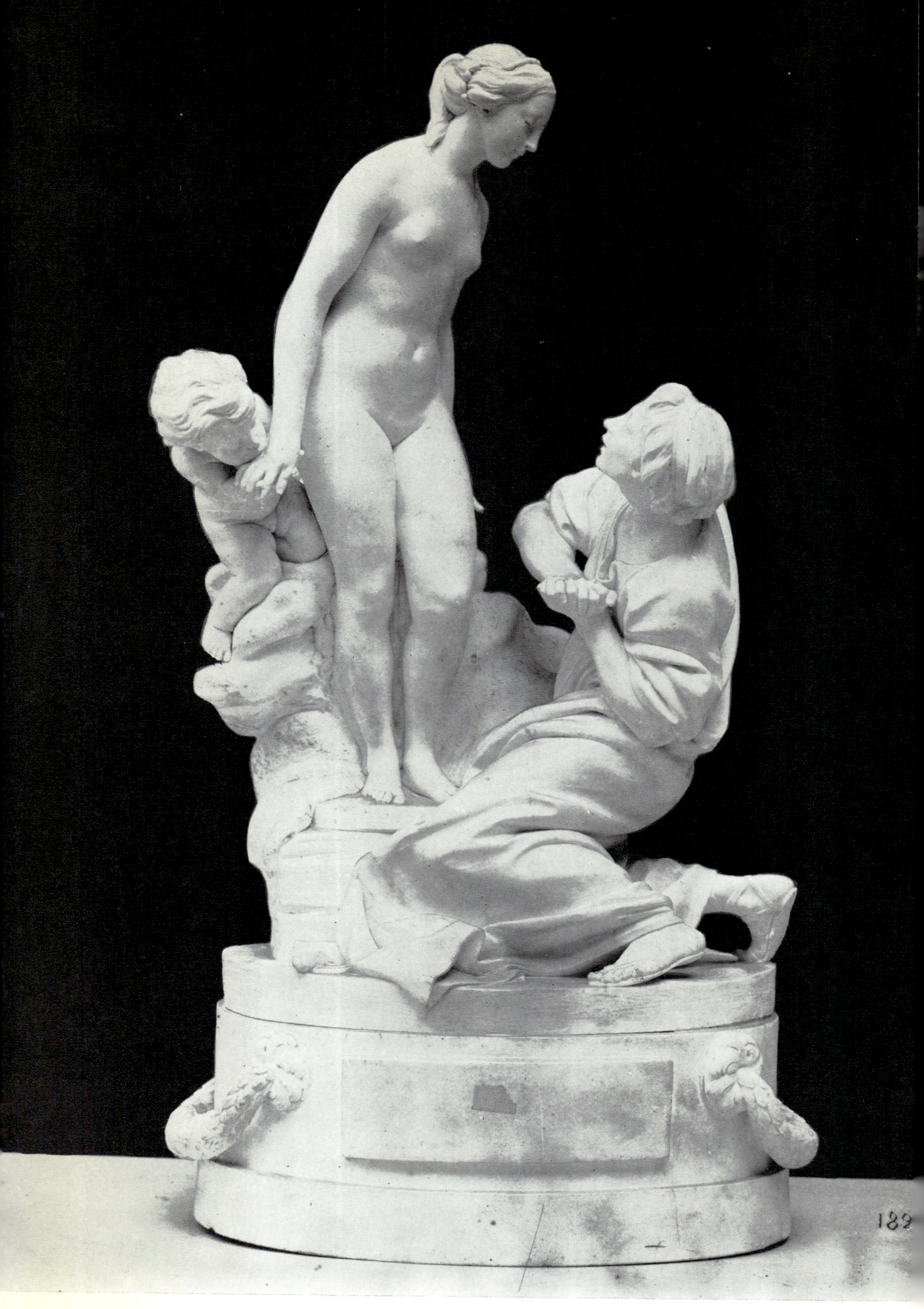

SEVRES. "Pygmalion and Galatea", a Falconet model, 1763, in biscuit. Height $17\frac{1}{2}$ ins.

Musée des Arts Décoratifs

Delemer, who were dealers in *faïence*. They made copies of Chantilly and Tournai which were simply decorated. In the nineteenth century some old Arras porcelain was over-decorated with intent to deceive.

AR — *1770–1790*, in underglaze blue.

ST. AMAND-LES-EAUX

A soft-paste porcelain was made between 1771 and 1778 by Jean-Baptiste-Joseph Fauquez (1742–1804), which was abandoned after unsuccessful competition with Tournai. It was resumed in 1800 by Maximilien-Joseph de Bettignies.

The early porcelain is very rare and of no great artistic merit. In the nineteenth century St. Amand was mainly concerned in the production of Sèvres forgeries.

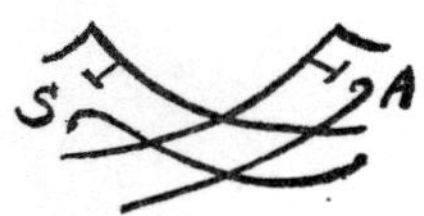

1800 onwards, in underglaze blue.

B.D. J — *1800* onwards, in underglaze blue.

[9] LUNÉVILLE, Lorraine
Porcelain 1755–1778

A pottery was established at Lunéville in 1731 and made *faïence fine* in the style of Strasbourg. Lorraine was the consolation prize offered to King Stanislas of Poland by his son-in-law, Louis XV, when he was deprived of his Polish throne. A brilliant Court surrounded the Monarch, and writers and artists out of favour at Versailles flocked to Lorraine. Voltaire was a frequent visitor.

The fame of Lunéville in ceramics rests on the skill and artistry of Paul-Louis Cyfflé. From 1755 he modelled charming unsophisticated figures and groups first in a *terre de pipe*, which was a soft clay pottery, and later in a warm-toned, fine grain hard-paste biscuit porcelain. The Royal monopoly at Sèvres demanded that these porcelain figures should be sold as *terre cuite* (terra cotta) or be discontinued, but Cyfflé appealed for the term *pâte de marbre*. It was in fact finally called *terre-de-Lorraine*.

Cyfflé's figures are sentimental and portray a childish innocence. Subjects included a Cobbler Whistling to his Caged Bird, paired with a Stocking Mender, Children with a Dead Bird and a Girl with a Broken Flowerpot.

Cyfflé became acutely financially embarrassed in about 1778, and his business was sold in 1780, when most of the moulds went to Niderviller.

The mark used on Cyfflé's figures were sometimes a capital TDL or Terre-de-Lorraine.

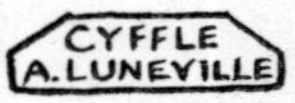

Impressed in relief.

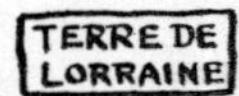

Impressed in relief.

[10] PARIS

After deposits of kaolin were discovered in St. Yrieix in 1768, a number of factories sprang up in the various *quartiers* of Paris and began to make hard-paste porcelain. Although the Royal edicts regarding porcelain manufacture were still in operation, they were openly flouted by these Paris factories, usually because they were protected by important members of the aristocracy.

With the continual difficulties at Sèvres and the reduction in staff, many workmen joined the Paris factories and the Sèvres style was avidly copied.

VINCENNES 1767–1786
(*Hannong*)

Pierre-Antoine Hannong sold his secrets of hard-paste manufacture to Sèvres, but he was denied the pension that he had been promised and was also prohibited from making porcelain in

France. However, despite this he contrived through the use of a proxy, or indeed using an alias, to obtain permission to found a *faïence* factory at the old Vincennes works. Later he was allowed to make hard and soft-paste porcelain as long as he did not infringe the privileges of Sèvres. Every-day table-ware was made but it was of no particular artistic merit. Hannong left in 1772, and the factory was continued by Sieurlenaire who protested against the restrictive edicts of Sèvres. Louis-Philippe, when visiting the Sèvres factory in the nineteenth century, is reported to have said that whilst he was Duke of Chartres he had been Hannong's patron, which enabled him to found the Vincennes factory.

The body was vitreous, hard and yellowish, and the glaze was pitted and uneven.

Registered *1777*, in underglaze blue.

FAUBOURG ST. DENIS 1769–1810
(*Manufacture du Comte d'Artois*)

Pierre-Antoine Hannong left Vincennes to direct this new factory, but he was soon replaced and the factory obtained the patronage of Charles-Philippe, Comte d'Artois, brother of Louis XVI, and with it the privilege of using the title, *Manufacture du Comte d'Artois*. The new Director, Bourdon-Deplanches (*c.* 1786), achieved the distinction of firing porcelain with the use of coal instead of wood, an advantage for the large number of porcelain factories around Paris were causing a general fuel shortage Because of the use of coal in this factory, the restrictive edict of 1784 was amended and they were allowed to make biscuit pieces as long as they were not more than eighteen inches high and to paint china in colours and gilding as long as the gold did not cover the whole of any one piece.

The factory was very prosperous until 1793, and when the worst of the Terror was over, it continued production making fine quality porcelain until 1810.

The hard-paste body for the first few years of production from this factory had a yellowish tinge similar to that which was made at Vincennes under Hannong, but later this was improved until the paste was pure white and translucent. Completely flawless, some fine pieces could be mistaken for opaline glass. The glaze under Hannong's directorship was pitted and imperfect, but as the body improved so the glaze was perfected. The factory made large quantities of every-day table-ware, but under Bourdon-Deplanches' direction the factory produced a large variety of articles in direct competition with Sèvres. Large decorative pieces were made as well as portrait busts and figures in biscuit. The first decorations were of scattered polychrome flowers with a conspicuous reddish-violet colour used in the decoration and in a thin line round the edges and rims of table-ware. Under Bourdon-Deplanches landscape and classical figure subjects were used, often in *en camaieu* in a soft grey, also bouquets and garlands of small flowers in polychrome and the blue Bourbon sprig. Gilding was judiciously and tastefully employed.

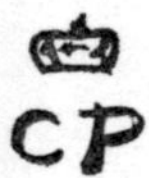

1779–1793, stencilled in red. Initials of Charles-Phillippe, Comte d'Artois.

1779–1793, in underglaze blue.

CLIGNANCOURT 1771–1798

Fabrique de Monsieur à Clignancourt

A factory was established at Clignancourt in 1771 by Pierre Deruelle. In 1775 he obtained the patronage of Monsieur, brother to King Louis XVI (later Louis XVIII), with the right to style his factory *Fabrique de Monsieur à Clignancourt*, and applied for official recognition from the authorities at Sèvres.

The products of the factory were so good and of such elegance that they hold their own in comparison with the work of Sèvres. Some pieces were daringly decorated in the styles reserved by Royal edict for Sèvres alone, and the crossed LLs beneath the Prince's coronet were clearly marked. The police confiscated them, and Deruelle was heavily fined.

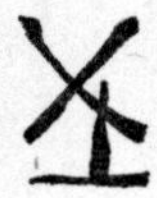

1771–1775, in underglaze blue. The "Windmill" mark.

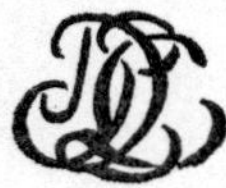

1775–1793, stencilled in red. Monogram of Louis-Stanislas-Xavier (*Monsieur*).

Crowned "M" for *Monsieur*. Stencilled in red.

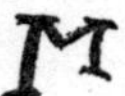

"M" for Moitte. In underglaze blue or other colour.

LA COURTILLE 1773–1794
La Fabrique de la Courtille

La Fabrique de la Courtille was founded by Locré de Roissy in the rue Fontaine-au-Roy in 1773, with the avowed intention of making Meissen copies. De Roissy was joined by Ruffinger in 1784, and the factory grew in importance very quickly.

The paste was excellent, pure white and hard. Biscuit also was of very fine quality and was finely modelled. Every-day services and small articles in common demand were manufactured in large quantities. Meissen flowers, Pompeiian scrolls and Bourbon sprigs were popular decorations. The mark, a pair of crossed torches, is often wrongly presumed by the novice to be the Meissen electoral swords, which mark it was obviously intended to imitate.

The factory closed in 1794 during the Revolution, and although it was revived later, the porcelain made is unworthy of attention.

CROSSED TORCHES

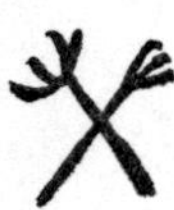

1773 onwards, in underglaze blue.

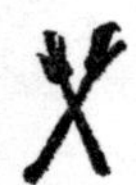

1773 onwards, in underglaze blue.

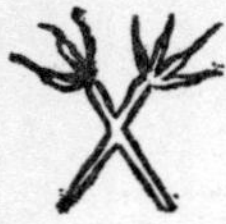

1773 onwards, incised.

RUE THIROUX 1778–1798
(*Fabrique de la Reine*)

A hard-paste porcelain factory was established in the rue Thiroux in 1778 by André-Marie le Boeuf. His products were so good that the following year he was heavily fined for infringing the privileges reserved for Sèvres.

The quality of the products of this factory caused the Sèvres authorities great concern, especially when Le Boeuf secured the patronage of Queen Marie Antoinette herself, who gave him the right to use her monogram as his factory mark. She encouraged him particularly by ordering the porcelain for her farm at Versailles, and bought many pieces from him to give as presents.

After the Revolution, the works changed hands and nothing more is known about them.

1775–1790, in underglaze blue. Monogram of Marie Antoinette.

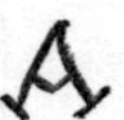

1775–1790, stencilled in red.

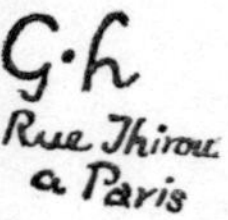

Guy and Housel mark. *1797–1798*. In red.

RUE DE BONDY 1780–1829
(*Le duc d'Angoulême*)

With the patronage of the duc d'Angoulême, and under the direction of Guerhard and Dihl, a hard-paste factory was established in 1780, and a large palette of colours was developed. Elaborately decorated, fine quality vases, ornaments and tableware, and many biscuit pieces were made.

After the Revolution, the factory continued but without the Duke, and the pieces were signed Dihl or Dihl and Guerhard, in various ways.

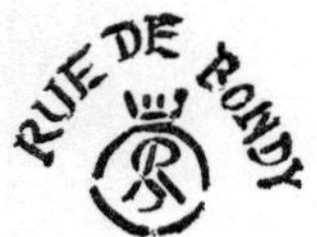

1780–1793, stencilled in red.

MANUFRE
de MOR Le Duc
d'Angouleme

1780–1793, stencilled in red.

MANUFRE
de MM
Guerhard et
Dihl a Paris

Late eighteenth to early nineteenth century. Stencilled in red.

Several other factories were flourishing in Paris about this time, the most important of which was the Fabrique de la Rue Popincourt founded by J. N. H. Nast in 1782 and continued by his sons until 1835.

RUE POPINCOURT

"Manfre de Porcelaine du Cen Nast. Rue Des Amandiers Don Popincourt."

1784, stencilled in red.

NAST.

Stencilled in red.

PARIS CHARACTERISTICS

1. Hard-paste.
2. Neo-classical and Empire styles.
3. Sèvres designs.
4. Usually marked, if they are not they are difficult to attribute, the output of all the factories being so similar.

Chapter Four

England and Wales

"To please the Noble Dame, the courtly Squire
Produced a tea-pot made in Staffordshire,
So Venus moaned and with such longing eyes,
When Paris first produced the golden prize,
'Such works as this (she cries) can England do?
It equals Dresden and excels St. Cloud',
All modern China now hide its head,
And e'en Chantilly must give o'er its trade,
For lace, let Flanders bear away the bell,
In finest linen let the Dutch excel,
For brightest fancied silks let France be famed,
Do thou, thrice happy England still prepare
Thy clay, and build they fame on earthenware."

SIMEON SHAW, 1829

TEA WAS INTRODUCED into Britain after the Restoration in about 1660.

Well-to-do Londoners flocked to the coffee houses to try the new exotic drinks imported by the East India Company.

Pepys wrote that he "did send for a cup of tee (*sic*) (a China drink) of which I had never drunk before". Alexander Pope wrote:

"Hear thou great Anna! whom three realms obey,
Dost sometimes council take, and sometimes tay."

At first an expensive luxury for the privileged, the tea-drinking habit subsequently spread right through the community. In

Scotland it was used as an expensive medicine. The changing social structure of the country led to new customs and habits. Beer and ale had been the beverages of men, women and children of all classes, for it was a great deal safer than the usually polluted water. Through misconceived notions that it helped the corn producers, cheap gin manufacture was encouraged and led to misery, degradation and death, well depicted by Hogarth in "Gin Lane". A series of laws culminating in the Act of 1751 heavily taxed spirits and controlled their sale, and as G. M. Trevelyan wrote in *English Social History*:

> "After the middle years of the century tea became a formidable rival to alcohol with all classes born in the capital and in the country at large."

"The cups that cheer but not inebriate" were as well known in the labourer's cottage as in Cowper's parlour, but until Pitt the Younger reduced the high tariffs, most of it was smuggled, for it was as precious as tobacco and brandy. Of the thirteen million pounds of tea that were consumed during 1784, it was calculated that only five-and-a-half millions had paid duty.

Fashionable out-door tea gardens became so prevalent that ultimately it was considered smart to drink tea only at home. In larger houses a small room was set aside as a tea room. Here the porcelain equipment was stored and here tea was taken in a genteel and elegant manner, improving the manners of the participants and replacing the earlier heavy drinking bouts which usually provided entertainment for the long winter evenings.

Hannah More wrote to her sister in 1788:

> "Perhaps you do not know that the *Thé* is among the stupid new follies of the winter. You are to invite 50 or a hundred people to come at eight o'clock: there is to be a long table, or little parties at small ones; the cloth is to be laid, as at breakfast; every one has a napkin;—tea and coffee are made by the company, as at a public breakfast; the table is covered with rolls, wafers, bread and butter; and what constitutes the very essence of a *Thé*, an immense load of hot buttered rolls, and muffins, all admirably contrived to create a nausea in persons fresh from the dinner table. Now, of all

nations under the sun, as I take it, the English are the greatest fools;—because the Duke of Dorset in Paris, where people dine at two, thought this would be a pretty fashion to introduce; we, who dine at six, must adopt this French translation of an English fashion, and fall into it, as if it were an original invention: taking up our own custom at third hand."

The arrival of East India Company vessels was eagerly awaited. Their cargoes of tea, porcelain, silks, lacquer work and all the other exciting produce of the Orient found a ready market. China tea required a delicate porcelain container, and the English potters, whose own wares were too clumsy for the purpose, feverishly experimented to discover the arcanum, in order to compete with first Chinese, then Continental porcelain.

A patent was granted to John Dwight of Fulham (*c.*1637–1703) in 1671, who claimed to have discovered the formula for a frit porcelain, but the project was abandoned.

By 1745, Bow and Chelsea had produced soft-paste porcelain, and were followed by André Planché (1727–1805) at Derby in 1750. The saltglaze factory at Longton Hall made soft-paste of the Chelsea type from 1750 and John Lund's experiments at Lowdin's Glassworks in Bristol in about 1748 led to the establishment of the Worcester factory in 1751. Liverpool and Lowestoft followed in 1756 and 1757, and William Cookworthy's (1705–1780) discoveries of kaolin in Cornwall led to the foundation of the Plymouth factory in 1768, where hard-paste was first made in England. Caughley began porcelain production of the steatitic Worcester type in 1772.

The county of Staffordshire had maintained potteries at various times throughout history, for remains of Roman and Saxon potteries have been found because the proximity of coal, marls and clay made the area eminently suitable.

During the seventeenth century the population of the county was about 4,000. There were a few thatched cottages and two Pot Works near the church. The roads were so bad that neither carts nor carriages, nor even pack horses, could travel. Coal for the ovens was carried on men's and women's backs, and water was sold at ½d. a pailful.

By 1762, there were 150 Pottery Works in the area, and the clear air which had been apparent in the preceding century was now full of coal-dust from the smoking kilns. The canal system, pioneered by Josiah Wedgwood, established during the eighteenth century and culminating in the opening of the Grand Trunk Canal in 1777, did much to facilitate the carriage of materials and finished products, and was the only form of transport until the railways were inaugurated in 1830. The five towns of Burslem, Stoke, Hanley, Tunstall and Longton were amalmated in the city of Stoke-on-Trent in 1910.

Simeon Shaw's observations in *The History of the Staffordshire Potteries* about the factory conditions in Staffordshire potteries are worth noting:

In 1780, a workman made four soup tureens from two moulds each day, for which he only received 10s. per week. But such was progress (and possibly the cost of living) that by 1819 a similar workman would make sixteen to eighteen tureens a day from six moulds, and he would receive as salary 15s. per week, house rent free, fire and the keep of a cow.

Royal patronage did not extend to the English arcanists. Apart from a cursory interest in Chelsea by the Duke of Cumberland, the Royal Georges were more interested in politics and their mistresses.

The prince of collectors, Horace Walpole, of whom it was written:

> "China's the passion of his soul:
> A cup, a plate, a dish, a bowl,
> Can kindle wishes in his breast,
> Inflame with joy, or break his rest."

—although not entirely free from Lord Shaftesbury's imputation that "he loves rarity for rarity's sake", wrote to a friend that a man named Turner, a great china man, had a jar cracked by the shock of an earthquake. The price of the pair of jars was originally ten guineas, but after the accident he asked twenty, because it was the only jar in Europe that had been cracked by an earthquake.

Porcelain objects were avidly collected and figures, vases,

trifles, were greedily acquired. A correspondent of the *Spectator*, No. 252, illustrating the absurdity to which china collecting had driven the fashionable of the eighteenth century, wrote that his home:

> "... is furnished with trophies of her (his wife's) eloquence, rich cabinets, piles of china, japan screens, and costly jars; and if you were to come into my great parlour, you would fancy yourself in an Indian warehouse. Besides this, she keeps a squirrel, and I am doubly taxed to pay for the china he breaks."

Chatham's foreign policy extended British spheres of influence all over the world. "We shall win Canada on the banks of the Elbe", he said, while he paid Frederick the Great £600,000 a year to take care of British interests in Hanover and distract the French while the British were Empire building.

The English tea-drinking custom spread throughout the Colonies, and with it went porcelain, both Chinese and English. These were two of the commodities that were subject to high tariffs, which the American colonists found insufferable, and it was in 1774 that the all-important tea in Boston Bay provided the spark for the War of Independence.

Tea and its attendant paraphernalia had become an issue of international importance.

[1] BOW, Stratford-le-Bow, Middlesex 1744–1776

A small row of wood-faced cottages called China Row existed up to the end of the nineteenth century on the north side of Stratford High Street about 250 yards from Bow Bridge. The Bow factory had been adjacent to these buildings but its exact position had been forgotten, for subsequently a match factory then a turpentine factory had been built on the site. Excavations were made in 1867 for some of London's first sewers and factory wasters and kiln equipment were found which established the identity of Bow porcelain. Further research on the site in 1921 and 1922 produced valuable quantities of wasters—including early blue and white, as well as kiln furniture and moulds. The Bow factory was called "New Canton" according to the inscription "Made in New Canton" on three documentary blue and white inkpots dated 1750 and 1751 and described by Thomas Craft in a note in his own handwriting attached to a fine punch bowl he made: "The model of the building was taken from that at Canton in China. The whole was heated by two stoves on the outside of the building and conveyed through flues or pipes and warmed the whole, sometimes to an intense heat 'unbarable' in winter."

The first patent was issued in December 1744 to Edward Heylyn (1695–1765), merchant, in the Parish of Stratford-le-Bow in the County of Middlesex and Thomas Frye (1710–1762), painter and mineral merchant, of West Ham, in the County of Essex, to make porcelain, using "unaker", the name given to an earth "the produce of the Cherokee Nation in America", together with potash, flint and other materials. Edward Heylyn was a merchant with Bristol connections, a saddler, and a Freeman of the City of London. Thomas Frye, one of the "Dublin School" of mezzotint engravers, was an artist of considerable ability and painted fine portraits of Frederick, Prince of Wales and Princess Augusta. Yet another proprietor of Bow was the wealthy and influential Alderman Arnold, who apparently helped finance the experiments and premises although he was not active in the actual porcelain production.

The "unaker" referred to in the patent was the Indian name of the kaolin André Duché (1710–1788) discovered and the popular theory is that Duché, newly arrived in England, encouraged Bow to patent the use of unaker so that he could ship it to them. Apparently he was unsuccessful for the only Customs record of any shipment which might be unaker imported into London from Carolina was "20 tons, value £5" in 1743–1744 classed as "earthy, unrated".

It has also been suggested that the Bow patent was lodged to forestall Duché, but although Cookworthy wrote that he had seen some of Duché's porcelain, there were only a few other witnesses and less than a handful of pieces have survived which have been attributed to him.

The second patent was taken out in 1749 by Thomas Frye alone, and amended details extended to the American Colonies and included the use of bone ash in the formula. All Bow porcelain appears to have been made with bone ash and none has survived from the previous patent.

John Weatherby and John Crowther, wholesale "Potters from St. Catherines near the Tower", became associated with the factory from 1750 and later became the proprietors.

No one quite knows when the production of Bow really started, but by 1748 it was reported that large quantities of tea-cups and saucers were being made.

By 7th February, 1753, a London showroom, "The Bow China Warehouse" was opened near the Royal Exchange in Cornhill. Production was enormous and sales were more than £10,000 in 1753, rising to over £12,000 in 1755. In November 1753, apparently short of hands they advertised in Aris's *Birmingham Gazette*:

> "This is to give notice to all painters in the blue and white potting way and enamellers on china ware, that by applying, at the counting house at the China-house, near Bow, they may meet with employment and proper encouragement according to their merit; likewise painters brought up in the snuff box way, japanning, fan painting etc., may have an opportunity on trial, wherein if they succeed they shall have due encouragement. *N.B.*—At the same house a person is wanted who can model small figures in clay neatly."

The first period, 1747–1754, was distinguished by large quantities of underglaze blue and white decoration in the Chinese manner. The name of the factory, "New Canton", epitomised the policy of the proprietors who attempted to supply the market created for China ware, and succeeded in being the most important manufacturers of blue and white wares in Europe. Copies of the Fukien *blanc-de-chine*, raised prunus pattern, were frequent and exquisite copies of the *famille rose* style in clear brilliant polychrome. The palette was simple and the colours transparently clean. Figures of children, groups of figures and many figures in the white were produced, which were decorated in the

London workshops of William Duesbury (1725–1786) and James Giles (*c.*1720–*c.*1780).

The second period, 1755–1760. Fine potting and elegant decoration were achieved and various foreign styles adapted and mixed to arrive at a naïve, individual style of its own. Typically English and often humorous these were table wares in Oriental styles, copies of Meissen figures, botanical flowers after Chelsea, and flowers in the soft colourings of Mennecy, and often Chinese designs in the Japanese pallete of red, blue and gold. Rococo scrolls were used, together with armorial designs and transfer printing with *famille rose* flowers and Meissen applied green leaves all on one piece.

During Frye's management until 1759 the output of the factory mirrored his great taste. The Bow sphinxes date from this period, when the original was probably modelled after another Dubliner, Peg Woffington.

Mr. Weatherby, one of the proprietors of the Bow China Warehouse in Cornhill, died at his house on Tower Hill on 15th October, 1762. A year later, his partner, John Crowther, was bankrupt together with Weatherby's son, Benjamin. This was the end of the Warehouse at Cornhill, but it did not affect the factory itself. Auction sales were held at the Cornhill Warehouse, arranged by Crowther's assignees, and included "curious figures, girandolles, dishes, compotiers, beautiful desserts in the fine old partridge and wheatsheaf pattern, knife and fork handles and branches for chimney pieces finely decorated with figures and flowers".

The Bow factory was continued by John Crowther alone, who subsequently opened a Warehouse in St. Paul's Churchyard in 1770, until 1775 when he sold his entire interest in Bow to William Duesbury of Derby. Duesbury closed down the whole business, and in 1776 transferred the moulds, models and equipment, along with those of Chelsea, James Giles' Studio and Vauxhall to Derby.

During the third period of Bow, 1760–1774, the paste became greyish and the colours were more varied, but without Thomas Frye's restraint the subjects were over-decorated and inclined to be crude. Dark blue was introduced, possibly to compete with the then popular mazarine blue of Chelsea and Worcester, but was not too successful.

From a memo book, once in the possession of Lady Charlotte Schreiber and now in the British Museum, belonging to John Bowcocke an agent for the Bow Works, interesting details of the products of the factory, the customers and the general day by day occurrences to do with the factory, are recorded for all time. In the front of the book is a note in pencil, written in 1866 and signed Thomas Bailey, "One hundred years since John Bowcocke died Tuesday Feb. 26th 1765 at 6 o'clock in the evening of lock jaw. He was brother to William Bowcocke of Chester, painter, my mother's father."

BOW CHARACTERISTICS

1. English soft-paste, phosphatic, milky-white, fracture close and compact.
2. Glaze carries greenish tinge.
3. Pieces heavy for their size.
4. Colours brilliant.
5. Cups and saucers thinly potted to egg-shell thickness.
6. Figure subjects vigorously modelled, with stupid faces.
7. Scrolled bases picked out in distinctive crimson veering to aubergine, crimson and blue, turquoise. Mound bases uncoloured with a few painted applied flowers and leaves.
8. Factory marks, Anchor and Dagger.

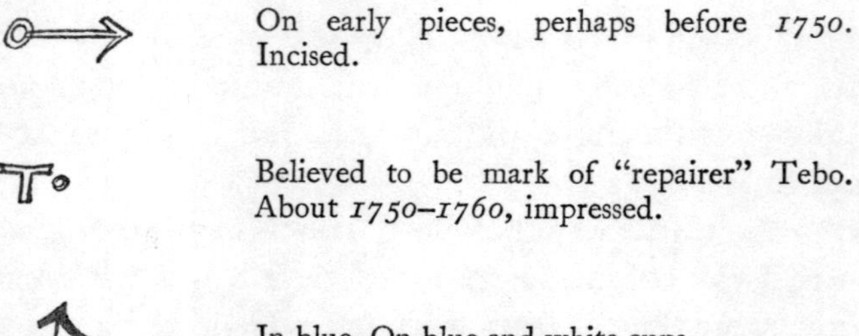

On early pieces, perhaps before *1750*. Incised.

Believed to be mark of "repairer" Tebo. About *1750–1760*, impressed.

In blue. On blue and white cups.

SPODE. Ice pail with painted floral sprays between ground laid crimson-purple borders and richly gilt. Marked Spode No. 4004 in red on the base. Height 13½ ins.

W. T. Copeland & Sons Ltd.

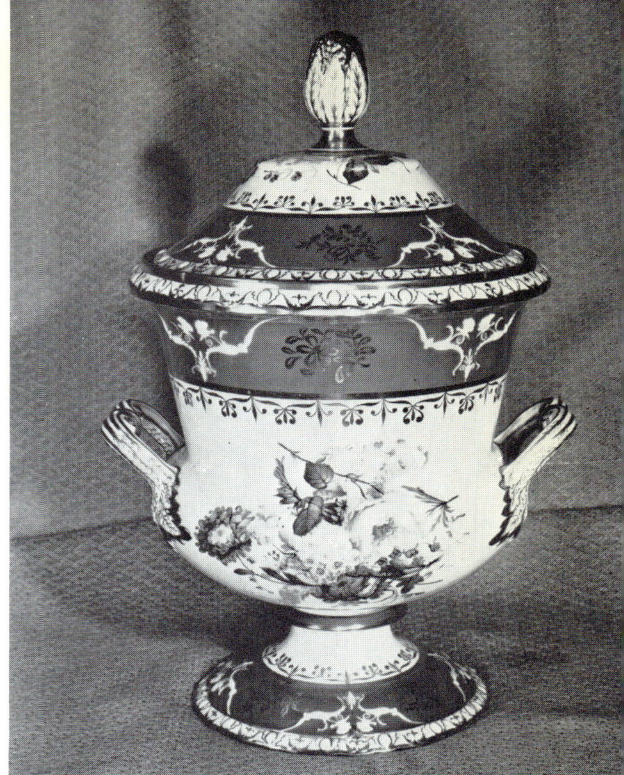

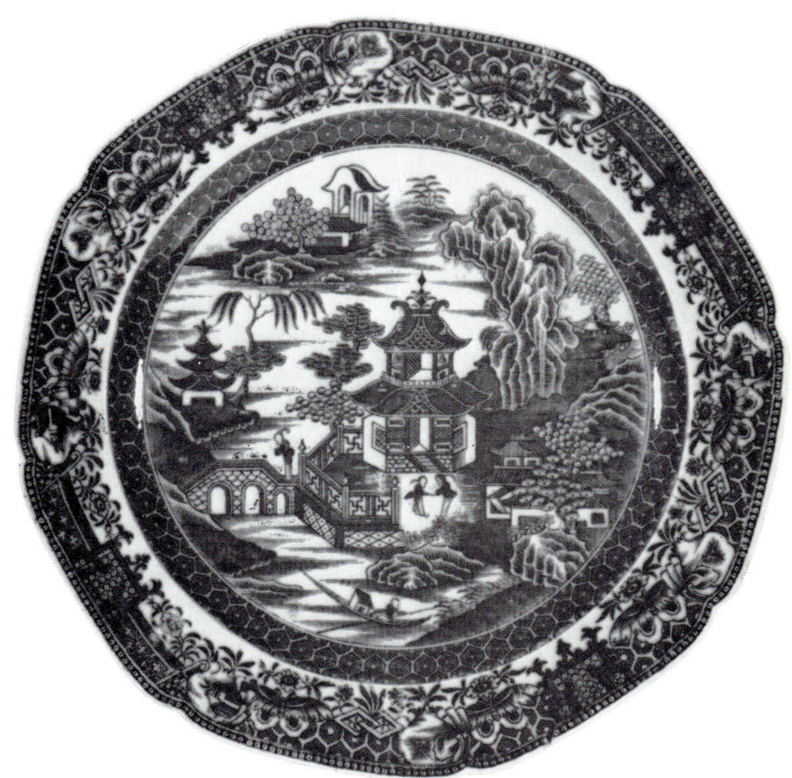

SPODE. Willow Plate. Earthenware body. Printed in underglaze blue. Impressed SPODE. Size 10 ins. diameter. This decoration was the first Willow Pattern produced by Josiah Spode, *c.* 1780

W. T. Copeland & Sons Ltd.

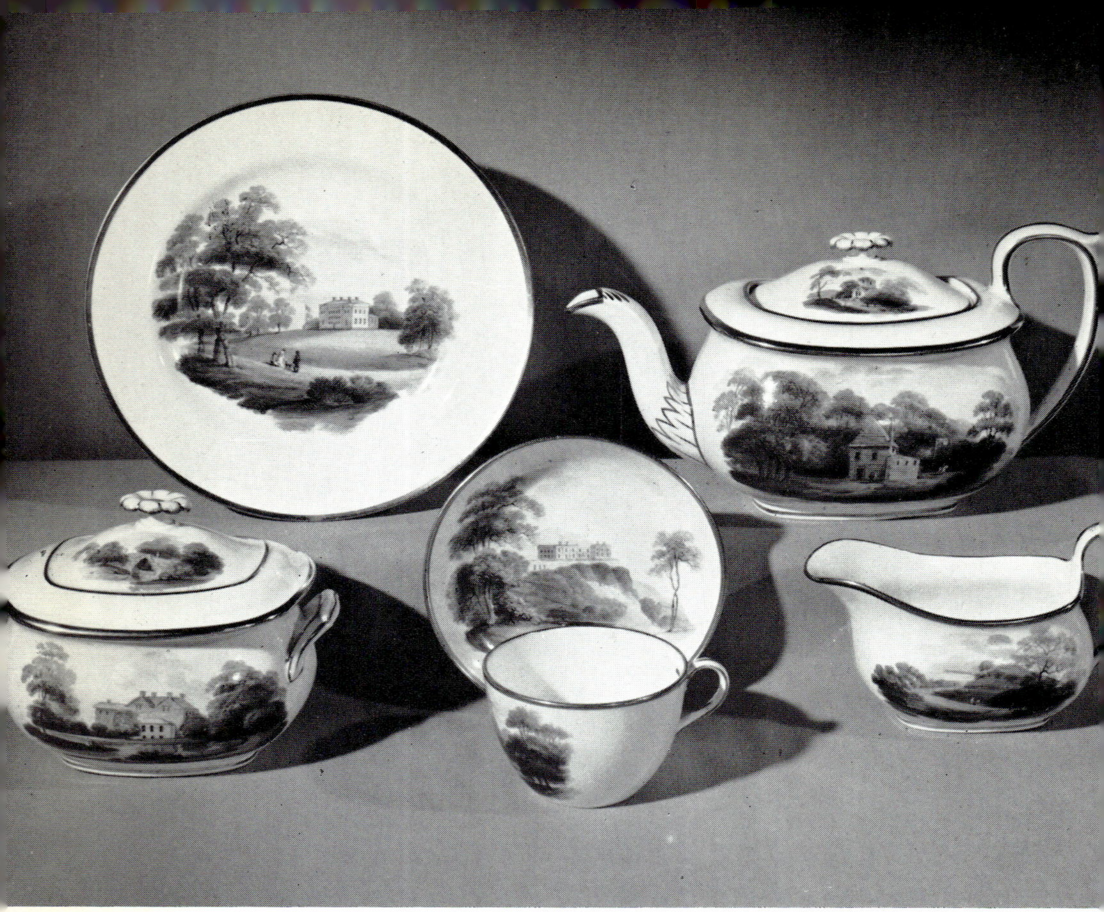

WEDGWOOD. Bone china tea-set painted by John Cutts, *c.* 1812–22

Josiah Wedgwood & Sons

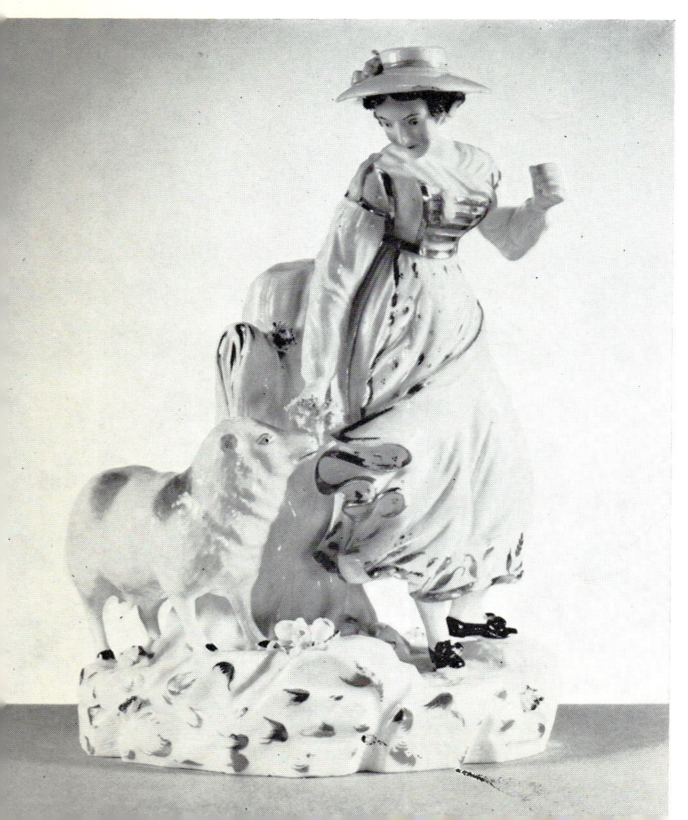

ROCKINGHAM

Figure decorated in enamel colours and gilt, *c.* 1826–30. Mark 'Rockingham Works Brameld', in red. Height $7\frac{1}{4}$ ins.

Victoria and Albert Museum

WEDGWOOD
Slave Medallion, 1786

Josiah Wedgwood & Sons Ltd.

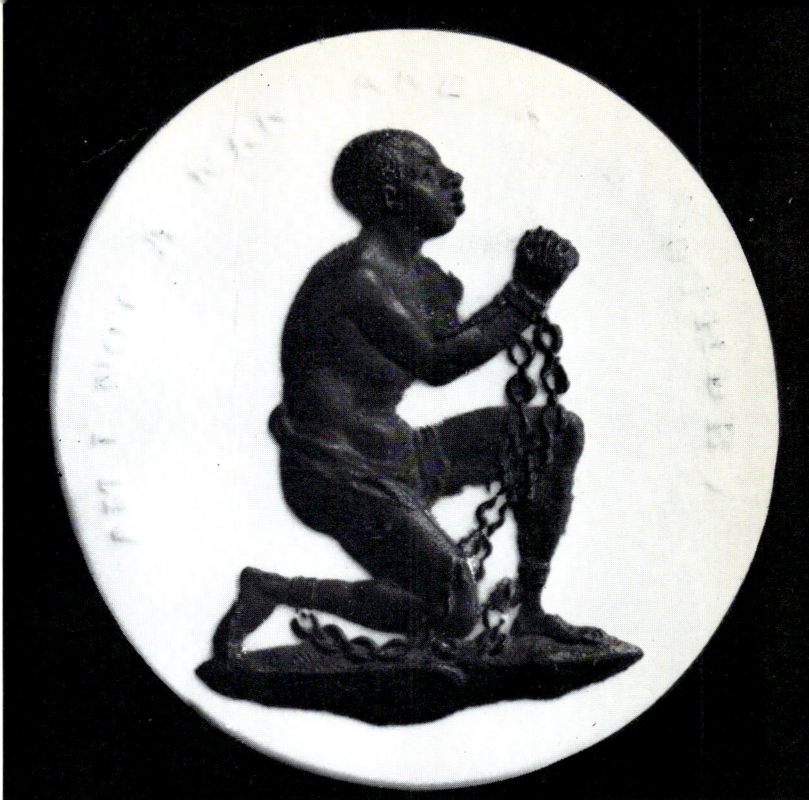

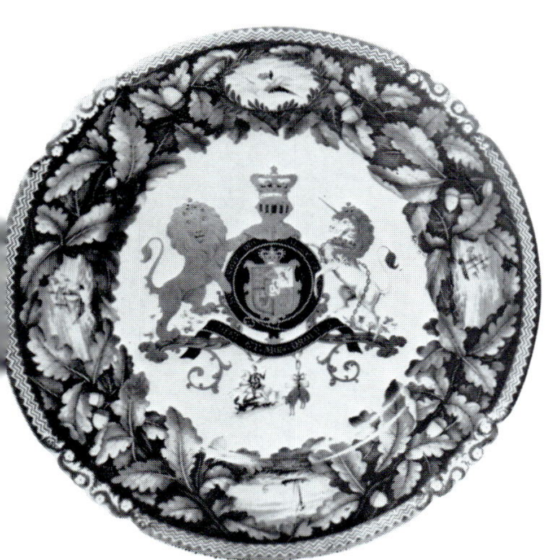

ROCKINGHAM
Plate from the William IV service, decorated in the centre with the Royal Arms hung with the George and Golden Fleece. Gilt-edged rim moulded with scrolls. 9½ ins. Griffin marked in puce

Sotheby & Co.

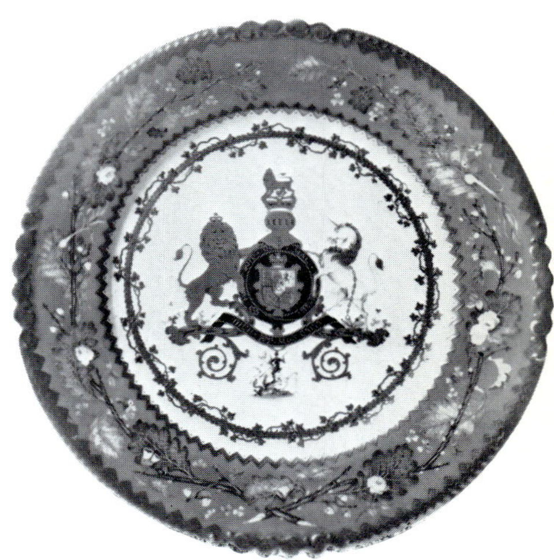

ROCKINGHAM
Plate painted with the Royal Arms hung with the George. Rim has brilliant red ground. 9½ ins. Griffin marked in puce

Sotheby & Co.

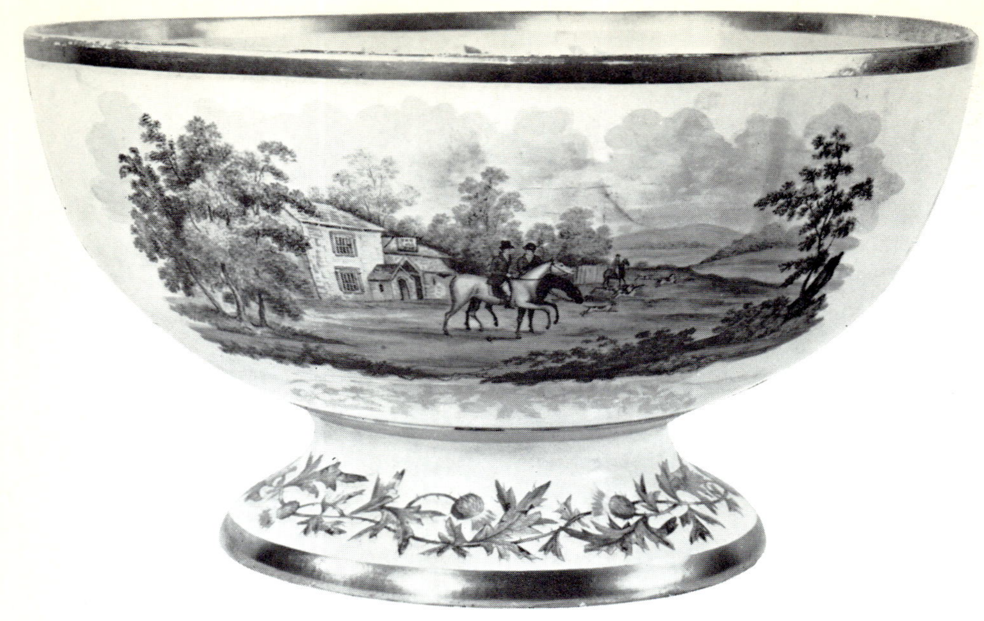

DAVENPORT. A punch bowl painted in colours and gilded edge. Diameter 19 ins.

Christie's

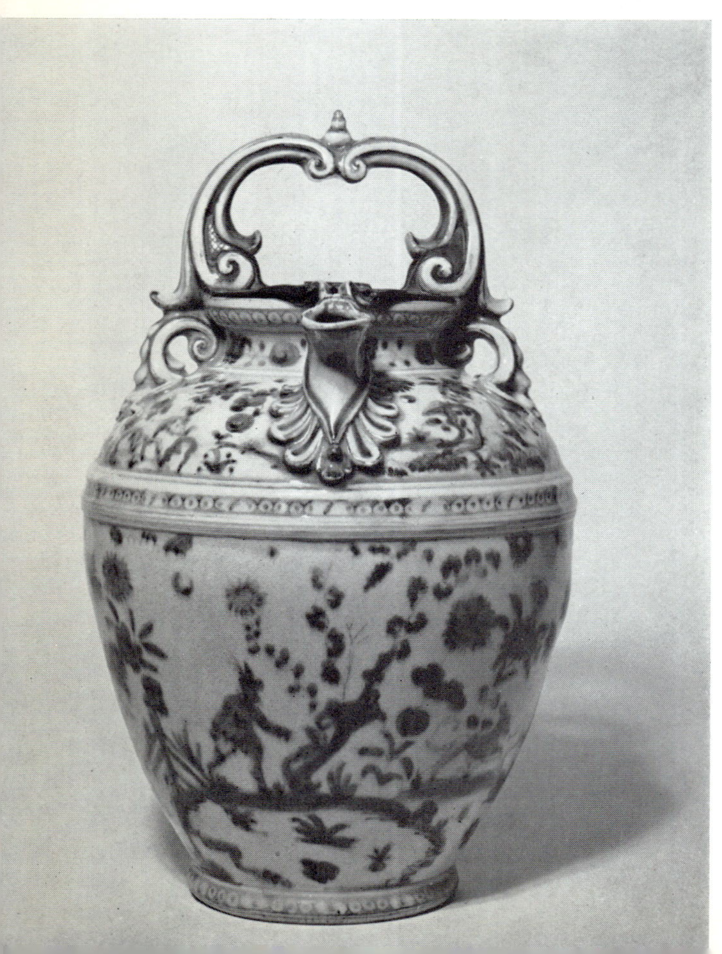

MEDICI

Large pitcher with monochrome *Chinoiserie* decoration. Last quarter of the sixteenth century

Museo Civico, Turin

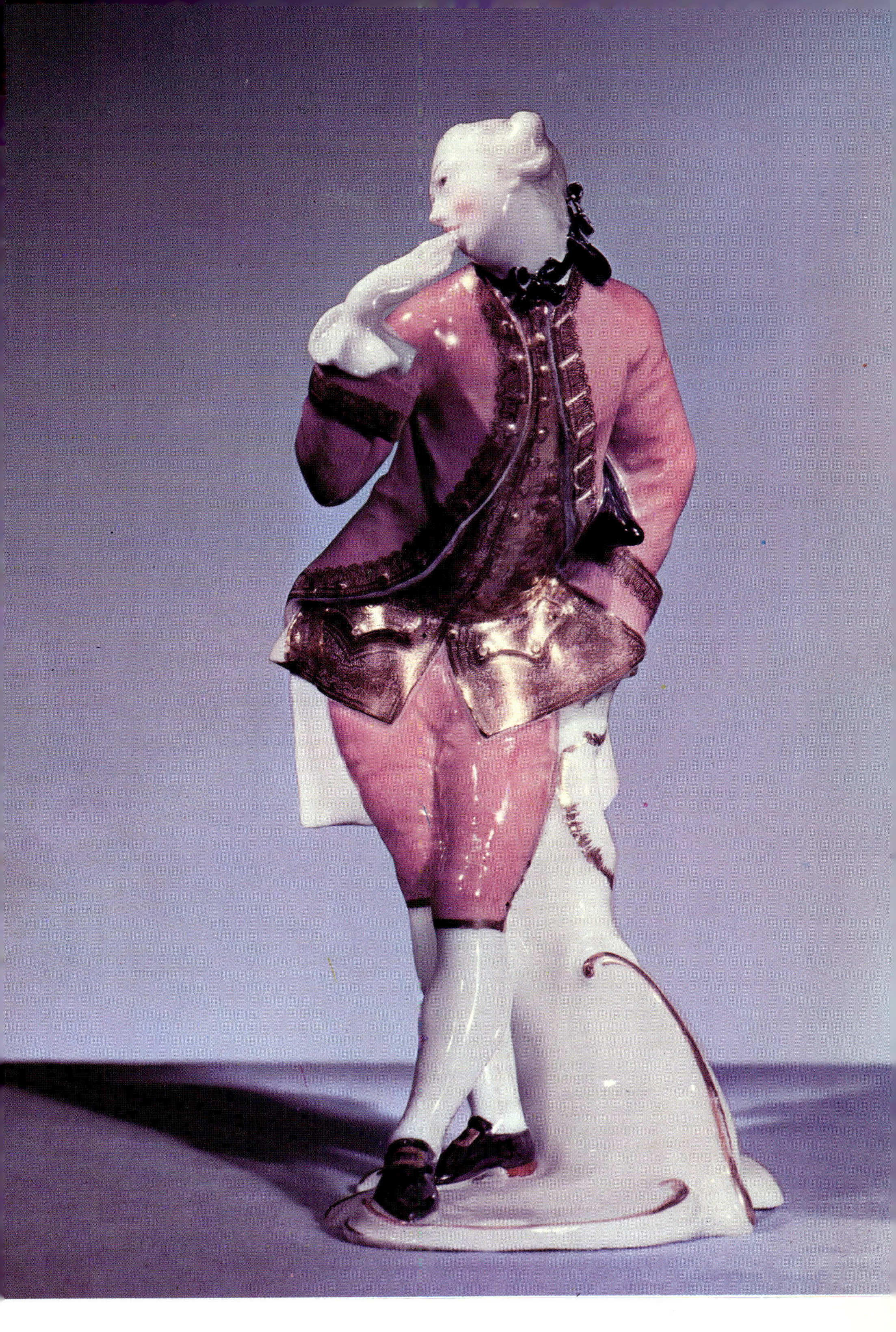

SECTION 6

NYMPHENBURG
Porcelain Ottavio (Italian Comedy), from a model by Franz Anton Bustelli, *c.* 1757.
7½ ins. high

Victoria and Albert Museum

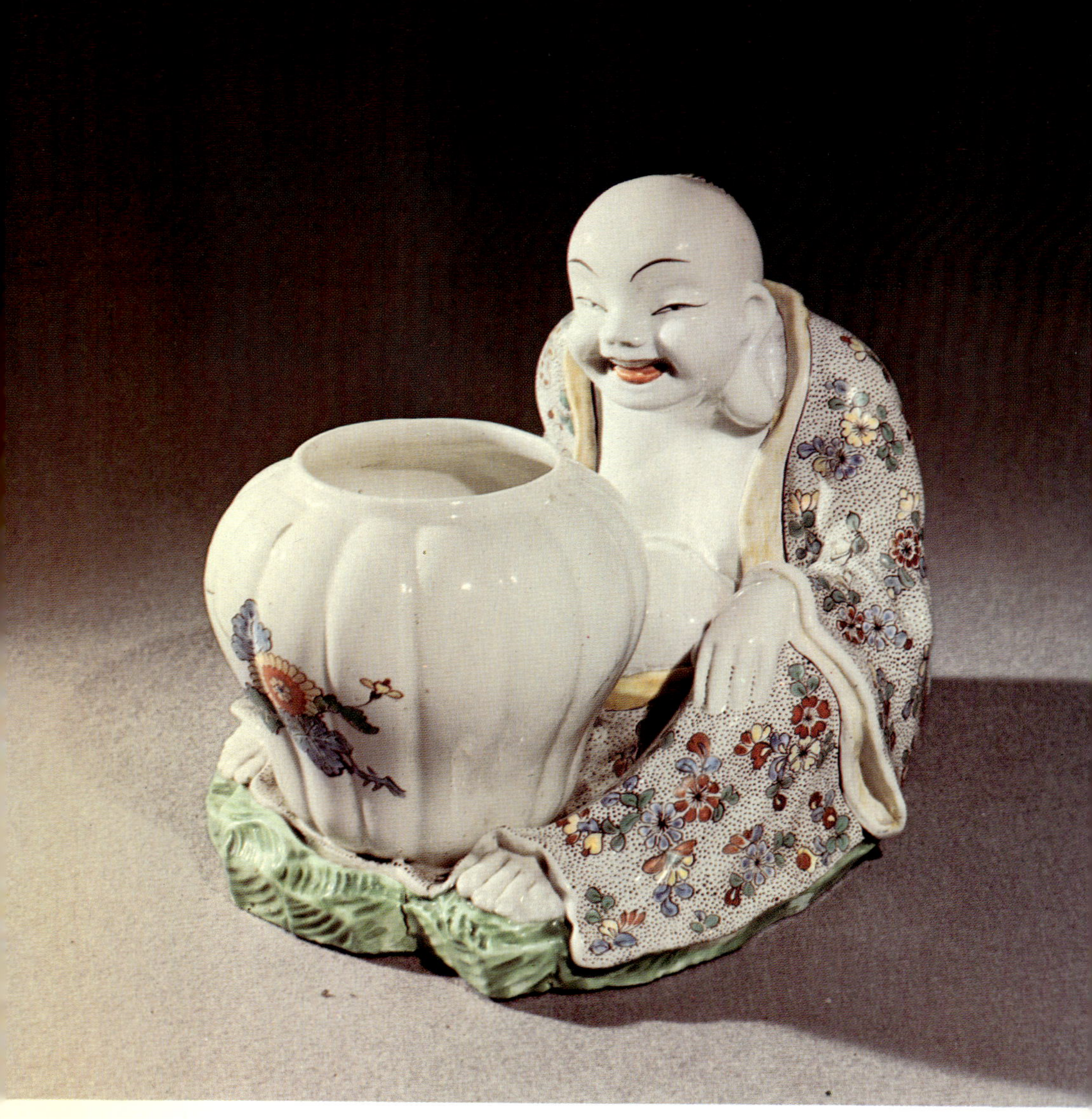

CHANTILLY
"Chinese Buddha"
Soft-paste porcelain, *c.* 1730
La Musée National de la Céramique de Sevres

In blue. On blue and white cups.

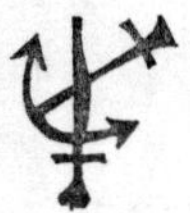

On late figures, in red or brown.

On late figures, in red or brown.

[2] CHELSEA 1745–1769

"*Calculated rather for ornament than for use*" (*Gentleman's Magazine*, Vol. XXXIII, 1763, p. 191)

Chelsea has been the subject of more books and articles than any other English porcelain factory. Presumably begun about 1745 because of some dated and inscribed cream jugs, moulded in the shape of a goat and bee, this remarkable factory produced the finest English porcelain figures of all.

No factory records have survived, and it is only in the last few decades that scholarly research into municipal and parochial archives, old newspapers and magazines, has caused many new facts to emerge which give a clearer historical picture.

Many myths surviving from the nineteenth century, recounted in lieu of documentary evidence, are now ignored, and new theories have been furnished, based partly on fact and subsequently on surmise, which doubtlessly will be challenged in time.

The factory was started by two Huguenots, Charles Gouyn (*c.*1700–1760), a jeweller, and Nicholas Sprimont (1716–1766), a silversmith. Little is known of Gouyn, but Sprimont's silver assay mark has made possible the identification of his work.

Born in Liège, he entered his mark at Goldsmith's Hall on 25th January, 1742 and apparently worked as a silversmith until 1748. In 1753 Sprimont described himself as a professional silversmith who had become interested in porcelain "from a casual acquaintance with a chymist who had some knowledge this way" (*sic*).

The similarity of the first paste made at Chelsea to that of Saint-Cloud has suggested that a French "chymist" may have been employed at Chelsea, and that it may have been Thomas Briand or Bryand who, in about 1743, had shown the Royal Society some specimens of china made with English materials.

The factory was situated at the river end and western side of Lawrence Street, with a small frontage on the river at Cheyne Walk. In 1843, during excavations for new houses, it was found that part of the factory must have been situated in the neighbourhood of Cheyne Row West, where quantities of broken porcelain were unearthed.

The Chelsea factory mark was altered to signify successive changes in paste and variety, and the porcelain falls into four approximate periods:

1. 1745–1749 Triangle period. An incised triangle or no mark at all.
2. 1749–1752 Raised Anchor period. An applied anchor on a raised pad, either round or oval.
3. 1753–1757 Red Anchor period. A small anchor in enamel painted in red, brown or purple.
4. 1758–1769 Gold Anchor period. A small anchor in gold.

During the first or Triangle period until 1749, Chelsea made tea and coffee services in silver forms, generally left unpainted. They also produced others in the Chinese Nankin style, painted in underglaze blue, which were referred to by Horace Walpole in his Strawberry Hill catalogue "specimens of early Chelsea blue and white".

Some figures were made from reproductions of popular contemporary bronzes, particularly children in various poses, after the seventeenth century sculptor "Il Fiammingo" and shell-shaped salts with crayfish in the manner of silverware.

All the early models were slip-cast and unpainted, although possibly some were decorated in unfired oil paint which subsequently has worn off—William Duesbury's account books refer to Chelsea figures painted in this manner between 1751 and 1753. The paste was like milky glass with black specks and fine transparent points seen by transmitted electric light. It was covered with a thick, ivory-tinted glaze, sometimes with air bubbles and crazing.

In 1749 there was a reshuffle in the factory and Charles Gouyn left, taking some of the workers with him.

According to Lane, (*English Porcelain Figures of the Eighteenth Century*) this nucleus of Chelsea defaulters became the rival to Chelsea when they produced the Girl-in-the-Swing series, a much debated and mysterious collection of figures and toys in the Chelsea style, which until recently was believed to have been a Chelsea experiment. The title of the series derived from a charming model of a young girl, dressed in eighteenth-century costume, seated on a swing, which was in a glassy paste, similar to the first period Chelsea, but obviously made during the second period. The large quantity of "toys" that were made, often with rich gilt mounts, has suggested that they were the invention of some jeweller—such as Charles Gouyn. These "toys" were miniature models, exquisitely executed, of historical, theatrical and allegorical subjects, forming a seal, a patchbox, a *bonbonnière*, a scent bottle, etc. Some bore inscriptions in French, frequently erroneously spelled: *Gage de mon amitié*, *Bachus nous invite*, *Fidèle* and *Je vis en esperance* to quote but a few. They were extremely popular in their day—and were exchanged as favours and gifts. The Girl-in-the-Swing factory closed without apparent reason in 1754, and lock, stock and barrel were placed under the hammer in a sale that lasted five days. Chelsea apparently bought the lot, as they continued the production of the models.

The Raised Anchor mark probably signified Sprimont's changeover to a more stable paste, less glassy than the previous one, but with a duller finish. He abandoned the manufacture of blue and white as the paste was still too fragile to survive the high temperature firing, and concentrated on enamel colours with which the porcelain fared better in the muffle kiln. During this period the "spur marks" began to appear. These were three rough, unglazed marks found on the base of dishes and plates where they had stood on a tripod in the kiln. Black specks were still frequent, although they were often disguised by the apparently erratic addition of an insect or leaf.

Chelsea was not favoured with royal patronage like its continental competitors. George II had no interest in porcelain although his son, William Augustus, Duke of Cumberland, is reputed to have had at least a porcelain chandelier made at Chelsea.

The factory was sponsored from 1748 to 1758 by the Duke's secretary, Sir Edward Fawkener, whose influence was considerable. In May 1751 he wrote to the British Ambassador to Saxony, Sir Charles Hanbury Williams, asking him to purchase some Meissen models for the Factory, as these were not freely available in England until after 1752. Hanbury Williams immediately made his own porcelain collection in London available. The close study of this considerable collection which included many Meissen models, enabled the Chelsea technicians to improve their production methods, and, what was most important, to demonstrate the range and virtuosity of the material. Comparatively few models were copied outright, but many were adapted. The difference between the Chelsea editions of the Meissen originals was the use of soft-paste, and the more romantic though none less vital rendering.

Great progress was made with figures of all kinds, and the hand of a master modeller soon became apparent when a definite Chelsea style emerged.

At one time it was believed that the sculptor Louis-François Roubiliac worked for the factory, but this has now been disproved. On the evidence of the rate books of the factory which show that it was occupied by Mr. Sprimont and Mr. Williams, and from some signed terra cotta models in the Ashmolean Museum, Oxford, it is now considered that he has been confused with the sculptor Joseph Willems (*b.*1716 Brussels, *d.*1766 Tournai).

Willems is thought to have joined Chelsea as early as 1749, for from that date models appeared which bear some relation to later Chelsea work, and which were not technically the same as previous models. Willems is presumed to have been the head designer until he left for Tournai in 1766. The figures made during this period were particularly fine. A series of highly decorated birds inspired by engravings in *The Natural History of Uncommon Birds* by George Edwards were made and followed by some excellent rather sturdy figures taken from engravings by Ravenet, Callot and others. Lane wrote "This whole range of rather large figures, mostly from 9 to 11 inches high, shows an increasingly confident breadth of handling, and a nobility of attitude that continued for the next thirteen years to be characteristic of the best work done at Chelsea".

From about 1753, during the Red Anchor period, Chelsea produced its finest work. The paste was improved and became harder and more adaptable, and oval transparent flecks, not points, seen against transmitted electric light known as "moons" were frequent.

Exquisite paintings in enamel, apparently haphazard, but actually carefully planned were enveloped by an unctuous glaze which clung like satin. Botanical flowers were meticulously and accurately reproduced in a free, bold style, and marvellous interpretations of Aesop's Fables were painted by Jeffrey Hamett O'Neale (*c.*1716–1780). The figures were outstanding. Although mainly inspired by Meissen there were many original Chelsea models which show the hand of Willems. Modelled in splendid baroque style on square bases there were allegorical and mythological subjects, Italian Comedy, peasants singly and in family groups, and *genre* figures in contemporary dress, the Gardener and his Companion, Fishermen, Beggars, Dancers, to name a few. They rank with the finest continental porcelain sculpture of the period.

Periodic auction sales were advertised to dispose of the factory output, and fortunately some of the catalogues have survived. In 1757 Sprimont announced that no sales would take place that year due to his illness and in 1758 Fawkener died. It was believed until recently that the factory closed for about a year, but it has now been discovered that a four-day sale was held in Dublin at this period which discounts this theory.

Possibly because of the experience of the workers who joined the factory from Bow, bone ash was added to the paste which considerably strengthened it, but gave it a chalky tone. The glaze inclined to be greenish and tended to serious crazing.

By this time, the popularity of Sèvres had outstripped Meissen, which was involved in the Seven Years War, and Chelsea turned to France for fresh ideas. Free use was made of strong ground colours, the most popular of which were Chelsea's glorious failure, claret, which was intended to be *rose pompadour* and mazarine blue, an adaptation of Sèvres *bleu-du-roi*. Everything was gilded profusely and it has been suggested that the anchor mark was changed to gold at this juncture to indicate the new factory style. Elaborate rococo vases, richly gilded, and heavily ornamented and with paintings in reserves after Watteau and Boucher became the main interest, whilst figures were given exaggerated asymmetrically scrolled bases and painted in elaborate, brocaded patterns with lush *bocage* and masses of gilding.

Whilst the figures of the Gold Anchor period are extremely fine, there is a certain stiffness which is less appealing than the vivacious Red Anchor models. The luxurious decoration is also inclined to detract from the sensuous soft-paste which, for most collectors, is the porcelain's most attractive feature.

Great interest was shown in the factory by people of fashion who collected new models and ordered services. The most important order came from George III as a gift for the Queen's brother, the Duke of Mecklenburg. Horace Walpole described it in his letter to Sir Horace Mann of 4th March, 1763:

> "There are dishes and plates without number, *épergnes*, candlesticks, saltcellars, sauce-boats, tea and coffee equipages. In short, it is complete and cost £1,200."

A pair of damaged candelabra were given to a steward in the Duke's household, and these fortunately found their way to the

Schreiber collection, now at the Victoria and Albert Museum, London.

The serious production of "toys" was begun after 1759 and many models were produced, some original and some based on the "Girl-on-the-Swing" style, with gilding.

Sprimont's health began to fail. He developed gout, and spent a great deal of time in continental spas. Competition became very keen from all the new porcelain factories, and business at Chelsea began to decline. "Having accumulated a comfortable fortune, a house in town, a country place in Dorset and his own carriage", Sprimont decided to retire. The last auction sale recorded was in 1763 when the premises and equipment were also offered, but the final sale was not completed until August 1769 when James Cox bought the lot for £600.

CHELSEA CHARACTERISTICS

1. Always soft-paste, smooth and soft to touch.
2. Does not bear doctoring, refiring causes glaze to craze.
3. Dishes and plates have raised shaped rim.
4. Triangle period, 1745–1749. Mark: Incised Triangle frequently unmarked. Milk-white glassy body and brilliant glaze. Black specks and other imperfections, small pinholes through transmitted light. Saint-Cloud type. Silver forms, modelling in relief, rarely coloured, some blue and white. White porcelain looks as though someone had just poured cream over it.
5. Raised Anchor period, 1749–1752. Mark: An Anchor moulded in relief on raised pad.
6. Red Anchor period, 1735–1757. A small Anchor painted in red, brown or purple enamel. Fine grained paste showing "moons", clear oval spots seen by transmitted light. Glaze cool white and slightly opaque. Footrims and bases ground level. Meissen influence. Figures baroque style, vivacious. Large range enamel colours, rarely gilded. Three or four "spur" marks on base. Anchor mark discreetly placed not always on base.

7. Gold Anchor period, 1758–1769. Small Anchor painted in gold. Bone ash added to paste. Glaze more lustrous and thickly applied forming greenish pools. Gilding heavy with strong ground colours. Sèvres influence. Figures elaborately decorated with lush *bocage*. Exaggerated rococo.

Chelsea 1745

1745, incised. On "goat and bee" jugs.

1745–1750 incised.

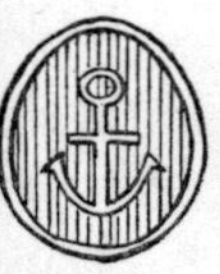

Raised Anchor. *1749–1752*. In relief on raised medallion.

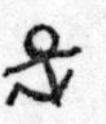

About *1752–1756* in red. Sometimes in underglaze blue, blue enamel or purple enamel.

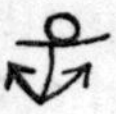

About *1752–1756* in red. Sometimes in underglaze blue, blue enamel or purple enamel.

About *1750–1756*, in underglaze blue.

[3] CHELSEA—DERBY 1770–1784

On 17th August, 1769 William Duesbury agreed to purchase the Chelsea Works, and completed the sale on 5th February, 1770 when payment of £400 as part of the purchase money was made. Jewitt records the actual document in *The Ceramic Art of Great Britain*:

> "Recd. London 5th Feby 1770, of Mr. Wm Duesbury, four hundred pounds, in part of the purchase of the Chelsea Porcelain Manufactory and its apurtenances and lease thereof, which I promise to assign over to him on or before the 8th instant. JAMES COX."

There followed a long legal action between Duesbury and an auctioneer called Burnsall relating to the last auction sale of finished Chelsea porcelain in 1770 which was included in Duesbury's transaction with Cox, which Burnsall disputed. Sprimont died in 1771 during the hearing, and the case was ultimately settled.

Duesbury was very proud to be associated with the illustrious Chelsea Works, and he tried to keep the factory going as before. His mark at this time was the Chelsea anchor and the letter D, presumably for Derby but more probably for Duesbury.

An interesting relic of the era is this weekly bill:

1770 *A weekly Bill at Chelsea from May* 12 *to the* 19

	£	s	d
Barton, 6 days at 3s. 6d.	1	1	0
Boyer, 6 days at 3s. 6d.	1	1	0
Seal, made overtime, 6 cocks			7
3 dozen Cupid crying by a Urn		3	6
1 dozen and 6 Gentle Man with a Muff		1	9
1 dozen and 6 Shephard Sheering of Sheep		1	9
6 Arliquens			7
Roberts, $6\frac{3}{4}$ days at 2s. 6d.		16	$10\frac{1}{2}$
Piggot, 7 days at 1s. 9d.		12	3
Ditto, Taking Care of the horse on Sunday		1	6

	£	s	d
Inglefield, 7 days at 1s. 8d.		11	8
Bleeding of the Horse, and a Broom and Soap......		1	0
Exd. and Entd.	£4	13	5½

Recd of Mr. Duesbury in full of all demands for Self and the a Bove.

RICHD. BARTON.

(The horse was used for turning the flint and clay mills)

Mr. Robert Boyer, the workman employed at Chelsea from 1770–1784, whose name features frequently in the weekly bills, was entrusted with the dismantling of the Chelsea Works. He wrote to Mr. Duesbury:

Laurence Strt., Chelsea
Feby. 18th, 1784.

Sir:

I Wright to Inform yow how we are pretty forward in the Pulling down of the buildings at Chelsea. I think a little better than a fortnight and they will all be down to the ground and Cleared of the primeses, wich I shall be glad to my hart, for I am tired of it. Mr. Lygo (Duesbury's London agent) says yow would wish to have the Ion Kiln Cum to Derby. Its hardley worth sending for the Corners are a good deail burnt at the Bottom, and the sides are opened or Drawd so much as 4 or 5 inches on each side. But if yow chuse to have it Cum, say how it shall be sent—by Land or Water and I will send it. I wish Yow will let me no if yow will have the mold of the large figur of Brittania sent to the warehous or Broake. Now, sir, as my time at Chelsea draws nigh to a conclution I should beg of yow to inform me by letter what yow mean to Imploy me abought at your manufactory. In case yow or myself should settle on Tirms agreable.

Yow now allow me one Ginue pr Week, house Rent and fire; and I dont make aney Doubght But I shall be found a very Uceful servant to yow if I cum, and must beg of Yow to say if 25/- pr week will be to much to Give me; and house rent free, as I have always had of yow. I make no Dought but yow will please to say what yow will allow me for the Removall of my Famaley. We have 4 children, my wife and self, wich will Cost a deal of money —and that a articall wich is scarce with mee. I have had severall offers of places's since the manufactory had bin pulling Down, but Refus'd them all Becaus it would have been Wicked in me to have Left yow till I had seen your property Cleared off. . . . I Due not like to Cum so maney miles from London on an Uncertinty, therefore it will be nesesary to have articals drawd for 3, five, or 7 years, as is agreable to yow. I have carrid Mr. Lygo above sixty-six pounds this week, wich I found to be very seasonable. I was very much shock'd, sir, when I heard yow had been so Dangeresly Ill, But an happy to find yow are so much better than yow was, & God send yow may Continue to Gett mending for the Best. Should I cum to Derby, I shall bring nothing with me but my Beds—Land Carridge cums to a Deal of Money; my Goods are But old, therefore they shall all be sold.

I am, with Respects, your Obt. Humble Servt.

Robt. Boyer.

Many of the artists and workmen from Chelsea transferred to Derby and in 1784 the Chelsea Works were closed. During the period of Duesbury's administration, little new work was developed. Old moulds and patterns were reproduced but were lacking in quality and finish.

[4] DERBY

Planché 1750–1756
Duesbury and Bloor 1756–1848

The first Derby porcelain was made about 1750 in a small factory near St. Mary's Bridge, by a jeweller and goldsmith, André Planché who is said to have been financed by the merchant banker John Heath. Some white cream jugs dated 1750 incised with the mark "D" or Derby, are the earliest known pieces in existence.

These were unpainted and modelled like silverware with strawberries, flowers and leaves. Other silver form objects made were salt-cellars and sauce-boats in the shape of sea-shells with marine incrustations. A range of excellent figures of high quality, comparable with Chelsea were modelled, either by Planché or an unknown sculptor, in a broad, free style and have a distinctive peculiarity in that the lower edge of the base was wiped free of glaze, which has caused them to be named the "dry edge" figures. These figures were hollow, but quite heavy for their size and were slip-cast in a rich non-phosphatic creamy paste made from Derbyshire or Dorset clay and glassy frit with a thick, well fitting, glassy glaze.

Some were apparently sent to Duesbury's London workshops to be decorated, for his account books show "Darby" or "Derbyshire" figures during 1752 and 1753.

Duesbury was working at Longton Hall during 1754 and was invited by Heath to become a partner in the Derby works which were extended down the Nottingham Road. A shrewd man of business, William Duesbury was the son of a currier and became an "enameller on china" learning his trade in the London factories, and rose by his energy and skill to be "the largest porcelain manufacturer in the kingdom".

Planché was appointed Works Manager in the new arrangement, but was apparently eased out of the business when all his knowledge had been imparted, for his name does not appear on later documents.

Duesbury found that the glassy paste was difficult to work, so he concentrated on complicated expensive models. Blue and white useful wares were made, but the footrings had to be ground level because of the uneven application of the glaze which caused unsightly drips. No blue and white bore factory marks before 1770, although some rare pieces had stilt marks on the base, similar to those on Longton Hall wares, presumably from Duesbury's experience at that factory. The designs were copied from silver forms from the Bow factory, and flat wares bore intricately enamelled Chinese style borders, which appear to have been a Derby obsession.

Duesbury launched a series of "pale colouring" figures of a

mediocre quality in emulation of Meissen. The announcement for the sale of 1756 read "Derby or second Dresden", and probably convinced provincial buyers.

By 1760, the models were increased in size—and the colours used all tended to be greyish and dirty. These are known as the "Patch family" of models and they were continued until about 1770.

Richard Holdship made an agreement with Duesbury in 1764 to supply him with the formula for a steatitic paste and to show him the secrets of transfer printing. Soapstone was added to the Derby paste for about five years, and enabled the wares to be more thinly potted than the earlier glassy body, so more tea services were made. Footrings no longer had to be ground level and the glaze became smooth and close fitting, but many objects had sandy black spots. Worcester style blue and white wares with inferior blurred engravings, some with Holdship's anchor mark in blue appeared, and the cobalt varied in tone from black to royal blue, both in transfers and painting. The body was very white, but by transmitted electric light tends to be a cloudy, greenish yellow.

Duesbury's concentration on commercial porcelain was financially successful, for by 1770 he was able, with the help of Heath, to buy up the Chelsea factory. He continued to run both factories, and then closed Chelsea for good in 1784, transferring men and equipment to Derby. The experienced Chelsea personnel caused many changes to be made. The formula of the body was altered to include bone ash and Cornish kaolin, which resulted in a close grained paste of remarkable purity, and the colours and finishes introduced gave the porcelain an outstanding quality.

The painting was superb. There were miniature landscapes by Zachariah Boreman (1738–1810) and John and Robert Brewer, naturalistic flowers by William (Quaker) Pegg, cupids by Richard Askew (*c.*1720–*c.*1800), exotic birds by Richard Dodson and the exquisite Billingsley roses.

William Billingsley (1758–1828), apprenticed to Duesbury at the age of sixteen in 1774, received considerable tuition from Boreman, and subsequently evolved an individualistic style of flower painting which depended upon rubbing out to obtain highlights on petals and leaves. When he tried to leave in 1796, the London agent Joseph Lygo wrote to Duesbury: "I hope that you will be able to make a bargain with Mr. Billingsley for him to continue with you, for it will be such a loss to lose such a great hand, and not only that, but his going into another factory will put them in the way of doing flowers in the same way, which at the present they are entirely ignorant of."

The work of anonymous artists has been identified by certain peculiarities of style. The "moth" painter who favoured large moths and insects, and another who painted very thin, thread-like stems and stalks to his Meissen style flowers.

Underglaze blue was unsuccessful on the new paste, so a reversion to the glassy paste was made for a time, but constant difficulties with supplies of cobalt led to the abandonment of blue and white altogether by 1786 except for special orders.

After 1770, Duesbury introduced a smooth, ivory-toned biscuit porcelain, which due to certain kiln conditions, had a slight trace of glaze depositied on it which gave it a warm, satin sheen. It was an admirable vehicle for figures, but apart from the later work of Spängler and Coffee, the modelling was too sentimental to be included amongst the "greats".

Jean Jacques Spängler (*c.*1750–1810), son of the director of the Zürich porcelain factory arrived in London in 1790 and his work was shown to Benjamin Vuillamy, clockmaker, one of Derby's most exacting clients. Spängler's obvious talent led to a contract with Derby where he modelled complicated figures and groups in biscuit for Vuillamy's elaborate clock cases. Spängler's erratic behaviour was a nuisance to his employers, who put up with him because he was valuable, but he only remained with them for about five years.

William James Coffee (*c.*1760–*c.*1810) began as a kiln-man at Coade's Artificial Stone factory in London, and joined Derby as a modeller in 1794. His first efforts brought a scornful letter from Lygo, for which we are indebted to Jewitt (*Ceramic Art of Great Britain*, VII, p. 97).

> "The figure No. 359 is one of the most stupid looking things I ever saw, and the figure of Apollo in group No. 379

is very vulgar about the bosom, for sure never such bubbys was seen and so much exposed—the design is pretty enough."

An interesting observation on contemporary English prudery was made by Josiah Wedgwood in a letter to Flaxman in Rome, 11th February, 1790, quoted by W. G. Constable (*John Flaxman*, London 1927, pp. 12–13):

"The history of Orestes is an excellent classic subject likewise—but there is one objection which I am afraid is insurmountable and that is the nakedness of the figures. The same objection applies to 'The Judgement of Paris' and the other pieces, and indeed the nude is so general in the works of the ancients, that it will be very difficult to avoid the introduction of naked figures. On the other hand, it is absolutely necessary to do so or to keep the pieces for our own use, for none either male or female, of the present generation, will take or apply them as furniture, if the figures are naked."

About 1770, Derby porcelain began to be marked with a factory insignia. Due to royal patronage and to the visit of George III in 1773 a crowned letter "D" came to be used. A crown with crossed batons and six dots over a "D" is thought to have been used after 1782. This is known generally as the Crown Derby period.

Derby porcelain made between 1770 and 1810 was one of the finest of its time, and justifiably found its way to the most discerning buyers.

In spite of Dr. Samuel Johnson's assertion during his visit to the factory in 1777 that if he could he would have had "vessels of silver of the same size, as cheap as what were here made of porcelain", he is recorded as a buyer of several lots of Derby at an annual auction sale at Christie's in 1783.

William Duesbury died in 1786, and was succeeded by his son William, born 1763. The factory gained in strength, but the responsibilities of the large business prompted him to take a partner, Michael Kean, an Irish miniature painter, but this proved to be a mistake. When Duesbury died in 1796, Michael Kean married the widow, and gave her five children. A poor manager, he was forced to retire when his misappropriation of funds was disclosed. The business passed to William Duesbury III, grandson of the founder, but in 1815 he leased the factory to his clerk Robert Bloor, who had managed the business during his minority.

Having to pay by instalments, Bloor decorated the large accumulations of seconds and auctioned them in neighbouring towns. While this solved his immediate financial problems, the subsequent deterioration in quality led to the decline of the factory. Bloor became insane and his brother Joseph managed the business until the end in 1848. The moulds and equipment were sold, and in recent years, some Chelsea moulds were found in the storerooms of W. T. Copeland and Sons Ltd., apparently bought with the Derby lots.

Some Derby employees formed a company known as Locker & Sons in King Street, and continued in the same style until the death of Locker in 1859. Various owners followed until 1862 when Sampson Hancock endeavoured to revive the Duesbury quality. His mark was the crowned "D" surmounting crossed batons with the letters S. and H.

The present Crown Derby Company was founded in 1877 in an entirely new factory to make high quality porcelain. After the visit of Queen Victoria in 1890, the prefix "Royal" was added to the name.

The present factory was built in 1935, and has since had several changes of ownership. The splendid collection of Derby porcelain which was once in the Company's possession mysteriously disappeared, but a new collection is now being formed. An excellent collection can be seen at the Derby Municipal Museum.

The modern factory makes technically excellent porcelain in modern and period designs. A curious fact is that some of their important customers for the modern version of Duesbury's *Imari* pattern, are the Romanys, who admire the rich colouring and heavy gilding which look so opulent in the dim lights of their caravans. When ordering they always refer to it as the "Tzigane" pattern.

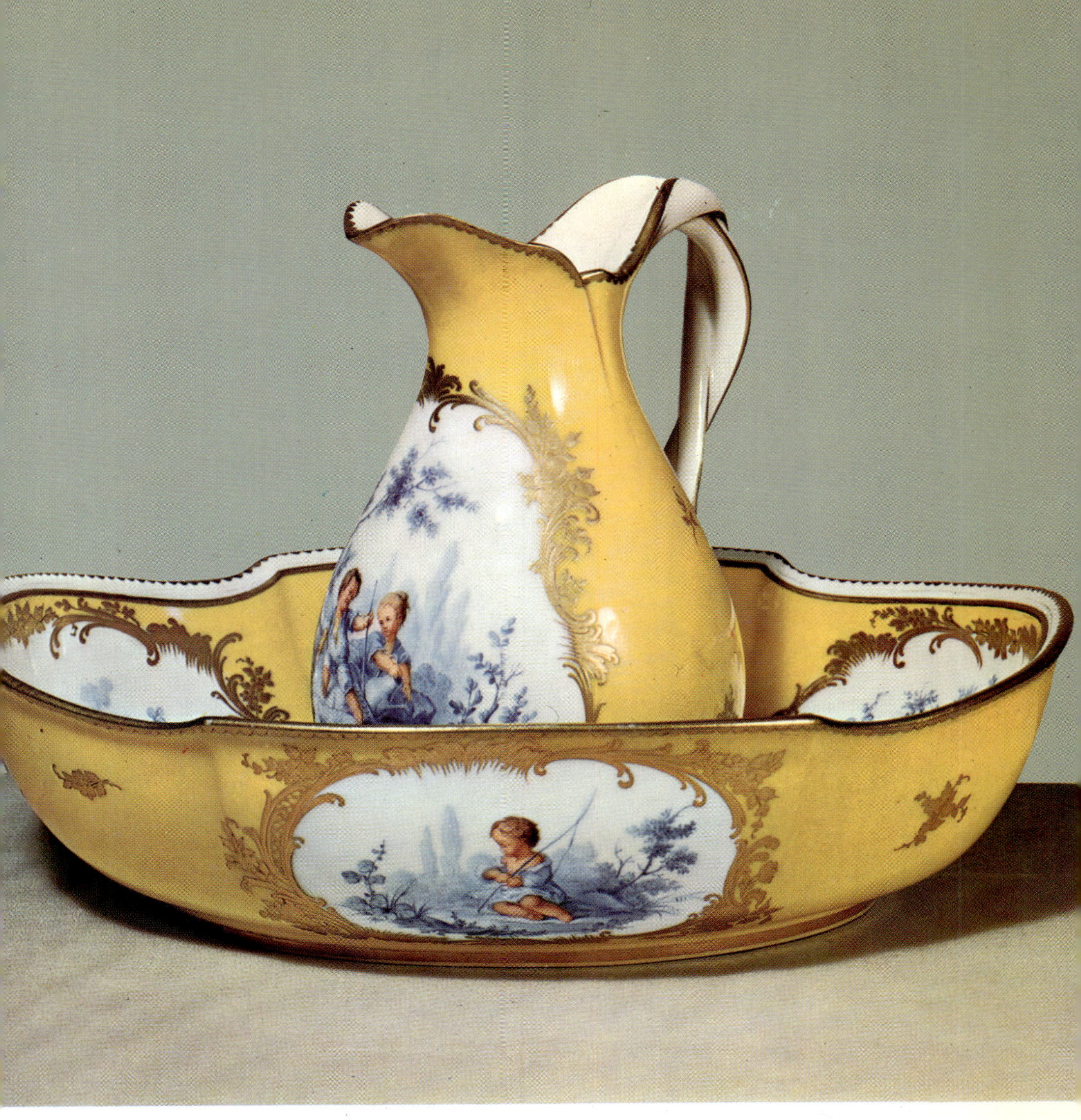

SEVRES
Ewer and basin, 1763, painted by Catrice. Marks, interlaced "L's" enclosing "K", the date letter of 1763, also interlaced "S's" in blue enamel. Basin length 10¾ ins.
The Victoria and Albert Museum

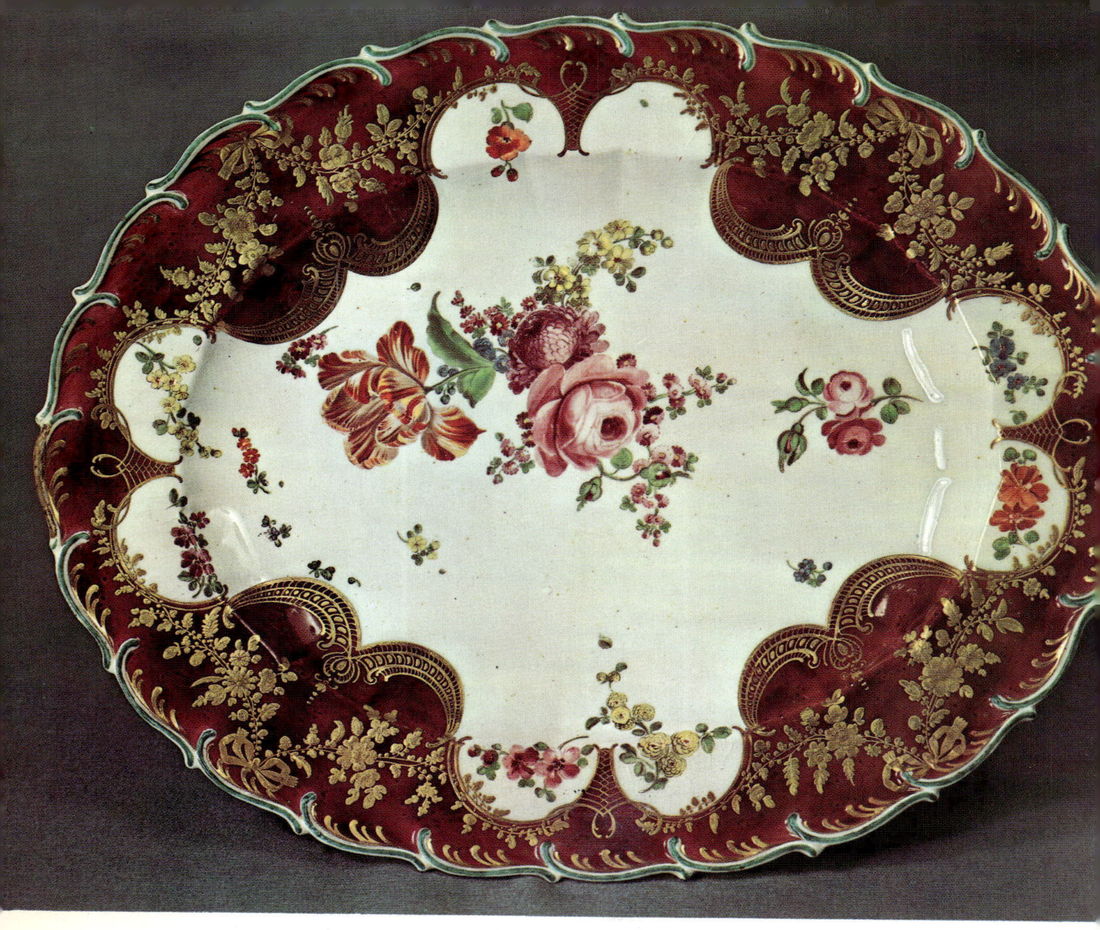

CHELSEA
Claret ground dish from Dessert Service painted by James Giles. Gold anchor marks. Belonged to Charles, eighth Lord Kinnaird, 1780–1826, a close friend of the Prince Regent to whom one of his sons was a page at the Pavilion, Brighton

By permission of Winifred Williams
Sotheby & Co.

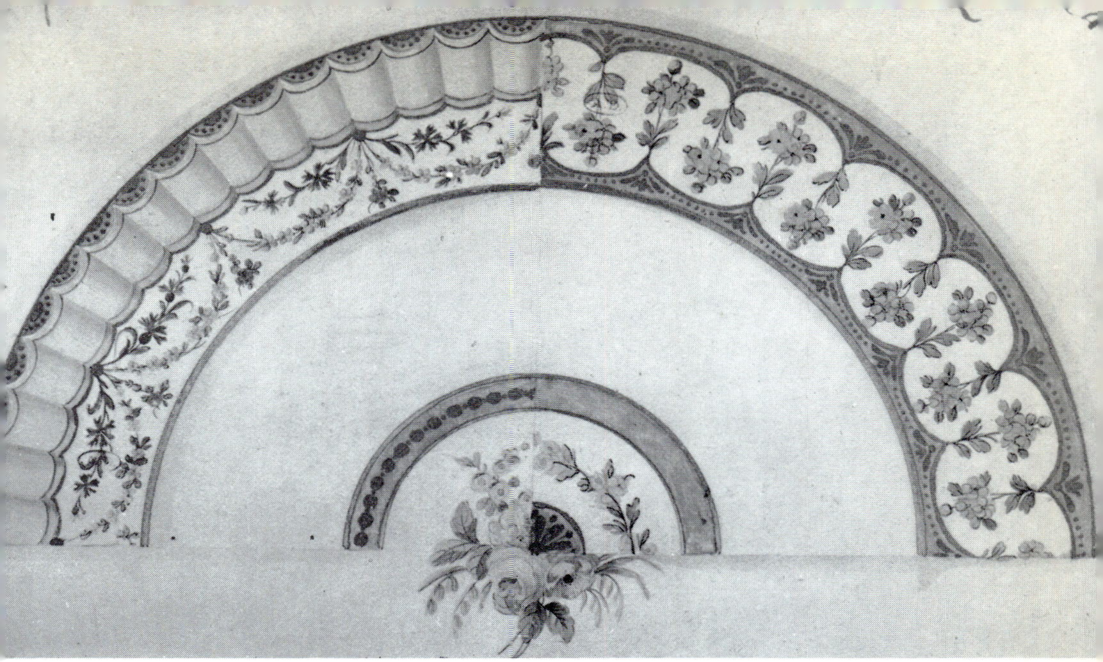

SEVRES. Design for a plate 8 ins. by 11 ins.

Vase in soft-paste porcelain, *c.* 1770, $12\frac{1}{2}$ ins. high

Vase in soft-paste porcelain, *c.* 1770 (one of a pair)

Musée des Arts Décoratifs, Paris

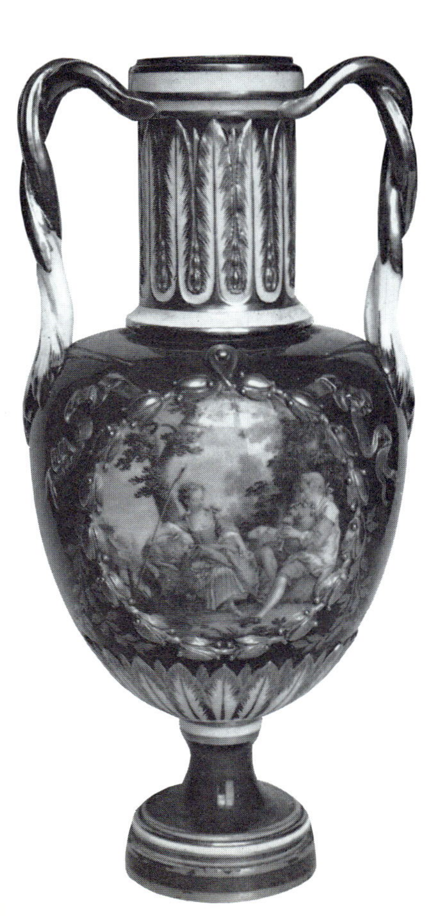

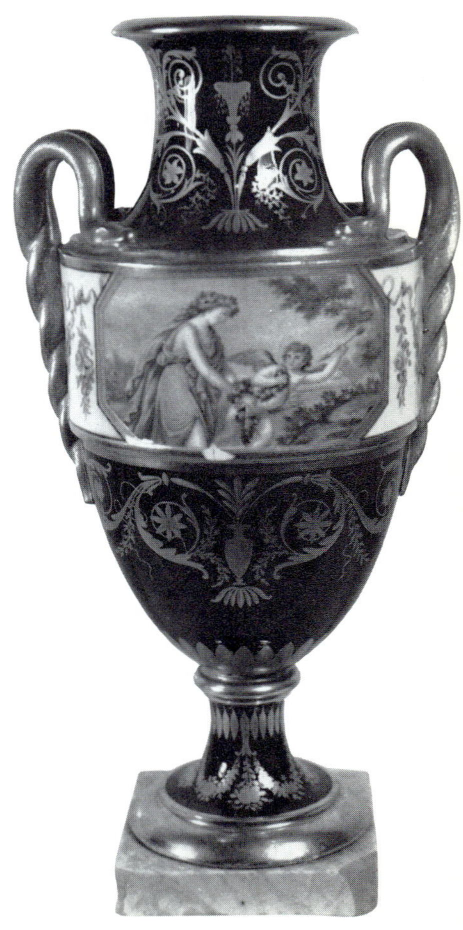

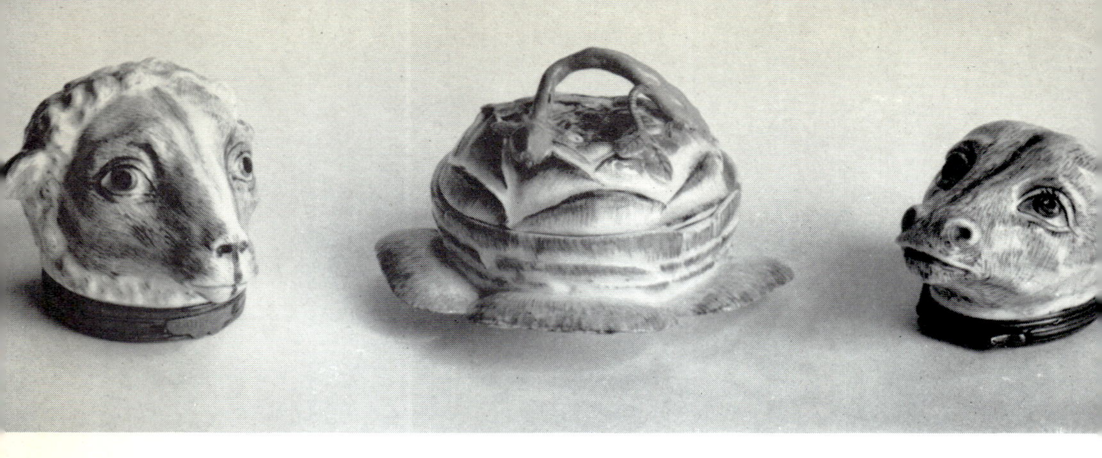

MENNECY

Small box in the form of a sheep's head, 1755. Height $2\frac{5}{8}$ ins., depth 2ins.

Box in the form of a rose, eighteenth century. Height $2\frac{3}{8}$ ins., depth 4 ins.

Small box in the form of a dog's head (mastiff) with silver setting, 1756–62

Musée des Arts Décoratifs, Paris

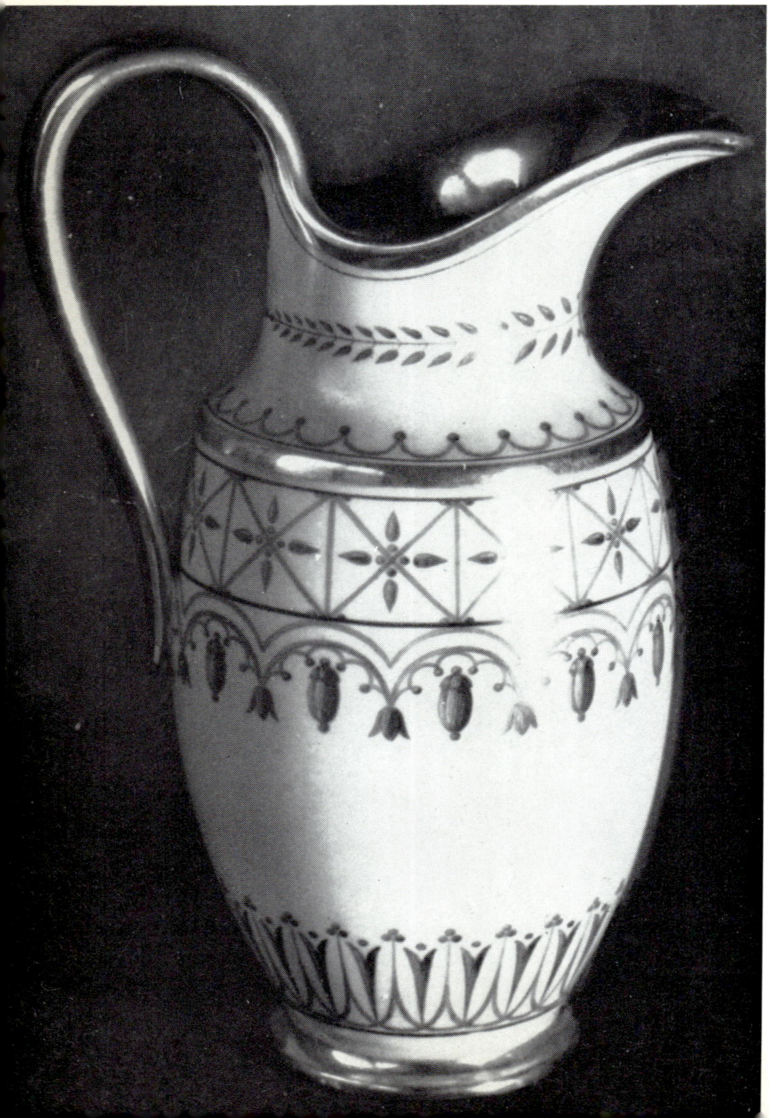

SEVRES

Jug from a *service à déjeuner* belonging to the Empress Josephine, 1813–15. Decorated in yellow and gold

Musée des Arts Décoratifs, Paris

ARRAS
Teapot with blue and white decoration. Soft-paste, *c.* 1770–90. Height $4\frac{1}{4}$ ins.

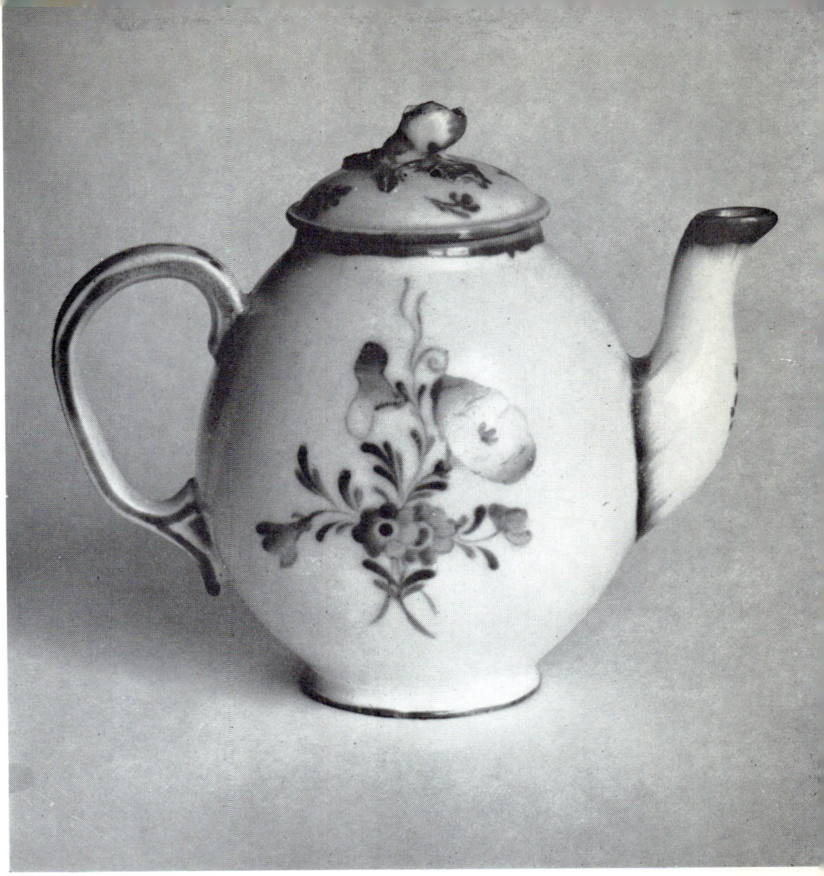

Both photographs from Le Musée des Arts Décoratifs, Paris

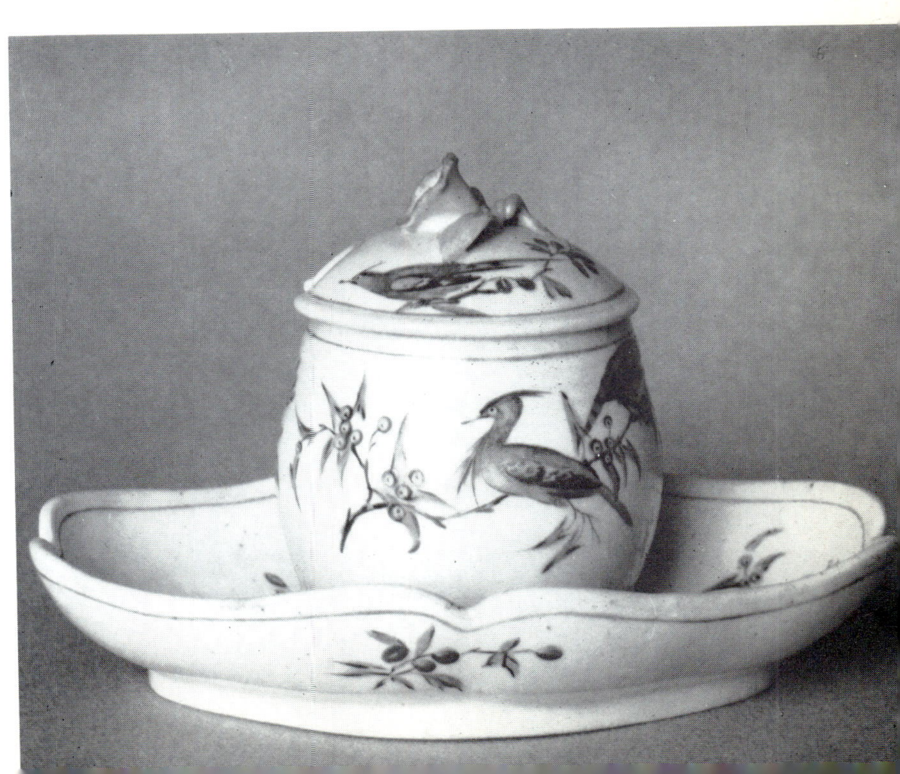

BOURG-LA-REINE
Mustard pot with polychrome decoration in soft-paste porcelain, *c.* 1779–1804. Height $4\frac{1}{2}$ ins. length $5\frac{3}{4}$ ins.

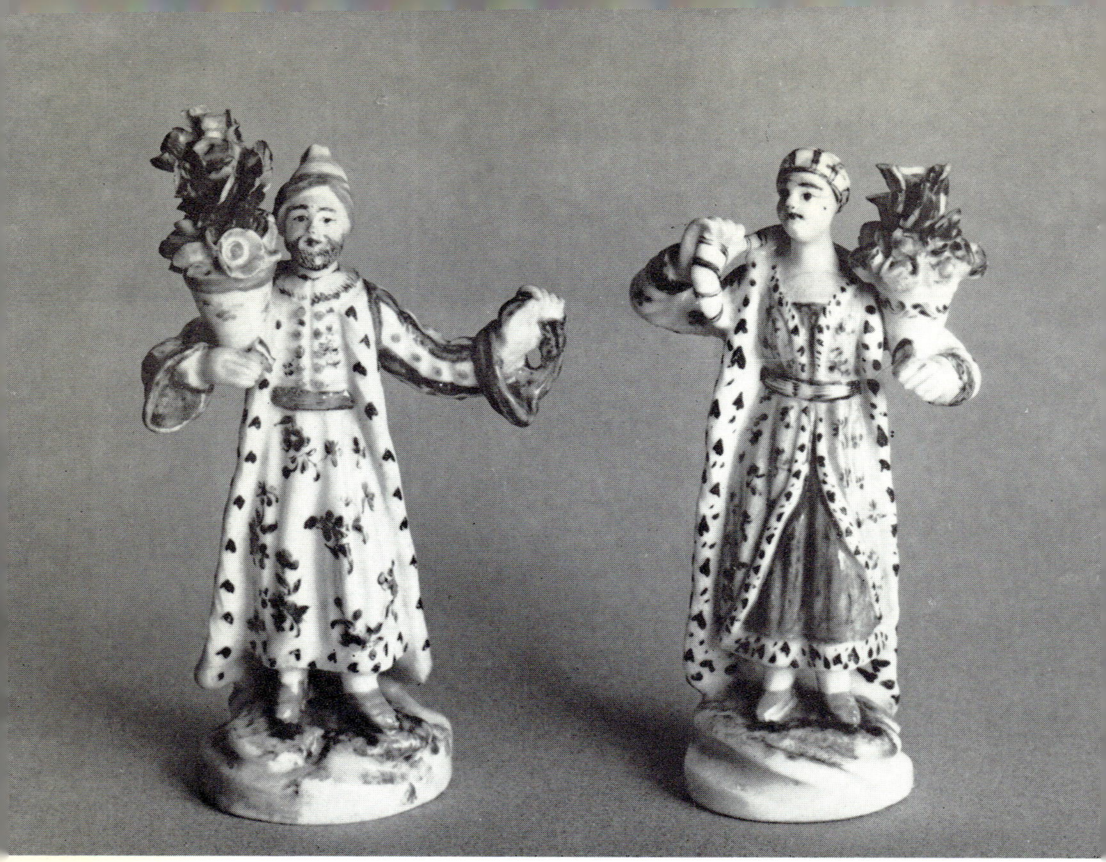

MENNECY— "Figurines de Persan et Persane" in soft-paste porcelain, eighteenth century. Length $1\frac{1}{2}$ ins., height 5 ins.

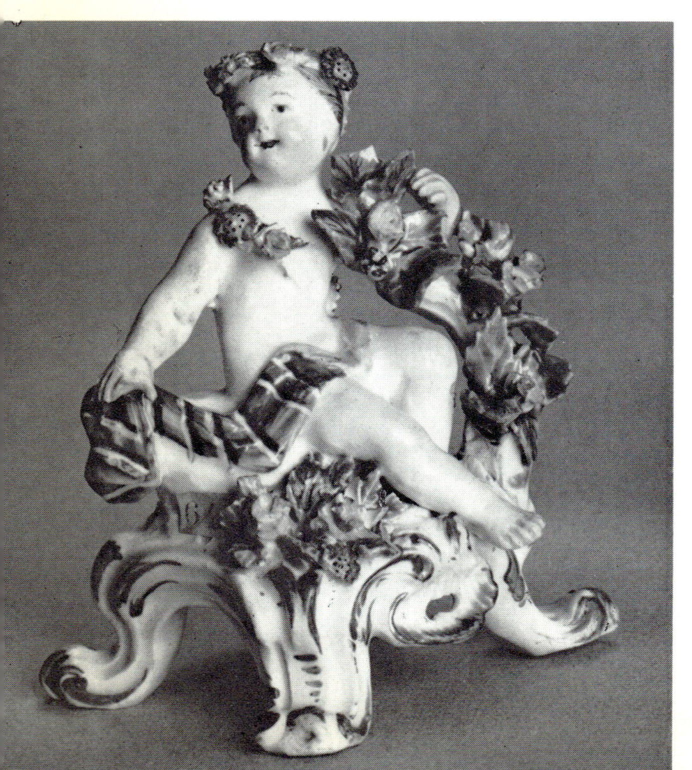

CREPY-EN-VALOIS
Cherub garlanded with flowers in soft-paste porcelain, eighteenth century. Height $4\frac{1}{2}$ ins.

Both photographs from Le Musée des Arts Décoratifs, Paris

DERBY CHARACTERISTICS

1. PLANCHÉ PERIOD 1750–1756

Soft Paste—heavy in weight, glassy glaze, creamy white by transmitted light. Strong modelling of figures—"dry edge". Duesbury colouring, but many pieces left undecorated.

2. "PALE COLOURING" PERIOD 1756–1760

Soft Paste—light in weight, greyish-white glaze. Blue-white by transmitted light. Dresden style figures in pale soft colours. Modelling stiff and lacking in vitality.

3. "PATCH" PERIOD 1760–1770

Very white soft paste with bluish glaze. Cloudy greenish yellow by transmitted light. Figures as "Pale Colouring" but larger. Three patch marks on base of figures.

4. CHELSEA-DERBY 1770–1784

Hybrid soft-paste, with thick clear glaze. Classical designs and patterns after Sèvres. Claret became brownish and mazarine blue became bright "Derby" blue.

5. DUESBURY DERBY 1770–1815

Bone China—beautifully finished with exquisite paintings. Sentimental figures and groups in biscuit. Factory mark now generally used.

6. BLOOR DERBY 1815–1848

Declining quality.

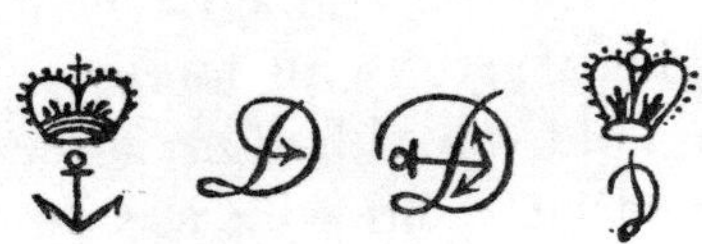

1769–1784, CHELSEA DERBY PERIOD.

1786–1796, PERIOD OF WILLIAM DUESBURY II, in puce, blue and sometimes in gold.

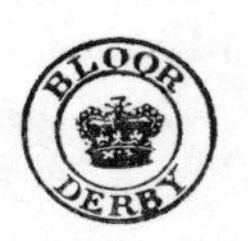

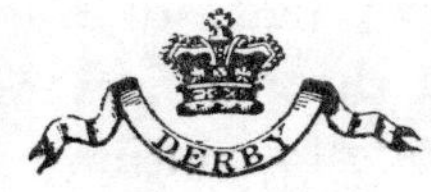

After about *1825*.

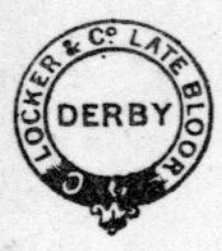

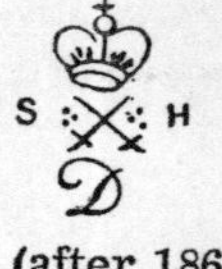

(after 1862)

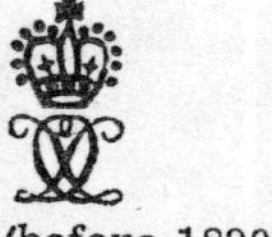

(before 1890)

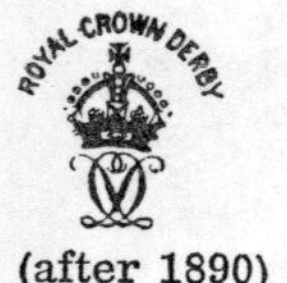

(after 1890)

Marks reproduced in facsimile by kind permission of THE ROYAL CROWN DERBY PORCELAIN CO. LTD.

[5] LONGTON HALL, NEAR NEWCASTLE-UNDER-LYME, STAFFORDSHIRE 1749–1760

A factory was started in an isolated Queen Anne country house (rented at £25 per annum) about 1749 by William Jenkinson who had "Obtained the Art, Secret or Mystery" in London, possibly at the short-lived Limehouse factory. In 1751 he took William Nicklin, a lawyer and William Littler (*c.*1724–1770), a saltglaze potter, into partnership but in 1753 he sold most of his shares to Nathaniel Firmin, a water gilder, and promised not to make porcelain nor to divulge the secrets of its manufacture, for the balance of the fourteen years left on the original agreement. Firmin died six months later and left his shares to his family.

William Littler was twenty-six years old when the first agreement was signed, and when he married later, his wife was employed in the factory at a guinea a week. They were both objured not to live away from Longton Hall without the consent of the other partners and to "employ the utmost application and diligence in the conduct, business and management of the factory".

The business would have failed in 1755, if a new partner Robert Charlesworth, lead mine owner, had not provided new capital. Five years later, he dissolved the partnership when he realised that it would be financial suicide to continue.

Confusing reports were made by early nineteenth-century writers on porcelain about the factory at Longton Hall, and many examples were wrongly attributed. Research begun by Sir Wollaston Franks in 1862 followed by others, culminated in the remarkable discoveries made by two doctors of medicine, Bernard Watney and Geoffrey Blake, who recently excavated on the site and categorically established the identity of Longton Hall.

1749–1753 FIRST PERIOD

The earliest pieces were made by artists still working in the pottery idiom and apparently unfamiliar with the new material. A series of figures were evolved, which have become known as the "Snowman" family. These were modelled with blurred details, usually uncoloured (although a few sparsely decorated specimens have survived) and buried in a thick, glistening glaze. They are not unlike, but not as fine as Planché's "dry edge" Derby figures and the "girl in the swing" series. Over thirty different models are known in this class, derived from Meissen, Chelsea and Chinese originals. Dr. Watney suggests in his book *Longton Hall* that the subjects which show a relative sophistication in spite of their primitive execution were probably suggested by Jenkinson, apparently an educated and cultured man.

Table wares in the fashionable blue and white of the period were executed in Littler's startling ultramarine ground colour, a deep underglaze blue tinged with indigo, violet or purple, derived from "zaffre" the Derbyshire cobalt, which was inferior to the expensive Swedish and Saxon varieties. Moulded and not thrown on the wheel, these show yellow on their bases and footrings, a characteristic noted by Dr. Pococke who wrote during his visit to the Potteries in 1750 that the potter from Limehouse could not bake his china "with coal, which turns it yellow, wood being the fuel which is proper for it".

A feeling for porcelain was soon developed, and polychrome enamel paintings of cabbage roses, birds and butterflies, the Oriental "quail" pattern and a free interpretation of Japanese designs followed.

During this period, the wares were unevenly glazed, free patches and pools of excess glaze were frequent on one piece. The undersides were typically glaze-free, and appear to have been wiped off before firing. A small conical hole was pierced in the base of figures, and "knife edge" stilt marks appeared on the base of useful wares, sometimes with fragments of fireclay embedded in them. Examples were thickly potted and heavy, and have a solid doughy appearance.

1754–1757 SECOND PERIOD

By 1754, the modelling had improved, and some fine, individual designs were created. "Curious parfume pots, vauses, figures and flowers" were produced in rococo form, in a glassy paste which appears opalescent green in transmitted light, covered in a sparkling glassy glaze, full of bubbles. Thickly potted and heavy, it is remarkably translucent and shows "moons" —irregularities in the paste due to air bubbles as in Chelsea. Littler's blue became greyer, and developed into a softer powder blue.

There were many technical faults in the potting, and it never reached the perfection of Chelsea or Meissen, but the faults only seem to enhance the appeal of this ingenuous porcelain.

The artists at Longton Hall seem to have been obsessed by the kitchen garden. A Harvest Festival must have inspired these realistic dishes and tureens, sauce-boats and platters that emerged in the shape of cauliflowers, cabbages and lettuces. Twigs served as handles and strawberries as finials, and skilfully modelled fruits and flowers were applied in reckless abundance. The models are exquisite and one can practically sense the enthusiasm of these provincial artists excelling with an indigenous subject, after their efforts at sophisticated work had not been as successful as their metropolitan competitors.

The painting improved considerably, and favourite subjects were romantic landscapes and harbour scenes, frequently with castles and churches. William Duesbury was employed as an enameller from 1754 to 1756 before he left for Derby.

This new and curious porcelain was advertised in the London

Public Advertiser in April 1757, "consisting of Tureens, Covers and Dishes, Large Cups, Covers, Jars and Beakers, with beautiful sprigs of Flowers, open-work'd Fruit Baskets and Plates, Variety of Services for Desserts, Tea and Coffee Equipages, Sauce Boats, leaf Basins and Plates, Melons, Colliflowers, elegant Epergnes and other ornamental and useful Porcelain, both white and enamelled".

1758–1760 THIRD PERIOD

Littler made a gallant effort to make Longton Hall profitable right up to the final sale in Salisbury on 20th September, 1760. He concentrated on table wares, expecially services in blue and white, rather than single pieces.

A London warehouse was opened in 1758 in St. Paul's Churchyard but due to competition from Bow and Chelsea it closed within the year.

Figure modelling, the quality of which had enhanced the reputation of the factory, was continued and new monumental forms of subjects and people of popular interest were developed.

Polychrome enamelled wares were painted less carefully apparently to get them out for sale as quickly as possible and shapes were simpler. Barrel-shaped teapots and tall cylindrical mugs were made in larger quantities and were decorated with signed transfers by Sadler in Liverpool. It was the practice of the printer Sadler to buy porcelain from "pot carriers" and "packmen" intermediaries who had bought from Staffordshire factories and apply his own decoration. It was earlier believed that the transfer-printed pieces were attributed to Liverpool but further research has defined that there were many which came from Longton Hall.

The subjects of the transfer pieces commemorated the heroes of the Seven Years War (1756–1763) and also depicted various coats of arms of societies and families.

The figure modellers continued with some fine work, particularly figures of horses such as one of a fine pair led by a Turk and a Blackamoor (after Meissen originals) and the magnificent Duke of Brunswick on his fettlesome mount trampling on French trophies. They also provided the Seasons, of which only Winter is known to have survived, but all were reproduced by Plymouth in hard-paste from the models, possibly held by an independent artist. The Four Continents made at Longton Hall were splendid and are considered to be amongst the finest works which emerged from the factory.

There was friction between Robert Charlesworth and William Littler in the final year, for Littler wished to continue for the full fourteen year term, but Charlesworth dissolved the partnership and his agents seized the stock and it was taken to Salisbury for the final sale. Salisbury was probably chosen because the London and Midland markets were already flooded with porcelain, and it was an important market town on the route used by the clay suppliers.

An exchange broker from London's Cheapside conducted the sale, which was advertised in *The Salisbury Journal*, 8th September, 1760:

> "upwards of ninety thousand Pieces of the greatest Variety of Dresden Patterns, in rich enamel'd pencil'd, Blues and Gold; as Figures and Flowers, mounted in Chandeliers, Essence Jars, Beakers, Vases, and Perfume Pots, magnificent Dessert Services; Sets of Bowls, Mugs, Dishes and Plates, ornamented with Columbines and Central Groups; Tea, Coffee and Toilet Equipages, of elegant Patterns, superbly furnish'd, equal to a National Factory, so eminently distinguish'd, with a profusion of useful and ornamental Articles."

William Littler's efforts in those ten strenuous years to emulate the porcelain of European State-aided factories was doomed to financial failure, but his originality and perseverance were none the less outstanding and a valuable addition to the development of English porcelain. He left Longton Hall saddened and disappointed, and is last recorded as opening a decorating establishment at West Pans near Musselburgh in Scotland, which enjoyed considerable success and several pieces by his hand, have now been identified.

LONGTON HALL CHARACTERISTICS

1. White, phosphatic soft-paste, glassy and frit similar to inferior Chelsea with "moons".
2. Paste. First Period, greenish-yellow to cloudy yellow by transmitted light. Second Period, opalescent green by transmitted light.
3. Heavy and translucent.
4. Glaze, pure glass, glittery colourless or greyish.
5. "Snowman" class, poorly defined modelling varying in quality. Not as crisp or fine as "dry-edge" Derby or "The Girl in a Swing". Glaze full of bubbles and glitters, thickly applied hiding details. Glaze uneven. Free patches and pools of glaze present on same figure. Undersides typically glaze-free, appear to have been wiped before firing. Small conical hole in base.
6. "Knife-edge" stilt marks on base of useful wares, sometimes fragments of fireclay embedded in them. Thickly potted and heavy, thick doughy appearance. Unfired enamel colours and gilding have not survived so examples seen unfinished.
7. Typical colours, pale yellow-green, pinks, strong red, yellow and strong dark blue and crude crimson.
8. Little gilding of poor quality.
9. Factory mark, crossed LLs with dots.

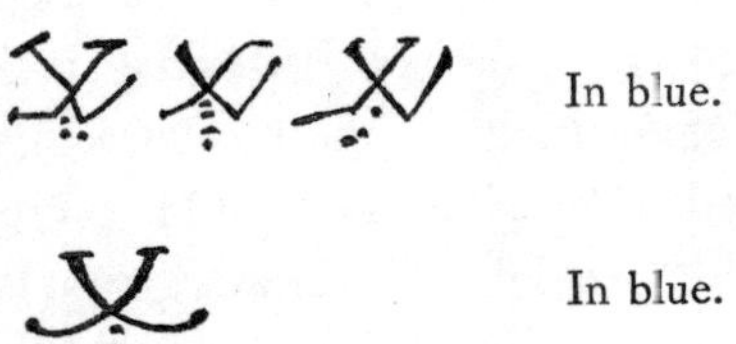

In blue.

In blue.

[6] WORCESTER 1751–Present Day

The use of soaprock (or soapstone) as a porcelain ingredient instead of kaolin was originated by the Chinese for a special class of fine grain porcelain. Père d'Entrecolles, in a letter dated

25th January, 1722, described the stone called *Hoa ché* and suggested that it might be found in Europe. He also noted that the *Hoa ché* could be used for medicinal purposes. Some time later steatites were discovered at The Lizard in Cornwall by Dr. J. Woodward, who apparently believed that he had found the English *Hoa ché*. He described his findings and reported that some experimental fine grain porcelain had been made from it successfully, and it could even be used for medicinal purposes in the manufacture of Epsom Salts.

The first commercial English steatic paste may have been made at the Limehouse factory, 1747–1748, but as no specimens have yet been identified it cannot be proved. Benjamin Lund obtained a licence to dig for soaprock in Cornwall in 1748 and started a steatitic porcelain factory in Bristol. Dr. Richard Pococke, later Bishop of Meath, in his *Travels through England* reported that the Bristol factory had been founded by "one of the principal manufacturers at Limehouse which failed". Lund's factory was in a glass works previously owned by William Lowdin, frequently known as Lowdin's Glasshouse, at Redcliffe Backs on a site which is now part of Bristol Docks. Dr. Pococke referred to this factory, "They make very beautiful white sauce boats, adorned with reliefs of festoons, which sell for sixteen shillings a pair".

In his History of The Worcester Factory R. W. Binns (*A Century of Pottery in the City of Worcester*) recounted that Worcester at that time was a Tory stronghold and Whig politicians decided that, after the loss of the cloth trade, a new industry in the town would entail more votes for their Party. Their disastrous failure in the 1747 Election caused them to re-double their efforts and by 1751 the Worcester Porcelain Company was founded. Two of the shareholders, Dr. John Wall (1708–1776) and the chemist William Davis were entrusted with the purchase of the Bristol process from Lund and his associates and the subsequent removal of moulds and equipment to Worcester. One of the associates, Robert Podmore, piqued that he was not offered shares in the new company, sold the soaprock secret to Richard Chaffers of Liverpool despite the fact that he had already been paid by Worcester. Because of recent discoveries, new periods have been suggested by Henry Sandon, Curator of the Dyson Perrins Museum.

1751–1776 DR WALL PERIOD

Dr. Wall studied medicine at Oxford and St. Thomas's Hospital, London. He was a successful practitioner, an excellent chemist and an artist of great ability. The shareholders included a goldsmith and the editor of *The Gentleman's Magazine*, also the potters Josiah and Richard Holdship who were partners at Worcester from 1751–1759. A fine old country mansion, Warmstry House, on the banks of the River Severn, was leased in Richard Holdship's name.

The first Worcester productions were supervised by Lund and porcelain decorated in *grand feu* underglaze blue was made in the Chinese Nankin style, similar to that which had been made at Bristol, and it is now difficult to distinguish between Lund's Bristol and early Worcester press moulded pieces. It is now considered that only pieces marked with "Bristol" in relief can be considered true examples of Lund's Bristol. This experimental period lasted until 1755 when the painting improved considerably, and by 1760 the potting shapes, patterns and designs had become standardized. The uniform high quality was now established and meticulously maintained throughout the first period. The finest English blue and white porcelain was made at that time at Worcester, and although the designs were copied by other factories their products always fell short of the Worcester quality.

In 1757 Robert Hancock, the engraver, joined the company from Bow, where he had worked since he left Battersea in 1756. The revolutionary process of transfer printing had been discovered in Birmingham to print on enamels no later than 1751. This process was also developed by John Sadler and Guy Green in Liverpool and at the enamelling factory at Battersea. Horace Walpole, writing to Richard Bentley in September 1755, said, "I send you a trifling snuff-box only as a sample of the new manufacture at Battersea, which is done with copper plates". At Worcester, under Hancock, it was brought to exquisite perfection and large quantities of porcelain were decorated in this manner.

Robert Hancock was responsible for many fine engravings, including the one on the famous tankard representing Frederick of Prussia. Richard Holdship, then head of the printing department, placed his mark, an anchor (a rebus on his name), on the productions of his department, thereby taking credit for the accomplishment of his subordinates. Jewitt reported the following exchange. A couplet appeared in Cave's *Gentleman's Magazine* for December 1757, with references to the portrait of Frederick the Great engraved by Hancock on the tankard just mentioned:

> "What praise is thine ingenious Holdship, who
> On the fair porcelain a portrait drew?"

The two lines were repeated in *The Worcester Journal* in January 1758, with the addition:

> "Hancock, my friend, don't grieve tho' Holdship has the praise,
> 'Tis yours to execute, 'tis his to wear the bays."

Animosity grew between the two men and ultimately led to Holdship's resignation from the company in 1759. He made a deal with Duesbury to sell the secret process of steatitic porcelain and transfer printing for the sum of "one hundred pounds of lawful British money" and for an annuity of £30 a year. Holdship appears to have arrived in Derby about 1764.

The successful manufacture of porcelain at Worcester was noted in the following extract from a correspondent in the *Annual Register* of 1763, "I have seen potteries in all the manufactories in Europe. Those of Dresden, and Chantilly in France, are well known for their elegance and beauty; with these I may class our own of Chelsea, which is scarce inferior to any of the others; but these are calculated rather for ornament than for use, and if they were equally useful with Oriental china, they could yet be used by few because they are sold at high prices. We have indeed many other manufacturers of porcelain, which are sold at a cheaper rate than any that is imported, but *except the Worcester*, they all wear brown, are subject to crack, especially the glazing, by boiling water".

After a reshuffle of ownership, Robert Hancock bought a sixth share in Worcester in 1769, but there were many disagreements and he finally left the factory in 1774 when he was paid £900 for his share. From Worcester he went to Caughley, and without producing anything new there, he turned to book illustration and his association with porcelain was ended.

The first transfer process consisted of engraved copper plates from which an inked impression was taken on fine paper and transferred on to the china. The clarity and sharpness of the results obtained were truly remarkable. Sometimes these transfers were retouched by hand, and between 1763 and 1770 James Giles, the London decorator, bought large quantities of transferred porcelain which he filled in with enamel colours and added gilding. Bat printing was invented in about 1815 and was a different and much cheaper process. The copper plate was oiled and the impression of the plate taken on a film of gelatine which was applied to china. When this was removed, a fine dusting of powdered colour was applied and adhered to the oiled design. The piece was then re-fired and the colour burned into the glaze. The effect is the same as transfer printing, but the outlines are inclined to be woolly. We are indebted to these mechanical processes of decoration for the enchanting scenes of contemporary life which were applied to table wares.

In 1768 many workmen arrived from the discontinued Chelsea works, with their fresh ideas and new techniques. New colours imported into the Worcester palette included dark blue, apple green, turquoise, yellow and claret. The rococo style crept into the Worcester shapes in a very modified form, and paintings of flowers and gilding were used together with subjects after Watteau, Boucher and Gainsborough, and charming *chinoiseries* after Pillement. A vogue for Meissen designs was also adopted and the fish scale pattern was introduced. Vases with ground colours in this scale pattern with reserves left blank were supplied to the workshop of James Giles for decoration, which frequently inserted the exquisite exotic birds for which Worcester is particularly renowned.

In 1776 Dr. Wall died and the influence of his good taste

was greatly missed, and when William Davis died in 1783 the remaining shareholders decided to sell.

DAVIS-FLIGHT PERIOD 1776–1793

Thomas Flight, the London agent for the Worcester Porcelain Company at their warehouse at 2 Bread Street, bought out the shareholders at Worcester for the benefit of his sons, Joseph and John. The transaction has been recorded by R. W. Binns in *A Century of Potting in the City of Worcester*, "The trade at this time, although not carried on with much spirit, doubtless yielded a reasonable profit, and only required the energy and experience of business-like men to ensure the continued production of works of equal merit with those which had already made the factory famous.

"In 1783, Mr. Vernon was either seventy or seventy-one years of age; Mr. Davis, Senior, could not have been much younger; and Mr. Davis, Junior, being the only active partner, it was resolved to dispose of the concern.

"Mr. Flight, having acted for so many years as London agent, was quite aware of the capabilities, the profits, and the high standing of the manufactory; and requiring occupations for his sons, Joseph and John, considered this a favourable opportunity to settle them in an important and lucrative establishment. We may be well assured that had not the business been profitable and well conducted, he would not have invested £3,000 in the purchase.

"The terms agreed upon were as follows: £500 to be paid on signing the transfer, £1,000 on or before July 24th, and £1,500 on March 25th, 1784.

"Mr. Flight took possession at Michaelmas, 1783 . . . . Messrs, Flight, Juniors, had no previous knowledge of the art (of porcelain making), having, we believe, been jewellers."

A new body and a new glaze were introduced and many difficulties were caused. King George III, Queen Charlotte and the Princesses paid a formal visit to the factory in 1788 and were so impressed that the King requested that the prefix Royal should be added to the name of the company. He also advised that a London showroom should be opened for the purpose of expansion, and the Royal Worcester Porcelain Company opened its showroom at No. 1 Coventry Street, London, W.1. The Royal crown was added to the china marks and the porcelain became very fashionable.

Changes of ownership took place, due to the death of the partners: 1793 Joseph Flight and Martin Barr (Flight and Barr); 1807 Martin Barr, Joseph Flight and Martin Barr, Junior (Barr, Flight and Barr); 1813 Joseph Flight, Martin Barr, Junior and George Barr (Flight, Barr and Barr); 1829 Martin Barr, Junior and George Barr (Barr and Barr). The factory mark at this time was the impressed initials of the proprietors surmounted by a crown.

During the "Flight" period the body assumed a greyish hue. There was some repetition of earlier styles and patterns, particularly *Imari*, but the colouring was brighter and the gilding was of the mercuric variety which, although of fine quality, was brash and cold compared with the earlier honey gold. Later, a whiter body was introduced which resembled that used at Derby. Fluted shapes were frequently used, and large quantities of tea wares were produced in dark blue and gold with small sprigs of flowers, of which examples are frequently found in modest antique shops. The neo-classical style was adopted, and vases and large services were made. Flowers were painted in the manner of Derby, and Thomas Baxter, who later went to Swansea, was responsible for the feathers and shells and topographical landscapes.

Robert Chamberlain an employee of the Worcester Porcelain Company since his apprenticeship, started business for himself in 1786. He bought his porcelain in the white from Caughley for decoration, as the Worcester factory probably would not supply him. He was soon making his own porcelain and was responsible for many services decorated in ground colours, flowers and armorial devices. The business was usually in financial difficulties, resulting in many changes of ownership, until 1840 when it was absorbed by Flight, Barr and Barr, who moved from Warmstry into Chamberlain's premises at Diglis. Yet a third factory was founded in Worcester in 1800 by Thomas Grainger, nephew of Humphrey Chamberlain, and the company was called Grainger, Lee and Company. Productions were not as good as those of the other two factories, and in style and taste were representative of the general decline in nineteenth century art.

1847–PRESENT DAY

The factory was carried on in the tradition of Chamberlain and Company. After some changes in proprietorship within the Chamberlain family and their partners, Mr. W. H. Kerr joined the concern in 1850, and then in January 1852 Chamberlain retired and Mr. R. W. Binns entered into partnership with Mr. Kerr and the firm was carried on under the style of Kerr and Binns, and W. H. Kerr and Company. The Works were considerably rebuilt and expanded. In 1888 Grainger was taken over by the main Worcester company, and the factory became the basis of the modern Royal Worcester Porcelain Company.

One of the few eighteenth century English porcelain factories to survive, Worcester has always been prudently managed, and paid its way. The early steatitic paste was reliable, producing few wasters, and the high standard of neat conservative designs, which did not follow extremes of fashion, were always in demand.

The present company continues the policies of the past, and fine porcelain and earthenware in old and new designs are being commercially produced with great success. The fine museum at the factory is open to the public and is well worth a visit.

WORCESTER CHARACTERISTICS

1. Paste. First Period, soft soapstone paste. Many changes in formula from 1770. Between 1783 and 1805 paste thin and of medium translucency. Biscuit made from 1840. Any hard-paste with Worcester decoration was imported from China in the white.
2. Glaze. First Period, glaze often greyish or bluish to counter the yellowish body. Thin, recedes from foot rings and is never crazed.

3. Early pieces thick, heavy and irregular in shape. Later pieces finely and neatly potted.
4. Decoration. First Period, very fine brushwork in underglaze blue, sometimes blurred. Later painting and gilding of fine quality. Very English.
5. Transfer printing in black on the earliest works; later in black, brown, lilac and red, sometimes covered with translucent enamel.
6. Lids well fitting, slightly overlapping or flush.
7. Colours, dark blue, turquoise, lavender, royal blue, sky blue, powder blue, pea green, grey green, sea green, purple, scarlet.
8. Gilding. First Period, honey gilding applied with great delicacy. Second Period, mercuric gilding still well applied.
9. The variety of products made is enormous, tea and chocolate cups, vases, dishes, plates, etc., but very few figures.
10. Factory marks various, perhaps the best known is the blue crescent, open when painted, cross-hatched when transferred. Also 1–9 Chinese style numerals previously thought to have been Caughley.

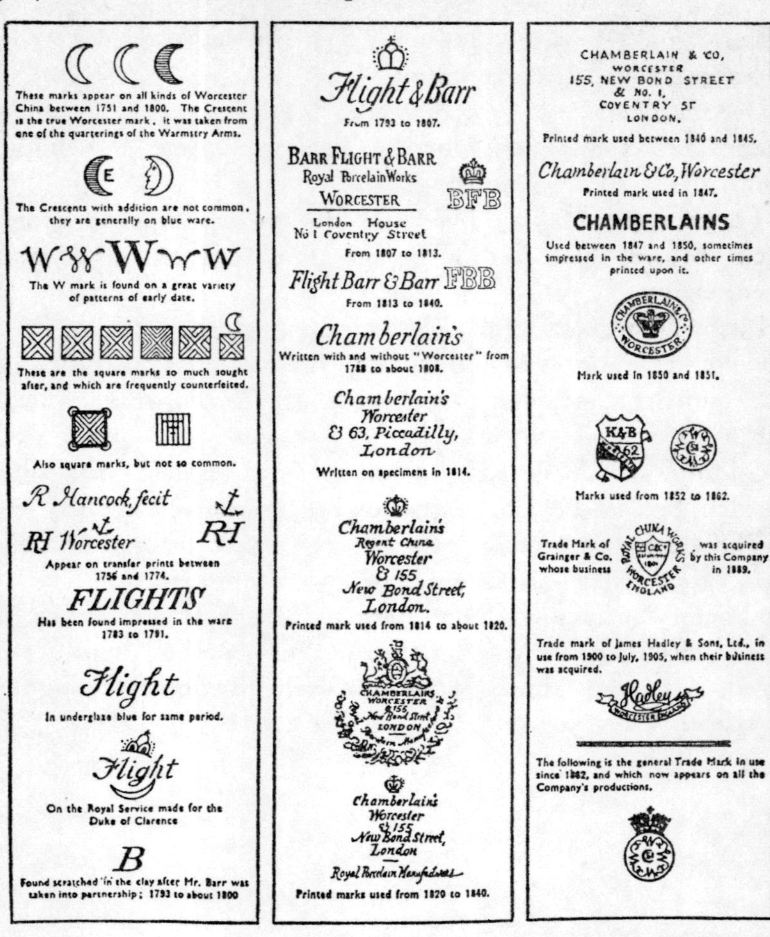

Marks reproduced in fascimile by kind permission of THE ROYAL WORCESTER PORCELAIN CO. LTD.

[7] LIVERPOOL (? 1754–1800)

Apart from bricks, clay pipes and crude drinking vessels, there was no ceramic tradition in Liverpool until the middle of the 18th century. Suddenly, with the aid of potters from other areas, about twenty pot banks were established within a few years, of which nine or ten are believed to have made porcelain. A large quantity of porcelain has been attributed to Liverpool

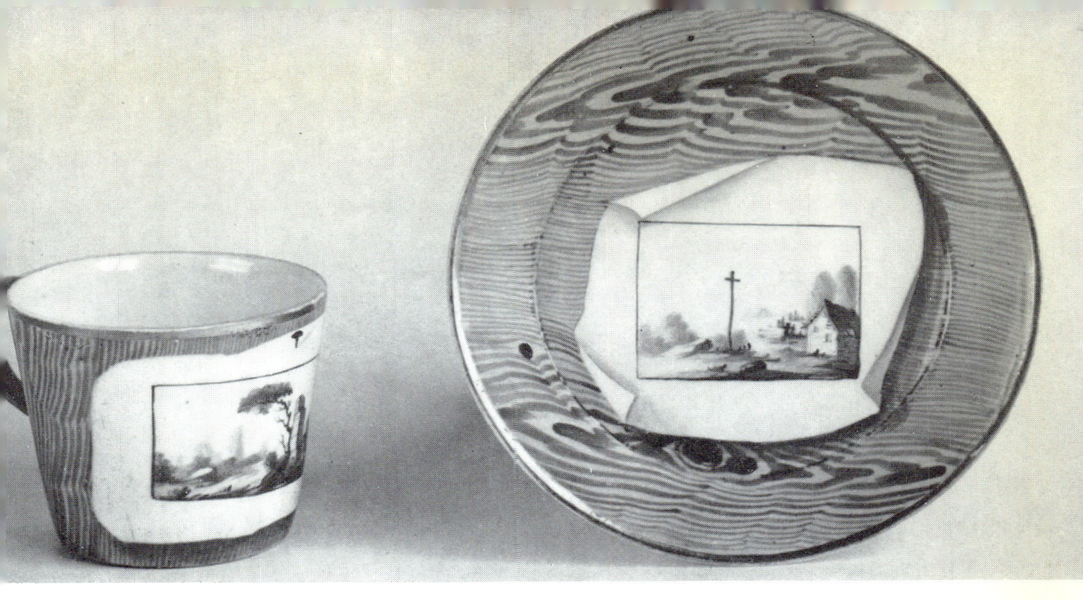

NIDERVILLER. Cup and saucer with *faux bois* decoration and landscape in carmine *en camaieu*, c. 1770. Height 2 ins., diameter $4\frac{1}{4}$ ins.

Musée des Arts Décoratifs, Paris

STRASBOURG. Oval dish in hard-paste porcelain by Joseph Hannong, decorated with polychrome bouquets. Marked in blue on reverse: HVL S 27. c. 1765 $10\frac{3}{8}$ ins. by $9\frac{5}{8}$ ins.

Musée des Arts Décoratifs, Paris

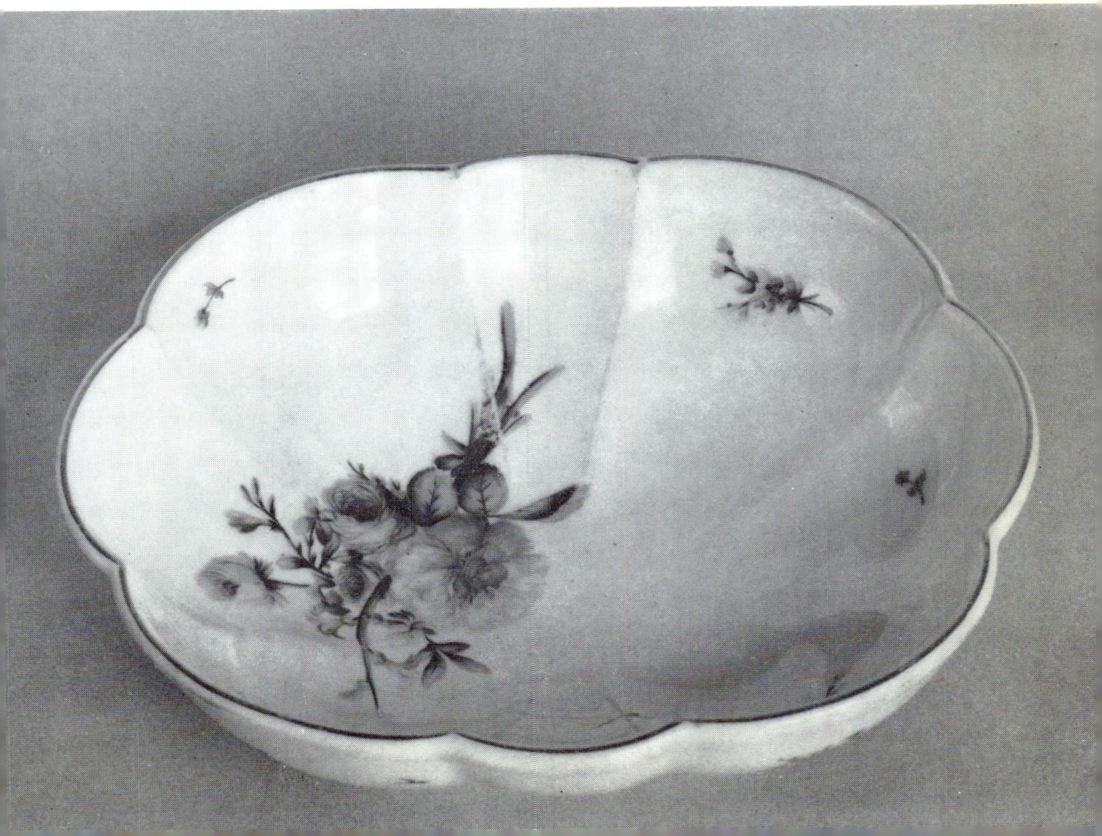

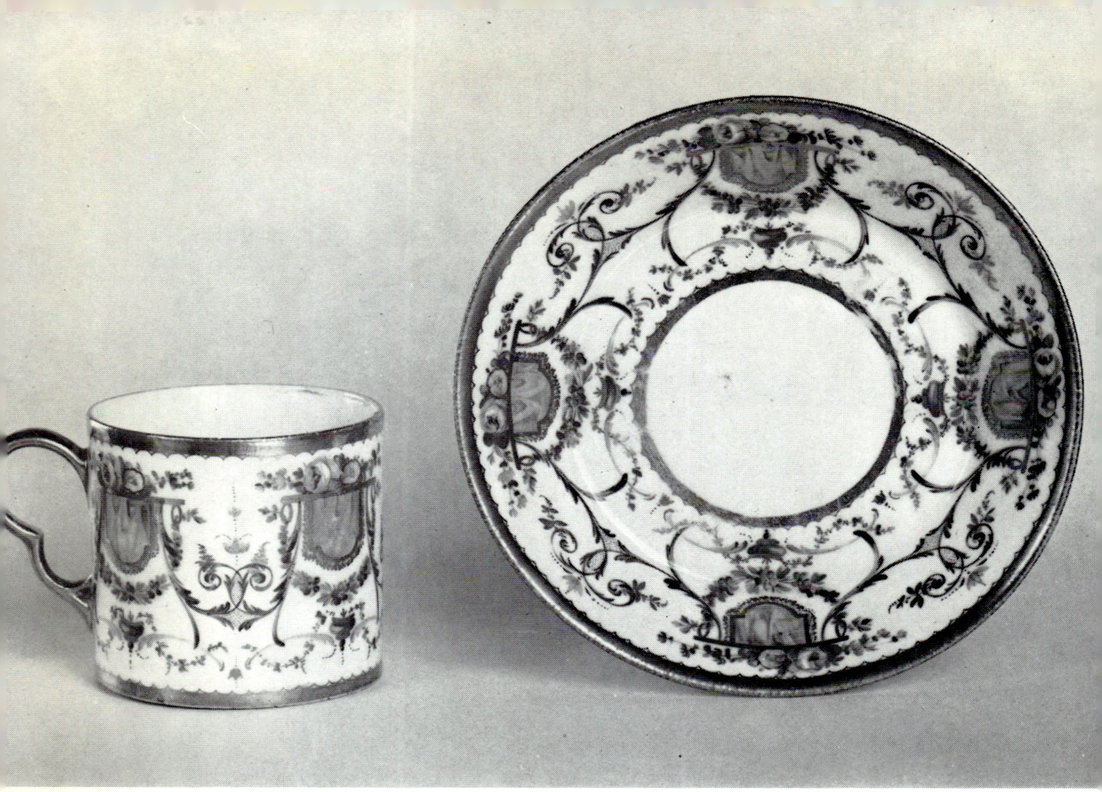

CLIGNANCOURT. Cup and saucer decorated with polychrome lambrequins, *c.* 1780. Marked in red: crowned M and L.S.X. interlaced. Height $2\frac{3}{4}$ ins.

Musée des Arts Décoratifs, Paris

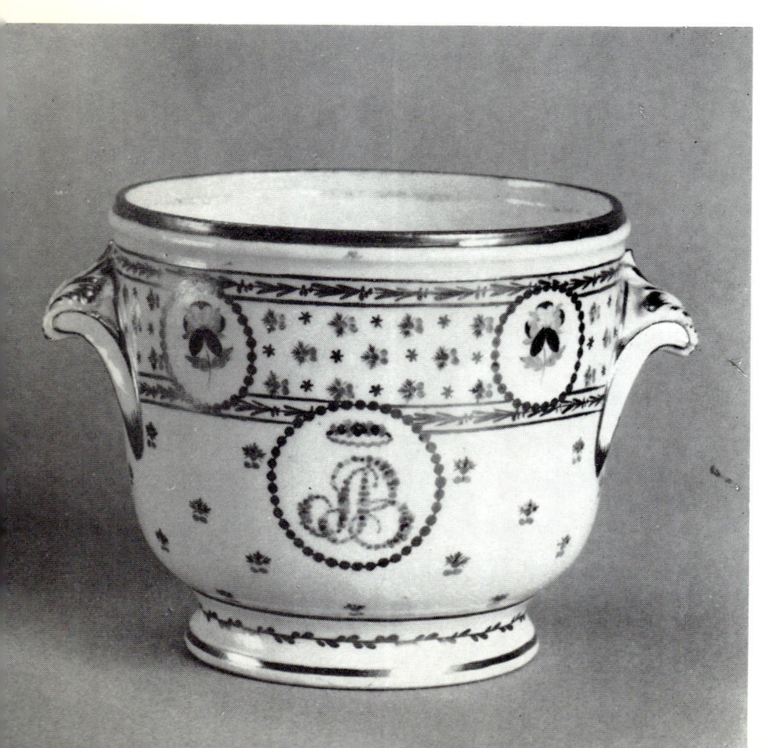

RUE THIROUX

Raffraichissoir.

Porcelain, *dite à la Reine.*

Mark: a crowned A.

Made by Le Boeuf, *c.* 1778–91. Height $4\frac{1}{4}$ ins.

Musée des Arts Décoratifs, Paris

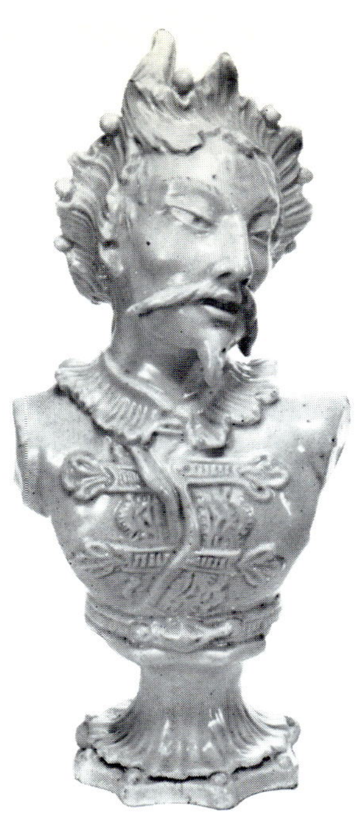

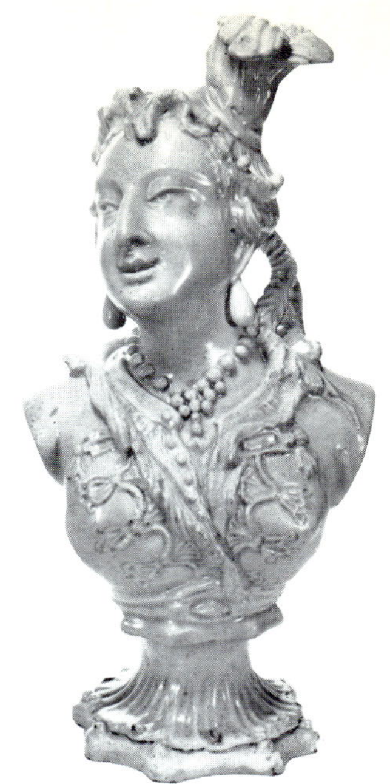

BOW. A pair of white busts of Mongolians, both flamboyantly modelled. Height 10½ ins.

Sotheby & Co.

BOW

A grotto group moulded in the form of a sportsman and his companion. They have puce hats and richly brocaded clothes. High scroll base picked out in green, puce and gilding. Height 8½ ins.

Sotheby & Co.

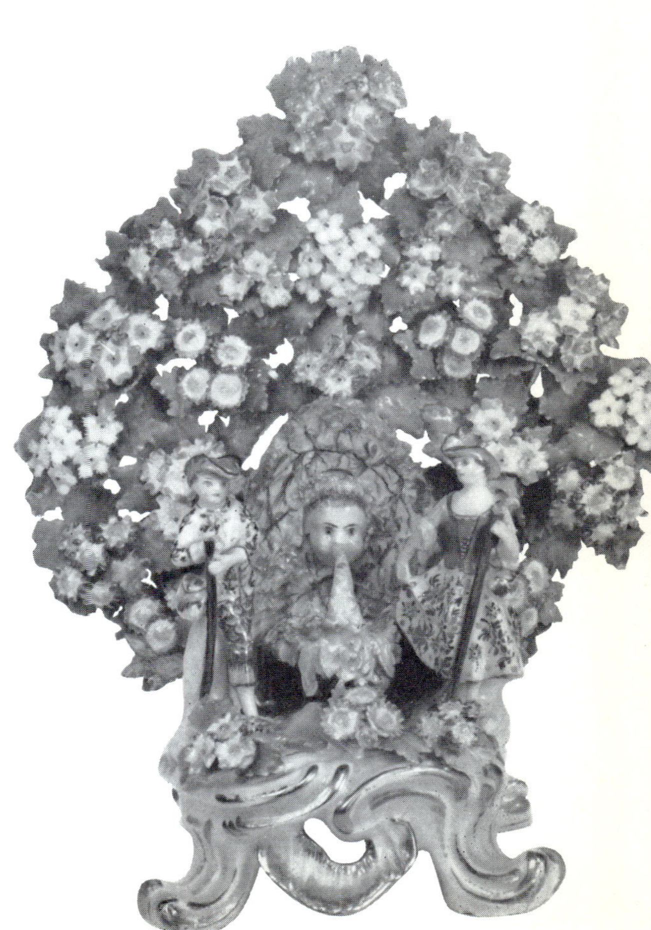

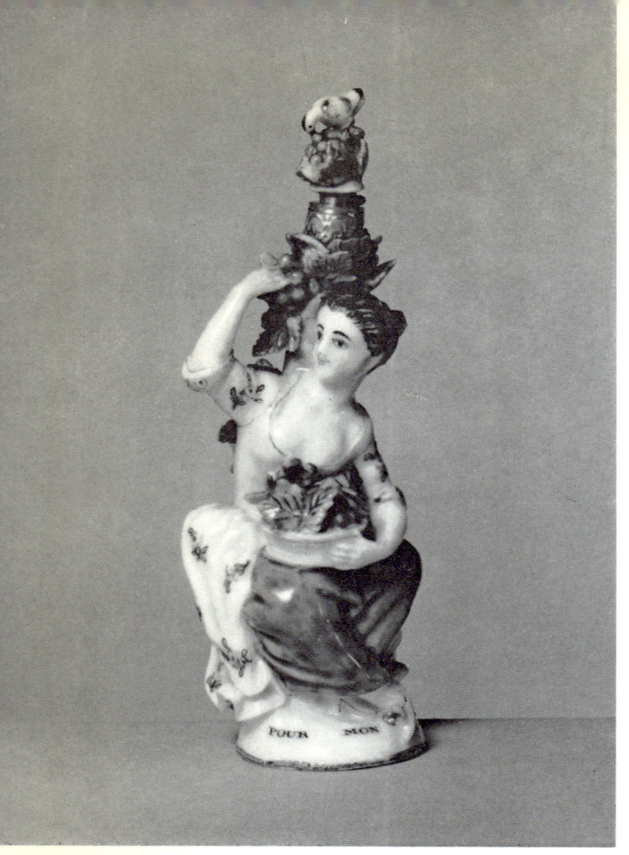

CHELSEA (GIRL-IN-THE-SWING) Scent Bottle enamelled in colours and gilt. Height $3\frac{1}{2}$ ins.

Victoria and Albert Museum

DERBY. Derby 'patchmark family', *c.* 1765.

Once in the author's collection

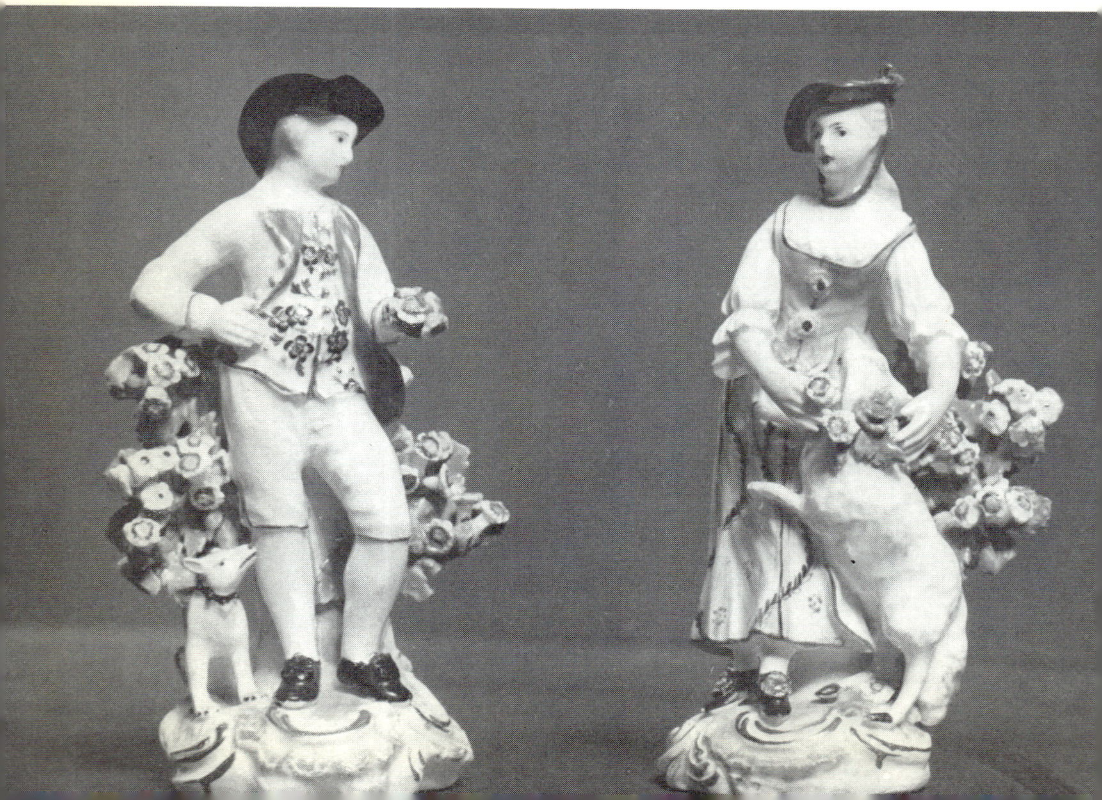

because it could not have been made anywhere else, and in spite of much scholarly research, there is still very little information available.

Dr. Watney has separated Liverpool into groups by spectrographic analysis. Grouping by visual examination is therefore proved by the chemical content of the wares.

In the central and commanding position then known as Shaw's Brow, now William Brown Street, and occupied by the Liverpool Museum, Library and Picture Galleries, a group of potteries came into being.

CHAFFERS AND CHRISTIAN (? 1754–1765)

The first to make porcelain on Shaw's Brow was Richard Chaffers (1731–1765) and Company who had been tenants since 1747. It is generally believed that at first they made phosphatic porcelain until in 1755 Robert Podmore illicitly sold them the Worcester formula for steatitic porcelain. In the agreement he signed with them he agreed to impart the methods "of making earthenware in imitation of or to resemble china ware".

Chaffer's journey to Cornwall in search of soapstone has been recounted by many writers from the original account of his grandson, John Rosson, but seems to me from this distance in time, to be so heroic, that it is worthy of repetition.

There were no roads, no public transport and no facilities. Chaffers left Liverpool on horseback, his change of linen in his saddlebags, 1,000 guineas in his purse and a pair of pistols at his waist. After a hazardous journey he arrived at his destination and hired men to dig for soapstone. Abundant supplies were located at Predannack, near Mullion and the mines were taken on a lease, which was subsequently renewed, and ultimately sold to Worcester in 1776 for £500. Chaffers left Cornwall in July 1756 and the first shipment arrived in Liverpool at the end of November.

On the 10th December 1756 the first advertisement appeared in Williamson's Liverpool Advertiser and Mercantile Register:

"Chaffers & Co., China Manufacturer. The porcelain or china ware made by Messrs. Richard Chaffers and Co., is sold nowhere in the town, but at the manufactory on Shaw's Brow. Considerable abatement for exportation, and to all wholesale dealers. N.B. All the ware is proved with boiling water before it is exposed for sale."

The proximity of the advertisement to the arrival of the soapstone suggests that sufficient steatitic porcelain could not have been finished in time and generally proves the theory that a quantity in phosphatic paste had already been manufactured.

It is also interesting to note that the main selling feature in the advertisement, "proved with boiling water" was borrowed from Worcester.

Worcester type blue and white porcelain followed, with neat potting and shapes, but the painting was inclined to be hasty and primitive. Curious Chinese style combinations of squat pagodas, bridges on thin stilts, triangular fir trees with birds flying straight upwards in "V" formation were usual, and the whole scene was generally peppered with dots. A copy of the Bow "Jumping Boy" pattern was produced.

The footrings were generally undercut and rounded—differing from Worcester's triangular section, and frequently had a glaze-free ring on the inside. Plates are rare, but are usually octagonal, and some of the best tea and coffee services have six straight sides. There was no Liverpool factory mark, but some pieces were marked with numerals as at Lowestoft. When Chaffers and Podmore died in 1765 "of the same fever" the factory was continued by Christian and Chaffer's widow until 1769 when he bought her out for £1,200.

PHILIP CHRISTIAN (1765–1776)

Christian's porcelain had a few characteristics which distinguished it from that of Chaffers'. The blue decoration was less intense and the slightly blued glaze was generally uniform. Designs attributed to this period are the "Biting snake" handle, the comma-shaped tag handle and the palm column and leaf moulded teapots. Jugs with a moulded mask on the lips were introduced, which depicted a youthful, courageous face, quite different from the face of an old man on Worcester jugs and that of a cynic on those of Caughley. He continued production until 1776 when he sold his soaprock rights in Cornwall and moved to Folly Lane with his son, to trade as merchants.

PENNINGTON AND PART (1769–1799)

In 1785 premises at Shaw's Brow were taken by Seth Pennington and John Part, who, having reverted to the manufacture of bone-ash porcelain, had been in production since 1769 elsewhere. John Sadler noted "Pennington's Body" in his notebook for March 1769. The "Biting Snake" and the comma-shaped tag handles, and the Christian teapot designs were continued and elaborate silver shape handles were frequently used on cups and cream jugs. A number of fine bowls and jugs painted with ships (most of which were Slavers), and a considerable number of transfer-printed pieces have been attributed to this factory. There were also some unusual duck-shaped tureens based on pottery counterparts.

The general standard of design, workmanship and finish were inferior to Christian, the glaze was thick and pitted and formed darkish blue pools in corners. In 1799, the Pottery was auctioned and the Pennington-Part partnership ended, although Pennington continued to make porcelain with a partner named Edwards until 1805 and then alone.

SAMUEL GILBODY (? 1754–1761)

Gilbody took over a pot works next door to Chaffers on Shaw's Brow when his father died, and advertised "wholesale and retail at the lowest prices, china ware of all sorts, equal to service and beauty to any made in England". He became bankrupt in 1760 and the following year "the large pot-house situate on Shaw's Brow taken in possession of Samuel Gilbody, a bankrupt, also chinaware belonging to the assignees of the said Gilbody" was advertised for sale on July 3rd, 1761 in *The Liverpool Advertiser*.

Gilbody made phosphatic porcelain which was either decorated with transfers, painted in underglaze blue with a distinctive overglaze or enamelled in iron red and gilded. Some of the designs follow Chaffer's work which was understandable as they were neighbours. He is now known to have made figures similar in style to Derby "pale-colour" family type.

REID & COMPANY (? 1755–1761)

A distinctive group of porcelain has been attributed to this small, short-lived firm, who finished their wares with a glaze containing tin, similar to that used on Delft. They made both phosphatic and steatitic bodies which are difficult to tell apart for the opaque glaze is identical on both. There is a similarity in style of decoration on the steatitic paste to Lund's Bristol and Dr. Watney wrote: "In fact, it is debatable whether this group was made at Limehouse, Bristol or Liverpool. However, the enamelled examples have a bold, rather amateur style of decoration which is fully in keeping with a Liverpool tradition." (*English Blue and White Porcelain.*)

WILLIAM BALL (? 1755–1769)

An important collection of porcelain of the steatitic group—with a slight trace of bone-ash has been attributed to this factory.

An unusual cobalt blue, exceptionally bright and covered with a very shiny soft glaze, distinguishes the blue and white wares of this factory. The blue looks as if it has just been freshly painted, and most writers refer to it as "sticky blue".

There is a resemblance to both Bow and Longton Hall in the style of potting and decoration, and a large variety of objects were made. Blue and white with iron-red and gilt transfers overpainted with enamels, and polychrome enamels were all used with distinction.

THOMAS WOLFE & CO. (1795–1800)

A small quantity of hybrid porcelain was made by Thomas Wolfe and his partners in the Folly Lane factory that had belonged to Pennington.

SADLER & GREEN

The art of transfer printing from copper plates was first invented in Birmingham in 1751. John Sadler is said to have invented or borrowed the idea in 1752. An engraver, he gave his spoiled impressions from the plates to the children playing outside his house, who stuck them on pieces of broken pottery. This romantic story is given by Jewitt (*The Ceramic Art of Great Britain*) as the origin of Sadler's idea to print earthenware commercially. Together with his partner, Guy Green, on the 27th July, 1756, he printed 1,200 earthenware tiles of different patterns in six hours in front of a group of witnesses who included Samuel Gilbody the potter.

Sadler and Green became the printers for many pot banks, and could have prevented the failure of so many Liverpool factories with his cheap and effective designs had not Wedgwood, who packed his Queen's Ware "in waggons and carts and even in the panniers of pack horses" before the canals opened, practically monopolised their production.

LIVERPOOL CHARACTERISTICS

1. Steatitic or Phosphatic Paste.
2. Glaze bluish with bubbles.
3. Rather heavy and opaque.
4. Shapes and designs reminiscent of other English factories.
5. Primitive painting—Delft style.
6. Bright "sticky" blue. (William Ball)
7. Sometimes tin-glazes. (Reid & Company)

[8] LOWESTOFT, Suffolk 1757–1803

We are indebted to the Gillingwaters, two erstwhile hairdressers from the High Street, Lowestoft, for the first historical evidence of the beginnings of the Lowestoft porcelain works. *An Historical Account of the Ancient Town of Lowestoft* dated 1790, by Edmund Gillingwater, records that the discovery of suitable clay led to experiments in London, possibly at Bow, culminating in the opening of a small factory in a property bought in Bell Lane (now Crown Street) by four Lowestoft men: Walker, Browne, Aldred and Rickman.

The county of Suffolk, conveniently situated geographically for the trip across the North Sea to Holland, had been for centuries a natural trading post for Dutch goods.

Delft and Chinese porcelain from Holland passed through Yarmouth and there was a Delft-ware industry, probably with Dutch potters at one time in Norwich.

With the local discovery of china clay, a porcelain industry developed, but it was unlike all its contemporaries. Whilst Chelsea, Worcester and the rest pandered to the elegant and fashionable, Lowestoft in its rugged provincialism fulfilled the requirements of a less demanding middle-class public. The surprisingly well-made objects, with their imperfect decorations boldly drawn and painted by untutored women and children, have a charm which is particularly appealing in these days of technical perfection. The individuality of these robust objects, with their local names and simple homilies have endeared them to many discriminating collectors, whereas in their time, they were probably sold in the village shop or direct from the factory to the local worthies whose simple pastoral taste these articles exemplified.

The small factory opened by Robert Browne (*c.* 1725–1771) and partners produced a phosphatic paste porcelain suspiciously similar to Bow in 1757 which lends conviction to the family legend recounted by Jewitt in *The Ceramic Art of Great Britain.*

Apparently Robert Browne, the most active partner, took a job as a labourer at the Bow works. He bribed a warehouseman to lock him into the mixing room, where he hid in an empty barrel while the principals assembled the secret paste formula. After a few weeks, Browne returned to Lowestoft, and immediately afterwards Bow type porcelain was produced.

From 1770 the firm went by the name of Robert Browne and Company and a London warehouse was established:

> "Clark Durnford, Lowestoft China Warehouse, No. 4 Great Thomas the Apostle, Queen St., Cheapside, London, where merchants and shopkeepers may be supplied with any quan-

tity of the said ware at the usual prices. *N.B.* Allowance of twenty per cent for Ready Money."

Jewitt quotes that the Brownes were also engaged in the herring fishing trade as well as the manufacture of porcelain; they were ship owners and "kept the vessels constantly running to the Isle of Wight for a peculiar sand which with pulverised glass and pipe clay form principally the ingredients of the ground work of the ware". They also sent to Newcastle for the coal required in the kilns. Robert Browne, manager and chemist died in 1771, aged sixty-eight, but the factory was continued by his son Robert Browne the younger, Philip Walker and Obed Aldred, with 50 per cent of the shares. The Lowestoft Directors were also engaged in the Holland shipping trade. They imported Chinese Porcelain in the white and decorated it, and for years it was considered to be completely the product of the factory. Excavations made in 1902 and 1903 are systematically recorded by Spelman and Crisp, who have documented the productions of this factory for future analysis.

Although in most circles it is a well-known fact that no hard paste was ever made at Lowestoft and that the myth of Chinese Lowestoft is in fact Chinese export porcelain which probably never went near Lowestoft, in some quarters, particularly American, the legend persists. Crude Chinoiseries were painted on white Chinese porcelain in the Lowestoft factory, often amusing in their malinterpretation of the Chinese drawings left to the factory by Lady Louth, but these are quite separate from the Canton decorated armorial and other services imported directly from China.

Dr. Watney (*English Blue and White Porcelain*) has well described the products of this factory and divided the output into three periods. The early period 1757–1760 is conspicuous for its Delft-like appearance with a greyish-blue glaze. The Chinese and silver forms were well made and finely drawn compared with later work. Moulded decoration was frequent, and models were frequently re-issued at a later date with or without modifications. Typical features of Lowestoft were straggling flowers and buds, often drawn in profile, willow trees with dots, a spray of three leaves at the side of spouts and handle terminals; fine single lines which are frequently to be found round the feet of pickle dishes and outlining spouts and handle terminals.

The middle period 1761–1770 abounds with dated pieces, but unfortunately these documentary items are hardly decorated, so they are comparatively useless for further identifications. Charming birthday plaques, inkwells, mugs, punch bowls, jugs and other simple items were made as well as a few animals and figures. Nöel Turner has pointed out that "a practice almost peculiar to Lowestoft among the English factories was the painting of blue strokes or dashes at handle and spout junctions—copied from the Chinese who started this practice to cover flaws at these points. Lowestoft teapots usually have seven strainer holes where the spout joins the body and footrims are most often triangular in sections and not undercut. There are, of course, the usual exceptions to all these points".

Lowestoft had no factory mark of its own although a crescent, crossed swords and other devices were "borrowed". However, there is a series of numbers, 1–17, which has helped in the identification of the artists; Number 5 has been attributed to Robert Allen (1744–1835), manager of the factory from 1780, who was later to paint the east window of the Church of St. Margaret's. He painted several fine pieces of Lowestoft with views of this church.

The late period 1771–1803 coincided with the death of Robert Browne senior and the opening in 1770 of the London Warehouse. Production was intensified to reach a wider market, and Bow and Worcester models were imitated. The glaze became clear and brilliant and the paste was translucent. Comparatively cheap production and materials enabled Lowestoft to produce a wide variety of models, which larger factories would not find economic. Knife handles, egg cups, mustard pots, pounce pots, pap warmers, caddy spoons, eye baths, jugs for salad oil, hors d'œuvres dishes moulded in one piece, bottles, salt-cellars, cream boats, leaf-shaped pickle trays, butter boats and miniature tea wares.

After 1770, the factory which had previously concentrated on painted blue and white, produced (according to Hunting) at least thirteen transfer-printed designs, more than half of which were original. These were sometimes filled in with blue washes in the Caughley and Derby manner. Polychrome painting was increased and the best artists were employed portraying scenes, flowers, insects, etc. A bright brick red was characteristic of the factory.

The factory closed in 1803 after the death of Philip Walker, probably through the reverses the company had suffered when one of their vessels was lost and the Rotterdam warehouse was destroyed by the Napoleonic Army.

The original charming idea of painting the motto: "A trifle from Lowestoft" on a simple object, to be a gift taken home from the Fair has become a victim of mass production, a fact which can be appreciated by any visitor to the gift shops in any sea-side resort.

LOWESTOFT CHARACTERISTICS

1. No factory mark—but numerals 1–17 appeared after 1773. Letters sometimes used concurrently.
2. Paste soft phosphatic, like Bow.
3. Light in weight.
4. Glaze easily scratched, inclined to discoloration.
5. By transmitted light the colours vary from white through cream to dirty yellow.
6. Silver shapes and copies of Bow and Worcester.
7. Flat pieces usually crazed.
8. Foot rings and triangle bases usually higher than Bow or Worcester. Three stilt marks on rims as in Bow.
9. Transfer printing.

[9] CAUGHLEY (pronounced Carflee) 1772–1799

A small pottery was built in about 1750 by a Mr. Browne of Caughley Hall and on his death it was leased for sixty-four years to a relative, Ambrose Gallimore. The pottery was admirably situated, built on a hill on the south side of the River Severn, about fifty miles from Worcester. Included in the lease, was a small colliery, and local supplies of clay for the saggers were freely available. The advantages of cheap materials and transport augered a sound commercial future. Porcelain was not made until 1772 when Gallimore's daughter married Thomas Turner (1749–1809), an experienced chemist from Worcester, who became a partner. Turner set about under-cutting the porcelain from Worcester, by making a cheaper product using less soap-rock, decorated with blue and white transfer printing. He flagrantly copied Worcester designs which together with some of his own, became an immediate financial success. The quality of his product was rather thick and opaque to start with, but it was soon improved to compare favourably with Worcester. The Caughley paste was brownish when seen in transmitted light and inclined to be creamy rather than white. The local newspaper on 1st November, 1775 gave the following report: "The Porcelain Manufactory erected near Bridgnorth, in this County, is now quite completed, and the proprietors have received and completed orders to a very large amount. Lately, we saw some of their productions, which in colour and fineness are truly elegant and beautiful, and have the bright and lovely white of the so much extolled Oriental."

Turner was unable to acquire a direct lease for a soap-rock mine until 1776 when he negotiated for a fourteen-year lease to commence from 1780, of the Gew Graze mine when the Worcester lease expired. Until that time he apparently bought his supplies from merchants.

Robert Hancock (1731–1817) left Worcester after some disputes and announced his association with the Salopian factory in 1774. His close copies of his Worcester designs together with the similarities in potting, make attribution nearly impossible. According to Bernard Watney (*English Blue and White Porcelain*) Hancock's designs for Caughley included the following: "Parrot and Fruit", "*La Pêche*" and "*La Promenade Chinoise*", "*La Terre*", two shooting scenes after George Stubbs and a fox hunting print with inscription "We shall catch him anon";

"Milkmaids" and "Classical Ruins". Fruit and flowers included the well-known "Mulberry" or "Pine Cone". Possibly a study of three birds on a stunted tree may have been his last design for Caughley. Turner also engraved designs of his own while continuing with those of Hancock after he had left. He is best known for his *chinoiseries*, of which there are at least ten with a willow tree, pagoda and islands in different variations.

This "willow pattern" was not the original of this celebrated romantic version of old China but the beginning of a tradition which was to be developed and copied by Spode and other factories until the mass production of cheap Staffordshire pottery in the nineteenth century when it achieved its enormous popular appeal. Turner employed several apprentice engravers including the famous Thomas Minton who subsequently founded a firm of his own.

Turner was fascinated by French porcelain. He visited France in 1780, returning with several experienced French potters and an architect, who built him a *château* style house known as Caughley Place, demolished in 1820. Several close imitations of Chantilly porcelain were produced. These included the wide basket-weave border (*osier*), the freely drawn sprays of flowers and cross-hatched sprigs (*à l'épi* or *à la brindille*) and the most famous "Chantilly" or "Salopian Sprig" which consisted of a cornflower and forget-me-nots with odd sprays and insects. These fine designs were used to great effect on large services which the factory produced economically due to mastery of the transfer technique. In two sales at Christies in 1789, two services comprising 115 and 126 pieces respectively were sold at high prices. The greater part of production was devoted to transfer printed wares (some in blue wash) and a little underglaze blue painting, but extremely fine potted articles were sold to the London decorator James Giles (1718–1780) for enamelling. Robert Chamberlain also bought Salopian porcelain for decorating, also blue and white transfer printed goods for which he was an agent. Flight, Barr and Barr at Worcester also dealt in Caughley blue and white.

There was also a Caughley warehouse in London at No. 5 Portugal Street. The colour of the underglaze varied from pale grey to an intense violet. Turner was continuously experimenting to find the most popular shade. The modelling generally was more robust than that of Worcester with small variations on the mask lips on jugs and knops on covers. Footrings were usually straight-sided and higher than those of Worcester. The marks were various, either "S" or "C" for Salopian or Caughley as well as the hunting horn in blue of Chantilly. The Caughley works were taken over by the Rose Brothers and Edward Blakeway of Coalport in 1799, as a going concern. The works were eventually pulled down in 1821.

CAUGHLEY CHARACTERISTICS

1. Paste steatitic, brownish by transmitted light, creamy rather than dead white.
2. Glaze—bluish.
3. Worcester and Chantilly shapes and designs.
4. Quality excellent rivalling Worcester.
5. Colours, painted underglaze blue—and transfer blue and white.
6. Footrings—straight-sided and high.
7. Designs—"sprigs" and *chinoiseries* usual.

S — In blue.

C SALOPIAN. — In blue.

C — In blue or gold.

[10] COALPORT 1795—PRESENT DAY

Destiny was unkind to Thomas Turner. He had left his Worcester employers to open in direct competition with them and enjoyed considerable material success for over twenty years. Then one of his own employees, an energetic and ambitious apprentice John Rose (1772–1841), opened a factory on the north bank of the Severn. Within four years, he had so depleted the markets of his former employer, that he was able to buy him out lock, stock and barrel.

Rose ran the two establishments successfully until 1815, when he incorporated them into the enlarged Coalport factory. One of the reasons for the closure was the exhaustion of the coal seam at Caughley. The unfinished porcelain was carried in baskets by women—usually on their heads, across the ferry to Coalport for firing.

The ferry was used extensively by many of the workers who lived at Broseley. On the night of 23rd October, 1799, thirty-two of them were crossing as usual after their long working day. Some said the ferryman was drunk, while more charitable folk said it was stormy. The boat sank in mid-stream and twenty-nine valuable personnel were lost.

The products of Caughley-Coalport period until 1815 included the transfer printed steatitic porcelain of Turner, plus a hard-paste porcelain like New Hall. Rose experimented with new pastes and evolved a fine bone china which was decorated in gorgeous ground colours and gilding in the French manner. After 1820 when the Billingsley–Walker concern was bought out by Rose, the paste was changed and it became almost as fine as that of Nantgarw, for which it is constantly mistaken. Coalport enjoyed considerable success throughout the nineteenth century, particularly in the United States. After many changes in ownership and policy, the Coalport brand is still in existence.

A word about Coalbrookdale. A mistaken belief exists that certain porcelain, usually in strong ground colours with encrusted flowers, comes under this heading. Coalbrookdale is the name of the district only and these wares were made by Coalport. No other factory existed in the vicinity.

COALPORT CHARACTERISTICS

1. Paste white and translucent.
2. Gilding brassy.
3. Colours like Sèvres.
4. Appearance—good, typical nineteenth-century splendour.

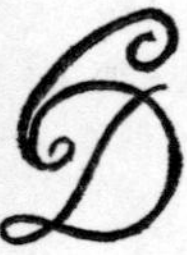

Second quarter of nineteenth century. (Coalbrookdale.)

Coalport.

[11] PLYMOUTH, DEVONSHIRE 1768–1770

Plymouth porcelain was the first hard-paste porcelain to be produced in England. W. B. Honey (*Dictionary of European Ceramic Art*) suggested that it would make for clarity to speak of Cookworthy's porcelain rather than Plymouth for the story of Plymouth is the story of William Cookworthy (1705–1780).

Born in Plymouth, the eldest of a poor Quaker family, William Cookworthy was apprenticed to Sylvanus Bevan, F.R.S., a London chemist of 2 Plough Court, Lombard Street (the firm later became Allen and Hanbury's). Fatherless at the age of fourteen, he had to walk to London to take up his appointment. Returning to Plymouth he set up in business as a wholesale chemist and druggist in Nut Street, and became one of the town's leading citizens. A friend of Captain Cook and Earl St. Vincent (then Captain Jervis), his home was the meeting place for the most interesting people of the time. He married a Quaker lady named Berry in 1735, but after only ten happy years she died and left him broken hearted with five small daughters. He never re-married.

About this time he became interested in the manufacture of porcelain, and was familar with the letters of the Jesuit missionary Père d'Entrecolles, who had described the materials and manufacture processes he had observed in China in 1712–1722. Cookworthy was convinced that deposits of the kaolin and petuntse would be found in England. America's first chinamaker, André Duché, showed Cookworthy some porcelain he had made from materials he had discovered in Carolina, on land leased from the Cherokees. Cookworthy described this in a letter to Richard Hingston, surgeon of Penryn, dated 30th May, 1745, "I had lately with me the person who hath discovered the china earth. He had several samples of the china ware of their making with him, which were, I think, equal to the Asiatic. 'Twas found in the back of Virginia, where he was in the quest of mines, and having read de Hald discovered both petuntse and the kaolin. 'Tis the latter earth, he says, is the essential thing towards the success of the manufacture. He has gone for a cargo of it, having bought the whole country of the Indians where it rises. He can import it for £13 per ton and by that means afford their china as cheap as common stoneware but they intend only to go about 30 per cent under the company. The man is a Quaker by profession but seems to be as thorough a deist as I ever met with". Nothing appears to have developed from the American clay.

About this time, in his research for a treatise on furnaces he was aware of the "growan" and "moorstone" as they were locally known, found near St. Austell, which were used in the manufacture of refractory firebricks for the tin-smelting furnaces. He frequently travelled through Cornwall on business and often stayed with John Nancarrow, a tin-mining superintendent and a "scientific person" and possibly through this acquaintanceship came to realise that the two materials were the kaolin and petuntse referred to by d'Entrecolles and Duché.

He experimented for years and finally perfected a formula which he patented in his sixty-third year on 17th March, 1768. A company was formed with fourteen shares of which Cookworthy retained three; the rest were distributed in single units amongst his family and Quaker merchant friends, including Richard Champion of Bristol. Production began at Coxside, Plymouth. Thomas Pitt (later Lord Camelford) granted the company a short lease for extracting clay and china stone from his land near St. Stephen's Parish, and this lease was later extended to ninety-nine years in 1770.

Cookworthy was anxious about the expense (they had spent between £2,000 and £3,000 according to Lord Camelford) and finding the production and management work too much for him he moved the works after only two years to Bristol where Champion could take an active part.

The porcelain produced at Plymouth was primitive and coarse, with many firing cracks and faults, but it was gradually improved by patient experiment. The first decoration was in underglaze blue from Cornish cobalt, but at first the blue became almost black until Cookworthy's experience as a chemist enabled him to overcome some of his difficulties and finely drawn outlines with the minimum of cobalt were more successful. The wood-fired kilns caused paste discolouration which was sometimes grey and often brownish. Some charming naïve figures were made, probably from Longton Hall models, which they so closely resemble. The effects of the Longton Hall factory were sold at Salisbury in 1760, and it is quite reasonable to suppose that Cookworthy took the opportunity to buy some ready made equipment, although it has been suggested that this would have been premature for his own porcelain factory did not open until eight years later.

The following advertisement appeared in 1770:

> "China Painters wanted for the Plymouth new invented Patent Porcelain Manufactory. A number of sober, ingenious artists capable of painting in enamel or blue may hear of constant employ by sending their proposals to Thomas Frank in Castle Street, Bristol."

Amongst those employed at Plymouth were the Repairer Tebo (*c.* 1730–*c.* 1790), who worked at Bow, Henry Bone (1755–1843) an excellent artist who became a Royal Academician, and

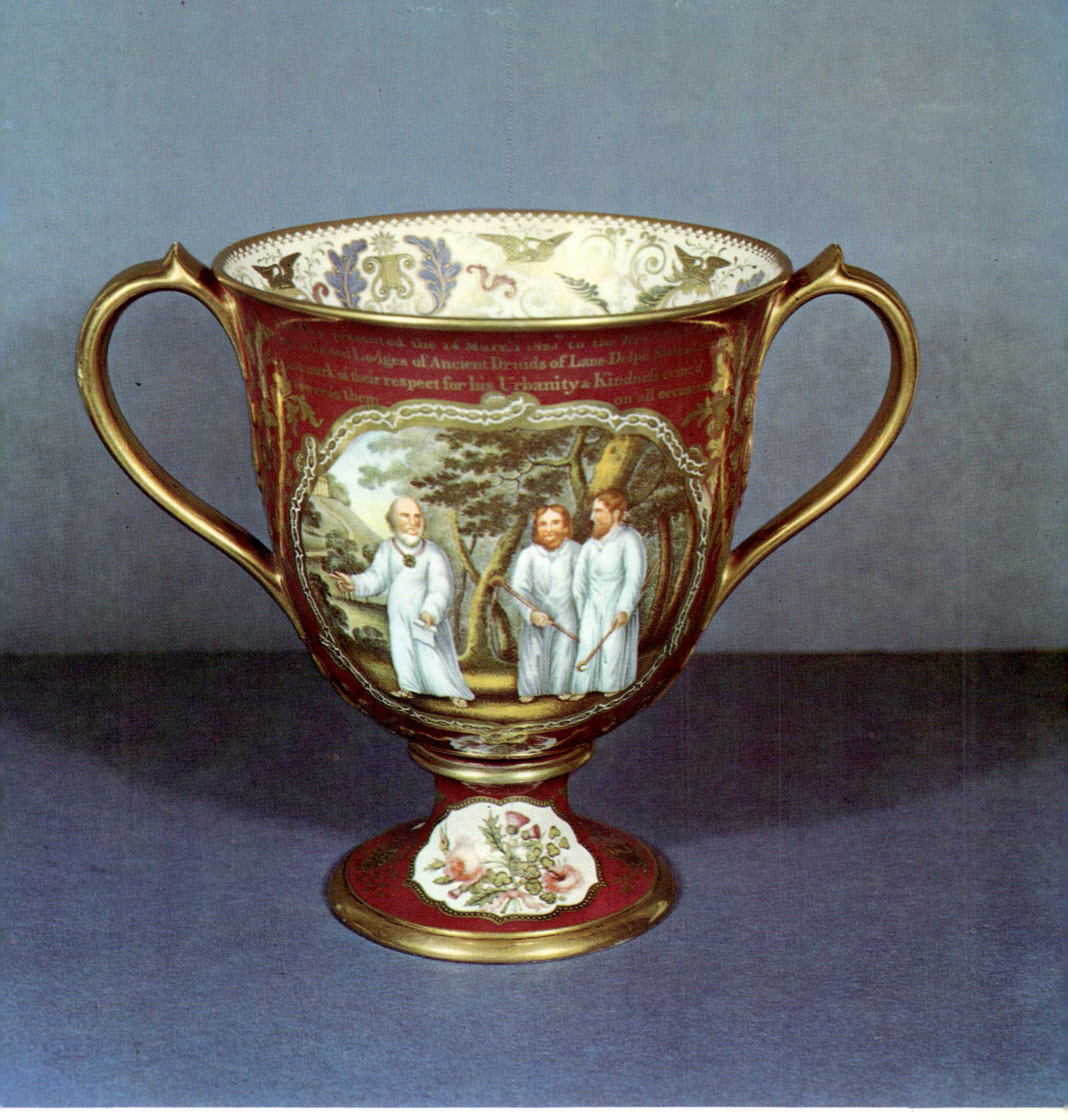

SPODE

A "two-handled loving-cup" dated 1825, with inscription and painting of three druids standing in an oak grove

W. T. Copeland & Sons Ltd.

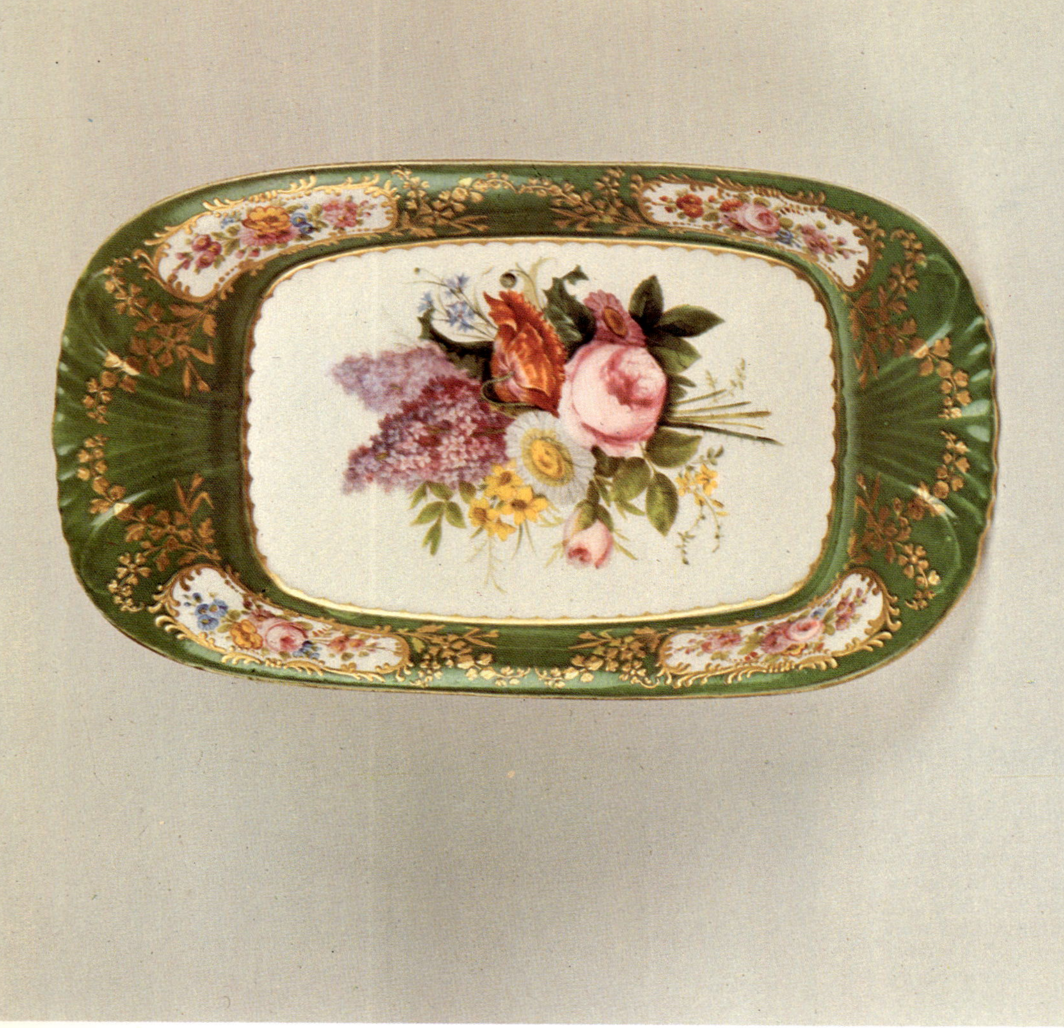

NANTGARW

A deep rectangular dish with an apple-green border, having four reserves of English flowers, profuse gilding, the whole of the centre painted with a large spray of flowers. Size 12 ins. by 7 ins. London decorated by Robins and Randall for Mortlocks

By Courtesy of Derek Hutchings

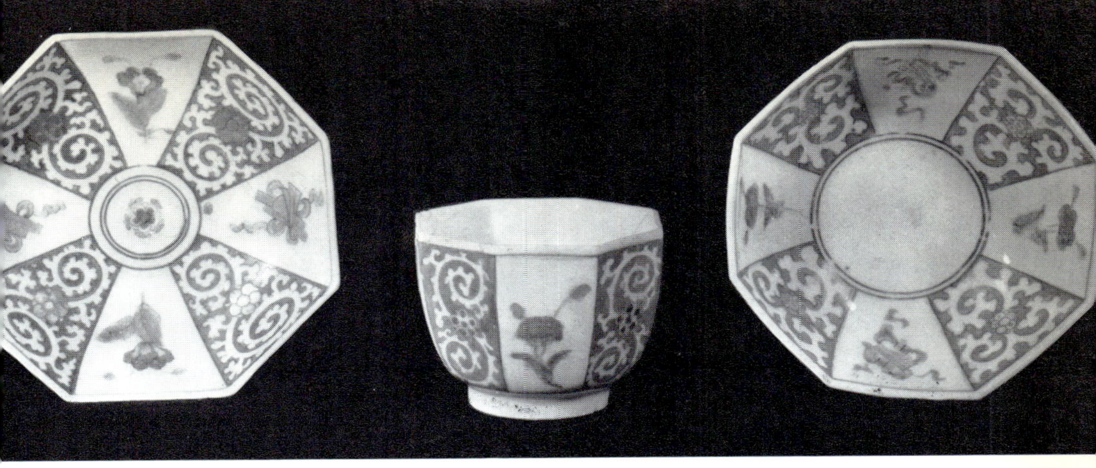

1. CHELSEA. Soft-paste porcelain saucer, *c.* 1752–56. Marked with Red Anchor. Diameter 5 ins.

2. MEISSEN. Octagonal cup, *c.* 1735. Marked with the crossed swords of Meissen, and the "Johanneum" Inventory incised marks. Height $2\frac{1}{2}$ ins.

3. Arita saucer-dish in hard-paste porcelain, made in Japan, *c.* 1680. Diameter 5 ins.

Grosvenor Antiques

CHELSEA. A group of "Perseus and Andromeda". He wears a yellow-lined puce cloak and iron-red tunic with turquoise blue breeches. She wears a pink-lined white dress and turquoise veil. The dragon is spotted russet. Height $11\frac{1}{2}$ ins. Red Anchor period

Sotheby & Co.

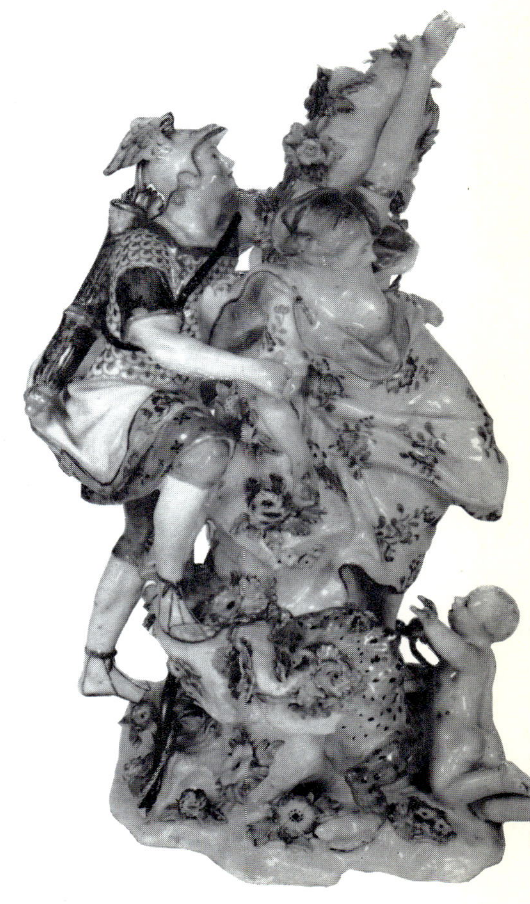

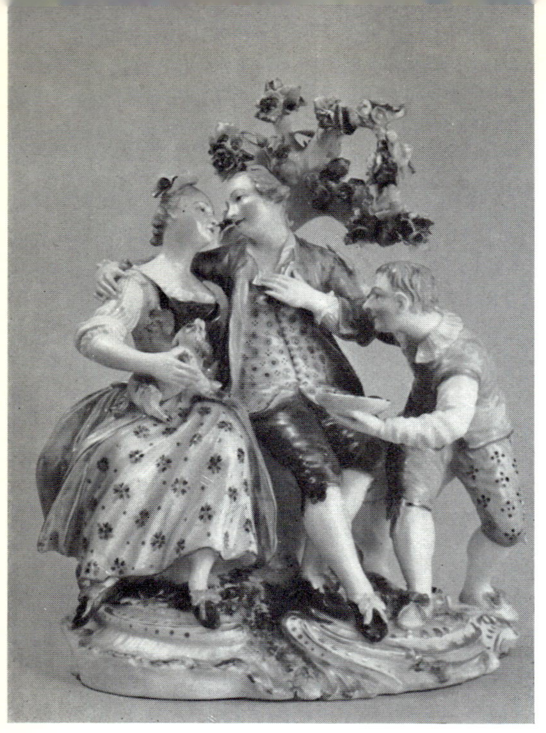

DERBY. A group of "Isabella, Gallant and Jester", from the Italian *Commedia del Arte*, *c.* 1756. William Duesbury 2nd period 1760–69

The Royal Crown Derby Museum

DERBY. Obelisk depicting "The Four Continents", *c.* 1795–1800. The period of William Duesbury and Michael Keen 1786–1811

The Royal Crown Derby Museum

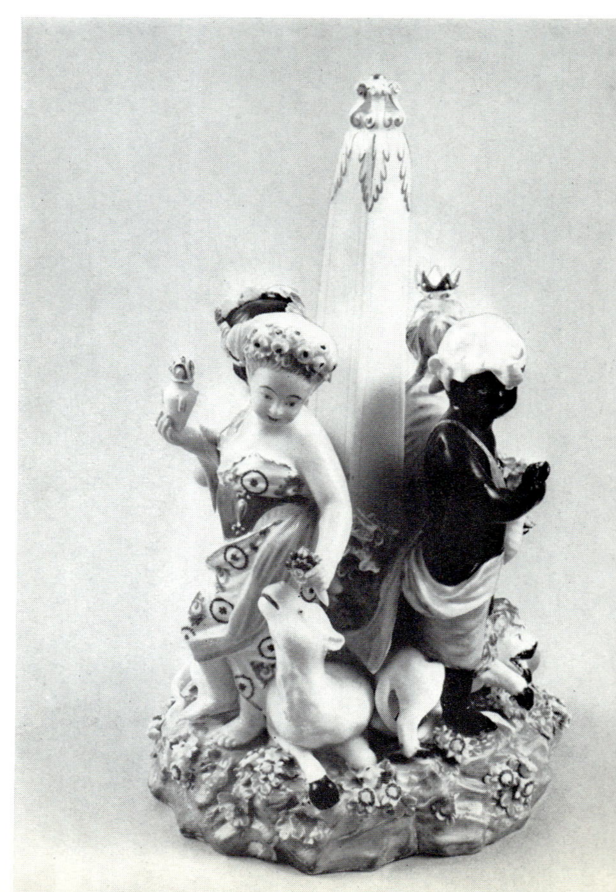

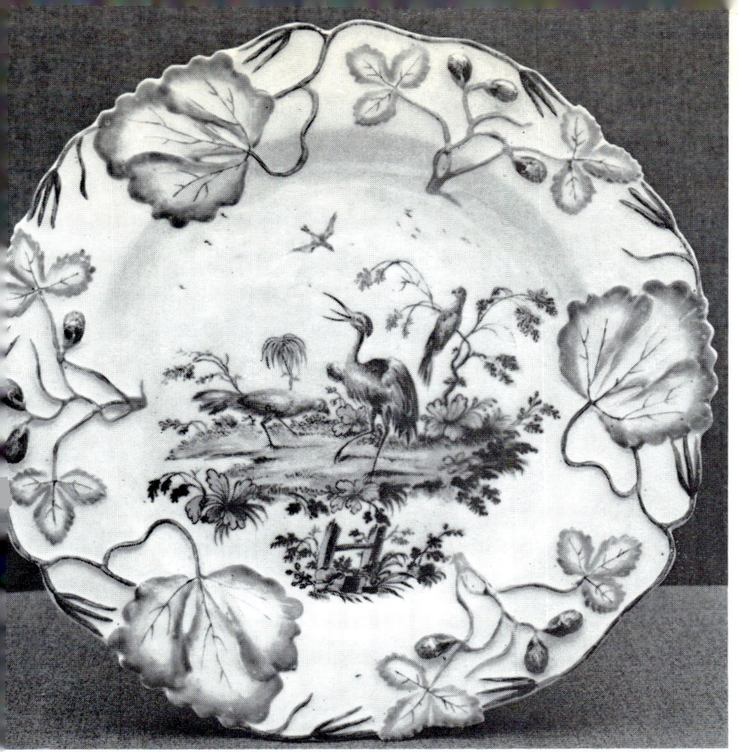

LONGTON HALL
Plate in softe-paste porcelain, decorated in enamel colours, *c.* 1755. 9 ins. diameter

Victoria and Albert Museum

WORCESTER
Jug with illustration of "King of Prussia", taken from a print by Robert Hancock, dated 1757

The Dyson Perrins Museum, Worcester

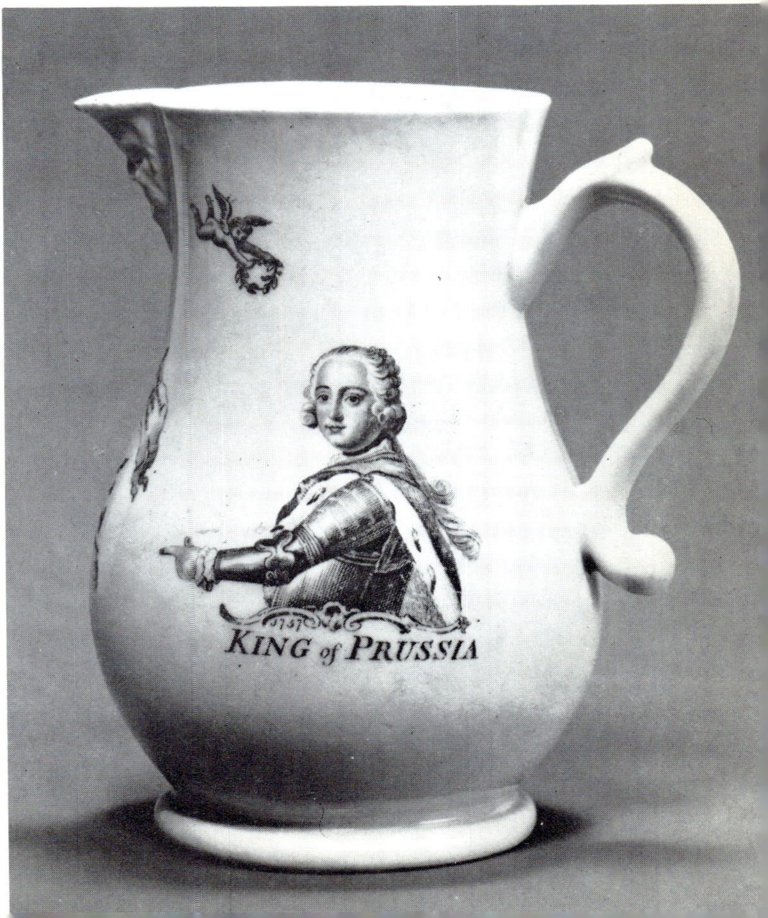

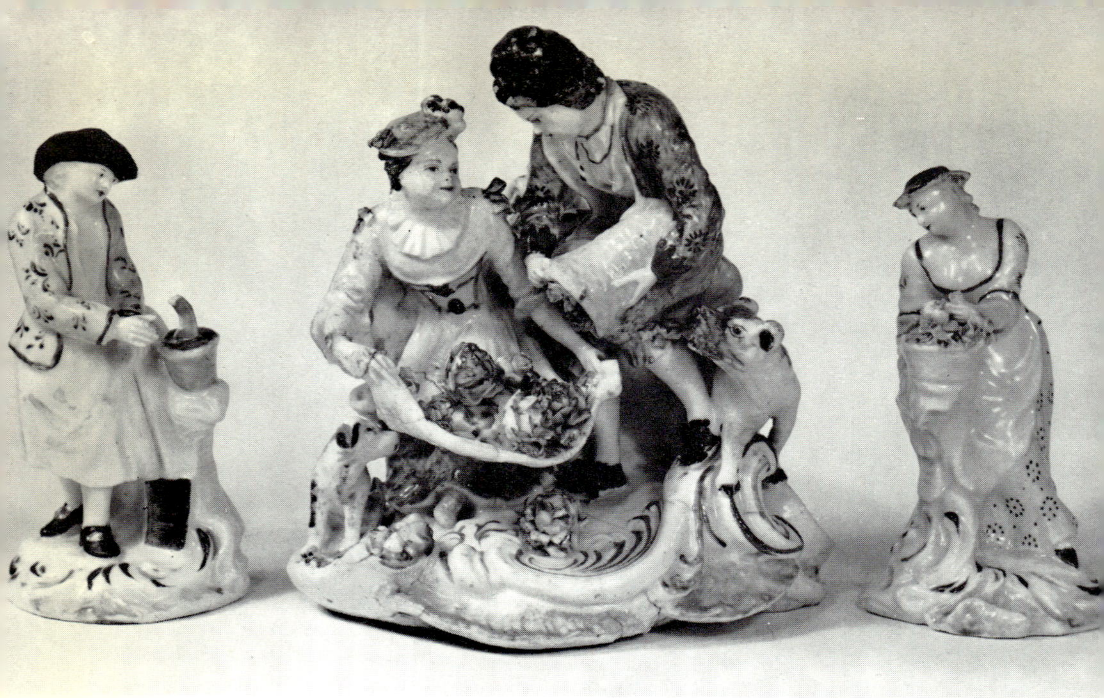

LONGTON HALL. A pair of figures, Gardner and Companion, height $4\frac{1}{4}$ ins., and centre, a rare Longton Hall group, height $5\frac{3}{4}$ ins.

Christie's

WORCESTER. 1st period Worcester sauce-boat

Dyson Perrins Museum, Worcester

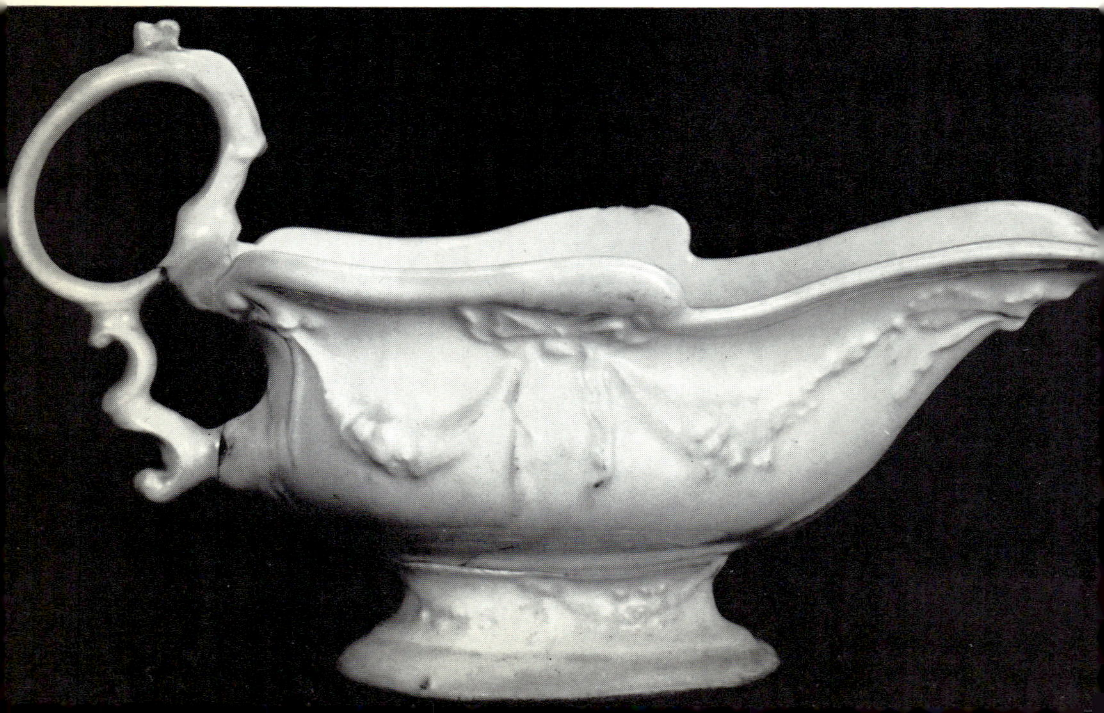

Etienne-Charles Le Guay (1762–1822) a French painter from Sèvres who was known as Saqui or Soqui. Both Bone and Saqui painted birds and flowers in polychrome with great success. Chinese subjects, copied from Worcester, were made and table-ware moulded in the shape of sea shells.

The high temperature at which the paste had to be fired caused even the rococo sauceboats and shell salts to "have a petrified remoteness which is in marked contrast to the sensuous quality of the finest soft paste" according to Dr. Watney (*English Blue and White Porcelain*). Flat-wares were virtually impossible to produce with the stubborn paste, but its poor plastic quality was used to advantage in massive ink-wells.

It is difficult to distinguish the late products of Plymouth from the early Bristol wares, so W. B. Honey designated the work of the two factories as "Cookworthy's Plymouth" to cover all that was made under his direction both at Plymouth and Bristol, and "Champion's Bristol" for that which was made at Bristol from 1774 onwards. (*Old English Porcelain.*)

Although the output of Plymouth was lacking in quality, it has a great appeal to the collector because of the obvious production faults, and imperfections. One feels close to the craftsmen who struggled with insurmountable difficulties to produce the first English hard-paste, and the results have individuality and charm which cannot be imitated.

PLYMOUTH CHARACTERISTICS

1. Always hard-paste.
2. Thrown specimens sometimes show spiral wreathing.
3. Glaze imperfect, thick and uneven in patches and full of tiny bubbles.
4. Appearance shows greyish tinge, sometimes brownish, from the smoke.
5. Firing cracks and imperfections common.
6. Style used, a form of rococo with scrolled bases.
7. Enamel colours raised from glaze.

8. Enamel colours used include a dirty brownish-red, green, gold, pale blue and brown, also underglaze blue.
9. No ground colours used.
10. Decoration usually birds and butterflies and sprays of flowers.
11. Shapes after Worcester, silver shapes and shell shapes.
12. Factory mark, the alchemical sign for tin.

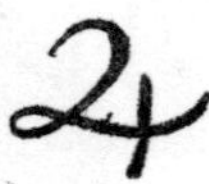

In underglaze blue, blue enamel, red or gold.

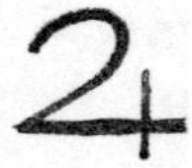

In underglaze blue, blue enamel, red or gold.

[12] BRISTOL, Gloucestershire 1770–1781

In 1770 Cookworthy removed his moulds, equipment and his apprentices to factory premises at No. 15 Castle Green, Bristol, where he continued his porcelain production in close co-operation with Richard Champion (1743–1791), who lived next door at No. 17. Champion was a go-ahead, public spirited Bristol merchant who had been engaged in the American trade before the war of Independence, and was an ardent supporter ofEdmund Burke. In a letter of November 1765, Champion wrote in reference to some clay sent to him by Duché from Carolina, "I sent part to Holdship (at Worcester) as you desired and gave part to a new Work just established. . . . This new work is from a clay and stone discovered in Cornwall and answers the description of the Chinese".

In 1774 Cookworthy retired and the Bristol factory by then known as Richard Champion and Co. was transferred to Champion. The royalty agreed was a sum equal to the value of Cornish materials bought for use at the factory. Cookworthy wrote to his cousin Anna in May 1774:

. . . I shall set out in the machine second day moving and reach Plymouth on fourth day . . . I have not had a least reason to complain of Richard Champion's behaviour and my acquaintance at Bristol have shown me much kindness and respect and on the whole my time hath been spent agreeably amongst them all things considered. For, considering my attention to china wares the closing of my business with Richard Champion, the settling the lovers' matters which were in a much worse situation than we imagined; all this and the attending meetings have made the last month the busiest one to me that I have known for many years."

The "machine" referred to was the stage coach, which it is interesting to note took two days to cover the 120 odd miles from Bristol to Plymouth. Presumably the lovers referred to were Champion's sister, Esther, and Cookworthy's cousin, who married in that year.

In 1775 Champion, having incurred large expenses without adequate return, sought an extension of the Patent which he had bought from Cookworthy so that he might benefit from the sole rights of the use of the Cornish materials for a longer period. Champion's petition to Parliament was challenged by Josiah Wedgwood and other Staffordshire Potters, who were anxious to use the Cornish materials themselves and so tried to prevent Champion from obtaining any form of renewal. With the help of Burke a fourteen-year extension was granted to Champion, but he had to make concessions, one of which was that the Cornish materials should be available to other potters but only for earthenware. The suit was therefore only a partial success, for Wedgwood and John Turner hastened to Cornwall to buy the comparatively inexpensive clay and stone. The cost of the suit and the loss of his trade caused by the war with America practically ruined Champion. He had no partners in his Castle Green enterprise, although many influential friends supported him, particularly the Quaker Joseph Fry, a chocolate manufacturer, Edmund Burke and the Duke of Portland. There is no record of Champion becoming bankrupt although a suit was preferred against him on the 29th August 1778 and withdrawn on the same day, so perhaps one can presume that the creditors were either repaid in full or in porcelain.

A London warehouse was opened in 1776 at 17 Salisbury Court, Fleet Street, and during the following two years the Bristol factory produced its finest work.

Champion endeavoured to make blue and white domestic wares, but the English hard-paste did not respond to this treatment and required rich enamel colours.

Richard Champion's Bristol produced models derived from Chelsea, Derby and Sèvres, but the hard-paste was less attractive. He produced elaborate services for his friends with their initials in festoons of tiny flowers, and also produced what is known as Bristol cottage china which consisted of simple domestic ware, lightly decorated with sprigs and festoons of flowers without gilding. His shapes were new and unusual, derived from the Chinese, and his figures were a great improvement on those of Plymouth for he spared no expense to obtain the designs he required. He also made plaques in biscuit with applied modelled flowers, and busts of the famous of the day, and coats-of-arms modelled in high relief. The artists employed at Bristol in addition to those who followed Cookworthy from Plymouth, were Thomas Bryand, a flower painter and the modeller Lequoi.

Constant experiments with the paste and glaze improved the quality of the shape, and difficulties in the production of flat-ware were surmounted and plates were made in quantity.

Josiah Wedgwood in a letter dated 24th August 1778 wrote, "Poor Champion you may have heard is quite demolished; it was never likely to be otherwise as he had neither professional knowledge, sufficient capability nor scarcely any real acquaintance with the materials he was working upon. I suppose we might buy some growan stone and growan clay now upon easy terms, for they have prepared a large quantity this year".

Champion decided to form a new company in Staffordshire and in conjunction with six potters a factory was started in 1781 at Tunstall. Champion sold out the following year when the factory moved to New Hall.

BRISTOL CHARACTERISTICS

1. Paste hard, with spiral wreathing and very translucent.
2. Glaze is greyish and clearer than Plymouth.
3. Appearance pale grey and more uniform than Plymouth.
4. Styles after Chelsea, Derby and Sèvres and the Chinese.
5. Colours used, smoky brown, clear yellow, greyish blue, watery red, clear bright green, and some gilding.
6. Grit often adheres to foot rings.
7. Concentric foot rings and S-shaped ribs to prevent articles from sagging during firing.
8. Factory mark, a cross in underglaze blue.

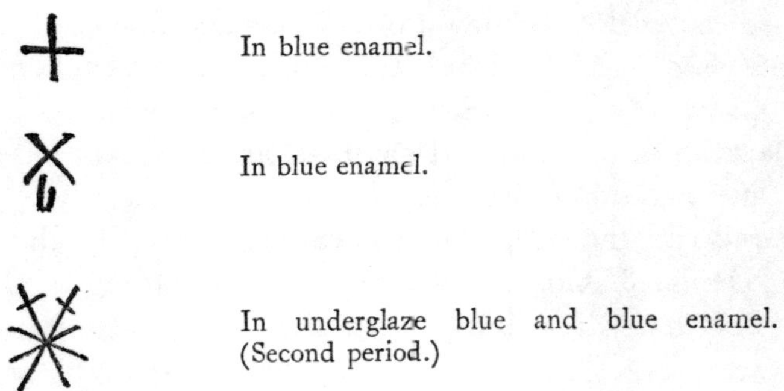

In blue enamel.

In blue enamel.

In underglaze blue and blue enamel. (Second period.)

[13] NEW HALL, Staffordshire 1781–1835

Champion, "a respectable merchant" of Bristol, formed a company with six potters, Sam Hollins, Anthony Keeling, John Turner, Jacob Warburton, William Clowes and Charles Bagnell and under his direction they commenced production of hard-paste porcelain in the factory of Anthony Keeling at Tunstall. After much disagreement amongst the seven men, Keeling, Turner and Champion withdrew, and John Daniel became a managing partner when the concern moved in 1782 to Shelton Hall, known as New Hall—hence the name.

Champion went to London where he became Deputy Paymaster of the Forces under Edmund Burke, the Member of Parliament for Bristol, in the short-lived Rockingham Ministry. When the Government was dissolved, Champion emigrated to America where he had many interests from his Bristol shipping days, and died at Charleston, South Carolina, in 1791.

Jacob Warburton (1740–1826) was the travelling salesman for the company, and by all accounts was energetic and intellectual. According to Simeon Shaw (*History of the Staffordshire Potteries*) he was interested in literature and read French, Dutch, German and Italian fluently. He had many friends and included Wedgwood amongst his intimates. When widowed and well advanced in years, he took a young second wife and lived on to the age of eighty-six.

John Turner, one of the founder members of New Hall, described as a "Red China Potter", a very fine potter was at one time associated with the Caughley factory. When he left New Hall he set up at Lane End and made figures and busts in both black and cane coloured basalt, from the local Staffordshire clay in the style of Wedgwood.

The records show that a firm calling itself "Hollins, Warburton, Daniel & Co." traded from the beginning of the nineteenth century, describing themselves on their invoices as "manufacturers of real china". However, although hard-paste was made until long after Champion's Patent expired in 1796, bone ash was introduced into the paste and bone china was made exclusively from about 1810 onwards.

No figures were made, only domestic and table-wares were produced. Designs were simple, rarely gilded, and resemble roses, daisies and chrysanthemums. The borders usually consist of wavy lines, sometimes in the form of ribbons, lightly decorated with odd sprigs or leaves. There were also *chinoiseries* copied from Chinese porcelain which were ill-drawn and completely missed the point of the emblems and styling, although they do have a certain quaintness which is not unattractive.

The New Hall patterns are easily recognisable. Rarely marked, they have been copied so extensively the amateur will probably find that he has several factories represented in his collection. Examples of the so-called New Hall design which were made earlier at Bristol are extremely rare, the danger lies in the Oriental export originals from which the New Hall copies were taken.

The experienced New Hall potters introduced great improvements in production and a new low temperature glaze was discovered to follow the Staffordshire traditional high temperature biscuit firing, which enabled them to use underglaze transfer.

Ten designs have so far been attributed to New Hall in blue and white transfer, which vary in colour from pale blue to dark indigo. These sometimes bear the Frankenthal mark of a crowned lion rampant in underglaze blue—probably used as a compliment to the only other European hard-paste factory which had succeeded in this method. The factory closed in 1835, but the extraordinary number of Staffordshire copies of New Hall still leave a great deal to be explained. No doubt further research will ultimately provide the answer. Since writing this chapter, I have learned that a forthcoming book by Holgate on New Hall should be most enlightening.

NEW HALL CHARACTERISTICS

1. Hard-paste until 1810, then a glassy bone china, greyish and opaque.
2. Glaze unctuous, and bare patches frequent on bases. On teapot bases frequently streaked as if fingers drawn across to wipe off excess.
3. Only tea wares produced with limited number of designs and shapes decorated in enamel colours. Ten patterns in blue and white transfer.
4. Unmarked until 1810–1835. Then marked New Hall. Blue and white transfer wares sometimes marked with crowned lion rampant of Frankenthal.

1810–1835, printed in red.

[14] PINXTON, Derbyshire 1796–1813

A factory was founded on the family estate by Mr. John Coke who, having spent some time in Dresden, was interested enough in porcelain to experiment with the local clays. He corresponded with William Duesbury at Derby who tried to discourage him.

Coke then approached Billingsley and persuaded him to join the new factory. Probably promised greater freedom and financial advantages, Billingsley left Derby, together with his wife, his mother-in-law, two daughters and son-in-law and settled in Pinxton.

Duesbury was naturally concerned to lose his finest flower painter, for, "Paintings with Billingsley's flowers" were constantly in demand.

Billingsley had perfected an individual technique of painting sprays of flowers and leaves, and Duesbury feared that the Derby business would suffer to the benefit of Pinxton. However, with the contrariness of an artist, Billingsley suddenly became interested, not in painting which had held him at the bench for twenty-two years, but in the production of porcelain itself. His experiments resulted in a white, transparent, granular soft-paste porcelain, containing bone-ash, with a brilliant glaze.

The products of Pinxton are restrained and elegant. The shapes pure in the neo-Greek taste, and the decoration simple and refined, reminiscent of Derby. Useful wares were made, sometimes with oval reserves of landscapes, as well as scattered flowers, Chantilly sprigs and some gilding. No figures were made. Billingsley left Pinxton in 1801 for Mansfield, taking his formula with him. There is a signed Billingsley decoration at Mansfield very similar to some Pinxton such as the arabesques under a primrose yellow ground.

The factory was taken over by John Cutts (*c.* 1804), who made an inferior product which was thick and opaque.

It closed in 1813.

PINXTON CHARACTERISTICS

1. Soft granular paste with brilliant glaze, very translucent.
2. Neo-Greek designs, simple and uncluttered.
3. Derby style decoration.
4. Domestic and table-wares.

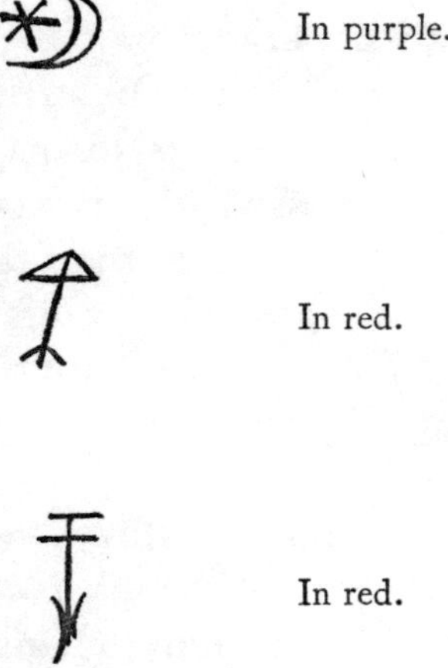

In purple.

In red.

In red.

[15] NANTGARW (pronounced Nantgarrwe), GLAMORGAN, WALES 1813–1814 and 1817–1820

In 1813, William Billingsley ceased his wanderings and settled in some primitive cottages alongside the Glamorgan Canal in the village of Nantgarw, eight miles from Cardiff.

He was obsessed with the idea of a pure white, translucent porcelain, and began to experiment at Pinxton, where he produced a new type hybrid granular body. For reasons which we do not know, he left Pinxton for Mansfield in 1801 and probably found a backer for a new factory, but it was short-lived. In 1804 we find him in Torksey, Lincolnshire, and then in Wirksworth in Derbyshire. Little is known about these factories so they are not mentioned elsewhere in this book. In 1811 at Worcester where he worked as a decorator—his theories on white porcelain were disregarded. Apparently he was forever short of funds—he was made bankrupt at least once, after which he sometimes called himself Beely, a diminutive of his name to avoid his creditors. He is also said to have had intemperate habits, and must have been the sort of character of whom Flight and Barr did not approve.

In 1813, Billingsley and his son-in-law Walker started their Welsh factory. As usual, funds were low, so Billingsley, calling himself Beely, applied to the Board of Trade for Government support. The Government instructed Lewis Dillwyn of the prosperous Cambrian Pottery Works at Swansea to inspect the new factory. Lewis Dillwyn was so impressed with the porcelain that had already been made, and presuming that the high percentage of wasters was due to the small trial kilns in use, invited the two men to transfer their moulds and equipment to his premises at Swansea, where they might have greater facilities for production.

After a short while, it became apparent to Dillwyn, who was essentially a business man, that the extremely high cost of the small production of perfect goods would lead him to bankruptcy. About this time he received a letter from Flight and Barr of Worcester informing him that the two men in his employ were runaway workmen from Worcester, where their porcelain body had been tried and found to be impractical for production. Dillwyn, already shocked by his own losses, dismissed the two men, so they returned to Nantgarw.

Liberal friends came forward and assisted them with capital. A total of £8,000 was subscribed, which was all dissipated in two years on alterations to buildings and experiments with the paste. So little porcelain was produced in comparison with the large number of wasters, it might have been more practical to sell the "seconds" at a reduced rate, but they refused to do so.

The astounding quality produced by the partners, now including William Young and Thomas Pardoe (1770–1823), who followed them from Swansea, attracted the attention of the London trade. Mortlocks, of Oxford Street, bought large quantities which were delivered to London in the white to be decorated locally.

The Derby painter Webster was employed to some extent, and the wares were fired in the enamel kiln belonging to the decorators Robins and Randall of Spa Fields, Islington. The porcelain resembled Sèvres soft-paste so closely that forgeries were made with gorgeous rococo decoration, which Mortlock's sold at enormous profits.

A service was made and decorated by Billingsley and Pardoe at Nantgarw and presented to the Prince of Wales (later Regent and then George IV). "The pattern was a green vase with a single rose on every piece, and every rose different."

Nantgarw porcelain began to supplant other favourites of the day. John Rose of Coalport, whose London agent was also the firm of Mortlocks, noted that this porcelain was inferior to that of Nantgarw, so he made a takeover bid. After some negotiations he persuaded them to sell out lock, stock and barrel with the sinecure of a job at Coalport. Billingsley, no match for Rose, and probably tired of the struggle, accepted the offer. He moved to Coalport, where he lived in a small cottage close to the china works, and died soon after, in 1828, in utter obscurity and poverty. Few have made a more important contribution to the greatness of English porcelain.

After Billingsley's death, Walker, whose wife Sarah had died in Swansea, removed his family to America, where he founded the factory in New Troy called the Temperance Hill Pottery, and where he became very prosperous. Pardoe died in 1823. William Young went to Droitwich, where he made salt glaze.

At a time when porcelain was becoming commercialised, and taste less demanding, Billingsley and Walker had produced a porcelain which was in the true tradition of the early soft-paste Sèvres. The beautiful granular paste, which on fracture looks like fine lump sugar, was painted tastefully in the neo-Greek style of the period. The qualities of the material itself were never overlooked, and it was never over-decorated or garish. Whilst in production they were asked to replace breakages in services made by other factories, but they did not falsify the marks. Pieces sold in the white for outside decoration were not marked at the factory.

[16] SWANSEA, Glamorgan, Billingsley 1814–1817 Bevington 1817–1823

In about 1750, a former copper works at Swansea became an earthenware factory. Thirty-three years later it was offered for sale and was purchased by a Mr. G. Haynes, who enlarged and improved and named it the "Cambrian Pottery". In 1802 he sold it to Lewis Weston Dillwyn, naturalist and author, who later became Member of Parliament for Glamorganshire, and under whose direction a fine earthenware, called "Opaque China" was artistically produced. It was generally painted by William Weston Young, an artist of considerable ability, with subjects of natural history; shells, flowers, butterflies and birds. In 1814 Dillwyn was requested by the Board of Trade to inspect the newly-formed porcelain factory at Nantgarw on their behalf.

After his unlucky experience with the two potters from Nantgarw, however, which I have already discussed, Dillwyn appointed the painter Timothy Bevington as production manager, and he changed the formula to make the paste harder, denser and more durable. This later paste had a yellowish tinge, and the glaze had a peculiar dead-white look. The texture became chalky and far less translucent; some of it being practically opaque.

Bevington, already a shareholder, became the sole owner for a period, during which he commissioned Morris to paint the magnificent dinner service with the royal blue and gold borders, and different basket of fruits on each piece.

Swansea porcelain was made and decorated in the neo-Greek style in a characteristic manner. Decorative themes included low relief mouldings with landscapes and figures, wild strawberries, wild flowers, botanical flowers, birds and other natural history subjects—feathers, shells, to name a few. A typical style of flower painting is associated with Swansea which is attributable to Billingsley, although according to Honey (*A Dictionary of European Ceramic Art*), Billingsley seldom, if ever, painted anything at Swansea.

The manner of painting flowers with the high-lights brushed out, and groups of light and dark flowers arranged together to intensify the effect was developed by Billingsley at Derby, and was much imitated. Swansea porcelain was frequently marblized and mottled to achieve unusual effects—ground colours in deep blue, pink, yellow, buff and green were frequent. No figures have been recorded, but biscuit flowers were made to be applied to vases.

Several fine artists were employed at Swansea, including David Evans (*c.* 1740–*c.* 1820), painter of flowers and wild strawberries; Reed and Hood, the modellers; Lenny, the gilder; Colclough, a painter of birds; George Beddow, a specialist in heraldic devices; Thomas Pardoe, the flower painter, and Baxter who produced the "Shakespeare Cup" and a dessert service of garden scenery amongst other subjects while at Swansea. Previously he had been principal of an Art School at Worcester, and later joined Flight and Barr, then Chamberlains where he remained until his death in 1821. At one time he was employed by a connoisseur who asserted that there was no decorative art in England and showed him a piece of porcelain purchased in France. Baxter replied that it was in fact he who had painted that particular piece of porcelain.

Swansea reverted to Dillwyn, then subsequently to his son, Lewis Llewellyn Dillwyn, who in 1823 sold the porcelain moulds and equipment to Rose of Coalport. The pottery continued production until 1869, when the site proved more valuable than the Pot Bank, and was sold for re-development.

CHARACTERISTICS OF BILLINGSLEY'S PORCELAIN MADE AT NANTGARW AND SWANSEA

1. Pure white granular hybrid soft-paste.
2. Neo-Greek forms.
3. Fracture like fine lump sugar.
4. No foot rings on saucers.
5. Unglazed bases.

6. Honey gilding.
7. High standard of decoration.
8. Transparent even when thickly potted.
9. Naturalistic painting of fruits, flowers, feathers and shells.

NANTGARW.	Impressed.
NANT GARW C.W.	Impressed.
Nantgarw	Impressed.
SWANSEA.	Impressed or printed in red.
Swansea.	Written, printed or impressed.
BEVINGTON & CO., SWANSEA.	*1818–1824.*

[17] MADELEY, Shropshire 1827–1840

The demand in England for Sèvres soft-paste porcelain was tremendous, and when production ceased in 1804 prices rose rapidly. It is not therefore difficult to understand why more forgeries of this factory were made than of any other. The accumulated stocks of "seconds" released by Brongniart found a ready market and were swiftly decorated in the Sèvres manner. When these were exhausted unscrupulous china dealers sold soft-paste Welsh china made by Billingsley and Walker at Swansea and Nantgarw as genuine Sèvres. The London dealer John Mortlock in particular bought all he could in the white, as well as sparsely decorated old Sèvres, and employed the decorators Robins and Randall of Islington to complete the pieces to his requirements.

The supply of Welsh china ceased when Billingsley and Walker sold out to Rose of Coalport in 1820 and it then occurred to Thomas Martin Randall that this profitable business might be continued. He was a capable chemist and decorator and knew all about soft-paste production. He opened a factory at Madeley in Shropshire in 1827, and retired with his fortune made in 1840. His patterns and styles of decoration were in the Sèvres soft-paste manner, but the London dealers were very annoyed when the "old Quaker" refused to forge the Sèvres factory mark. However, he very conveniently did not mark his porcelain at all.

Randall's soft-paste body was very similar to that made by Billingsley. The main difference was that Randall's could be described as rich cream, while Billingsley's was like rich milk.

There has now been a revival of interest in the Madeley factory, whose productions were previously considered only as Sèvres forgeries. The workmanship was so superb that they are now appreciated for themselves. The exquisite shapes, colours and decoration deserve their place in the collector's cabinet.

MADELEY CHARACTERISTICS

1. Granular hybrid soft-paste.
2. Creamy rather than white.
3. Sèvres shapes and patterns.
4. No factory mark.

[18] SPODE, Stoke-on-Trent, Staffordshire
1776 Earthenware
1794–Present Day
Porcelain, Semi-Porcelain and Earthenware

Josiah Spode I was apprenticed as a lad of twelve to Thomas Whieldon in 1745 at the starting rate of 2s. 3d. per week, or 2s. 6d. per week "if he deserved it". Apparently he did, and progressed so well that he eventually broke away and by 1776 had acquired a pottery of his own. He was a practical, cultured, intelligent man and a brilliant potter. There is some doubt as to the actual date he first went to London, but he is recorded as a member of the Spectacle Makers' Company from 16th June, 1778 and his address was given as 5 Portugal Street, Lincolns Inn Fields, formerly of 29 Fore Street, Cripplegate.

The Fore Street warehouse where his son, married in 1773, went to live, was opened soon after 1770. The business was so prosperous that by 1776 larger premises at Portugal Street had to be taken in what was once the Theatre Royal where Gay's *Beggar's Opera* had first been produced in 1727.

About this time, Spode met a Staffordshire-born merchant in the tea trade, William Copeland, who saw the possibilities of selling Spode's productions to his own customers. He was useful in obtaining Oriental porcelain and decorative Chinese tea wrappers to provide patterns for the new porcelain Spode introduced. He was extremely successful and in the year 1796 the profit made by the firm exceeded £13,000, from which Copeland received £1,000 as a gift "in recognition of his services".

According to the firm's books of 1902, Copeland the salesman became a partner in 1776, but this seems doubtful. It is believed that he was probably employed from that year and made a partner later on.

Spode I took his son and Copeland into partnership some time before his death in 1797 so that the firm became known as Spode, Son and Copeland. Josiah II's wife Sara also died in 1797, and the double tragedy may have decided him to leave London to live in Stoke permanently, where he brought up his

WORCESTER. Hexagonal-shaped vase and cover, painted with underglaze scale blue ground reserving panels in which are painted fabulous birds and insects in onglaze enamels. Mark: a fretted square in underglaze-blue. Dr. Wall Period, *c.* 1770. Height 14 ins.

Dyson Perrins Museum, Worcester

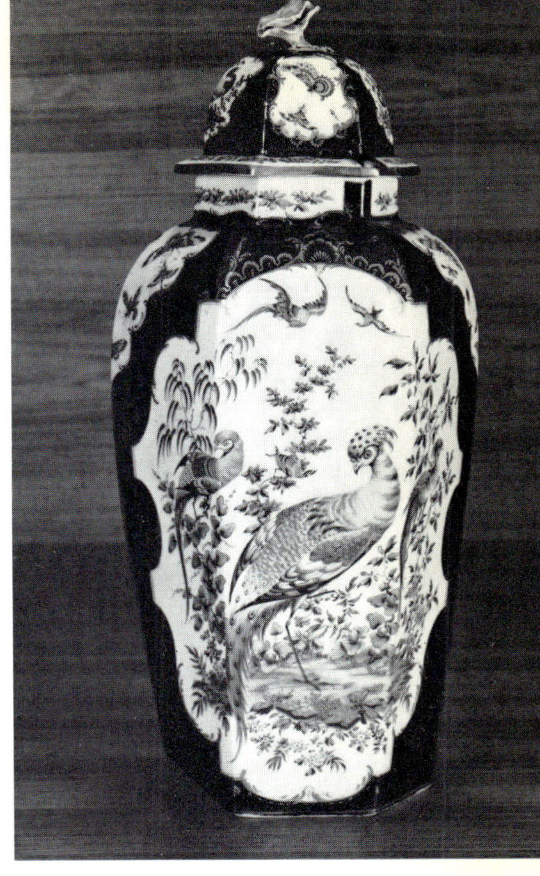

WORCESTER. Japan-pattern dish, *c.* 1765–70 *Dyson Perrins Museum, Worcester*

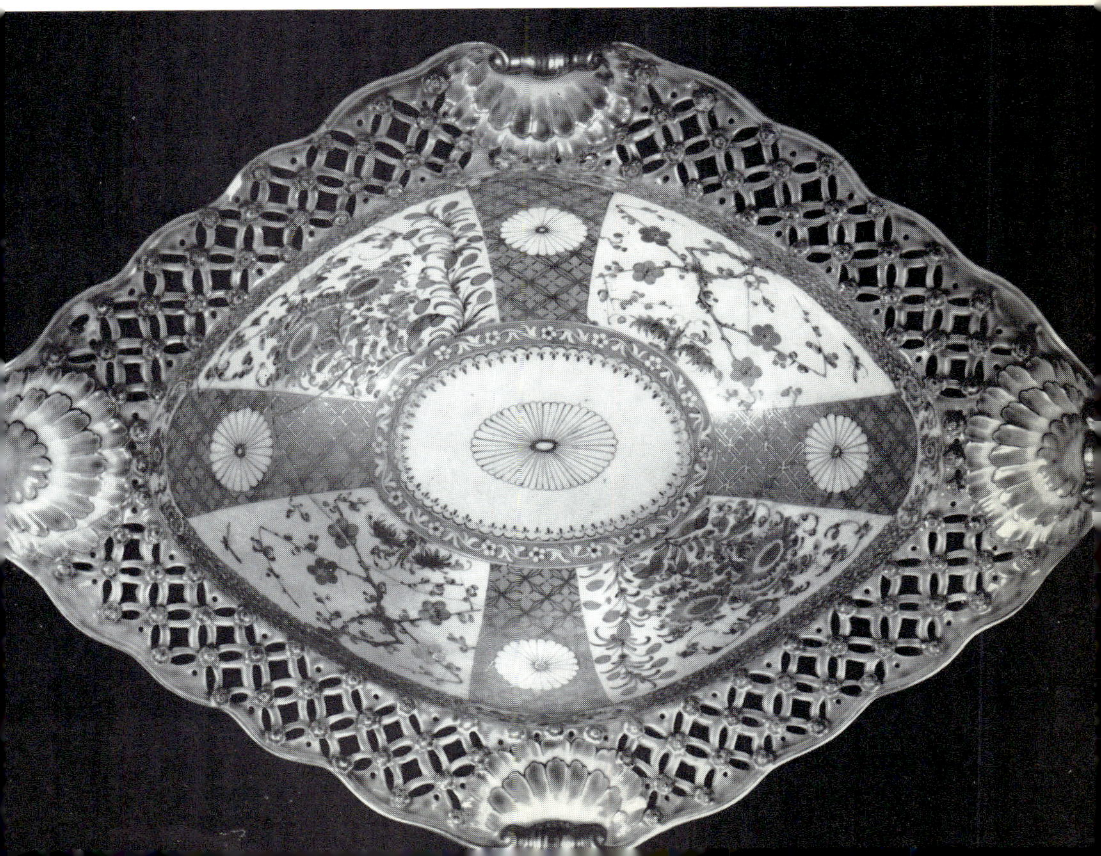

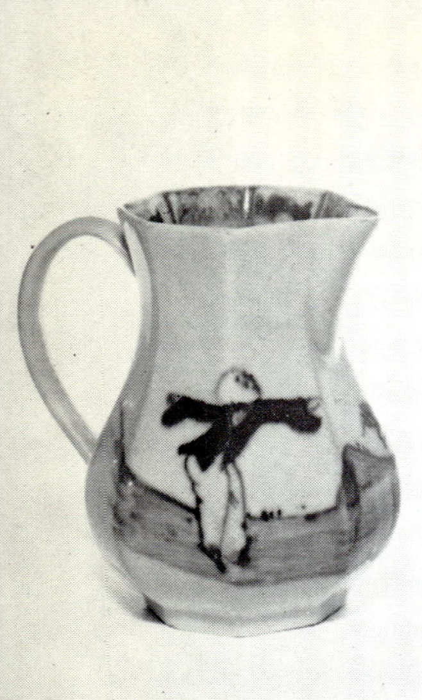
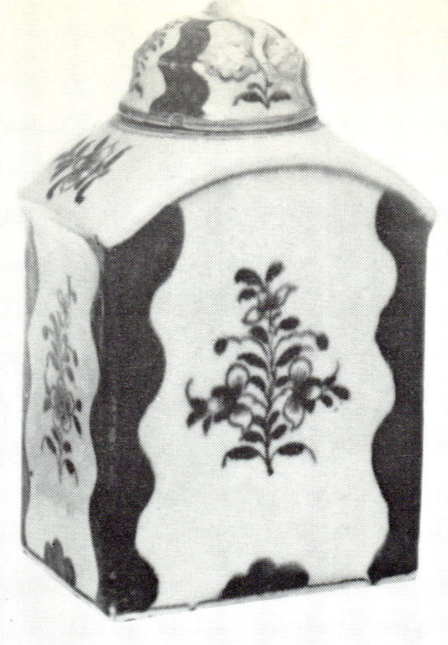
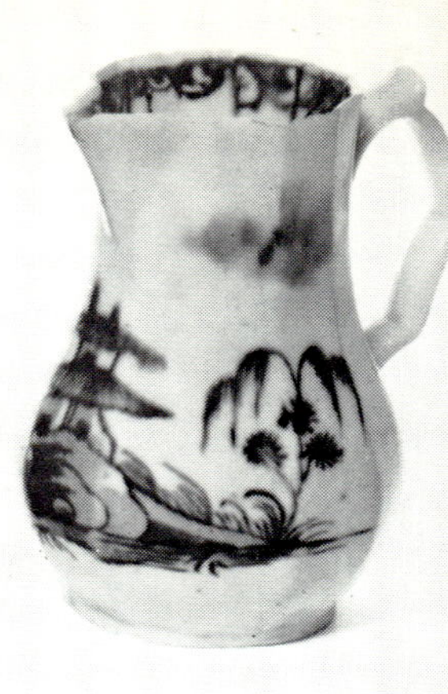

LIVERPOOL (left). A cream-jug with broadly faceted pear-shaped body and loop handle, painted in a dark tone of blue with The Jumping Boy pattern under a bluish glaze. Height $3\frac{1}{8}$ ins. Simulated Chinese marks, Chaffers Factory

LOWESTOFT (centre). A tea-caddy and cover, painted in underglaze blue with spray flanked by blue trellis diaper. Height $4\frac{1}{2}$ ins. Crescent mark

LONGTON HALL (right). Cream-jug with faceted pear-shaped body and angular handle. Height $3\frac{1}{2}$ ins. P. mark in underglaze blue

Sotheby & Co.

LOWESTOFT. Sugar-basin and sauce-boat, in soft-paste porcelain decorated in underglaze blue, *c.* 1757–60. Basin height $5\frac{5}{8}$ ins.; sauceboat length $5\frac{1}{2}$ ins.

Victoria and Albert Museum

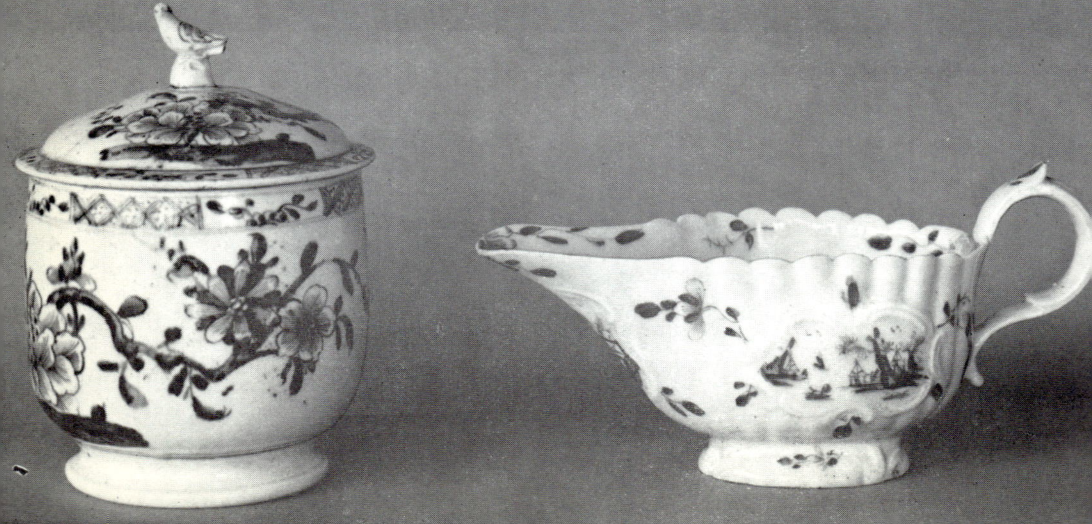

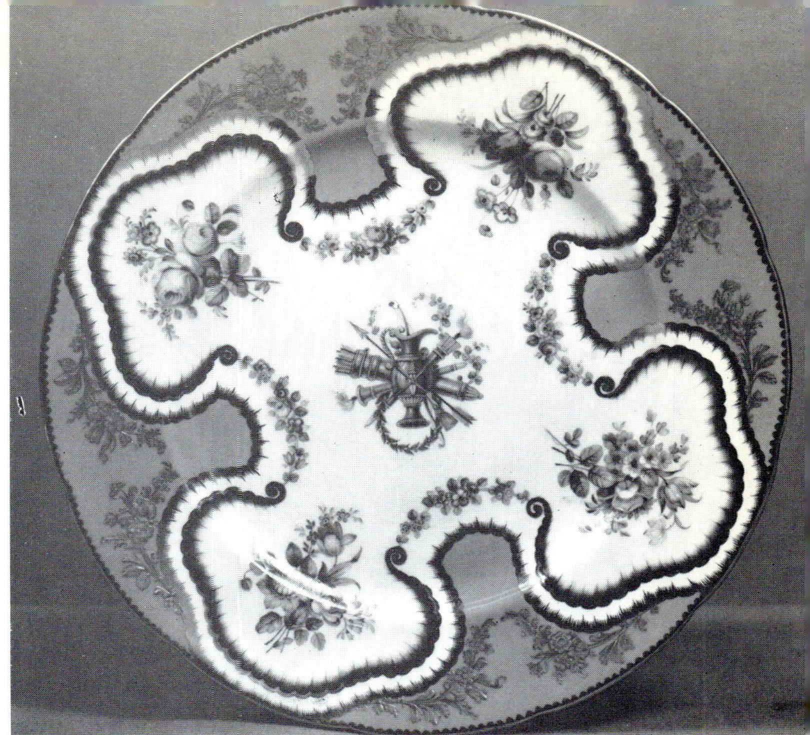

COALPORT. Plate painted in enamel colours and gilt, in imitation Sèvres porcelain, 1850. Diameter 9½ ins.

Victoria and Albert Museum

BRISTOL. Teapot and stand in hard-paste porcelain, decorated in enamel colours and gilt, *c.* 1775. Diameter 5 ins.

Victoria and Albert Museum

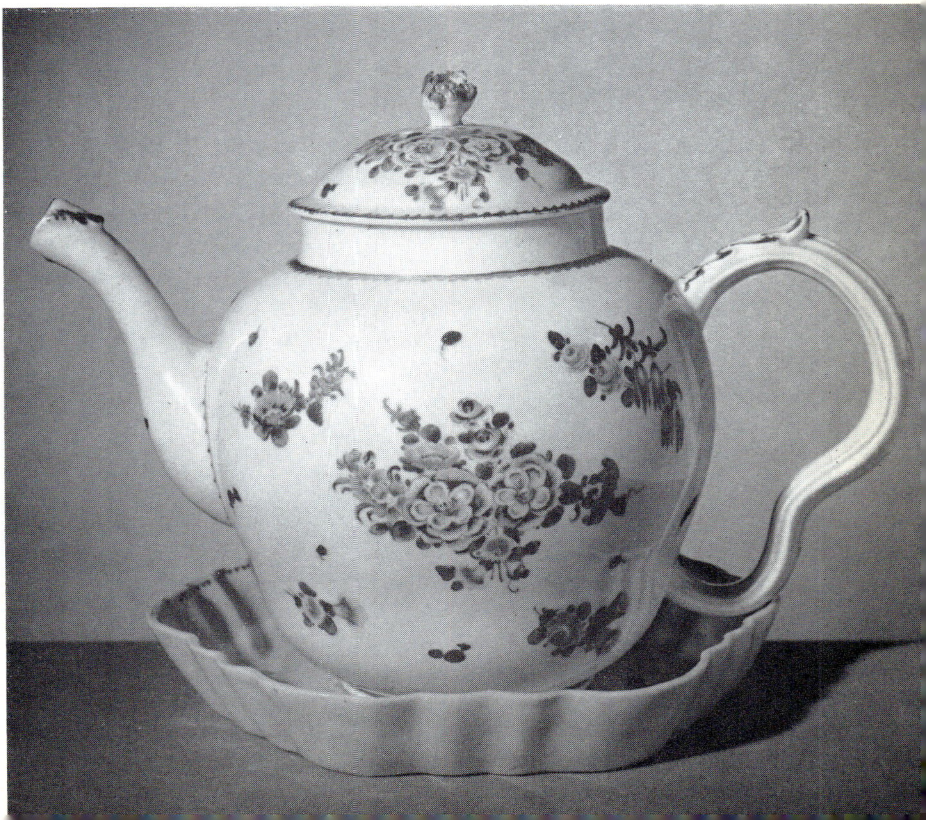

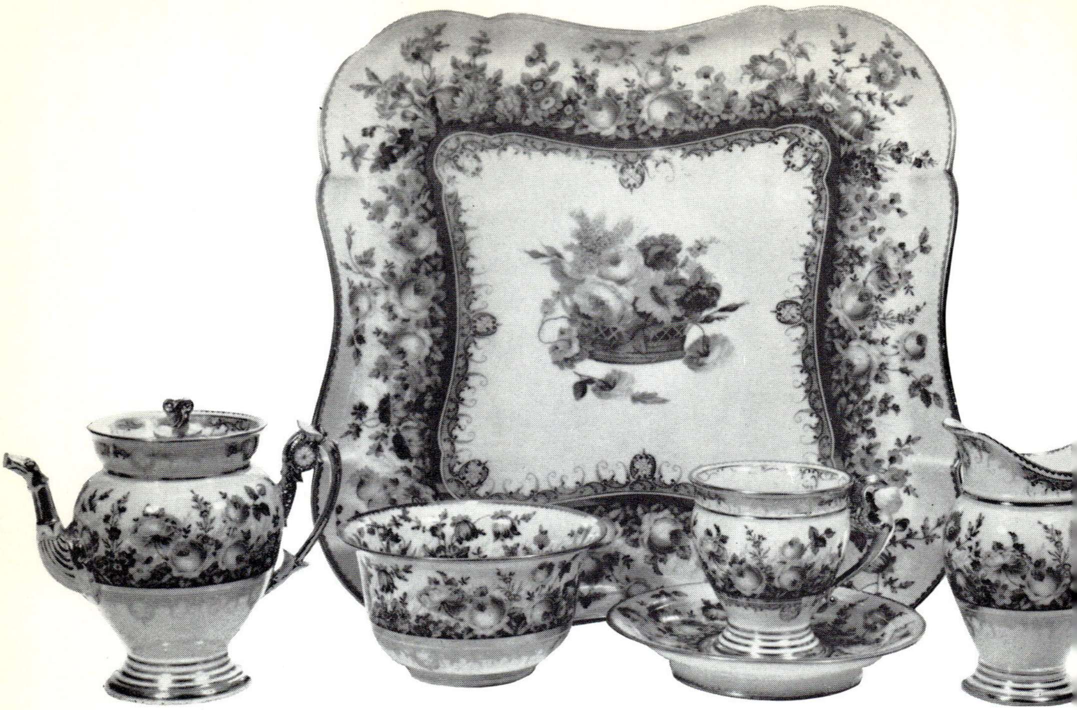

SWANSEA. Cabaret set, decorated in London, Empire style with burnished gilt handles. Impressed mark Swansea, c. 1815

Sotheby & Co.

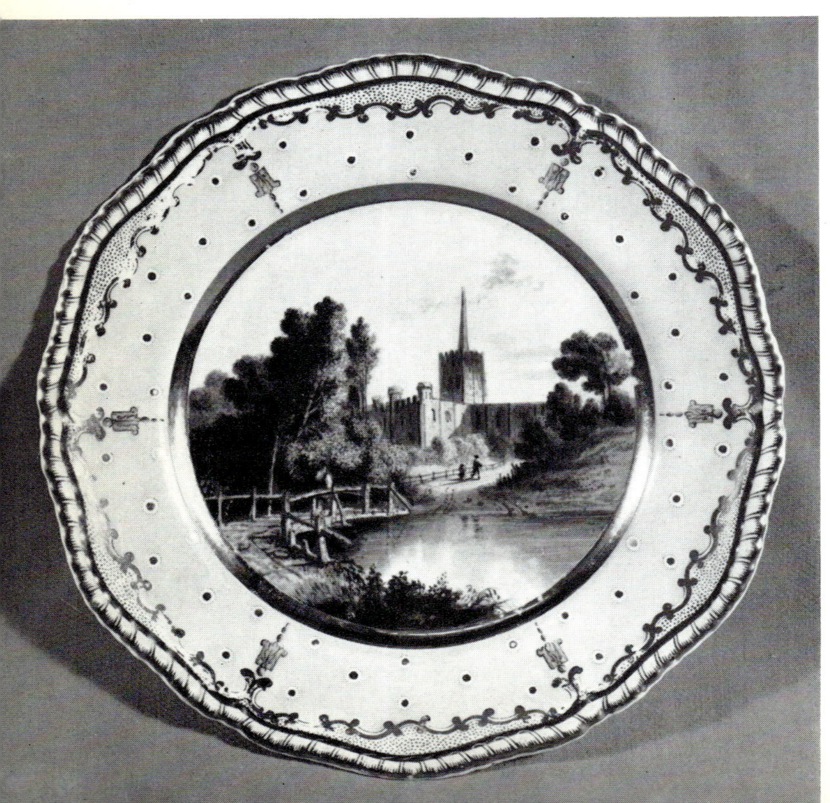

SPODE. Dessert plate Pale fawn ground Richly gilt, with hand-painted English land-scape. Diameter 9 ins Mark on back—St Albans Abbey Herts—in script lettering

W. T. Copeland & Sons Ltd

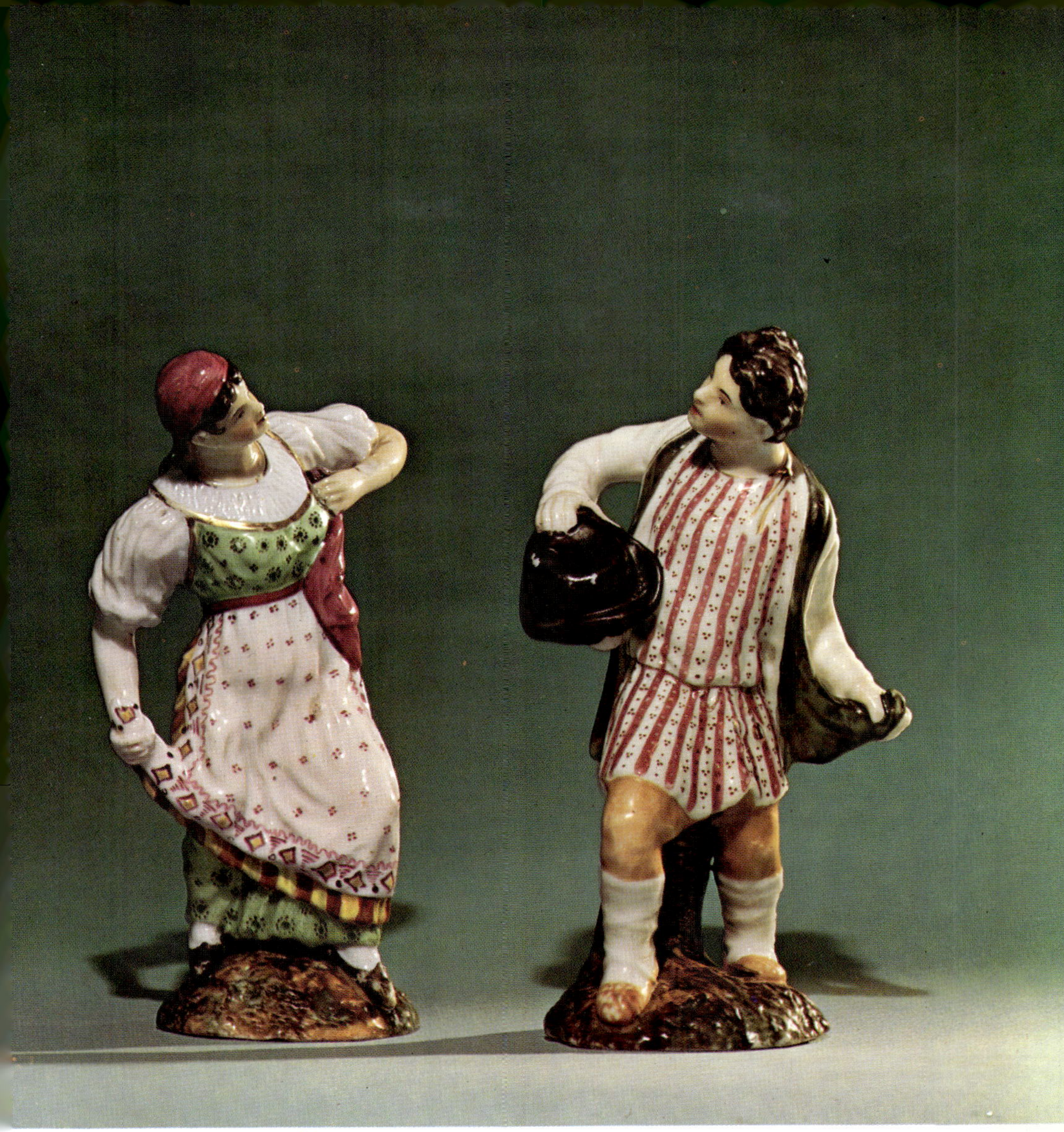

GARDNER PORCELAIN
"Pair of Dancing Figures", *c.* 1840
The Hermitage Museum, Leningrad, U.S.S.R.

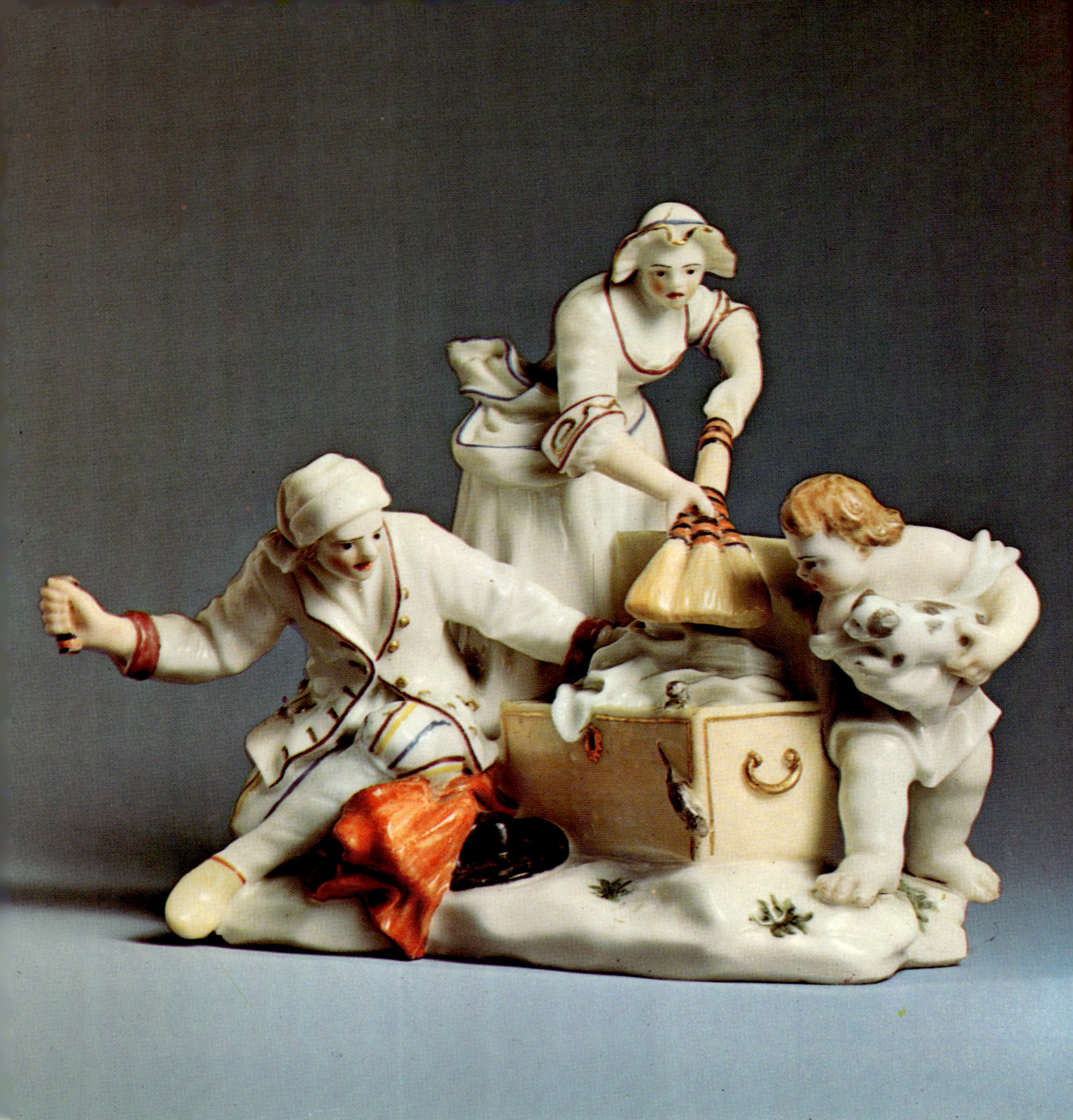

CAPODIMONTE (Carlo III)
"Group of Mice Catchers", $7\frac{1}{4}$ ins. high
Modelled by Giuseppe Gricci.
An important and rare piece

Christie's

children alone, never remarrying, and the Sales Warehouse was left in the charge of his partner Copeland. He built himself a fine house, known as "The Mount", and after a worthy and successful life, left a fortune of £250,000 when he died in 1827.

William Copeland died in 1826, and the two founders were succeeded by their sons, William Taylor Copeland and Josiah Spode III.

Spode III was also an excellent potter, learning his trade from his grandfather. A tragic accident in 1803 probably caused his retirement in 1810, when he became interested in the farming of his estate. "A lamentable accident", reported by the *Staffordshire Advertiser*, 1829. He was inspecting a newly erected Boulton and Watt engine, when, "a crown wheel struck his hat; and, in lifting his left arm to protect himself, the hand passed between the cogs of the wheels". The injury necessitated an immediate amputation. When Josiah III died in 1829, his executors continued the partnership under the title Spode and Copeland. In 1833 W. T. Copeland bought out the executors for £11,000, and became the sole proprietor.

Apart from being a pioneer in the porcelain works, where he introduced production methods which are still in use today, W. T. Copeland was also a respected citizen. He became Lord Mayor of London in 1835, at the early age of thirty-eight, then Tory Member of Parliament for Stoke in 1837 until 1852. He was beaten in the following election by the Whig candidate, and during the campaign the usual turbulent political incidents of the period which disturbed the town, resulted in the windows of his factory being smashed. He was re-elected in 1857, and remained the representative for Stoke until his death. His epitaph, spoken by the Rev. John Cox at his funeral epitomises not only him but all the Spodes and Copelands:- "It is our joy to believe that wordly prosperity and high position had not elevated the man whose loss we so much deplore, to think highly of himself".

Calcined animal bones had been used in porcelain production previously, but Spode I is credited with the standardisation of a formula for English bone china, which the rest of the country was soon to imitate. Brongniart wrote, "Spode produced a better porcelain than any other that has hitherto been made in England. He endeavoured to equal the soft porcelain of Sèvres which his paste closely resembled. He introduced, or at any rate perfected, the use of calcined bones in the body of his ware". This bone china was made from about 1790. The firm's record books show that it was sold in quantity from 1794.

A feldspar porcelain was produced in 1800, and was an immediate success, and was made in large quantities until 1824. It was a very translucent porcelain, and was clearly marked Spode Felspar Porcelain, printed in puce and surrounded by a wreath of roses, shamrocks and thistles.

In 1805, stone china, an opaque semi-porcelain, was introduced, and this also became an immediate success and rivalled Wedgwood's Queens-ware in the European markets. It had a bluish-grey body and a fine texture, and was usually decorated by transfer or bat printing, or enamel colours, or a combination. Spode also made black basalt and other coloured stone-ware bodies, including cane, red, lavender and green with bas-reliefs in the style of Wedgwood.

The Spodes were men of taste, and their productions of quasi-Oriental patterns after the Japanese *Imari* porcelain are delightful. The rich red and blues with gold elegantly used were the forerunners of the multitude of Derby Oriental patterns which followed, and were vastly superior to them.

Josiah Spode II was versatile and energetic. He imitated the best of his contemporary competition of Sèvres and Dresden, which could almost be taken for the originals were it not for the paste. His finest copies were those of Worcester, Nantgarw and of course the Chinese.

Copies of the Chinese patterns had been made to order during the troubled times of the Napoleonic Wars, when replacements were impossible. The Spode copies were excellent, and in the Spode Museum in Stoke one can see them side by side with the originals.

The great success of these replacements encouraged Spode to produce services decorated in the Chinese taste. Amongst them was the Willow Pattern, printed from engravings by

Thomas Minton when he joined the firm. The unprecedented fame of this English *Chinoiserie* led to fourteen known versions of the design from this factory alone.

A great variety of porcelain was produced decorated with fruits, flowers and birds, which were occasionally applied as well as painted, and bas-relief moulded decoration was frequent. A few figures were also made, but they were unmarked and are now so rare that attribution is difficult. Parian biscuit figures were made from about 1850. The porcelain trade turned a full circle in 1823 when Spode supplied the East India Company in Canton with a 1,300-piece service for the sum of £400.

The early porcelain products of Spode did not fall into the category of over-decorated wares which were predominant in the neo-Greek period, for the discernment of the Spodes maintained the tradition of the eighteenth century.

From 1833 to 1847, the title of the company was Copeland and Garrett, until Garrett, a traveller with the firm, retired, then Copeland (late Spode), then W. T. Copeland and Sons, until 1932 when it became a limited company.

The firm still exists and is under the direction of descendants of the founders, and is known as W. T. Copeland and Sons Ltd. They make excellent porcelain and earthenware, and seem to have recaptured the magic of the eighteenth century. On the same site as the original factory, with the necessary modern additions, elegant designs in modern and traditional idioms are produced with taste, restraint and quality.

One of the original porcelain "bottle ovens" (so called from its shape) is left standing as a memorial. It was in use until 1961, but has now been superseded by a modern electric tunnel kiln. The old bottle oven required sixteen tons of best coal to fire it, and the fireman (usually a temperamental gentleman on whose shoulders the responsibility of a firing rested) directed the delicate operation. ("We were always in the hands of the fireman.") The tunnel kiln, although impractical for large monumental pieces, is more suitable for production.

The factory is well worth a visit, for through the original wrought-iron gates at the entrance, one steps into the cobbled court-yard of another era.

SPODE CHARACTERISTICS

1. Paste, English bone china, rich and white, not glassy.
2. Glaze, clear and transparent, but warm-toned.
3. Usually clearly marked, with pattern number.

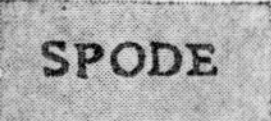

Impressed
(c. 1770)

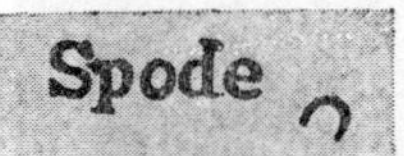

Impressed
(c. 1770)

SPODE
2417

Painted in Red
(c. 1790)

The numbers indicate design numbers

1989
Spode

Painted in Red
(c. 1790)

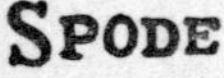

Printed in Blue
(1784-1789)

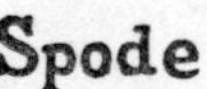

Printed in Blue
(1790-1800)

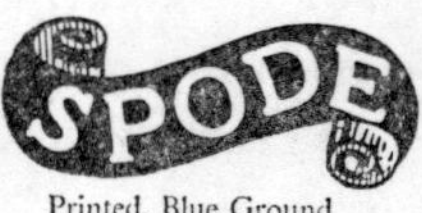

Printed, Blue Ground
(1795-1805)

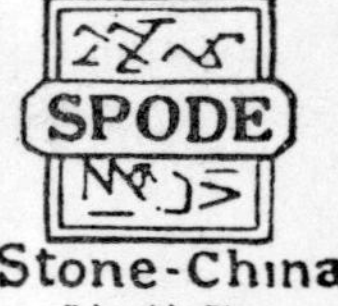

Printed in Blue
(c. 1805)

Printed in Blue
(c. 1805)

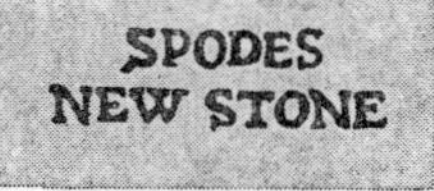

Impressed
(1810-1815)

Printed in Puce
(1800-1833)

SPODE
Felspar Porcelain

Printed in Blue
(1800-1833)

Printed in Blue
(From 1810)

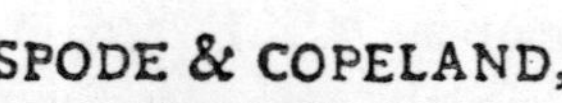

Printed in Blue
(First used in 1815)

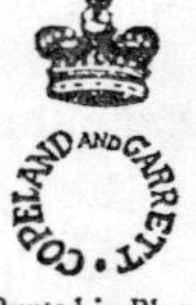

Printed in Blue
(1833-1846)

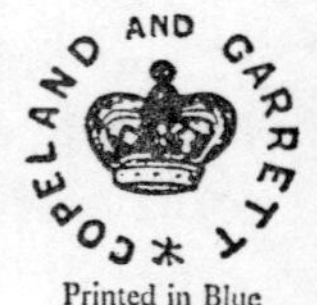
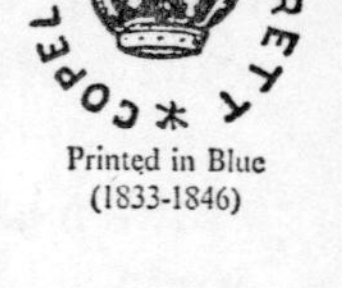

Printed in Blue
(1833-1846)

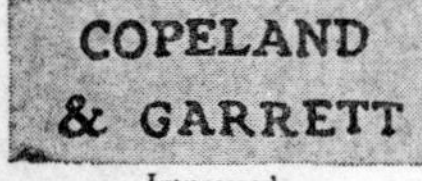

Impressed
(1833-1846)

COPELAND & GARRETT
LATE
SPODE
THE TIBER

Printed in Blue
(1833-1846)

Copeland
Late Spode.

Printed in Blue
(1847-1867)

Copeland late Spode

Impressed
(1847-1867)

COPELAND

Printed in Green
or Blue

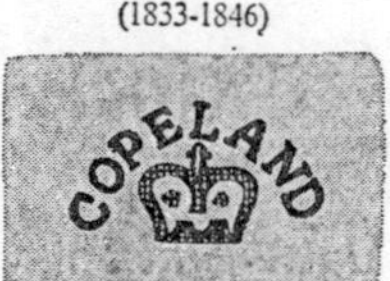

Impressed

Copeland
Stone China

Printed in Blue

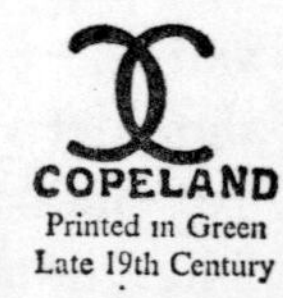

Printed in Green
Late 19th Century

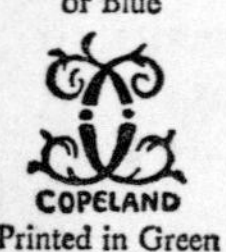

Printed in Green
Late 19th Century

SPODE
COPELANDS CHINA
ENGLAND

Modern Mark
Printed in Green

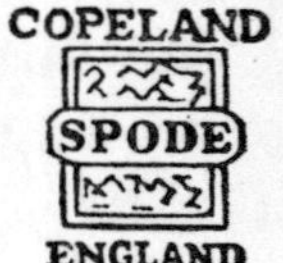

COPELAND
SPODE
ENGLAND
New Stone

Modern Marks, Printed in Various Colours

SPODE & COPELAND TRADE MARKS

Marks reproduced in facsimile by kind permission of W. T. COPELAND & SONS LTD.

[19] ROCKINGHAM, SWINTON, YORKSHIRE
Pottery 1745–1842
Porcelain 1826–1842

A factory was opened by Edward Butler in 1745 on the property of Earl Fitzwilliam, Marquis of Rockingham, for the manufacture of common earthenware, and so began the long association of the Brameld family with Rockingham. Between the years 1787 and 1796, the factory was owned by a company of Leeds potters, and following several changes in ownership, the second period began in 1806, when John Brameld, son William and successors, carried on the business as Brameld and Company. By 1825 the company was bankrupt, and the landlord (who was the main creditor) paid the sad factory a visit. He was shown specimens of porcelain that Thomas Brameld had produced experimentally, and was so impressed that he decided to finance the Bramelds so that porcelain could be made commercially. He also allowed his family crest—a griffin's head—to be used as a factory trade mark.

Encouraged by his patron, Thomas Brameld enlarged the factory and engaged more artists. Production increased and large quantities of a great variety of goods were placed on the market and sold without difficulty. During this third period the mark was printed in red. John Brameld's brother George Frederick managed the sales department, and for some time lived in St. Petersburg, where he supervised the large Russian market he had established. Another brother, John Wager Brameld, was a fine artist, and specialised in botanical flowers which he painted exquisitely. Unfortunately they were not produced in great quantity for he spent most of his time in London as the agent for the firm. The Bramelds were avid copyists, and inspiration for their porcelain was derived from Coalport, Worcester and Derby. They made candelabra, coffee sets, ornaments, scent bottles, spill cases, pen trays, ewers, pastille burners, cottages and castles, candlesticks, figures, animals, bedposts, tea, dessert, and dinner services, etc.

The fourth "Royal" period began in 1830 and lasted until

the accession of Queen Victoria in 1837. King William IV and Queen Adelaide visited Earl Fitzwilliam, and having admired the porcelain products of the factory, ordered a dessert service. This dessert service, which according to Jewitt was first used at the Coronation of Queen Victoria, consisted of 144 plates and 56 large pieces. Every ceramic decorative device was used to adorn it. It was heavily gilded over a raised lace pattern, with raised oak-leaf borders converging on to a painted Royal coat of arms. The centres were decorated with paintings of landscapes, and each of the large pieces was decorated with plastic work to represent its use. The mark for the seven years of this period was the griffin printed in puce, together with the motto, "Royal Rockingham Works. China manufacturers to the King, Queen and Royal Family". Royal patronage stimulated trade. Jewitt (*The Ceramic Art of Great Britain*) records the dessert services made at Swinton for the Duchess of Cumberland in 1830, and the Duke of Sussex in 1833.

An interesting fact for the porcelain collectors are the prices charged at that time:

4 Large Dress Plates
4 Second size do.
8 Small do. do.
4 Ice Pails (Handles à la Warwick)
4 Pine and Grape Baskets
8 Peach Baskets—say 4 Mulberry and 4 Pine
4 Fruit Comports
4 Shell ,,
—

40 pieces	perhaps	500 guineas
6 doz. of Plates	will be	360 ,,
		860 ,,

The display pieces cost the Duke an average of 12½ guineas each, and the dessert plates 5 guineas each. With the devaluation of sterling since 1833, the present day value of such a service, if indeed one were offered for sale, would not be excessive by comparison.

Extended credit and bad debts at home and abroad, reduced the factory to near bankruptcy and led to its ultimate closure. By 1842, the Fitzwilliams decided they had lost too much money in the venture, so withdrew their support and the factory closed down.

For some time afterwards, a former employee Isaac Baguly and his son Alfred (who had come to Swinton from Derby) bought china-ware in the white from Staffordshire and decorated it at Swinton. They used the griffin mark, with the caption added, "Manufacturers to the Queen", printed in red. This was the fifth and final period of Rockingham.

Rockingham porcelain was made in a florid rococo style, painted in bright colours with brassy gilding and was always well-made and finished. Recent research has determined that much of the porcelain previously attributed to Rockingham was never made there at all. For many years certain types of unidentifiable porcelain sheep, poodles, cottages, castles, dessert and tea sets in the familiar biscuit, grey or green ground colour, were attributed to Rockingham. It has now been proved that the quality of Rockingham porcelain was always excellent, and these clumsy imitations were manufactured by other Staffordshire potteries. Only marked pieces are now considered to be genuine, with the exception of services where a marked piece identifies the rest. A fine collection in the Rotherham Museum is well worth a visit.

It is worth remembering that the Rockingham factory was also a great pottery. Porridge bowls, bleeding bowls, ewers and basins and other domestic paraphernalia of Regency England found their way into thousands of homes. These utensils evoke a bygone era and have become part of social history.

ROCKINGHAM CHARACTERISTICS

1. Phosphatic English soft-paste.
2. Florid rococo revival styles.
3. Light in weight.

4. Unmarked pieces, unless part of services, highly suspect.
5. Lavish brassy gilding.
6. Well made and finished.
7. Factory marks clear and in various ways.

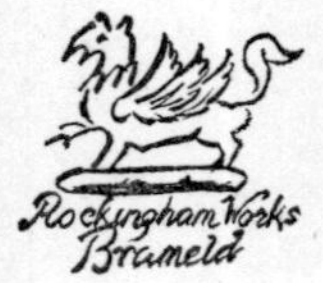

Printed, generally in red.

[20] MINTON, Stoke-on-Trent, Staffordshire 1796—Present Day

Thomas Minton was apprenticed to an engraver (possibly Hancock) at the Caughley China Works. He became extremely skilful and amongst many others he created the celebrated Willow Pattern design.

From Caughley he went to London where he worked for Josiah Spode, and got married. He then returned to Staffordshire where he set himself up as a master engraver, in a house close to Trent Bridge in Stoke which had been built by Whieldon, the first partner of Wedgwood. He became very successful and designed many patterns which were in constant demand.

In 1793, at the age of twenty-eight he decided to build a factory to manufacture earthenware on his own account. He bought some land, and from modest beginnings the famous factory was born. Minton engaged the Poulson brothers, practical potters in a small way of business, and by 1796 production had begun of cream coloured earthenware printed in blue. Thomas's brother Arthur became the London agent, and William Pownall, a Liverpool merchant, provided the capital.

From 1798 the factory made porcelain from Cornish china clay until 1811 when production was temporarily abandoned, although it was resumed later. Jewitt's account of the difficulties of obtaining supplies of clay from Cornwall are interesting as they illustrate the period so succinctly (*The Ceramic Art of Great Britain*):

"Difficulties of all kinds sprung up. Sometimes the water courses were obstructed; robbery of all kinds was going on; and there were also the exacting demands of lords of the manor to battle with and satisfy. Bad roads, imperfect machinery and methods of getting the minerals were other stubborn facts tending to abate 'the pleasures of landlordism'. The property was within three miles of St. Austell, but Charlestown was then the port of shipment, and the cost of transit thither in waggons over the wretched roads was 8s. per ton; cost of raising, working, and casking, £1.15s., and other expenses, raised the value free on board there to £4.15s. Freight from Charlestown to Liverpool 12s., dues 2s. 6d., canal freight to the Potteries, 11s. 6d., and making a moderate allowance for capital invested, the clay could not be delivered at less than £6.15s. per ton."

Thomas had four sons and six daughters. The two elder sons, Thomas and Herbert, were made partners in the business in 1817, but Thomas left in 1821 in order to study for the Church. Herbert Minton, after his education at a Dame school, then at a Grammar school, showed a remarkable aptitude for the family business. After only two years with the company and only sixteen years of age, he became a travelling salesman and represented the firm all over England. He resumed porcelain production in about 1821 and workmen from the closed Derby works were readily absorbed. Their techniques and practical experience improved the quality and variety of the Minton wares and the firm prospered.

In 1836 the company was known as Minton and Boyle (Herbert Minton and John Boyle), until 1841 when Boyle withdrew to join Wedgwood. In 1845 the title of the firm was Herbert Minton and Co. (Herbert and Michael Hollins). In 1858, upon the death of Herbert Minton, his nephew, Colin Minton Campbell, Member of Parliament for North Staffordshire, became the Director, first with Michael Hollins and then with the grandsons of Thomas Minton. The present company was formed in 1883 and became known as Mintons.

The early porcelain wares were of high quality and were nearly as good as Sèvres, whose models they copied. These early products were sometimes marked with M or the Sèvres crossed LL's with M between.

Minton is the only English factory which produced a new technique in the nineteenth century. This was the *pâte-sur-pâte* which was a process invented by Marc Solon, the artist from Sèvres, and consisted of painting in white slip instead of enamel, before glazing. The subjects were classical figures or flowers, and show great elegance of design if a rather cool interpretation.

Extremely prosperous during the nineteenth century, Mintons supplied many services with special decorations and coats-of-arms to Heads of State. One cannot fail to admire the technical virtuosity of the nineteenth century potters, who achieved results that even with all our modern equipment we can no longer equal. Large Parian figures and monumental Majolica pieces cannot be fired in electric kilns, and it is even doubtful whether they could be produced at all, for the cost would be prohibitive.

The factory is still in existence and produces high quality bone china table ware.

MINTON CHARACTERISTICS

1. English bone china, finely finished.
2. Prim, English versions of French models and decoration.
3. Favourite colour, brilliant turquoise blue.
4. Most popular nineteenth century factory for custom made services for Embassies and foreign V.I.P.'s.
5. *Pâte-sur-pâte.*
6. Parian figures.
7. Large majolica pieces.
8. Factory mark, M, or M, between crossed LL's. After 1883, Mintons.

1820–1830, in blue enamel.

1820–1830, in underglaze blue.

After *1851*, printed or impressed.

MINTON After *1865*, impressed.

[21] WEDGWOOD, Stoke-on-Trent, Staffordshire
1759—Present Day
Bone China 1812–1822

Josiah Wedgwood was born in Burslem in July 1730 of an old established Staffordshire family of potters. He became apprenticed to his brother Thomas in 1744 for a period of five years, and stayed as an employee for some time afterwards.

Josiah then went to Stoke, where he began the manufacture of imitation agate and other types of knife handles which were then in demand. He entered into partnership with John Harrison in 1752, and continued the same productions, and two years later they both joined Thomas Whieldon the potter for a five-year partnership. When this expired in 1759, Wedgwood returned to Burslem where he rented premises from his family and started business on his own account. He moved his factory several times, first to "Ivy House" and then to "Bell Works" where he successfully produced his Cream-ware. Although the main products of Wedgwood were not in porcelain, its influence on porcelain in Europe was so great that a brief description of his other work is necessary.

Cream-ware was perfected as an imitation of porcelain and contains in its formula many of the ingredients of its inspiration.

Cream-ware was opaque and as the name implies of a deep creamy colour. The paste was stable and was inexpensive to produce, and was the first mass production so-called porcelain to be made.

In 1762, on the confinement of Queen Charlotte, Wedgwood astutely presented her with a breakfast service which was graciously accepted. Cream-ware was re-named Queen's-ware and Wedgwood, his success assured, was permitted to call himself "Potter to Her Majesty".

The Queen ordered a complete dinner service and this was swiftly followed by an order for another from the King. Orders for Queen's-ware came pouring in from England and abroad, and many copyists sprang up in the surrounding potteries, but there was work for all.

Some of the Queen's-ware was undecorated except for ribs and other moulded ornaments, while some were painted in enamel colours and others sent to Sadler and Green in Liverpool for transfer printing.

Queen's-ware was to have a revolutionary effect on the *faïence* and Delft factories. When import restrictions were lifted in France in 1786, Queen's-ware became very popular to the detriment of the more expensive *faïence*. One by one the *faïence* factories closed, until by the end of the eighteenth century there were only a few left in business.

In 1764, Josiah married a distant cousin, Sara Wedgwood, who was heiress to a fortune of some £20,000. He looked around for new and larger premises, and in 1766 purchased the Ridge House Estate which he afterwards named Etruria because he believed, without foundation, that the new basalts he was producing were of Etruscan origin.

Thomas Bentley, the Liverpool agent, was made a partner in the ornamental department only of the business in 1768, and opened a London branch in Chelsea in 1769.

Six commemorative vases of antique form based on designs taken from Sir William Hamilton's book *Ancient Greek and Etruscan Vases* were made in 1769, and were thrown by Wedgwood himself, with Bentley turning the wheel.

By 1773, three kinds of ware were made by Wedgwood for

ornamental purposes, terra cotta, black basalt and a white biscuit ware. A fourth was added in 1774, a "fine white terra cotta of great beauty and delicacy proper for cameos, portraits and bas reliefs". This Jasper-ware was to become one of Wedgwood's most popular productions. At first it was made in colours throughout, and from 1785 it was "dipped" so that the body remained white inside, but from 1858 "solid" Jasper was re-introduced.

The twenty-year old sculptor John Flaxman, son of an intaglio moulder, began his twelve years association with Wedgwood in 1775, during which he modelled vast numbers of low reliefs used as decoration on the Wedgwood Jasper, as well as many fine cameo high relief portraits of Dr. Johnson, Captain Cook, Sir William Hamilton and others.

A great auction sale was held in 1786 of a tremendous collection of antiquities and *objets de Vertu* belonging to the deceased Duchess of Portland. In the catalogue was the magnificent Portland or Barberini vase, described by Sir William Hamilton, "Except the Apollo Belvedere, the Niobes, and two or three others of the first-class marbles, I do not believe that there are any monuments of antiquity existing that were executed by so great an artist". Wedgwood was determined to buy it, but it was sold to the Duke of Portland for £1,029. When he learned why Wedgwood wished to buy the vase, the Duke of Portland kindly loaned it to him for twelve months. The vase, which was made in glass and now rests in the British Museum, was of superb workmanship and featured a white classical frieze modelled in low relief. Wedgwood determined to produce fifty copies in Jasper, which he proceeded to make against subscription at fifty guineas a time, but it cost him far more. Some indeed were sold for less than the full price because of some minor defect, and one of these is now to be found in the Wedgwood Museum at Barlaston. It was originally sold to Thomas Hope of Amsterdam in 1793 for £31.10s. plus £2.10s. for the display case.

Towards the end of the eighteenth century, public support for the Abolition of Slavery Movement increased. The plight of the unfortunates who had been kidnapped and transported to work in the American plantations outraged the conscience of decent people. Josiah Wedgwood commissioned William Hackwood to design a Jasper medallion in 1786 as a campaign button. The Slave medallion depicted a kneeling African slave, his manacled wrists upheld, and the motto "Am I not a man and a brother?". Wedgwood wrote to the Rev. Thomas Clarkson in January 1792, offering to pay for a woodcut to be made of it for the title page of a pamphlet in connection with the Abolition of Slavery Movement.

Wedgwood took his three sons, John, Josiah and Thomas, and his nephew Thomas Byerley, into partnership in 1790, and upon his death in 1795, the management of the business passed into the hands of Byerley, who introduced the manufacture of bone china at Etruria from 1812 to 1822. It was of extremely good quality and is now extremely rare. Porcelain was soon abandoned for it was expensive to produce for a highly competitive market. The specialisation in Jasper and Queen's-ware became the obvious practical and commercial policy for the factory, and porcelain was not made again until the 1880's.

Wedgwood today is housed in a modern factory at Barlaston, and makes fine quality porcelain and earthenware table ware and reproductions of their old Jasper models.

WEDGWOOD CHARACTERISTICS
Bone china 1812–1822

1. English bone china.
2. Botanical flowers, bouquets, landscapes (John Cutts) ground colours, purple monochromes, blue transfer, some gilding.
3. No figures.
4. Clean, fresh work but unoriginal.
5. Mark Wedgwood printed in colour, usually red.

WEDGWOOD

1812–1822, printed in red, blue or gold. Reproduced in facsimile by kind permission of JOSIAH WEDGWOOD & SONS LTD.

[22] DAVENPORT, LONGPORT, STAFFORDSHIRE 1793–1882

In 1793 John Davenport bought a pottery founded some twenty years earlier, and made both earthenware and porcelain, and added a glass works in 1801.

The porcelain was of excellent quality and was fresh and clean in appearance.

The Prince of Wales (later George IV) together with his brother the Duke of Clarence (later William IV), visited the factory in 1806. Later, on the accession of William IV, a royal service was ordered to be used at the Coronation banquet, and from then onwards the crown was incorporated into the trade mark.

An English bone china, the paste is indistinguishable from its contemporaries. Domestic ware was made in great abundance, technically very good and decorated in the nineteenth century taste for lush splendour with masses of gilding. Intricate patterns in a fine dark blue enamel and a wide range of reds were popular and designs were sometimes printed and finished by hand. The pieces are usually well marked.

DAVENPORT CHARACTERISTICS

1. Good quality bone china.
2. Decoration mechanically rendered.
3. Lush brassy gilding.
4. Pieces generally clearly marked Davenport, sometimes with crown.

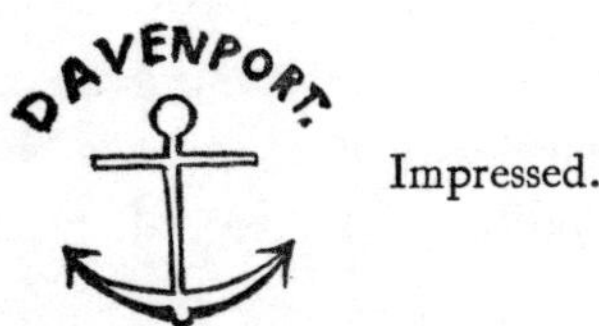

Impressed.

Chapter Five

Italy and Spain

THE RENAISSANCE OF the fifteenth century, begun in the Italian cities, spread to the rest of Europe. Established as the leader in arts and sciences, Italy was the light and hope of the civilised world after the gloom and repression of thought in the Middle Ages.

The surge of talent thrown up in this intellectual explosion is too well known to be described here. In the field of ceramics Italian maiolica developed into a splendid industry, which was imitated in France, Holland and England.

Porcelain shared modestly in this success. A *porcellana contrefacto* was said to have been made in Venice in 1470 by an alchemist, but as no examples have survived it cannot be proved.

The first recorded European porcelain was made at Florence in the Medici factory from 1575, and was Persian inspired. It was not a true porcelain, but a soft-paste, of which some sixty specimens have survived. Production ceased in 1587.

In 1700, Philip Duc d'Anjou, grandson of Louis XIV, became Philip V King of Spain and ruler of her possessions in the Indies, the Spanish Netherlands (modern Belgium), the Italian Kingdoms of Naples and Sicily, and the Duchies of Tuscany and Milan. The Papal States and Venice were independent.

The next enterprising factory was launched in Naples by the King, whose passion it became. He took an active part in all parts of the production, and when he became King Charles III of Spain in 1759, he took his artists and workmen with him to Madrid, where he established a factory at his palace at Buen Retiro.

Other factories were established in the eighteenth century, but their work was derivative and lacking in originality.

The lead taken by Italy in the Arts had been lost by this time. The baroque style of the Counter-Reformation was not seriously adopted abroad, and the rest of Europe developed independently.

Generally speaking the contribution of Italy and Spain during the great porcelain epoch of the eighteenth century was floridly imitative and lacking in restraint.

[1] FLORENCE
MEDICI, Florence, Italy
1575–1587

A factory was founded by the Grand Duke of Tuscany, Francesco I de Medici "with the assistance of a Levantine" (probably Persian), and fine quality soft-paste porcelain was made, the first porcelain in Europe. Only about sixty surviving specimens are known to exist, and these are all in collections or museums. The decoration was in underglaze blue, in the maiolica idiom. Porcelain in the possession of Queen Elizabeth I and other contemporary monarchs was probably of this origin, although there is no substantiating evidence. It is known that English ships had traded with Italian cities since the reign of Henry VII.

The mark, in blue, was a drawing of the dome of Florence Cathedral surmounting a capital letter "F", and sometimes the Medici device.

MEDICI CHARACTERISTICS

1. Soft-paste.
2. Substantial forms reminiscent of Persian earthenware.
3. Decoration in the maiolica style in underglaze blue.
4. Glaze rarely white, with small bubbles.
5. Mark Dome above F.
6. Stylised flowers, birds, view of Florence.

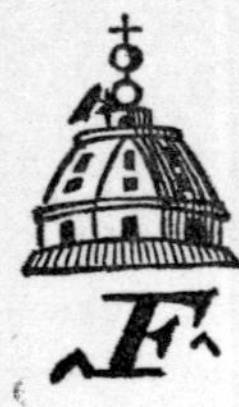

In underglaze blue.

DOCCIA, near Florence, Italy 1735—Present Day

The Marchesi Ginori was a man of cultivated tastes and important social position. He carried out many public works in order to promote agriculture and fisheries in his native Tuscany. In the tradition of the Italian nobility, who frequently indulged in trade, he realised the importance of reviving a porcelain industry in Florence, which was justly proud of its tradition of Medici porcelain. He founded a factory at Doccia on part of his estates, and travelled widely collecting men, materials and ideas for his favourite enterprise.

Visiting Vienna during 1737 on a diplomatic mission, he met Carl Wandhelein (1702–1747), an experienced porcelain chemist, and invited him to manage his factory. Artists from Vienna and Meissen followed, and even the early works show mature appreciation of form and decoration. A nursery of artists was formed so that the tradition could be handed on through the generations. Ginori's energy was immense. While Governor of Livorno he sent a ship to China to the East India Company, expressly for a cargo of china clay so that the much admired Chinese porcelain could be exactly copied. Later, local materials from the Island of Elba were used, as importation proved too expensive.

The first products were a form of soft-paste, a hybrid porcelain as Brongniart called it, and later products were a type of true porcelain, a hard-paste—*masso bastardo*—following the tradition of Meissen without the perfection of paste. Later, when kaolin was discovered in the South of France at St. Yrieix, this was conveniently imported, and the paste became whiter.

The Ginori factory followed the fashionable styles. They were avid copyists, and developed no particular style of their own. First there were the forms and colours after the Chinese, the Fukien *blanc-de-chine* and the blue and white Nankin. Due to the connection with Vienna, much work was done in the baroque Vienna style and many of the early Doccia pieces which were never marked, have probably been attributed to other factories. Then followed the rococo style with copies of Meissen, Sèvres and Menneçy, all admirably executed, but nevertheless unoriginal. Then came the cameos and medallions after Wedgwood and the neo-classical styles after Capodimonte. Etruscan and Pompeian styles were popular, Bourbon sprigs, landscapes in polychrome and *en camaieu*, rims laid with heavy ground colours with rich gilding in the French Empire manner.

The factory later bought the Capodimonte moulds when that factory closed down in 1806, and continued to produce the well-known raised figure designs using the mark of the letter "N" surmounted by a crown. The preceding period used a star in blue, red or gold as the factory mark.

DOCCIA CHARACTERISTICS

So many different types and classes of porcelain were made that it is impossible to generalise on the characteristics of this versatile factory. Factory records are obscure and the works of the factory have never been well documented.

In blue, red or gold.

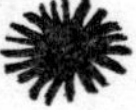

In blue, red or gold.

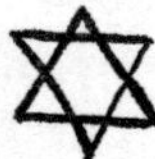

Impressed.

[2] VENICE

Venice was an important port and trading centre. Her merchant adventurers established a vast mercantile network throughout the Middle East, and made Venice the clearing ground for goods from the Orient which had been transported to the Levant by camel train. It is hard to imagine that porcelain made that long, arduous journey and arrived intact. For some time porcelain was called "Venus ware", as it emanated from Venice.

The area is notable for some fine maiolica which was made from the sixteenth century and the famous glass works at Murano which are still in existence. The earliest porcelain recorded in a letter dated 1470 possibly referred to milky glass, fine and transparent, decorated in colours "as good as, or even superior to that of Barbary" made by *Maestro* Antonio of S. Simion.

In 1504 some *porcellana contrafacto* (imitation porcelain) was made for the Duke Alfonso I of Ferrara, but no surviving examples of either of these exist. Four porcelain factories were opened in the area during the eighteenth century. These were the brothers Vezzi (1719–20 to 1740?), Nathaniel Friedrich Hewelcke (1757–1763), Geminiano Cozzi (1764–65 to 1812), and Nove (1752 to ?).

VEZZI, Venice, Italy 1720–1740

Two wealthy goldsmiths, the brothers Francesco and Guiseppe Vezzi, opened a factory at S. Nicolo in 1720 and are said to have bought the arcanum from Christoph Konrad Hunger or one of his associates and bought their kaolin from the Meissen source at Aue in Germany.

A German type hard-paste porcelain was made at Vezzi. Inclined to be smoky and yellowish, it is variable in quality and distinguishable by a singular glassy appearance. The earliest documented pieces are two armorial cups and saucers now in the

Museo Civico at Turin marked in red "Ven[a] A.G. 1726". Some Vienna style sugar-boxes with covers and octagonal shaped teapots in the style of silver were made, some with acanthus leaves and others painted with figures from the Italian Comedy. The style developed into an exaggerated form of Venetian rococo. Fantastic subjects were painted in a wide range of enamel colours (often imperfect) and gilding, and Chinese and Japanese plants and flowers were often mixed with Venetian motifs. Handleless cups and globular teapots are the most numerous items surviving which are painted with naturalistic flowers to charming effect.

The marks were "Ven[a]" or "Venezia" or variations, incised or painted in red or blue. When Francesco Vezzi died in 1740, the factory was discontinued.

VEZZI CHARACTERISTICS

1. German type hard-paste—characteristic glassy finish.
2. Exaggerated rococo shapes. Interesting moulded ornament. Fantastic subjects.
3. Painting inferior, inelegant. Some gilding.
4. Colours include browny-red, ochre yellow, bright blue, apple green.

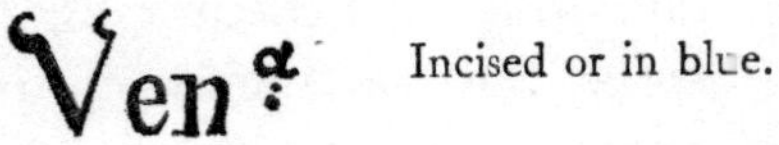

Incised or in blue.

HEWELCKE, VENICE, ITALY 1757–1763

The Dresden dealers, Nathaniel Friedrich Hewelcke and his wife Maria Dorothea left Saxony because of the Seven Years War, and applied in 1757 and 1758 for the privilege to manufacture porcelain in the style of Meissen. This was granted on condition that their products were marked with a "V" to signify Venice. This mark was adopted, either incised or painted in red or both. Whilst there is very little Hewelcke to collect, the pieces in the museums are charming. Usually full of imperfections and greyish in colour, the porcelain is painted with a characteristic border of feathery scrolls or lines in a solid dark red.

V[a] In red.

COZZI, VENICE, ITALY 1764–1812

With financial help from the Venetian State, Geminiano Cozzi (*c.* 1730–1812) founded a porcelain factory at San Giobbe in Venice in 1764. Although he described his porcelain as "in the style of the Japanese" it was a hybrid soft-paste made from kaolin found at Tretto on the Venetian mainland. It had a slightly greyish tinge and the glaze was thin and watery. The extremes of rococo had been abandoned by this time, and the large variety of services for every day use, the enamelled and biscuit figures and small vases they made were charming, if unoriginal. Obviously intended as copies of Meissen, most of it is without merit, but there are some pieces which have a whimsical Italian flavour that suggests the mellowness of an artistic race warmed by the Mediterranean sun. Odd masquerade figures, local scenes executed in red monochrome and copies of paintings after Tintoretto are individual and memorable.

The mark used by this factory was an anchor in red, or rarely in gold, sometimes with the painter's initials.

COZZI CHARACTERISTICS

1. Hybrid soft-paste, greyish. Watery glaze.
2. Mark, Anchor in red.
3. Colours thick and solid. Red, olive green and purple and some gilding.
4. Meissen shapes and designs.

In red.

NOVE, Venice, Italy
Porcelain 1752—Late Nineteenth Century

A factory was opened in 1728 by Giovanni Battista Antonibon to make *faïence*. Porcelain was made from about 1752 onwards by Sigismund Fischer "a porcelain maker from Dresden" who may have been the same man who worked as a painter at Vienna 1751 to 1770 or/and at Capodimonte 1754 to 1758. No German type hard-paste was made and from surviving examples attributed to this factory, their product was a hybrid soft-paste similar to that made at Cozzi.

The mark, a six or eight pointed star, roughly drawn in red—and more rarely in blue or gold, sometimes with and generally without "Nove", is not easily distinguishable from that of Doccia of the same period.

The paste was greyish and inclined to be opaque but the enamel colours used were gay and vivacious. A glossy deep red and a yellowish green are typical of the clean pallette of colours that were used in the painting of fanciful Italian subjects, In addition to *faïence* and porcelain the factory also made cream-coloured earthenware of fine quality.

Apart from the interval between 1802 and 1824 when Giovanni Baroni and his son Paulo were lessees, the factory remained in the hands of the Antonibon family until the late nineteenth century.

Nove
*

In gold or red.

[3] CAPODIMONTE, Naples, Italy
1743–1759 (Charles III)
1771–1806 (Ferdinand IV)
1818–1834 (Post-Royal)

Charles Bourbon, King of the Two Sicilies (Naples and Sicily), married Princess Amalia, daughter of Augustus III of Poland, Elector of Saxony, in 1738, and brought her to Naples. The lively, artistic young Queen, brought up in the strong cultural background of her native Dresden, admired the antique statuary littered around the palace grounds. Discovering that these had been unearthed by General d'Elboeuf around Vesuvius more than twenty years before, she persuaded the King to initiate further excavations. Vesuvius had been quiet for some time, and so he agreed.

There followed the exciting discovery on December 11th, 1738, of an inscription declaring that a certain Rufus had built, with his own money, the "Theatrum Herculanese". The diggers had found Herculaneum.

Ancient sources had recorded that Pompeii had perished at the same time as the city of Hercules, so more excavations were begun in 1748, when wonderful wall paintings were revealed for the first time in nearly 1700 years.

The excavators were not archaeologists in the present day sense. At least half the labour force were criminals, and gold coins and ornaments were the main prizes. As soon as a pit had been explored and emptied, it was filled in and other holes excavated. This unsystematic process was followed without protest from the Royal couple, who now possessed more antiquities than any other contemporary Monarch. They were now interested in porcelain. A factory was opened in 1743 and the management was in the hands of a chemist, Schepers, and a painter and gem-cutter, Caselli.

Charles took an active interest and actually worked there himself. A contemporary letter to Mr. Pitt stated, "He is particularly fond of the china manufacture at Capodimonte. During a fair held annually in the Square before his palace at

Naples, there is a shop solely for the sale of part of this china; and a note was daily brought to the King of what was sold, together with the names of those who bought; and it is said he looked often favourably upon the persons who made any purchases".

The character of the early porcelain produced was quite exceptional, and differed considerably from that of any other European factory. Original models were the jugs, vases and snuff-boxes made in the form of shells, periwinkles, coral, dolphins—the so-called *fritti-di-mare*. Frequently unpainted, they are reminiscent of the Chinese Fukien porcelain, and were the inspiration of the crustacea subjects produced at Bow.

The porcelain was extremely transparent and as thinly potted as the Oriental, but was a creamy soft-paste. When painting was applied, it was of the highest standard of the miniaturist.

A series of figures have also been attributed to Capodimonte which have distinctive small heads and are modelled on irregular mounds. Where firing cracks appeared they were hidden by applied green leaves. Honey writes "They are modelled with an admirably rhythmical movement and softness of outline. Their colouring is slight and effective". (*Dictionary of European Ceramic Art*). Subjects were from the Italian Comedy and Neapolitan folk-types.

The pieces were rarely marked, but occasionally the Bourbon *fleur-de-lys*, either impressed or painted blue, was used. After 1759 this mark was used at Buen Retiro, and most objects with this mark have been attributed to that factory.

Another factory was founded at Portici in 1771 by his successor Ferdinand II, who then moved it to Capodimonte where production was continued until 1806, when the moulds and equipment were acquired by Doccia.

Lord Nelson, appointed to the Mediterranian Fleet to secure the Kingdom of the Two Sicilies, wrote to Lord St. Vincent:

"A little circumstance has also happened, which does honour to the King of Naples, and is not unpleasant to me. I went to view the magnificent manufactory of china. After admiring all the fine things, sufficient to seduce the money from my pocket, I came to some busts in china of all the Royal family; these I immediately ordered, and when I wanted to pay for them, I was informed that the King had directed whatever I chose should be delivered free of all cost; it was handsome of the King!"

During Ferdinand's reign the paste became greyer and was changed to a hybrid variety. The high cost of the soft-paste and the difficulties of manufacturing useful wares were probably the cause. Classical figures were made either glazed or in biscuit, and later a series of figures, sympathetic Neapolitan folk-types, were produced in white glazed porcelain or in a yellow biscuit similar to the *terre de pipe* of Lunéville.

Classical decorative motifs were freely adapted, Bourbon sprigs, key pattern, Pompeiian scrolls, as well as local views and figure painting.

Honey wrote "The porcelain material was usually of a pleasant ivory tone and texture of great charm'.'

Ferdinand's products were marked with a crowned N for Naples, or a monogram FR for Ferdinand Rex, or RF, *Real Fabbrica*.

In the "Post-Royal" period more classical figures in white enamelled and biscuit were made, but the productions of this period are of little merit.

CAPODIMONTE CHARACTERISTICS

1. Soft creamy-white paste.
2. Very translucent.
3. Thinly potted.
4. Doccia copies greyish, enamelled on crude colours.
5. Most coloured low-relief decoration with crowned N either Doccia or German reproductions.

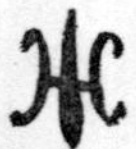

1736–1759.

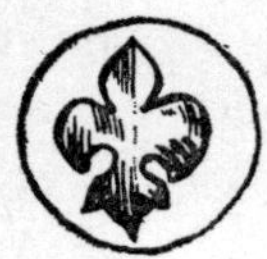

1736–1759, usually impressed.

Naples, not Capodimonte after *1771*. Underglaze blue or impressed.

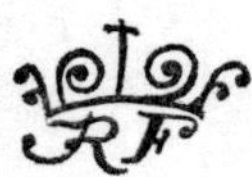

Presumed to be Portici. In various colours.

Presumed to be Portici. In various colours.

[4] SPAIN
BUEN RETIRO, Near Madrid 1760–1808
LA MONCLOA, Near Madrid 1817–1850

When Charles III Bourbon of Naples inherited the Spanish throne in 1759, he removed most of his artists and workmen from the Capodimonte factory and founded the Buen Retiro factory in 1760 in the gardens of his palace near Madrid.

Bourgoanne, a visitor to Spain in 1777, wrote, "In the gardens of Buen Retiro the monarch has established a china manufactory which strangers have not hitherto been permitted to examine. It is undoubtedly intended that experiments shall be secretly made, and the manufactory brought to some perfection before it be exposed to the eyes of the curious. These productions are to be seen nowhere except in the palace of the sovereign, or in some Italian Courts to which they have been sent as presents. Charles III rendered then due homage to our French manufactories, when he excepted the Court of Versailles from his distribution, notwithstanding the latter regularly forwarded some of the finest works of our Sèvres manufactory to the Princess of Asturias. Louis XV established this custom on account of his grand daughter, and his successor did not discontinue the practice".

Management was at first under Schepers and Gricci, and upon their deaths it was continued by their sons who constantly quarrelled.

The formula of the paste brought from Italy, which produced very vitreous porcelain, contained small crystals and although excellent for figurines, was unsatisfactory for dishes. Experiments followed with new pastes, and caused disputes between the Italian element who wished to keep their original formula and the Spaniards who wished to develop a purely Spanish paste.

Bartolome Sureda (*c.* 1760–1829) was sent to Sèvres in 1802 in order to study their methods. He returned in 1803 with new ideas and experienced potters. He was appointed Director in 1804 and introduced a satisfactory new hybrid paste containing magnesium, made from kaolin discovered in the vicinity.

At first the production at Buen Retiro was almost identical to that which had been made in Naples, which was characterised by the rococo style and the high relief moulded ornament, but the Louis Seize style was quickly adopted.

The models were of Sèvres inspiration and well finished. The paste was soft and yellowish, reminiscent of Saint-Cloud, and was the basis of delightful *Putti* and humorous Peasants, vigorously modelled in massive proportions.

The colouring is distinctive on all the Buen Retiro products. The enamels are stippled on in a purely individualistic manner—evidently the style of painting dictated by the painting school adjoining the factory.

All the painting was excellent. The delicate colouring—coloured grounds were rarely used—and the soft honey gilding were rich and tasteful. The style of the neo-classical vases was individually Spanish and many were filled with porcelain flowers in the style of Vincennes, long after that fashion had been abandoned elsewhere.

Biscuit figures of classical subjects were also made, as well as reliefs and plaques in the style of Wedgwood.

The high standard of quality was maintained throughout the lifetime of Charles III, who died in 1788, but the productions were derivative and lacking in originality.

In 1808, when the Peninsula was invaded by Napoleon, Madrid was occupied, together with the Palace of Buen Retiro, which was the scene of a terrible massacre. The factory was used as an arsenal and was finally completely destroyed in 1812.

A factory was built in 1817 at La Moncloa by Ferdinand VII, but on the 7th July, 1825 it was burned down by the British. It was rebuilt and in production until 1850. It was under the management of Sureda until 1829 and produced copies of contemporary English and French models of declining merit.

BUEN RETIRO CHARACTERISTICS

1. Yellowish soft-paste.
2. Opaque and creamy lead glaze.
3. Generally very heavy for its size.
4. Could pass for fine earthenware.
5. After 1804 hybrid paste with a magnesium composition.

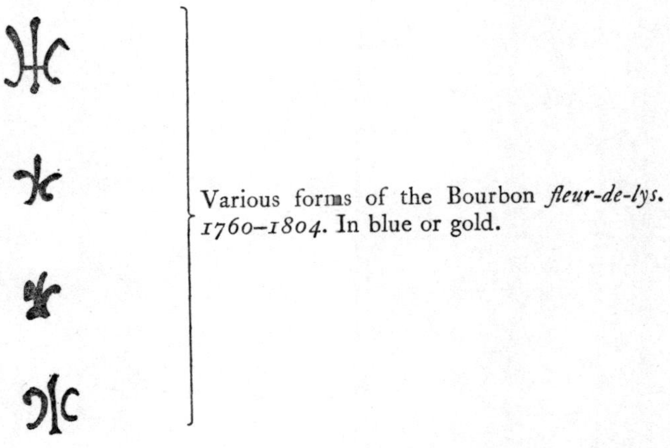

Various forms of the Bourbon *fleur-de-lys*. *1760–1804*. In blue or gold.

In red. The factory mark under Sureda (*1804–1808*).

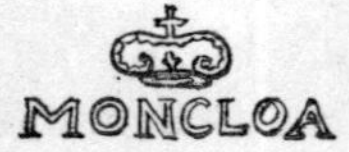

Impressed.

Chapter Six

The Rest of Europe

DURING THE EIGHTEENTH century, borders changed and Kingdoms convulsed from Treaty to Treaty. The power of Spain had diminished, and her territories in Italy and the Netherlands (modern Belgium) were hotly contested by France and Austria. Sweden under Gustavus Adolphus had been the great power in the Baltic during the seventeenth century, but after his death it was won by the newly-emerging Russia of Peter the Great, and his successors, particularly the German born Catherine the Great. Switzerland had won her independence, and the United Provinces were established under the leadership of Holland, guaranteed by her ties with England through William of Orange and their mutual Protestant religion.

The wars of the seventeenth century which had torn Europe apart had been mainly religious explosions (the Counter-Reformation versus Lutheranism and the newer Calvinism, and rebellion against the Holy Roman Empire), and the pattern had been complicated by the grand expansion schemes of Louis XIV.

The eighteenth century saw the emergence of the new strong peoples, Prussia and Russia, at the expense of their neighbours, and the new great overseas colonisations by England.

Social life was divided into two groups, the very rich and the very poor. The poor were treated little better than slaves and their lives were pathetically short and bitter. The rich had leisure and cultivated the Arts. Patronage was extended to creative artists in every field, including the exciting new porcelain.

The leaders in the field of porcelain production have already been mentioned, and the rest of Europe produced fine work, but it was for the most part derivative and unoriginal.

[1] BELGIUM
TOURNAI 1751—Present Time

When Belgium was part of the Austrian Empire, the Empress Maria-Theresa granted the privilege to make soft-paste porcelain to F. J. Peterinck, and with capital provided by the Corporation, this important factory was founded in 1751 at Tournai.

Robert Dubois, the so-called arcanist from Chantilly and Vincennes, was at Tournai for a time in 1753, and probably helped to develop the formula.

The factory remained in the Peterinck family until 1800, when it was managed by Peterinck's son-in-law, Jean-Maximilien-Joseph de Bettignies, and passed into the hands of his family until 1850 when it belonged to the brothers Boch.

Tournai is especially interesting in England because of its similarity to Chelsea and Worcester. English workmen were in fact engaged in 1754 and 1759, and Peterinck's son is said to have worked at Chelsea.

The early products of Tournai were not marked and were frankly forgeries of their contemporaries. Some original work was done—a fine reeding on plates and dishes and a rococo style handle is peculiar to this factory. The products were simple and restrained and very "English" in character. The paste was greyish at first, but developed into a warm creamy tone. Paintings were made of *deutsche blumen* in rather pale colouring, and a frequent pattern was the blue and white underglaze *zwiebelmuster* copied from Meissen.

The finest artist produced by Tournai was Henri-Joseph Duvivier, who was the chief painter between 1763 and 1771. His father, William had gone to England in the 1740's to work at Chelsea, and the son returned to Tournai as an experienced painter in 1763. Peterinck referred to him as "a certain Henri-Joseph Duvivier who had learned the art of painting in England

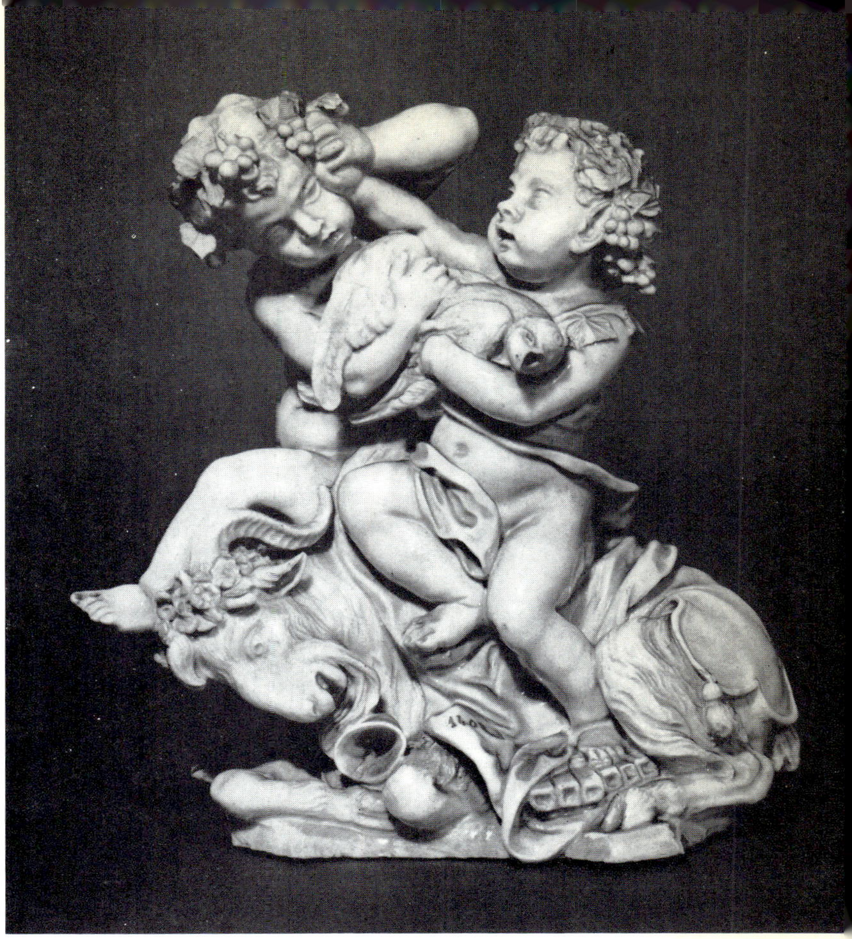

DOCCIA. *Putti* enjoying themselves, seated on a goat. White porcelain group, c. 1755

Museo Civico, Turin

COZZI

Soup tureen, c. 1770

Museo Civico, Turin

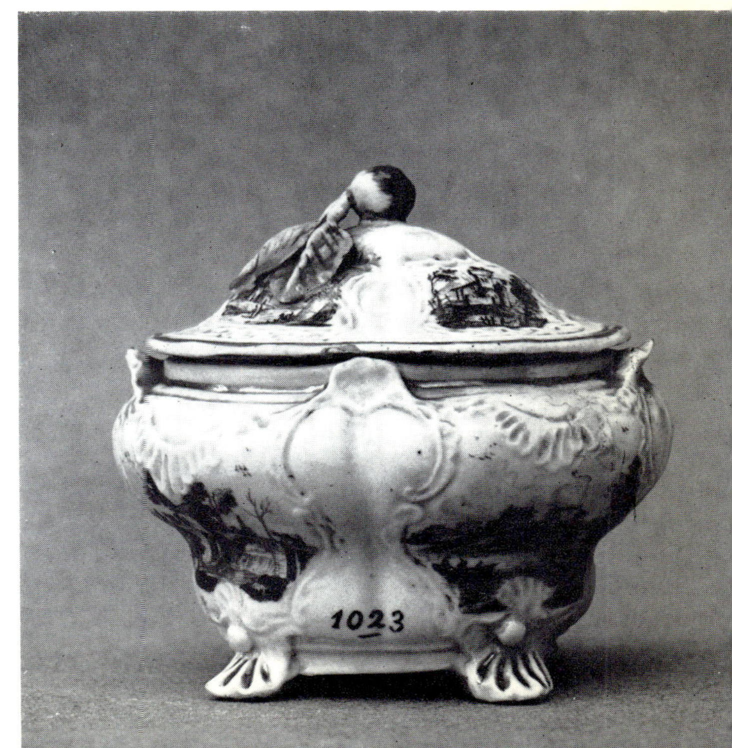

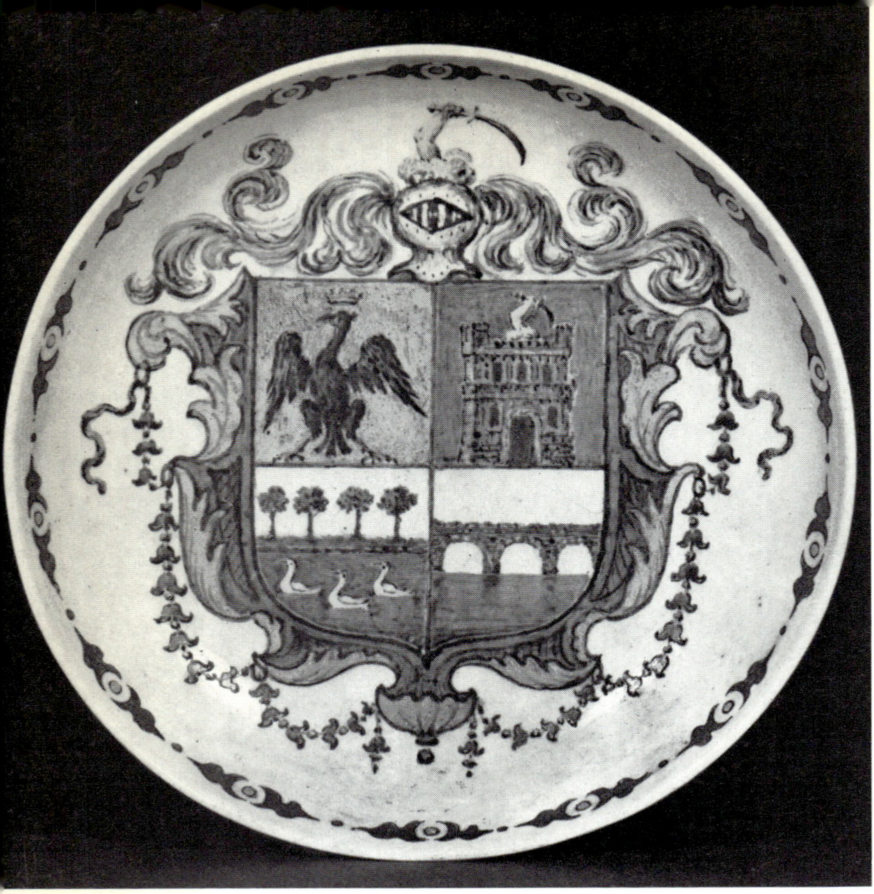

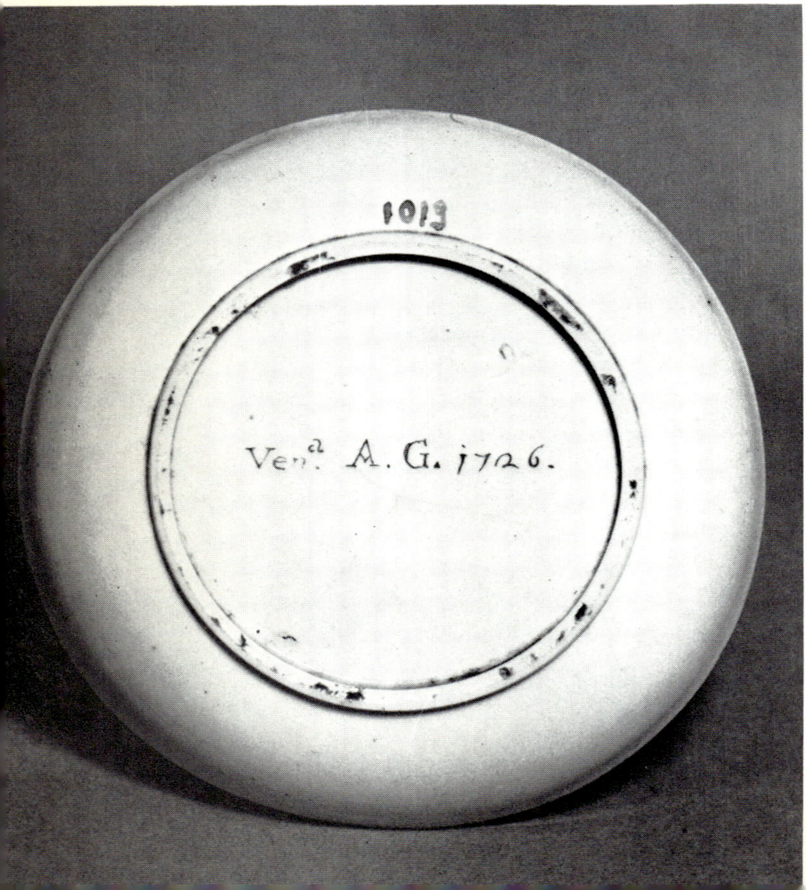

VEZZI. Small plate with coat of arms, 1726; reverse side showing date 1726 and mark

Museo Civico, Turin

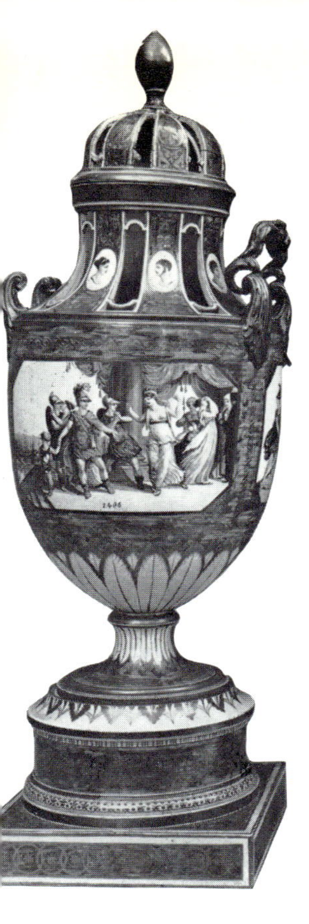

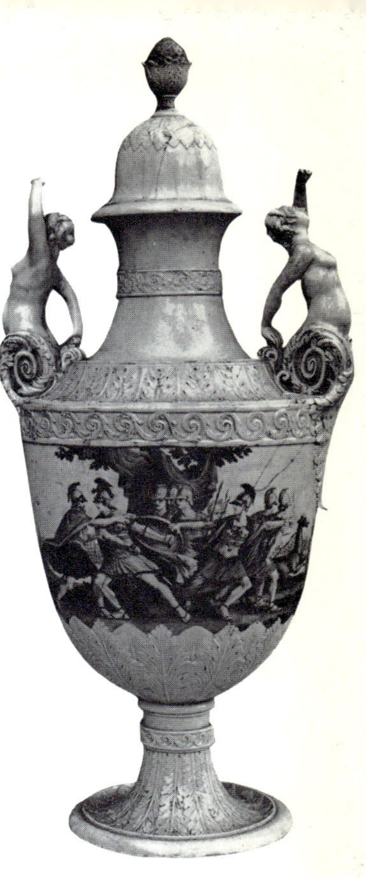

NOVE
Two vases, late 18th century

Museo Civico, Turin

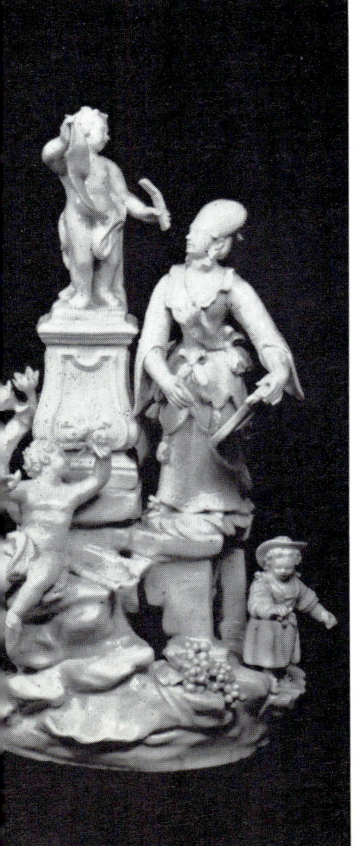

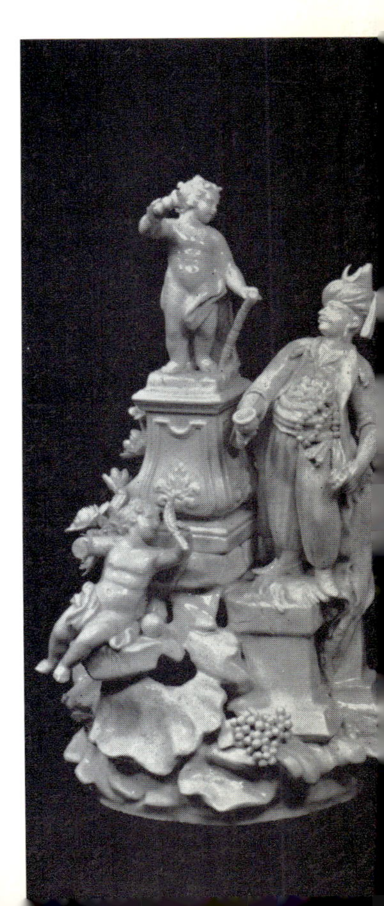

NOVE
A rare pair of Nove white groups of "a Lady" and "a Turk". Height 10 ins. c. 1780

Christie's

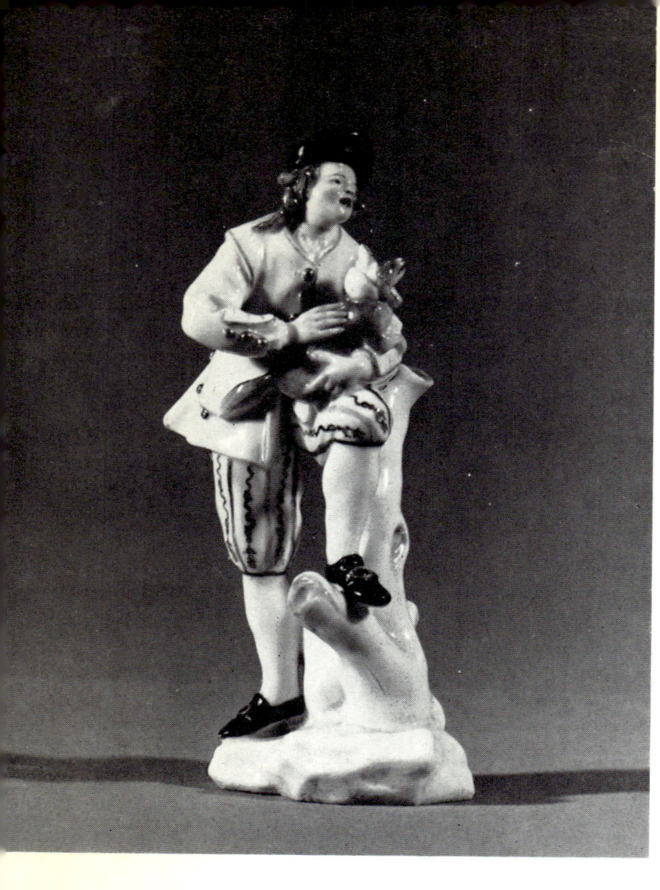

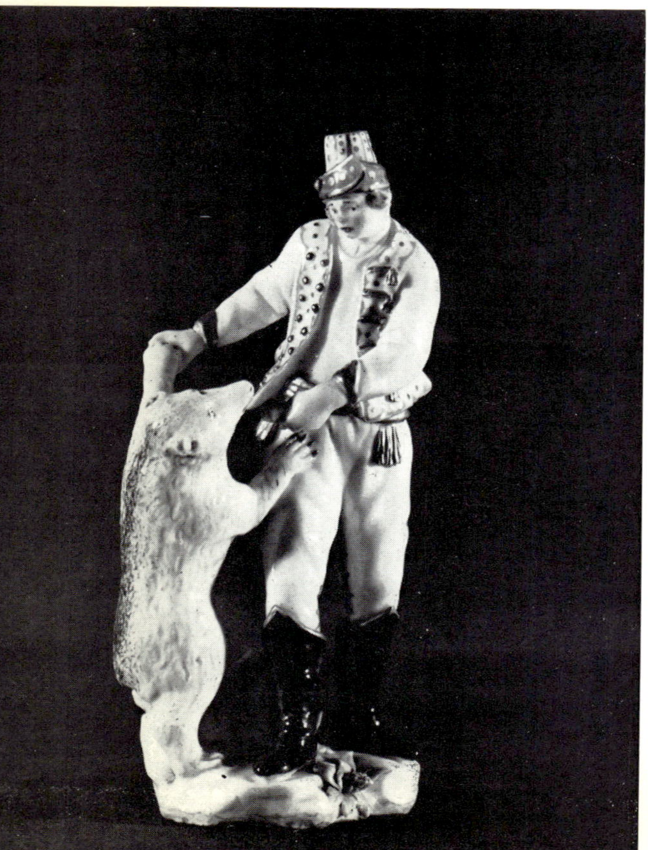

CAPODIMONTE
Two figures of Charles III period (1743–1759).

Naples Museum of Capodimonte (De Ciccio)

under the tuition of the Great Masters of that art". The crimson monochrome paintings of landscapes, with figures, horsemen and castles, copied from Meissen, and cupids in the same tone copied from Sèvres, are attributed to him. He also painted exotic birds on a plain white ground similar to those produced at Worcester and Chelsea.

Tournai gilding was distinctive in that it was thick and pasty and applied more liberally than on the Sèvres originals. Colour grounds in blue and yellow, after the style of Sèvres, were imitated but never quite achieved the same tone.

Towards the end of the eighteenth century a restrained neo-classical style was adopted, and armorial services were painted with looped ribbons. A famous service was that made for the Duke of Orleans in 1787, which was painted with birds from Buffon's *Natural History*.

Tournai provided porcelain for The Hague, where it was decorated. Honey suggests that Chantilly porcelain is sometimes found with paintings in panels reserved on a colour, usually blue, ground, apparently done at Tournai but almost certainly St. Amand work of nineteenth century date.

Many figures were made but were never marked and their identification is doubtful. They are in the style of Chelsea and Menneçy, and a favourite form was the "round group" arranged round a tree with Lovers, Cupids or Peasants. Most of the figures were white glazed, although some colour and biscuit ones were also made.

The Bettignies were deeply involved in the faking of old porcelain in the nineteenth century, when early Tournai was re-painted with colour grounds and gilding.

Whilst the Tournai porcelain is of certain merit, it is not the most popular amongst collectors. Its derivative and imitative qualities are irritating and the mass of forgeries perpetrated in the nineteenth century make collecting a dangerous field to tread.

TOURNAI CHARACTERISTICS

1. Paste greyish or creamy.
2. Colours pale, not quite recognisable as Sèvres or Meissen.
3. Continental characteristics with a trim "English look".

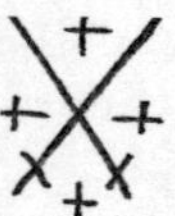

In blue, gold, crimson or other colour.

[2] RUSSIA
ST. PETERSBURG, Imperial Factory 1744–1917

An Imperial Russian factory under the protection of the Empress Elizabeth Petrovna was founded in 1744 and directed by Christoph Konrad Hunger. Hunger who had been an enameller at Meissen had founded the porcelain factory in Vienna, and then the Vezzi factory in Venice where he had been for the previous five years. He experimented with kaolin, discovered near St. Petersburg, without great success. He was replaced by Dmitri Vinogradoff, who had studied porcelain production in Saxony, and who succeeded in making a beautiful white hard-paste formula. He died in 1758, but his discoveries were developed and the factory flourished. A speciality of Vinogradoff, whose work was exquisite, was a series of tiny snuff boxes, the most famous of which was in the shape of an envelope addressed to the recipient.

About 1763 a change took place. Under the protection of Catherine the Great the factory became more commercial and considerable quantities of work were completed. These included the Arabesque service of over 1,000 pieces, based on a Sèvres design, and was decorated with Pompeiian scrolls and cameo medallions. The designs generally followed the decoration of Sèvres and Meissen, together with gold Chinamen and monochrome landscapes and flowers painted in green or purple and gold or black.

The factory was considerably enlarged in 1786, and Catherine took great personal interest in its affairs. She invited artists from rival European factories to join the imperial Works, and Falconet, the modeller from Sèvres, was amongst those who accepted. The Empress particularly liked the models of Russian Peasants which were produced as figurines. Artistically satisfying in themselves, they are even more valuable as a documentary record of the period.

The finest period of the Imperial factory was during the direction of Prince Youssopoff from 1792 to 1802. Made in the Russian Empire style, a series of fine works were produced which included classical figures in white enamel and biscuit and massive vases covered with heavy gilding.

Louis XVI and Marie Antoinette presented Youssopoff with a magnificent dinner service of a flower design on a brown ground, originally intended for the Dauphin. In 1912 two French Professors, making a study of Sèvres porcelain, visited the family and Youssopoff's descendant, who was later to achieve fame as Rasputin's executioner, instigated a search. The service was found lying in the far corner of one of his furniture warehouses where it had been forgotten.

The output of the factory was derivative, and models and decoration were based on Sèvres and Meissen designs. Even the Russian Peasant figures were probably inspired by the Berlin centrepiece presented by Frederick the Great to Catherine the Great in 1776. The finish was not as good as it should have been, and the gilding is inclined to be over-done.

During the nineteenth century the factory continued commercially, following the general deterioration in artistic standards, until the death of Tzar Nicholas II in 1917. The porcelain was marked with the Russian eagle, with the initials or monogram of the reigning Sovereign.

ST. PETERSBURG CHARACTERISTICS

1. Hard-paste.
2. Meissen, Sèvres and sometimes Vienna styling.
3. Painting inclined to be tasteless and gilding over-done.
4. In the neo-classical and Empire style.

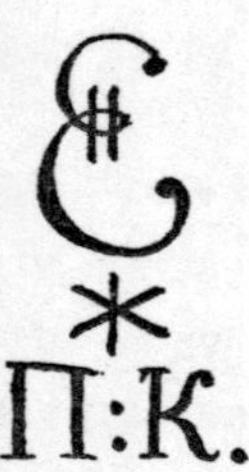

1762–1796. Cipher of Catherine II. On pieces intended for Court use.

1796–1801. Cipher of Emperor Paul I.

MOSCOW—Gardner 1755–1891

A mysterious Englishman named Francis Joseph Gardner went to Russia in 1746, and there are no records to confirm or deny whether he learnt ceramics before or after he arrived. He opened a factory at Verbilki in the suburbs of Moscow in 1754/5, first making *faïence*, and then porcelain.

The porcelain was excellent, and was in fact superior in quality to that of the Imperial Factory. Particularly outstanding were the vigorously modelled figurines of Russian Peasants and Dancers painted in bright colours. Domestic wares were made in great quantity and found a ready market outside Russia, in the Baltic and east to Persia, Afghanistan, and Pakistan. I am indebted to Frank Davis in the *Sunday Times* (May 1967) who was informed by two gentlemen who had served in India, that the Gardner Ware was popular in the East, because the quality of the paste was such, that the teapots could sit in the ashes of a wood fire. Old frontier families had large services of dark red and dark blue patterns. This pattern was the most popular for surviving teapots are to be found in practically every Asian caravanserai, usually repaired, or reinforced with new metal spouts.

In 1919, Gardner china sets of six small coffee cups and saucers, milk jug, teapot, sugar basin and cover could be bought for 25 rupees in Peshawar (about 35s.). The factory was continued by Gardner's descendants throughout the nineteenth century making these delectable items. The mark was "Fabrik Gardner" in Russian characters, or "Gardner" or "G". In 1891 the factory was sold to S. Konznelzoff.

ΓΑΡΔΗΕΡΖ — Early nineteenth century. Impressed. Sometimes with "G".

C — In blue—early mark.

MOSCOW—Popoff 1805–1872

A factory was founded in about 1805 near Gorbunovo, near Moscow, by A. Popoff with the help of yet another Englishman, Charles Milly.

Their products were finer than those of the other two factories, and were made in small quantities for the Russian Court.

AΠ — *1812–1872.*

MOSCOW CHARACTERISTICS

1. Hard-paste.
2. Coarse, naïve enamelling.
3. Vigorous "barbaric" modelling of Russian folk-types.
4. Sèvres styling but broader—less refined.

[3] DENMARK
COPENHAGEN

Fournier 1759–1765 (Soft-paste)
Müller 1772–1779 (Hard-paste)
Royal 1779–Present Day

Arcanists and artists from Meissen were either invited or volunteered to make porcelain at Copenhagen. Hunger was recorded there between 1730 and 1737, and Ludwig Lück, with his son Karl Gottlieb Lück, went to Copenhagen at some time between 1752 and 1757, but it was a Frenchman, Louis Fournier of Vincennes and Chantilly, who finally succeeded in making porcelain in 1759. He produced a faintly yellow soft-paste with a dull glaze, and made modest pieces in the French taste, mostly table wares decorated with flowers and cupids. The mark was an F in script with the numeral 5 (for Frederick V King of Denmark).

In 1774, another company was formed by Franz Heinrich Müller, a capable chemist who had experimented with the kaolin found at Bornholm in 1755. The Queen was a principal shareholder in the company, but by 1779 the company was taken over by the King and has since been a Government establishment. The mark adopted consisted of three wavy lines signifying the Sound and Great and Little Belts.

The Fürstenburg modeller, A. K. Luplau, was engaged in 1776, as well as other painters from Berlin.

Müller's early porcelain was a greyish-blue tone, painted in underglaze blue, iron red or purple. Fürstenburg and Meissen models were copied with rococo-scrolled panels and *ozier* border patterns.

The neo-classical style was adopted from 1779. Architectural motifs, medallion portrait heads, portraits of historical characters and cupids were painted in *grisaille* with wreaths of polychrome flowers on useful wares and vases.

Copenhagen is famous for the fabulous service completed for Catherine the Great of Russia in 1802. It is known as the *Flora Danica* and consisted of 1,602 pieces decorated with copies of paintings of Danish flowers by Oeder. The naturalistic painting was beautifully executed by Johann Christoph Bayer, previously from Nüremburg. Classical moulded borders with basket-work piercing and the large modelled flowers with thick leaves are typical of the factory.

Domestic wares made for daily use were painted in underglaze blue, and these continued to be made for some time. A number of figures were made, the models for which were taken from other factories, particularly Sèvres and Meissen. According to Honey (*Dictionary of European Ceramic Art*), Luplau's own work as a modeller was apparently inconsiderable and cannot easily be identified. He is known to have made twenty-one figures of Norwegian peasants, which rank amongst the finest made at Copenhagen.

In one of his letters to Lady Hamilton, dated 14th April, 1801, at Copenhagen, Lord Nelson wrote:

"I was in hopes that I should have got off some Copenhagen china, to have sent you by Captain Bligh, who was one of my Seconds on the 2nd. He is a steady seaman, and a good and brave man. If he calls I hope you will admit him. I have half promised him that pleasure, and if he can get hold of the China, he is to take charge of it."—and again on the 15th of the same month:

"I can get nothing here worth your acceptance but as I know you have a valuable collection of china, I send you some of the Copenhagen manufacture; It will bring to your recollection that here your attached friend Nelson fought and conquered."

The factory declined in the nineteenth century, and by 1822 only two painters were employed. It revived in 1885 with the appointment of Arnold Krog, to whom may be attributed the development of the successful modern factory.

The Copenhagen State factory is still in existence, it has developed a magnificent style of its own and produces porcelain of a high quality.

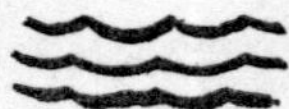

Formally adopted *1775*.

[4] SWEDEN
MARIEBERG, Nr. STOCKHOLM 1766–1778

A pottery making excellent *faïence* was established at Marieberg, near Stockholm, in 1760, and some porcelain was made when Pierre Berthevin of Menneçy and Copenhagen became manager in 1766.

For three-years a soft paste porcelain was made, very similar to that of Menneçy.

When Henrik Sten succeeded Berthevin in 1769, a chalky opaque porcelain was made in the same French style as his predecessor. Later under the management of Jacob Dortu, 1777–1778, a hard-paste was made.

The pottery was taken over by Rorstrand.

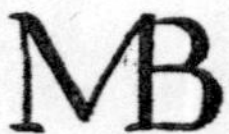

Incised.

[5] SWITZERLAND
ZURICH 1763–1768
NYON 1790–1800

A factory was established in Zurich by one of Ringler's workmen and was carried on by Spängler and Hearacher from 1763–1768. Its products were very similar to German porcelain and without especial merit. The mark used was the letter Z.

Another Swiss factory was formed at Nyon, in the Canton de Vaud, by a French decorator, Maubrée of Paris, in 1790–1800. The character of the porcelain resembles that of Sèvres soft-paste. The mark was a fish, probably suggested by the site of the factory which was on the shores of Lake Geneva.

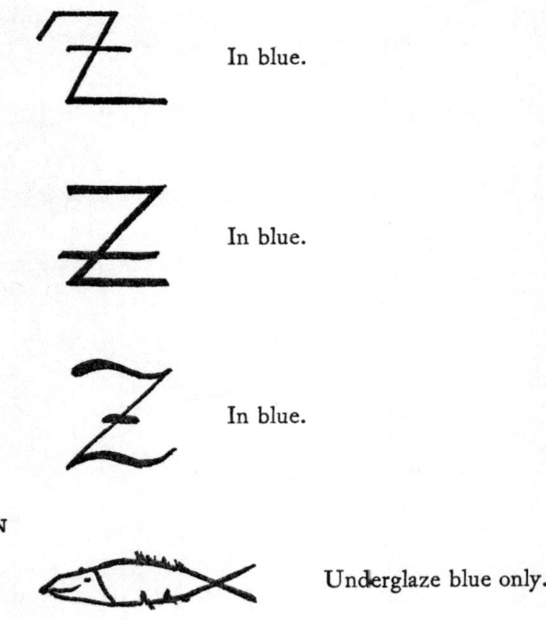

[6] HOLLAND
THE HAGUE 1773–1790

A German, Anton Lyncker (or Leichner) is recorded as a dealer in Saxon or Thuringian porcelain in 1773. A decorating establishment followed, and porcelain for finishing was imported from Tournai, and probably from various lesser German factories.

Some porcelain was made in about 1776, but although it was continued by Lyncker's son, the business closed in 1790.

The mark was a stork holding a fish in its beak, the insignia of the Hague, but this is often found on porcelain of other origins, sometimes together with the mark of the originating factory. Honey states that the best Hague decoration is found on the Tournai porcelain with narrow wavy borders in *bleu de roi* and gilt and neat painting of birds and landscapes in colour (*Dictionary of European Ceramic Art*).

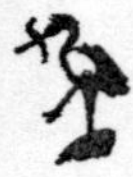

In blue enamel or underglaze blue.

Chapter Seven

[1] COPIES, FORGERIES AND FAKES

" 'Tis not in mortals to command success,
But we'll do more, Sempronius: we'll deserve it."

CATO ii 43.

DURING THE EIGHTEENTH century, porcelain makers eagerly collected each others successful models and copied them. The talent of the copyists was such that their copies had individuality, originality and quality and can be judged on their own merits. These are not considered to be fraudulent and we are not concerned with them in this chapter.

Mechanisation in the nineteenth century sacrificed craftsmanship in many fields of artistic endeavour, and none more surely than in the applied art of porcelain. Taste and refinement were replaced by ostentation and vulgarity, and in an age when people expected a lot for their money decoration was used for decoration's sake. Porcelain manufacturers now had the techniques for mass production, but lacked the talent for design. They turned to the popular models of the previous century—the golden age of porcelain.

An industry was started in the reproduction of valuable old models, exact to the smallest detail and excellent in finish and brushwork, bearing the old marks, and these are deemed to be forgeries in that they were made with intent to deceive. Another category of fakes are genuine old pieces which have been altered in some way in order to make them more valuable. The over painting of Sèvres soft-paste falls into this category.

Very fine copies were made at Coalport and Minton of the

splendid early Sèvres models and colours in hard-paste, but as they were generally marked clearly with the manufacturer's name with or without the crossed LL's there was no deliberate fraudulent intention.

It has been recorded that London dealers were persistent in their demands that the manufacturers should omit their own marks, which may account for the number of Coalport pieces marked solely with the LL's while the pairs to them bear the Coalport mark CBD.

The unenviable reputation of the firm of Samson et Cie, 7 Rue Béranger, Paris, is that they were and indeed still are reproducing old models from many early factories. Founded in 1845 by Edmé Samson, they insist that their reproductions are marked with S in addition to the imitated early mark. This is true for a number of English-style figures, but certainly not for the vast range of copies that the unwary collector may have bought at the price of an original. The copies are well executed in finish and painting, but are always hard-paste and do not have the warmth of the soft-paste originals. Their imitations range from Chelsea Goat and Bee jugs and figures, Derby Dwarfs, Bow and Worcester to Chinese Export vases and services. These imitations are so good that it requires some experience to be able to identify them.

The imitated marks are usually inaccurate. Chelsea anchors are always small and discreetly placed on the back of the model; on Samson imitations it is underneath and very large. The Worcester square mark is always a dark indigo blue, whereas the Samson copy is generally light blue. Derby is marked underneath, but for some odd reason Samson imitations, roughly drawn in brown, are placed on the back above the base.

Some mention must be made of the Welsh soft-paste which was decorated in London to the orders of the London dealers. It arrived from Swansea and Nantgarw unmarked and in the white and the most gorgeous decoration was applied by Webster and Robins and Randall at Islington. No doubt the crossed LL's were also painted on the base.

Randall's creamy soft-paste from Madeley was also decorated in the French manner, although "the old Quaker" refused to apply forged marks. He did not mark his goods at all except on a rare occasion, so there was nothing to stop the dealers having it marked as they pleased.

These so-called forgeries are now excused for they can be identified, and have a beauty of their own.

The soft-paste of Sèvres has been the subject of more convincing forgeries than any other European eighteenth century factory. The elegance of French taste, the superb palette of colours, the exquisite honey gilding and the thick unctuous glaze which caused the colours to sink deep into the paste, are so enchanting that examples have always fetched high prices.

Much Sèvres porcelain was decorated with simple sprigs of flowers for every day use, and forgers both in England and France discovered that the decoration could be removed with acid and a more elaborate design applied in the manner of the presentation pieces, which were much more valuable. The beauty of the thick glaze was a boon to the forger. When the re-decorated pieces were re-fired at low temperatures in a muffle kiln, the glaze spread and re-covered the new decoration. Many collections have contained examples of these "cuckoos".

Louis XVIII was the unknowing owner of a breakfast service with portraits of the King and his Court for two years before it was detected as a fraud. It was painted by Soirons, a nineteenth century artist. It is fairly safe to assume that specimens with portraits of famous people bearing the Sèvres mark and year letter before the Revolution are always forgeries.

We are indebted to Lady Charlotte Schreiber who described what she had seen at first hand in 1877 at the factories at Tournai and St. Amand-les-Eaux. Although the soft-paste of Saint Cloud and Menneçy was difficult to reproduce, she saw copies being made with imitated old marks. She also saw them making reproduction Sèvres, Sceaux, Chelsea and Worcester models in soft-paste.

Favourite designs used for fakes were yellow and blue grounds with reserves framed with gilt palm leaves, painted on cleaned-off eighteenth century soft-paste pieces from Chantilly, Sceaux, Tournai and Arras, which still bore their original factory marks.

Honey (*German Porcelain*) has pointed out that German porcelain is particularly dangerous as there is basically no difference between eighteenth and nineteenth century paste. Salient features of these copies, which are still being made at Nymphenburg, Fürstenberg and Württemberg, are:

1. Over-brilliant glassy dead white paste and clean finish.
2. Neat round pin-hole in tree stump.
3. Peculiar glossiness.

Copies of old Ludwigsburg models from original moulds were made at Amberg in the nineteenth century. They bear the impressed mould numbers without mark.

Meissen copies made by Wolfsohn, Thienne, etc. are easy to discover.

More dangerous forgeries were made by Weise of Dresden on porcelain less white than that of the eighteenth century, but skilfully painted in old colours.

Frankenthal, Ludwigsburg and Höchst were frequently copied at Passau in a credible creamy white paste, with dirty blue marks.

Mid-nineteenth century copies were made of eighteenth century Höchst figures in earthenware from Damm moulds and after the closure of the Vienna factory in 1864, genuine old Vienna pieces were redecorated richly in the Sorgenthal style with false signatures, i.e. "Angelica Kauffmann".

Nor were the Swiss factories neglected. A nineteenth century German firm adopted the Fish mark as their emblem, probably with intent to deceive as eighteenth century Nyon. Zurich forgeries include one with a crazed glaze and another with a white paste instead of a smoky one and a bright under-glaze blue mark.

Copies of Italian and Spanish models were and are still being reproduced. Doccia bought the Capodimonte moulds in the early nineteenth century and produced the familiar boxes, cups, etc., with decoration in relief marked with a crowned N for Naples. Cruder versions of these with the same mark were made in Germany at the end of the nineteenth century.

All these dangers might deter a timid would-be collector, but to the intrepid they are a challenge. Great experts have been known to err, when decades later more information and scientific tests have become available. Honey quotes in his *Dictionary of European Ceramic Art* the classic example of the nineteenth century expert Solon, who in his great work on ceramics over confidently stated that a fake could easily be discovered, and illustrated—a fake.

[2] HINTS FOR COLLECTORS

An awful lot of nonsense is talked about the expertise of porcelain. The ability to distinguish good from bad, true from false is not some god-given sixth sense; it is largely a matter of common sense, experience and trusting your own instincts.

Once you have decided to start collecting the first thing is to try to pick on some style, some subject, or some category of objects. Specialisation is all important; for it is more worthwhile to have a collection which has a unity of its own, no matter how small, or apparently unimportant such a collection may be.

Having once decided and started buying, the important thing is to get as much experience as you can. Never miss out on any chance of looking at actual pieces of porcelain, and when possible actually handling them. Go to museums—and most museums both in London (the collection at the Victoria and Albert is probably the finest in the country) and the provinces have many pieces of value. Foreign museums have interesting collections too, which are well worth a visit. Go to sales; go to shops which specialise in porcelain—dealers are nearly always helpful and cooperative. Examine your friends' pieces; never let slip an opportunity of widening your experience.

This goes for books and articles too. Apart from the short list of books included in the *Bibliography* at the end of this one, pay special attention to articles in magazines such as *The Connoisseur*, *Apollo*, *The Burlington Magazine*, *The Transactions of The English Porcelain Society*, *Country Life*, *Collector's Guide*, etc. Papers such as *The Times* also often contain articles of great interest to the collector, and are of especial value in giving indications of current prices.

The Keepers of the Ceramic Departments in most of the national collections are prepared to give advice about attributions and the like. They will not however make any evaluation of the price of an object, and it is always advisable to book an appointment beforehand.

There are all kinds of complex scientific methods of determining the composition and nature of any piece of porcelain, but these are not available to the ordinary collector who must rely on his own eyes and good sense. Here then are a few hints about how to set about examining and evaluating a piece of porcelain.

1. *Hold it up against the light* (a bare electric lamp is excellent) as this is the only method of evaluating the nature of the paste, which, as you will have discovered in reading the text of this book, is an invaluable guide to authenticity. Porcelain, as opposed to pottery or *faïence* is translucent.
2. *Feel it carefully.* In soft-paste porcelain the painting melted into the glaze so that the surface is smooth. Hard-paste porcelain painting can be detected by touch.
3. *Hold it at an angle to the light.* The final beauty of any piece of porcelain depends on the way in which the light is reflected from its glaze, and this is especially apparent on projections and mouldings.
4. *Tap it gently with your finger nail.* Perfect porcelain gives a clear sonorous ring, against a dull thump which denotes a repaired piece.
5. *Examine the appearance carefully*, paying special attention to colour and subject matter. As you discovered whilst reading this book, both of these are of immense importance in determining the source and date of any piece of porcelain. Each of the famous European factories has its own style, its own variety of form and colour, and if these do not correspond there is something wrong. If there is a pattern on a plate or flat surface look at the edges (with a magnifying glass) and make sure that what seems to be hand painting is not a transfer. See how true the colours are, and by tilting the object slightly against the light look out for any variation of lustre effects.
6. *Examine the base of the objects.* Here you are most likely to find evidence of the nature of the paste in the unglazed portions and the quality of the glaze. Factory marks, which are fully

BUEN RETIRO

A *chinoiserie* group. c. 1770. He wears a long pale lilac coat edged in yellow. The *rocaillerie* and the scroll-edged base picked out in puce. Height 11½ ins.

Sotheby & Co.

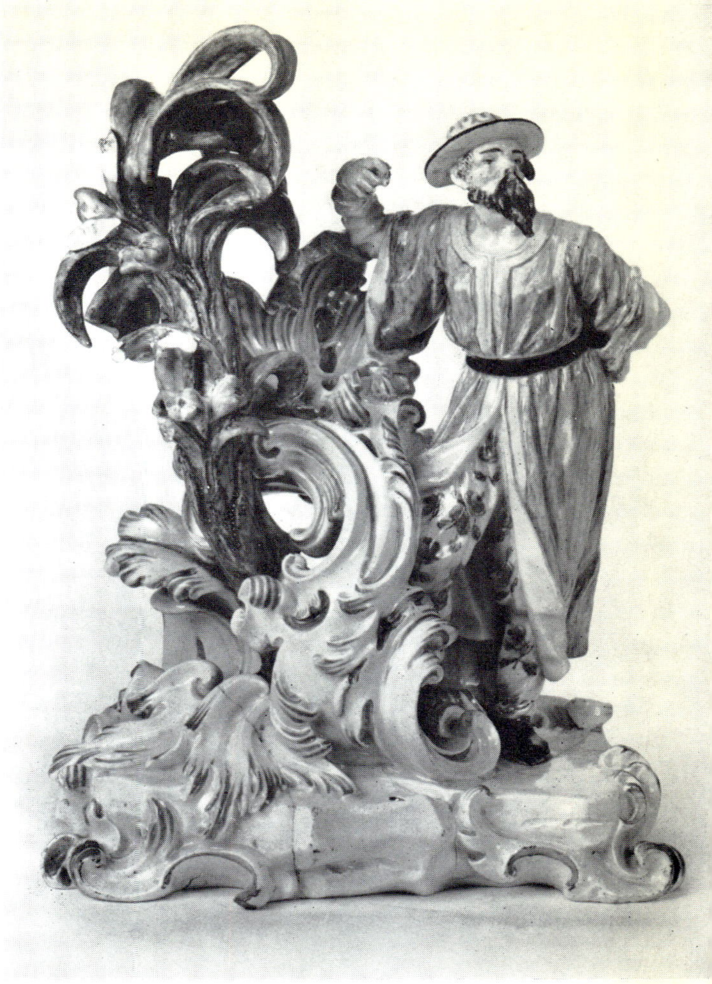

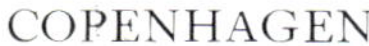

COPENHAGEN

Bowl in hard-paste porcelain, decorated in enamel colours and gilt, late eighteenth century. Mark: three wavy lines in underglaze blue. c. 1780. Diameter 9⅝ ins.

Victoria and Albert Museum

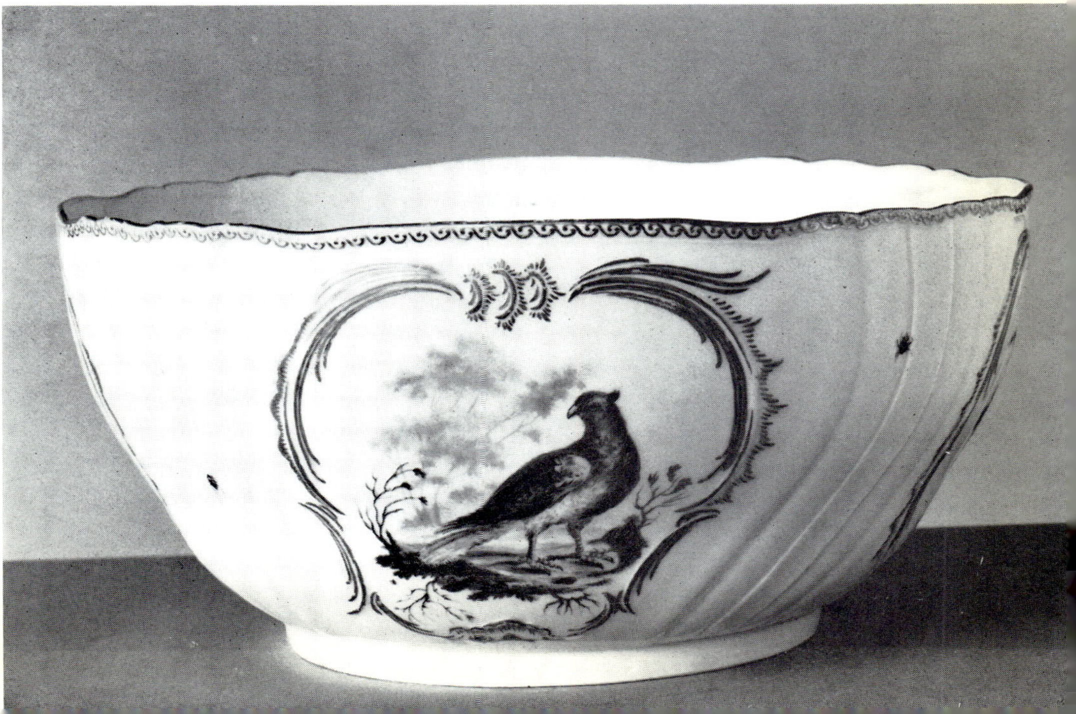

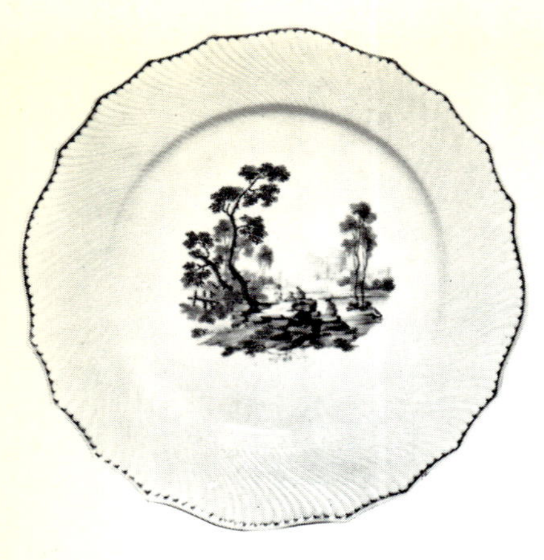

TOURNAI. Third quarter of the Eighteenth century.

Landscape plate, with spirally moulded narrow flutes, painted in the manner of Duvivier in a palette of coloured enamels. $9\frac{3}{4}$ ins. Mark: crossed swords and three crosses in gilding

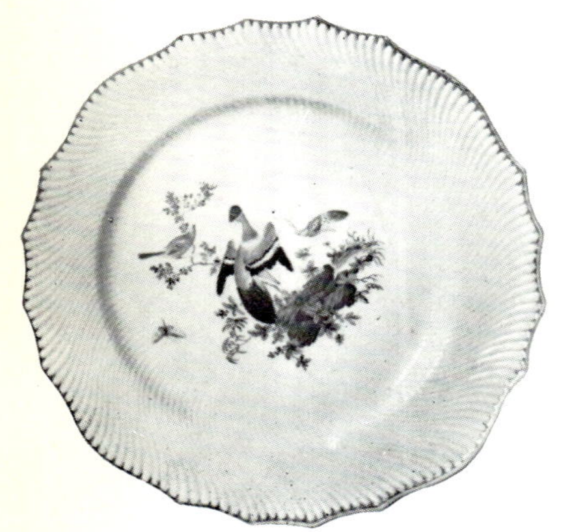

Bird-decorated plate, the well and rim moulded with narrow flutes, arranged spirally. Gilt edged rim. $9\frac{3}{8}$ ins. Mark: crossed swords and three crosses in gilding

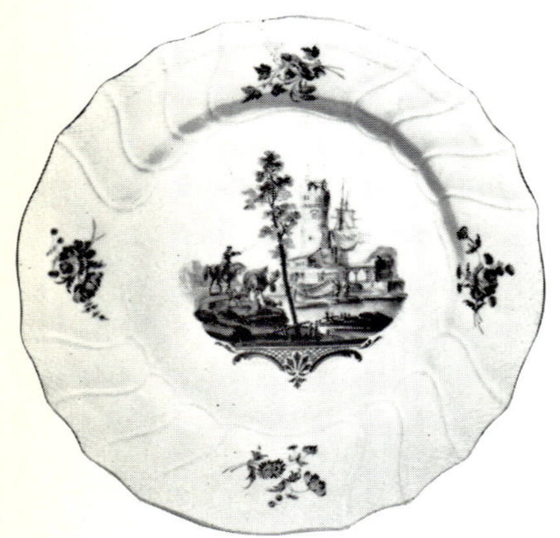

One of a pair of plates painted by Duvivier, signed I.D., painted in puce *camaieu* with island scenes. $9\frac{1}{8}$ ins. Mark: crossed swords and three crosses in gilding, I.D. and three dots in puce, incised P and R

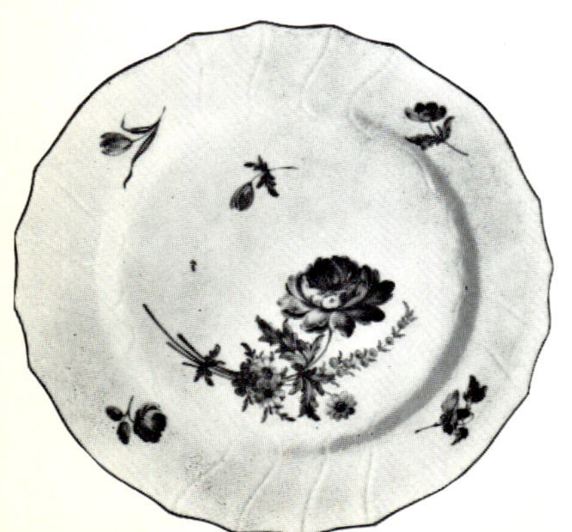

A plate with spirally moulded rim. $9\frac{1}{4}$ ins. Mark: incised initials P and ij

All photographs from Sotheby & Co.

ST. PETERSBURG
Large dessert plate from Imperial Russian Banqueting Service. Brilliantly decorated in gold, green and blue. c. 1820. Diameter 14 ins.

Christie's

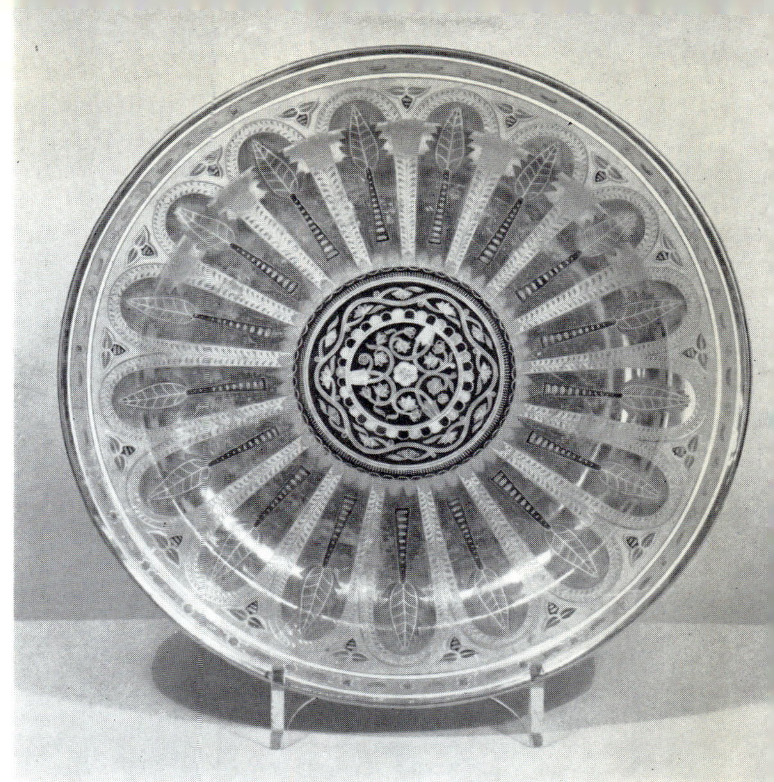

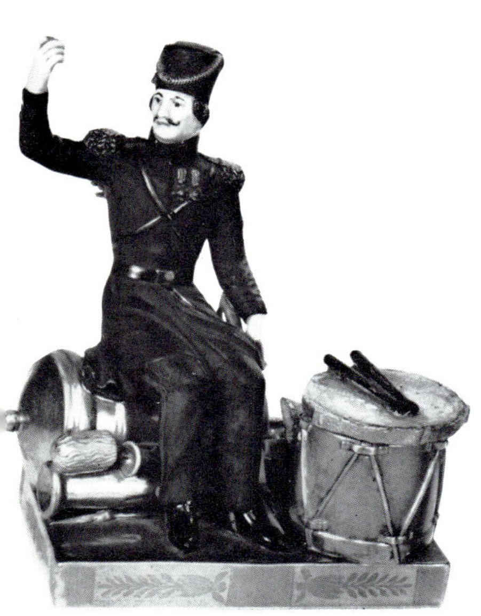

POPOFF. Inkwell in the form of an officer seated on a cannon, with an inkwell pounce pot concealed in a drum at his side. Height 6½ ins. Impressed mark in underglaze blue.

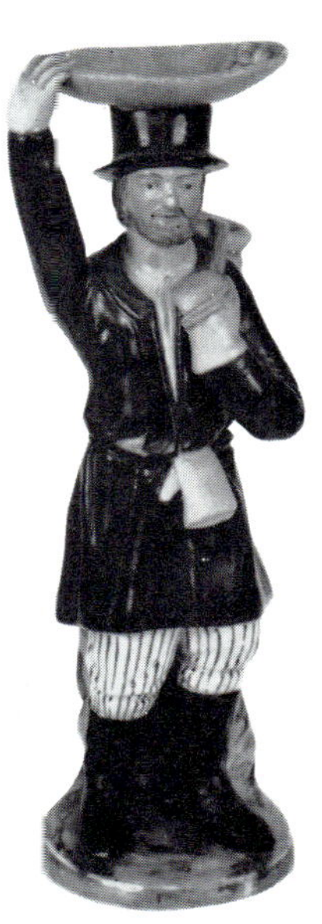

GARDNER. Figure of pastry seller. Height 8 ins. G mark in underglaze blue

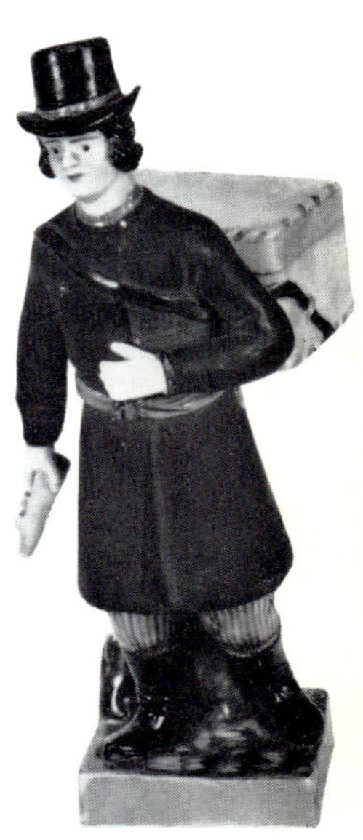

GARDNER. Figure of shoe seller. Basket strapped to his back with inkwell and pounce pot. Height 7¾ ins. G mark in underglaze blue

All photographs from Sotheby & Co.

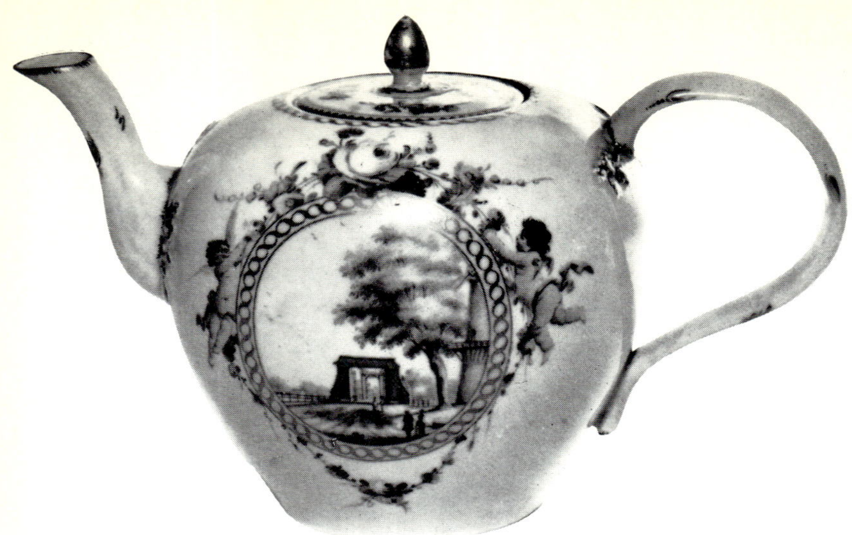

THE HAGUE. A teapot and cover of ovoid shape, with crabstock handle and spout, painted on each side in puce *camaieu* with an oval landscape medallion within a yellow border. Height 5 ins. Stork mark in blue

Sotheby & Co.

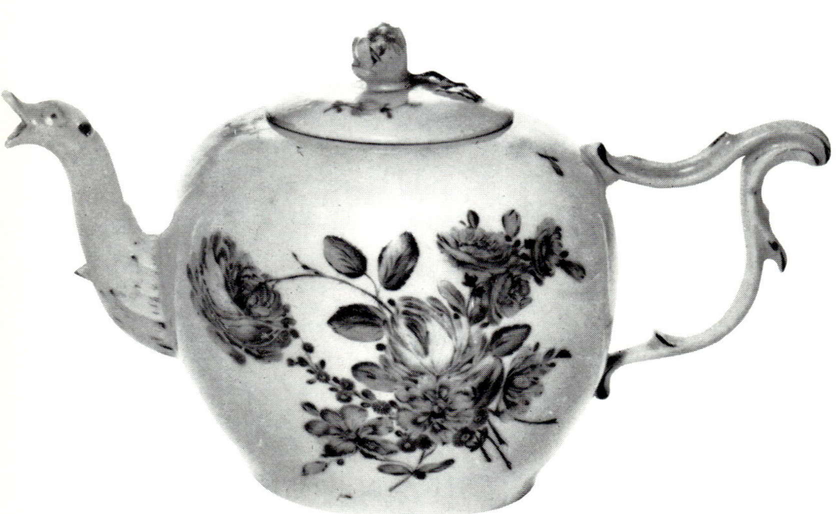

ZURICH. A teapot and cover of almost globular shape, with *tau* handle and serpent spout, painted in a soft palette, Height 4½ ins. Z mark and two dots in underglaze blue

Sotheby & Co.

described in the book; signatures or symbols of the potter or artist concerned are generally found on the base; and these can all be identified by reference to the diagrams of marks given in the text or in one or other of the following works: William Chaffers *Marks and Monograms on European and Oriental Pottery and Porcelain*, 2 volumes, London, William Reeves—15th edition 1965. (This also contains valuable information about prices and the like.) G. A. Godden *Encyclopaedia of British Pottery and Porcelain Marks* London, Herbert Jenkins, 1964.

A word of warning is necessary, however. Porcelain marks are not nearly as reliable, as for instance hall marks are. Marking was not compulsory, it was haphazard, and it has lent itself to forgery on a large scale. You have found constant warnings on this score in the body of the book, and you must remember that a piece may be genuine without the accepted mark, and false with it. Chaffers himself utters the warning:

"The amateur must be upon his guard in collecting porcelain and not place too much reliance on the marks he may find on the ware. When the mark is not indented on the paste or baked with the porcelain when at its greatest heat, usually in blue, it gives no guarantee for its genuineness; the mark was nearly always affixed before glazing. It is necessary in forming a correct judgement of the authenticity of a piece of valuable china such as Sèvres that many things be taken into consideration. First, above all, it is most important to be satisfied whether the porcelain be of hard or soft paste, and whether such types of paste were made at the time represented by the mark; then if the decoration be in keeping with the style adopted at the time indicated; the colours, the finish, the manner of decoration and various other *indica* must be taken into account." Vol. 1, p. 427–8.

It would be foolhardy to collect Sèvres or Meissen if the collector is of modest means, in the hope that bargains will be "picked up". Small country shops are daily combed by the more experienced traders, and the great shortage of fine goods makes the possibility of a "find" even more remote. It would be far more sensible to pay a fair price to a dealer who will actively cooperate in finding suitable pieces.

If the experience of the past twenty years is an example, and there is no reason to believe it is not, the price of fine porcelain will continue to rise. The collection should actually prove a profitable one.

Glossary

Arcanist: A workman professing to possess secret information about the making of porcelain, but generally used to indicate a master of the craft.

Arcanum: From the Latin *arcanus* meaning secret. An alchemical term applied to the secret process of porcelain production.

Ball clay: Kaolin from Devon and Cornwall.

Bauxite: Hydrated aluminium (increases heat resistance of refractory materials).

Biscuit: Meaning "twice cooked"; a rather vague term applied especially to porcelain, usually meaning that part or all of the surface has been left unglazed.

Blanc-de-Chine: A white unpainted porcelain made originally at Fukien in China and imported into Europe in the eighteenth century, where it served as a model for various factories.

Bocage: A background of flowers, etc., attached to a porcelain figure group, originally intended as a support.

Bone ash: Calcined animal bones.

Camaieu, en: The deliberate restriction of colours to create a cameo effect.

Ceramics: From Greek *keramos*, pottery. The art of pottery.

China clay: See kaolin.

Cornish Stone: See feldspar.

Crazed: The accidental splitting up of the surface into a mesh of fine cracks.

Décor Bois: A style of decoration imitating grained wood to

which a sheet with a landscape painted on it is made to appear attached.

DELFT: Distinctive glazed earthenware (lead containing tin oxide) of Dutch origin, Chinese inspired.

DELFT-WARE: English made *faïence*.

DEUTSCHE BLUMEN: Literally "German flowers"; naturalistically painted flowers—as opposed to the more stylised approach of the Oriental tradition.

EPERGNE: Table centre to hold fruit or flowers.

FAÏENCE, OR FAYENCE: From Italian town of Faenza. Distinctive glazed earthenware (lead containing tin oxide), made in France and Germany from seventeenth century to original designs.

FAÏENCE FINE: The French term for white or cream coloured lead glazed earthenware.

FAMILLE ROSE: Enamelled Chinese porcelain from about 1720 onwards. Predominant colour, rose-pink.

FAMILLE VERTE: Enamelled Chinese porcelain of the reign of K'ang Hsi (1662–1722). Painted over the glaze with five colours; green, red, blue, purple and yellow.

FELDSPAR: From the German *feldspat*. Potassium aluminium silicate, sometimes known as Cornish stone, soaprock or petuntse. Being non-plastic it has the advantage of a large difference between softening and melting temperature. Above 1,200° C. it becomes viscous liquid and dissolves kaolin.

FINIAL: An ornament or similar object finishing off a lid or such like.

FRIT: Made by melting water soluble chemicals (sodium carbonate, potassium carbonate, borax—boracic acid) with silica and clay to produce low melting point silicates.

GADROONING: Convex curves in series forming ornamental edge, like inverted fluting.

GALANTERIES: Subjects of an erotic or amorous character. Also means toys q.v.

GIRANDOLE: Originally revolving firework with centre piece; hence branched candlestick or candelabra.

GLASS: Made of silica and metallic oxides (sand, sodium or potassium carbonate, lime, etc.).

GLAZE: Vitreous substance fixed to pottery and porcelain by fusion.

GRAND FEU: The high temperature kiln used to fire porcelain, etc., at a temperature of *c.* 1,300° C.

KAOLIN: From the Chinese meaning "high ridge", probably from where it came. Decomposed feldspar—clay for the manufacture of porcelain. First analysed by R. E. Reamur of Paris in 1725.

LAMBREQUIN: A pelmet fitted to three sides of a door or a window. Originally a scarf worn on a helmet.

LAMBREQUINED: Adorned with frilly lace-like ornaments—sometimes called "vandyked".

LAUB-UND-BANDELWERK: (Literally "leaf and strap work") a late Baroque type of ornament common in eighteenth century German porcelain.

IMARI: The European name applied to Japanese porcelain imported from ARITA (which name is sometimes used as an alternative) in the eighteenth century.

MAIOLICA: General term covering all types of tin oxide glazed earthenware painted in polychrome in the Italian manner.

MAJOLICA: Earthenware with clear glaze made in the nineteenth century in imitation of the French Pallissy style.

OZIER: Basket-work like pattern in relief, usually on table wares.

PAP-WARMERS: Small dishes for keeping food warm for children or invalids.

PARIAN-WARE: Variety of hard paste introduced by Copeland in 1846.

PASTE: Combination of ingredients to make the porcelain body.

PETUNTSE: French name derived from Chinese word meaning "little bricks". See feldspar.

PHOSPHATIC: Containing a salt of phosphoric acid derived from interaction with iron or aluminium.

PIPE-CLAY: A white clay used as a slip-coating on other colours;

also used for the soft white earthenware known as *terre de pipe.*

POUNCING: A technique by which charcoal or some other powder is blown through holes in a transfer paper to provide the outlines for painter to follow on porcelain.

PUTTI: Small cupid-like figures usually shown flying.

RESERVES: Areas left blank for a painter to fill in.

SAGGERS: Fireclay box in which ceramics are placed for protection while in the kiln.

SALTGLAZE: Thin film on high-fired finish applied to stoneware caused by the addition of common salt to the firing kiln, at the point of greatest heat.

SCHWARZLOT: (Literally black lead), the name used to describe decorations in black enamel.

S'GRAFFITO: Decoration by scratching the surface of the coloured glaze to show the body, then re-glazed.

SLIP: Plastic clay converted into a liquid of cream-like consistency by the addition of a small quantity of an alkaline solution such as sodium carbonate. Used for joining moulded parts, as a brush applied decoration, and mainly for slip casting.

SLIP-WARE: An earthenware body of coarse character and decoration produced by trailing a pattern of different coloured slips.

SOAPROCK: See feldspar.

STONEWARE: Greyish-white body very hard, very dense and where thin slightly translucent. Sometimes referred to as porcelain.

TERRE DE LORRAINE: A fine grained porcelain produced at Lunéville by Cyfflé *c.* 1766.

TERRE DE PIPE: Soft white-bodied earthenware.

TOYS: Scent bottles, snuff boxes and other small objects usually made in fanciful forms.

TREMBLEUSE: The name given to a saucer which has deep cavity or a raised gallery in the centre into which cup is inserted. Usually made for chocolate cups when chocolate was served in bed.

TROMPE-L'OEIL: An extremely realistic manner of painting objects, etc., so as to "deceive the eye" and give the impression of actuality.

UNCTUOUS: A word usually applied to minerals meaning that they have a soft, soapy touch.

WASTERS: Firing rejects, caused by malformation in the kiln.

Bibliography

General

Boswell, J. *Life of Johnson*, Oxford, 1934.

Bright, M. *Diary of Samuel Pepys* (Transcribed from shorthand manuscript in the Pepysian Library, Magdalen College, Cambridge.) Edited by H. B. Wheatley.

Ceram, C. W. *Gods, Graves and Scholars*, London, 1952.

Chaffers, W. *Marks and Monograms on Pottery and Porcelain*, London, 1863 and subsequent editions.

Cushion, J.P. *Continental China Collecting for Amateurs*, London 1970.

Eberlein, H. D. and Ramsdell, R. W. *The Practical Book of Chinaware*, New York, 1948.

Fisher, Stanley W., f.r.s.a. *The Antique Dealer and Collector's Guide*, May 1959.

Fletcher, Sir Banister. *A History of Architecture*, London, 1956.

Hannover, E. *Pottery and Porcelain* (Edited by B. Rackham), London, 1924. Vols. 1, 2 and 3.

Honey, W. B. *The Art of the Potter*, London, 1946.

Dictionary of European Ceramic Art, London, 1952.

Klaus, Thelma N. *Harlequin Phoenix*, London, 1956.

Lewis, W. H. (Editor). *Memoires of the Duc de Saint-Simon*, London, 1964.

Lloyd Hyde, J. A. *Oriental Lowestoft*, New York, 1936.

Miller, Alec. *Tradition in Sculpture*, London and New York, 1949.

Reed Brett, S., m.a. *Europe Since The Renaissance*, London, 1931.

Renouard, J. *La Céramique Ancienne*, Paris, 1930.

Rosenthal, Ernest. *Pottery and Ceramics*, London, 1949.

Trevelyan, G. M., o.m. *English Social History*, London, 1942.

Tudor Craig, Sir Algernon, k.b.e., f.s.a. *Armorial Porcelain of the Eighteenth Century*, London, 1925.

Germany

BALET, L. *Ludwigsburger Porzellan*, Stuttgart and Leipzig, 1911.
BAYER, ADOLPH. *Ansbacher Porzellan*, Ansbach, 1933.
DUCRET, SIEGFRIED. *Les Porcelaines de Meissen*, Berne, 1954.
ERNST, RICHARD. *Weiner Porzellan das Klassizismus*, Vienna, 1925.
HAYWARD, J. F. *Vienna Porcelain of the Du Paquier Period*, Apollo XLVIII April, May, August, October 1948.
HEUSER, E. *Porzellan von Strassburg und Frankenthal*, Neustadt-an-der-Haardt, 1922.
HOFMANN, F. H. *Frankenthaler Porzellan*, Munich, 1911.
Geschichte der bayerischen Porzellan-Manufaktur Nymphenburg, Leipzig, 1922.
Das Porzellan der europäischen Manufakturen im. 18 Jahrhundert, Berlin, 1932.
HONEY, W. B. *Dresden China*, London, 1934.
German Porcelain, London, 1947.
LENZ, G. *Berliner Porzellan: Die Manufaktur Friedrichs des Grossen*, Berlin, 1913.
MCCLELLAN, GEORGE B. *The McClellan Collection of German and Austrian Porcelain*, New York, 1946.
RÖDER, KURT and OPPENHEIM, MICHEL. *Das Höchster Porzellan auf der Jahrtausend-Ausstellung in Mainz* 1925, Mainz, 1930.
SCHERER, C. *Das Fürstenberger Porzellan*, Berlin, 1909.
SCHNORR, VON CAROLSFELD, L. *Porzellan der europäischen Fabriken des 18. Jahrhunderts*, Berlin, 1920.
WARE, GEORGE. *German and Austrian Porcelain*, Frankfurt.

France

ALFASSA, P. and GUÉRIN, J. *La Porcelaine Française*, Paris, 1932.
Porcelaine Française du XVIIe au milieu de XIXe Siècle, Paris, 1932.
AUSCHER, E. S. *A History and Description of French Porcelain*, London, 1905.
BACHELIER, J. J. *Mémoire Historique sur la Manufacture Royale de Porcelaine de France* (Edited by G. Gouellain), Paris, 1878.
CHAVAGNAC, X. DE. *Catalogues des Porcelaines Françaises de M. J. Pierpont Morgan*, Paris, 1910.
CHAVAGNAC, X. DE and GROLLIER, A. DE. *Histoire des Manufactures Françaises de Porcelaine*, Paris, 1906.
GARNIER, E. *Catalogue du Musée Céramique de Sèvres: Faïences*, Paris, 1897.
HONEY, W. B. *French Porcelain of the 18th Century*, London, 1950.
KING, W. *Catalogue of the Jones Collection (Part II Ceramics)*, Victoria & Albert Museum, London, 1924.
LANDAIS, HUBERT. *French Porcelain*, London, 1961.

MACON, GUSTAVE. *Chantilly et le Musée Condé*, Paris, 1910.
SCHREIBER, LADY CHARLOTTE. *Lady Charlotte Schreiber's Journals*, Vols. I and II, London, 1911.

England

BARRETT. F. A. *Caughley and Coalport Porcelain*, Leigh-on-Sea, 1951.
Worcester Porcelain, London, 1953.
BEDFORD, John. *Chelsea and Derby China*, London, 1967.
BINNS, R. W. *A Century of Pottery in the City of Worcester*, London and Worcester, 1865.
CANNON, T. G. *Old Spode*, London, 1925.
CUSHION, J. P. *English China Collecting for Amateurs*. London, 1967.
DIXON J. L. *English Porcelain of the Eighteenth Century*, London, 1952.
EXLEY, C. L. *The Pinxton China Factory*, Derby, 1963.
FISHER, STANLEY W., F.R.S.A. *English Blue and White Porcelain of the Eighteenth Century*, London, 1949.
GILLESPIE, F. BRAYSHAW. *Crown Derby Porcelain*, Leigh-on-Sea, 1951.
Derby Porcelain, London, 1961.
GODDEN, G. A. *British Pottery and Porcelain 1780–1850*, London, 1963.
An Illustrated Encyclopedia of British Pottery and Porcelain, London, 1966.
HAYDEN, ARTHUR. *Spode and His Successors*, London, 1925.
HONEY, W. B. *English Pottery and Porcelain*, London, 1962.
Old English Porcelain, London, 1948.
Wedgwood Ware, London, 1948.
HUGHES, BERNARD and THERLE. *English Porcelain and Bone China 1743–1850*, London, 1955.
JEWITT, LLEWELLEN, F.S.A. *The Ceramic Art of Great Britain*, Vols.I and II, London, 1878.
JOHN, W. D. *Swansea Porcelain*, Newport, 1957.
LANE, A. *English Porcelain Figures of the Eighteenth Century*, London, 1961.
MACKENNA, F. SEVERNE. *Champion's Bristol Porcelain*, Leigh-on-Sea, 1947.
Chelsea Porcelain—The Gold Anchor Period, Leigh-on-Sea, 1952.
Chelsea Porcelain—The Red Anchor Wares, Leigh-on-Sea, 1951.
Worcestershire Porcelain, Leigh-on-Sea, 1950.
MANKOWITZ, W. *Wedgwood*, London, 1953.
MARRYAT, JOSEPH. *Pottery and Porcelain*, London, 1850.
SHAW, SIMEON. *History of the Staffordshire Potteries*, London, 1829.
STRINGER, G. E. *Histories of The Old and New Hall Potteries*, London, 1941.
Jubilee Souvenir of The New Hall Pottery Co. Ltd.
New Hall Porcelain, London, 1949.

WATNEY, B. *English Blue and White Porcelain*, London, 1963.
Longton Hall, London, 1957.

Italy and Spain

DAVILLIER, J. C. *Les Origines de la Porcelaine en Europe*, Paris, 1882.
LANE, ARTHUR, *Italian Porcelain*, London, 1954.
LIVERANI, G. *Catalogo delle Porcellane dei Medici*, Faenze, 1936.
PEREZ-VILLAMIL, M. *Catalogo de la Coleccion de Porcelanas del Buen Retiro del Francisco de Laiglesia*, Madrid, 1908.
RACKHAM, B. *Spanish Art* (Burlington Magazine), London, 1927.
STAZZI, FRANCESCO. *Italian Porcelain*, 1967.

The Rest of Europe

GELDER, H. E. VON. *Catalogus van de Verzameling Haagsch Porselein* (catalogue of the Hague Museum collection), The Hague, 1916.
HANNOVER, E. *Pottery and Porcelain*, (Vols. 1 and 3), London, 1924.
HAYDEN, A. *Royal Copenhagen Porcelain*, London, 1911.
HONEY, W. B. *A Centre-Piece of Zurich Porcelain*, Burlington Magazine LVIII, p. 96, London, 1931.
ROZENBERGH, A. *Les Marques sur la Porcelaine Russe*, Paris, 1926.
SOIL DE MORIAMÉ, E. J. *Les Porcelaines de Tournay*, Tournay, 1937.
STRÅLE, G. H. *Mariebergs Historie och Tillverkningar, 1758–1788*, Stockholm, 1880.

Index

Metric Conversion Table

1 inch	= 2.54 cm	= 25.4	mm
½ inch	= 1.27 cm	= 12.7	mm
¼ inch	= 0.635 cm	= 6.35	mm
⅛ inch	= 0.3175 cm	= 3.175	mm